Many Rāmāyaṇas

Many Rāmāyaṇas

The Diversity of a Narrative Tradition in South Asia

EDITED BY

Paula Richman

UNIVERSITY OF CALIFORNIA PRESS
Berkeley Los Angeles London

University of California Press
Berkeley and Los Angeles, California

University of California Press, Ltd.
London, England

Cover illustration (1878) reproduced by permission of the India Office Library (British Library), London. Call number: Tamil D. 3037.
"By Rāma's Grace" reprinted by kind permission of Princeton University Press.

All royalties from the sale of this volume have been donated to the American Institute of Indian Studies.

Library of Congress Cataloging-in-Publication Data

Many Rāmāyaṇas : the diversity of a narrative tradition in South Asia /edited by Paula Richman.
p. cm.
Includes bibliographical references and index.
ISBN 978-0-520-07589-4 (paper)
1. Indic literature—History and criticism. 2. Rāma (Hindu deity) in literature. 3. Sītā (Hindu deity) in literature. 4. Vālmīki. Rāmāyaṇa. 5. Kampar, 9th cent. Rāmāyaṇam. 6. Tulasīdāsa, 1532–1623 Rāmacaritamānasa. I. Richman, Paula.
PK2907.R25M36 1991
294.5'922—dc20 91-7273
CIP

Printed in the United States of America

12 11 10 09 08
9 8 7 6 5

The paper used in this publication is both acid-free and totally chlorine-free (TCF). It meets the minimum requirements of ANSI/NISO Z39.48-1992 (R 1997) (*Permanence of Paper*). ∞

To Doris and Nathan Richman

it spreads, ceaselessly various,
one and many at once

Kampaṉ

CONTENTS

PART THREE · TELLINGS AS COMMENTARY AND PROGRAMS FOR ACTION

PREFACE

This book began owing to my puzzlement. For years I had heard people refer to E. V. Ramasami's interpretation of the *Rāmāyaṇa* in a mocking and dismissive way. When I actually analyzed his reading of the story of Rāma, however, I found much of it strikingly compelling and coherent if viewed in light of his anti–North Indian ideology. While I was talking one day with A. K. Ramanujan about my attempts to make sense of this particular reading of the Rāma story, he gave me a copy of a paper he had presented entitled "Three Hundred *Rāmāyaṇas*." I read this piece again and again because it challenges us to look at the *Rāmāyaṇa* tradition in a new way. Each contributor to the volume also read Ramanujan's essay, which now comprises Chapter 2 of this volume. Every other chapter can be seen, in some way, as a response to some of the questions that Ramanujan raises.

As individual essays developed, intriguing patterns within the *Rāmāyaṇa* tradition were revealed. I encouraged authors to explore the exact ways in which the tellings of the Rāma story that they had studied related to particular theological, social, political, regional, performance, or gender contexts. Slowly the book grew in the direction of a study of tellings of the *Rāmāyaṇa* that refashion or contest Vālmīki's text. I am grateful to Raman for giving us his essay and to each contributor for the many revisions made to ensure the overall coherence of the volume.

A number of scholars encouraged me during the many stages of this book: Michael Fisher, whose initial enthusiasm for the project encouraged me to pursue it and whose advice at every stage I have deeply valued; Clint Seely, who believed in the worth of the endeavor and invited two authors to contribute to the volume; Robert Goldman and Sally Sutherland, who offered both textual and practical advice during the period when I was conceptualizing the volume's overall structure; David Shulman, from whom I have learned a great deal about the *Rāmāyaṇa* tradition and whose suggestions for revising the introduction were greatly appreciated; Philip Lutgendorf and H. Daniel Smith, both of whom shared their knowledge of *Rāmāyaṇa* tradition and gave me a number of valuable comments; Sandria Freitag, Wendy Doniger, and an anonymous reader on the Editorial Committee of the University of California Press, whose challenging questions and insightful suggestions for revisions made this book more coherent, complete, and concise; Lynne Withey, my editor, whose intelligence, efficiency, and graciousness have been greatly appreciated; Pamela MacFarland, whose attention to detail has improved this volume in myriad ways. To all these people I express my thanks; I alone am responsible for any shortcomings.

The research, editing, and completion of this book would have been impossible without a great deal of assistance. At Oberlin College's Mudd Library I want to thank Ray English, Kerry Langan, Valerie MacGowan-Doyle, and Anne Zald, and at Western Washington University's Miller Library Evelyn Darrow and Jo Dereske, for tracking down unbelievably obscure works in a number of South Asian languages. Similar feats were performed by James Nye, William Alsbaugh, and Lynn Bigelow in Regenstein Library of the University of Chicago. I am also grateful to Kenneth Logan, Barbara Gaerlan, and Sumathi Ramaswamy for assisting me at the South Asia Center at the University of California, Berkeley. A grant from the Research and Development Fund at Oberlin College made research trips to Berkeley and Chicago possible. Susan Munkres and Daniel Gardiner read drafts of each paper in the volume, making insightful and helpful suggestions for improving clarity. Many of my students during 1989 and 1990 came to share my enthusiasm for the *Rāmāyaṇa* tradition; I am grateful for their interest and intriguing queries. Thanks goes to the office of Ira Steinberg, which funded part of the cost of duplicating the manuscript. I appreciate the institutional support provided by William Stoever at Western Washington University during the summer of 1989. Thelma Kime and Terri Mitchell typed innumerable drafts of several of the papers in this volume. I appreciate their patience and dedication.

Paula Richman
Oberlin, Ohio

A NOTE ON TRANSLITERATION

Except where noted, standard scholarly transliteration systems have been used for each South Asian language. Authors whose papers deal primarily with Hindi materials have decided to drop the final short *a* of syllables in order to reflect Hindi usage most faithfully. (For example, Sanskrit Rāma becomes Hindi Rām.) Place names, such as Lanka and Ayodhya, are given without diacritical marks.

PART ONE

Larger Patterns

ONE

Introduction: The Diversity of the *Rāmāyaṇa* Tradition

Paula Richman

In January 1987 viewers in India began to tune in each Sunday morning for a Hindi television serial based on the *Rāmāyaṇa* story. Observers estimate that over eighty million people watched the weekly broadcasts.[1] In a land where most people do not own televisions and electricity remains in short supply, many gathered at the homes of relatives or at local tea shops to view the epic, while engineers worked overtime to supply adequate current. In some places entire villages joined together to rent a television set. It was not just that people watched the show: they became so involved in it that they were loath to see it end. Despite the fact that Doordarshan, the government-run network, had only contracted with the producer for a year's worth of episodes, the audience demanded more. In fact, sanitation workers in Jalandhar went on strike because the serial was due to end without depicting the events of the seventh, and final, book of the *Rāmāyaṇa*.[2] The strike spread among sanitation workers in many major cities in North India, compelling the government to sponsor the desired episodes in order to prevent a major health hazard. Quite apart from such militant enthusiasm, the manner in which viewers watched the serial was also striking. Many people responded to the image of Rāma on the television screen as if it were an icon in a temple. They bathed before watching, garlanded the set like a shrine, and considered the viewing of Rāma to be a religious experience.

The size, response, and nature of the television *Rāmāyaṇa*'s audience led Philip Lutgendorf, a scholar of Hindi *Rāmāyaṇa* traditions, to comment:

> The Ramayan serial had become the most popular program ever shown on Indian television—and something more: an event, a phenomenon of such proportions that intellectuals and policy makers struggled to come to terms with its significance and long-range import. Never before had such a large percentage

> of South Asia's population been united in a single activity; never before had a single message instantaneously reached so enormous a regional audience.[3]

Throughout Indian history many authors and performers have produced, and many patrons have supported, diverse tellings of the *Rāmāyaṇa* in numerous media. Perhaps not surprisingly, enthusiasm welcomed this new entrant into what has been an unending series of *Rāmāyaṇas* in India and beyond.

The televised *Rāmāyaṇa* did, however, disturb some observers, who worried that the Doordarshan version might come to dominate other tellings of the story. Romila Thapar, a noted scholar of Indian history, is among such observers. When the state acts as patron of the arts, argues Thapar, it often favors social groups that wield relatively great influence in that society. In Thapar's analysis, Doordarshan presented a *Rāmāyaṇa* telling that reflected the concerns not of the vast majority of Indians but of what she calls "the middle class and other aspirants to the same status."[4] For Thapar, the television *Rāmāyaṇa* possessed a dangerous and unprecedented authority. In the past, many performances of the *Rāmāyaṇa* have been sponsored by those in political power, but never before had a *Rāmāyaṇa* performance been seen simultaneously by such a huge audience through a medium which so clearly presented itself as authoritative.[5] In addition, its broadcasters were self-consciously presenting their version of the story as an expression of mainstream "national culture." Through such a presentation, would something of the *Rāmāyaṇa* tradition's richness be lost?

In her critique of the television production, Thapar calls attention to the plurality of *Rāmāyaṇas* in Indian history: "The *Ramayana* does not belong to any one moment in history for it has its own history which lies embedded in the many versions which were woven around the theme at different times and places."[6] Not only do diverse *Rāmāyaṇas* exist; each *Rāmāyaṇa* text reflects the social location and ideology of those who appropriate it:

> The appropriation of the story by a multiplicity of groups meant a multiplicity of versions through which the social aspirations and ideological concerns of each group were articulated. The story in these versions included significant variations which changed the conceptualization of character, event and meaning.[7]

Thapar emphasizes that, traditionally, local references and topical remarks play crucial roles in many performances of the *Rāmāyaṇa*. Were the television *Rāmāyaṇa* and the broadly distributed videocassette tapes of it to achieve widespread acceptance as *the* version of the epic, Thapar warns of possible negative effects for Indian culture. The homogenization of any narrative tradition results in cultural loss; other tellings of the *Rāmāyaṇa* story might be irretrievably submerged or marginalized.

The contributors to this volume desire an opposite fate—that the public discourse and scholarship stimulated by current interest in the *Rāmāyaṇa* draw even greater attention to the manifold *Rāmāyaṇa* tradition in India.[8] We take the popularity of the televised *Rāmāyaṇa* not as heralding the demise of other tellings but as affirming the creation of yet another rendition of the *Rāmāyaṇa*, the latest product of an ongoing process of telling and retelling the story of Rāma. In order to illuminate the nature of this process, our essays analyze an array of tellings, the better to display the vitality and diversity of the *Rāmāyaṇa* tradition.[9]

SYNOPSIS OF THE RĀMA STORY

Scholars familiar with the *Rāmāyaṇa* story will want to move on to the next section of this introduction. Meanwhile, for other readers, it is useful to provide an outline of the story's basic events. Such an enterprise, however, is fraught with difficulties, for "the story" is inseparable from the different forms it takes, forms which reflect differences in religious affiliation, linguistic allegiance, and social location. Nonetheless, those who are not *Rāmāyaṇa* specialists need at least a skeletal knowledge of incidents, characters, and locations in the *Rāmāyaṇa* tradition in order to appreciate the essays in this volume, which analyze different ways in which the *Rāmāyaṇa* has been told.

I have therefore chosen to present a synopsis of the story of Rāma based on Vālmīki's *Rāmāyaṇa*. Most scholars would agree that Vālmīki's *Rāmāyaṇa*, the most extensive early literary treatment of the life of Rāma, has wielded enormous influence in India, Southeast Asia, and beyond. Many later *Rāmāyaṇa* authors explicitly refer to it either as an authoritative source or as a telling with which they disagree. For centuries it has been regarded as the most prestigious *Rāmāyaṇa* text in many Indian circles. It has also drawn the most attention from Western scholars.[10]

However, I present Vālmīki's rendition here not as an *Ur*-text but only as the story of Rāma with which the majority of Western *Rāmāyaṇa* scholars are most familiar. My goal is not to privilege Vālmīki's *Rāmāyaṇa* but to give the nonspecialist reader some necessary background, since in explaining the components of other tellings of the story the contributors to this volume often take a knowledge of Vālmīki for granted. In addition, to tell other *Rāmāyaṇas* here would be to preempt the work of the rest of this volume.[11]

In order to maintain our perspective on Vālmīki's telling as one of many *Rāmāyaṇas* rather than as the authoritative *Rāmāyaṇa*, I will summarize the story in as neutral a way as possible, avoiding, for example, moral evaluation of the characters and their actions. My aim is to present readers with the plot of an extremely influential *Rāmāyaṇa* without encouraging them to view as normative the events, characterizations, and particular ideological commitments of Vālmīki's *Rāmāyaṇa*.

As the story opens the ruler of Lanka, the demon Rāvaṇa, has gained apparent invincibility by winning a promise from the gods that he cannot be destroyed by any divine or demonic creature: he is vulnerable only to human beings, who are too weak to be of account. Meanwhile in the city of Ayodhya, we learn, King Daśaratha has no male heir. In order to remedy this problem his ministers urge him to perform a special sacrifice, which causes his three wives to conceive sons. Firstborn among them is Rāma, son of Queen Kausalyā; then come his three half-brothers, Bharata, son of Queen Kaikeyī, and Lakṣmaṇa and Śatrughna, the twin sons of Queen Sumitrā. Rāma begins his career as a warrior while still a youth, when he defends a sage's sacrifice by killing the demons that threaten its success. Subsequently, Rāma wins his bride, Sītā, by stringing an enormous divine bow.

When King Daśaratha decides to retire, he chooses as his successor Rāma, beloved among Ayodhya's citizens for his wisdom and compassion. Soon, however, the king's youngest queen, Kaikeyī, becomes convinced that if Rāma were to become the sovereign, her fortunes and those of her son, Bharata, would suffer disastrous consequences. So Kaikeyī calls for the king to redeem two boons that he awarded her when once she saved his life on the battlefield: she asks first that Rāma be banished to the forest for fourteen years and, second, that her own son, Bharata, be crowned in his place. Rāma willingly accepts his fate, vowing to honor his father's wishes, and sets off at once for the forest, accompanied by his wife, Sītā, and his half-brother Lakṣmaṇa. When Bharata returns from a visit to his uncle and hears of the events that have transpired while he was away, he goes to the forest to persuade Rāma to return. Rāma, however, adheres to his vow, whereupon Bharata installs Rāma's sandals on the royal throne, agreeing only to serve as regent until Rāma's return from exile.

In the forest the threesome meet ascetic sages, travel through both beautiful and frightening landscapes, and eventually settle in a little hermitage. One day there appears a demoness named Śūrpaṇakhā who falls in love with Rāma and boldly offers herself to him in marriage. When Rāma refuses her offer, she deems Sītā the obstacle to her plan and prepares to eat her. In response, Lakṣmaṇa mutilates Śūrpaṇakhā, prompting the demoness to flee to her brother, Rāvaṇa. When she complains of the cruelty of the two princes and tells of the extraordinary beauty of Sītā, her words arouse in Rāvaṇa a passionate desire for Sītā. By enlisting the aid of another demon, who takes the form of a golden deer, Rāvaṇa lures first Rāma and then Lakṣmaṇa away from their hermitage. Then, posing as a wandering holy man, Rāvaṇa gains entrance to the dwelling and carries Sītā off to his island kingdom of Lanka.

In the course of his attempt to determine where Sītā has been taken and then to gather allies for the fight against Rāvaṇa, Rāma becomes involved in the politics of a monkey kingdom. There Rāma meets Hanumān, who becomes his staunch devotee, and Sugrīva, an exiled prince who, like Rāma, has also suffered the loss of wife and kingdom. Sugrīva and Rāma make a pact: if Rāma will help Sugrīva win back his wife and throne—both currently under the control of his brother, Vālin—then Sugrīva will aid Rāma in his search for Sītā. During a battle between Sugrīva and Vālin, Rāma conceals himself behind a tree and shoots Vālin from this position of hiding, an act that violates the warrior's code. Some time later Sugrīva sends his warriors off in every direction seeking news of Sītā's whereabouts. Finally they learn that Sītā has been imprisoned in Lanka.

Hanumān crosses the ocean to Lanka and locates Sītā, dwelling under guard in a grove near Rāvaṇa's palace. After he watches Rāvaṇa alternately threaten her life and attempt to seduce her, he gives her Rāma's signet ring, assuring her of imminent rescue. Then, when he allows himself to be brought to Rāvaṇa's court, his tail is set afire. Escaping his captors, he sets the city on fire and then returns to help Rāma's forces prepare for war, adding the intelligence about the walled city of Lanka that he has gathered to information provided by Vibhīṣaṇa, a brother of Rāvaṇa who has repudiated him to join Rāma. The monkeys build a bridge to Lanka so that the army can cross. The ensuing battle sees great losses on both sides. Rāma ultimately kills Rāvaṇa in one-to-one combat, whereupon Rāma makes Vibhīṣaṇa the new ruler of Lanka.

Rāma at first refuses to take Sītā back, since she has lived in the household of another man. After she successfully undergoes a trial by fire, however, he deems her worthy to take her place by his side. But continuing rumors questioning his wife's chastity cause Rāma to banish Sītā—who is now pregnant—from his kingdom. Banished, she finds refuge with the venerable sage Vālmīki, to whom the composition of the *Rāmāyaṇa* is traditionally attributed, and in the shelter of his hermitage gives birth to twin sons, Lava and Kuśa. Eventually, Sītā abandons this world to return to the bosom of the earth, whence she came. Bereft by the loss of his wife, Rāma finally ascends to heaven with members of his retinue.

THE ASSUMPTIONS AND GOALS OF THIS VOLUME

Along with Vālmīki's *Rāmāyaṇa*, there are hundreds of other tellings of the story of Rāma in India, Southeast Asia, and beyond. In confronting the diversity of the tradition, we are challenged to find ways of articulating relationships among these *Rāmāyaṇas*. In the lead essay of this volume, Ramanujan takes up the challenge by looking at five different *Rāmāyaṇas*: Vālmīki's Sanskrit poem, summarized above; Kampaṉ's *Irāmāvatāram*, a Tamil literary account that incorporates characteristically South Indian material;[12] Jain tellings, which provide a non-Hindu perspective on familiar events;[13] a Kannada folktale that reflects preoccupations with sexuality and childbearing;[14] and the *Ramakien*, produced for a Thai rather than an Indian audience.

Ramanujan's exploration of these texts suggests several ways to conceptualize the relations between *Rāmāyaṇas*. He urges us to view different tellings neither as totally individual stories nor as "divergences" from the "real" version by Vālmīki, but as the expression of an extraordinarily rich set of resources existing, throughout history, both within India and wherever Indian culture took root. Like the set of landscape conventions of classical Tamil poetry, the elements of the *Rāmāyaṇa* tradition can be seen as a source on which poets can draw to produce a potentially infinite series of varied and sometimes contradictory tellings.[15] Ramanujan likens the *Rāmāyaṇa* tradition to a pool of signifiers that includes plot, characters, names, geography, incidents, and relations, arguing that each *Rāmāyaṇa* can be seen as a "crystallization":

> These various texts not only relate to prior texts directly, to borrow or refute, but they relate to each other through this common code or common pool. Every author, if one may hazard a metaphor, dips into it and brings out a unique crystallization, a new text with a unique texture and a fresh context.

Creation of *Rāmāyaṇas*, Ramanujan's metaphor implies, involves both constraints and fluidity: while certain sets of codes structure expression, the fluidity of tradition accounts for the diversity of tellings. Like Thapar, he also calls attention to the fact that *Rāmāyaṇa* tellings take shape in particular contexts. They may be influenced, for example, by the beliefs of individual religious communities, the literary conventions of regional cultures, and the specific configurations of social relations.

In responding to Ramanujan's suggestion that we explore *Rāmāyaṇa* tellings in light of their structure, diversity, and context, the contributors to this volume have both reconsidered familiar *Rāmāyaṇas* and explored lesser-known tellings of the story. Those familiar with *Rāmāyaṇa* scholarship will recognize the extent to which we have used and built upon the careful research of earlier studies that trace the historical and literary peregrinations of Rāma's story. We are grateful to those who preceded us, scholars of extraordinary patience who meticulously charted the many tellings of the tale.[16] Our present goal is somewhat different: to consider the logic that informs, and the relations that exist between, selected tellings of the *Rāmāyaṇa*, as well as the cultural contexts of those tellings.

The essays share five assumptions about the plurality of *Rāmāyaṇa* tradition in India and Thailand. First, we deem all the incidents connected with the story of Rāma and Sītā equally worthy of our attention. Philological scholarship on Vālmīki's *Rāmāyaṇa* has argued that the *Bālakāṇḍa* (the first book, which tells of Rāma's youth) and the *Uttarakāṇḍa* (the last book, which tells of the events that transpire after Rāma's rescue of Sītā, including her banishment to the forest) are "late" additions.[17] Their status as possible interpolations into Vālmīki's text, however, has had little effect on the popularity of their contents in Indian culture. Whether these events from Rāma's early life and from the end of the story were original to Vālmīki's text or not, the contributors to this volume treat them in the same way as they treat incidents from other periods in Rāma's life.

Second, we accept the idea of many *Rāmāyaṇas* and place Vālmīki's text within that framework. Some scholars assume, either implicitly or explicitly, that Vālmīki has written *the* definitive *Rāmāyaṇa*. Hence, the diverse non-Vālmīki *Rāmāyaṇas*—the "other *Rāmāyaṇas*"—have often been assessed against that standard, according to their angle of divergence from Vālmīki's version. While Vālmīki's importance is undeniable, we learn more about the diversity of the *Rāmāyaṇa* tradition when we abandon the notion of Vālmīki as the *Ur*-text from which all the other *Rāmāyaṇas* descended.[18] We need instead to consider the "many *Rāmāyaṇas*," of which Vālmīki's telling is one, Tulsī's another, Kampaṉ's another, the Buddhist *jātaka* yet another, and so forth. Like other authors, Vālmīki is rooted in a particular social and ideological context. His text represents an intriguing telling, but it is one among many.

Third, in part to offset the prevalent attitude toward Vālmīki, the contributors seek to foreground non-Vālmīki *Rāmāyaṇa* texts in order to set out the key assumptions informing different tellings of the story. For example, although in many cases Vālmīki and Kampaṉ adhere to the same basic outline of events, Kampaṉ's rendition of particular incidents is shaped by the Tamil *bhakti* tradition, which gives radically different religious nuances to those events. Kampaṉ's *Rāmāyaṇa* is not a divergence from Vālmīki; the two are different tellings. Their differences intrigue us because they testify to the diversity of Indian culture, indicating that throughout history multiple voices were heard within the *Rāmāyaṇa* tradition.

Fourth, in addition to analyzing textual diversity, we want to emphasize the diversity and significance of renderings of the *Rāmāyaṇa* in other genres. Recent scholarship on Indian *Rāmāyaṇa* dramas and public culture testifies to the vitality and social significance of epic-related performances.[19] Building on this research, this volume highlights *Rāmāyaṇa* tellings found in puppet theater, debate, song cycles, and iconographic traditions. These tellings possess their own logic, their own intended audience, and their own richness.

Finally, we seek to demonstrate that the telling of the *Rāmāyaṇa* in India has included stories that conflict with one another. It is true that particular tellings have attained various degrees of dominance and/or popularity (Vālmīki, Tulsī, the televised *Rāmāyaṇa*). Nonetheless, there have always been contesting voices. Where Hindu *Rāmāyaṇas* have predominated, Jain and Buddhist *Rāmāyaṇa* poets have criticized or questioned those texts by producing their own tellings. Where male dominance has been prescribed in textual traditions, women's *Rāmāyaṇa* songs have expressed alternative perspectives that are more in keeping with women's own concerns. Our essays suggest that the *Rāmāyaṇa* tradition permits endless refashioning of the story, sometimes in actual opposition to the ways in which the story has previously been told.

The influence of two competing sets of religious tellings of the Rāma story are examined in the essay by Reynolds. He points out that, despite widespread privileging of Hindu tellings of the *Rāmāyaṇa*, Buddhist tellings of the story form an ancient, continuous, and coherent tradition in South Asia and beyond. He then goes on to show how both Hindu narrative elements and Buddhist values have influenced the composition of the complex and sophisticated Thai *Ramakien*, shedding light on the ways in which that text has been shaped by the multireligious diversity of the South Asian *Rāmāyaṇa* tradition.

TELLINGS AS REFASHIONING AND OPPOSITION

Despite the widespread belief that Rāma acts as the embodiment of righteous action, certain deeds that he performs have troubled various authors of *Rāmāyaṇa* texts over the centuries.[20] Because the textual treatment of these morally ambiguous deeds often involves dealing with them in creative ways, the study of such incidents can reveal some of the sources of diversity within the *Rāmāyaṇa* tradition.[21] In Part Two of this volume, Kathleen Erndl and David Shulman examine how these incidents can be seen as nodes of narrative capable of generating different tellings, each pursuing its own logic.

A number of authors and commentators have puzzled over the ethically problematic way that Rāma and Lakṣmaṇa treat Śūrpaṇakhā, Rāvaṇa's sister. In her chapter for this volume, Erndl brings structural analysis to bear on the mutilation of Śūrpaṇakhā, an event which ultimately leads to Sītā's abduction. The incident's ambiguities stem in various texts from the way that Lakṣmaṇa contravenes the prescription that a warrior must never harm a woman; from Śūrpaṇakhā's status as demoness and disguise as a beautiful woman; and from the attempts of Rāma and Lakṣmaṇa to tease and trick her. By examining the portrayal of this incident in a selected set of Sanskrit, Tamil, and Hindi *Rāmāyaṇa* texts, Erndl demonstrates how its moral ambiguities have generated a whole array of renditions and commentaries. In doing so, she reveals a fascination within the *Rāmāyaṇa* tradition for Śūrpaṇakhā, a woman who moves about the forest independent of a male protector and boldly articulates her passionate feelings, as a kind of alter ego of Sītā, often considered the model of the chaste and submissive wife.[22]

Shulman's essay considers another nodal incident in the narrative, the scene in which Rāma repudiates Sītā and then is informed by the gods that he is divine. Shulman juxtaposes Vālmīki's account of the incident with Kampaṉ's rendition, examining the fundamental motivations of each telling by considering two foci of ambiguity and literary creativity. One dilemma concerns Rāma's relationship to his wife, now returned from a sojourn in another male's house: her ambiguous status—there is no proof that she remained chaste—dismays Rāma's supporters. Rāma's response to her return also raises issues about his own hybrid status as a deity in human form. Vālmīki's account of the incident explores the extent to which Rāma has forgotten his divine identity; in contrast, Kampaṉ's account raises questions about the limited extent to which human beings can know the divine and attain union with him. Shulman brings to light both the differences in the two accounts and the ways in which these differences are embedded in different theological contexts.

If Erndl and Shulman focus upon diversity within the *Rāmāyaṇa* tradition inspired by moral ambiguities, that tradition also encompasses ways of telling the story that contest the character portrayals, values, and concerns of dominant *Rāmāyaṇas*. Jain and Buddhist writers are not alone in this endeavor. Other tellings that oppose influential Hindu tellings (which I have labeled "oppositional tellings") exist as well. Two papers in Part Two explore the specific ways in which certain texts resist a dominant presentation of the story.

Narayana Rao's essay for this volume, an account of folksongs collected from Telugu women, focuses on a *Rāmāyaṇa* tradition that contests the prevailing ideology of male dominance. Narayana Rao sees these songs as statements against what he calls "the public *Rāmāyaṇas*," pointing out that the latter glorify "the accepted values of a male-dominated world," whereas the Telugu songs relate a story in which public events (coronation, war) are displaced by domestic ones such as Kausalyā's morning sickness or Rāma getting bathed by his mother. The overall emphasis in these songs differs as well. While Vālmīki's *Rāmāyaṇa*, for example, concentrates on the virtues of Rāma, several of the women's folksongs question Rāma's integrity and foreground the theme of the suffering that husbandly neglect causes a wife. Gloria Raheja, an anthropologist studying North Indian women's songs, has cautioned against assuming that "the identity and self-perceptions of Hindu women depend heavily on the set of male-authored mythic themes [such as wifely devotion, subservience to in-laws, and suppression of desire for marital intimacy] condensed into the figure of Sītā."[23] Narayana Rao's analysis gives us another perspective, a way to hear another set of voices singing about the relationship between Sītā and Rāma.

Oppositional tellings of the *Rāmāyaṇa* also emerged from the colonial context in South Asia, as Clinton Seely's paper about Michael Madhusudan Dutt shows. Dutt's *Meghanādavadha Kāvya* reflects the complexity of contact between Indian and British culture. Dutt adored Milton, converted to Christianity, embraced blank verse, and composed some major poems in English. Yet he loved Hindu mythology and created a whole new tradition in Bengali writing. Both the rejections and the acceptances in his telling of the *Rāmāyaṇa* reveal much about its author and his colonial context. As Seely points out, Dutt based the plot of his epic upon that of the dominant Bengali *Rāmāyaṇa* by Kṛttivāsa. Yet at the same time he subtly subverted the image of Rāma by carefully interweaving three additional stories that serve to identify Rāvaṇa with heroic figures. As a result, the perplexed reader, expecting a more conventional characterization, often ends up admiring or feeling sympathy for the expected villain of the story. Dutt admitted to a friend that his character portrayal was the result of his contempt for traditional Hindu values like asceticism and his admiration for the enjoyment of possessions and power that was associated with colonial Calcutta.[24]

Such oppositional texts demonstrate the potential plurality of characterization and plot in the *Rāmāyaṇa* tradition; analysis of kinds of audience in performance reveals another component of the tradition's diversity. Stuart Blackburn's essay examines a shadow-puppet tradition in present-day Kerala (based on Kampaṉ's twelfth-century Tamil *Irāmāvatāram*), focusing on the play's "internal" audience. Unlike the Rām Līlā of Banaras, performed before huge crowds, the spectators at the Kerala puppet plays are few—and those few often doze off soon after the performance begins. As a result, the puppeteers perform principally for one another. Aficionados of the genre, they strive to outdo each other in voluminous commentary and witty remarks, incorporating into the telling of the *Rāmāyaṇa* verbal treatises on grammar, local references, and satire of pious ideals. This internal audience has thus shaped the many layers and frames of the drama, giving rise to yet another kind of diversity within the *Rāmāyaṇa* tradition.

TELLINGS AS COMMENTARY AND PROGRAMS FOR ACTION

Rāmāyaṇa tellings provide a set of resources on which people have drawn—in their own way and for their own purposes—in order to accuse, justify, meditate, debate, and more. The papers in the final section of the volume, Part Three, explore how and why people select particular incidents from the *Rāmāyaṇa* to express their view of reality. Such selective tellings—ones which adopt a nontraditional perspective on otherwise familiar features of the tale—have proved an effective means for conveying political views and for inculcating religious teachings. In Indian exegesis as well as tellings, the diversity of *Rāmāyaṇa* tradition makes itself known.[25]

Paula Richman's paper analyzes the logic of E. V. Ramasami's exegesis of the *Rāmāyaṇa*. In an oft-reprinted pamphlet intended for a popular readership, he argues that morally ambiguous episodes such as the killing of Vālin, Rāma's harsh treatment of Sītā, and the mutilation of Śūrpaṇakhā constitute the real core of the *Rāmāyaṇa*. Using these incidents to guide his assessment of *Rāmāyaṇa* characters and their values, he scathingly attacks Hinduism—especially the worship of Rāma—as a North Indian way of subjugating South Indians, while glorifying Rāvaṇa, whom he identifies with the values of "Dravidian" culture.[26] Labeling the sanctity accorded the *Rāmāyaṇa*, as well as the high status of the Brahmins that the *Rāmāyaṇa* seeks to justify, as forms of North Indian domination, he exhorts fellow South Indians to liberate themselves by rejecting belief in Rāma both as moral paradigm and as god. Such a reading of the Rāma story functions as a clarion call to cultural separatism.

Medieval Śrīvaiṣṇava commentators used their own form of *Rāmāyaṇa* exegesis to explain a different kind of freedom: spiritual liberation. Patricia Mumme's paper shows how Teṉkalai Śrīvaiṣṇavas regard the actions of *Rāmāyaṇa* characters as revealing truths about the relationship between the devotee and the divine Lord. In contrast to theologians from the rival Vaṭakalai sect, who wrote primarily for an elite audience of learned Brahmins, the Teṉkalais addressed themselves to a broader lay audience that included women and non-Brahmin men, edifying this diverse group by incorporating incidents from the *Rāmāyaṇa*. In their exegesis, the Teṉkalai commentators select what other tellings usually regard as minor incidents, remove them from their usual narrative context, and use them in unexpected ways as parables to thwart the expectations of their audience. Such incidents shock hearers into questioning their ordinary assumptions about the nature of salvation, preparing them to accept Śrīvaiṣṇava theological claims.

Selectivity generates another kind of power in the *rasik sampradāy* based in Ayodhya, a sect whose religious beliefs and meditational practices Philip Lutgendorf analyzes in his essay. The theology and practices of the *rasik* tradition assume a telling of the *Rāmāyaṇa* that foregrounds the time right after the wedding of Rāma and Sītā, when the couple savors the pleasures of love in their golden palace. The *Rāmcaritmānas* of Tulsīdās (generally known by the shorter title *Mānas*) portrays this incident only briefly and discreetly; yet members of the *rasik* tradition elaborate on this account, prescribing various means to identify meditatively with the companions and servants of Sītā and Rāma during this period. Here we find not the heroic Rāma but the erotic one, not the long-suffering Sītā but one engaged in exploring life's pleasures. *Rasik* adepts say that the traditionally emphasized events—exile, war, coronation—constitute the conventional *Rāmāyaṇa*, which is easily known; in contrast, true devotees seek the transcendent *Rāmāyaṇa* of the love play between Rāma and Sītā, revealed only to initiates. Their interpretation of the *Rāmāyaṇa* enables adherents to actualize heavenly play on earth through meditation.

If selectivity enables *rasiks* to attain their meditative goals, it is also, as Ramdas Lamb shows in his essay, key to the telling of the *Rāmāyaṇa* among the Rāmnāmīs, a militant Untouchable sect of the Chhattisgarh region in eastern Madhya Pradesh. Although the Rāmnāmīs view the *Mānas* as their official text, they reject some sections and stress others, reducing the text of 24,000 stanzas to a corpus of some four to five hundred individual verses. In addition, through ritual chanting and debates, members of the sect continue to personalize their *Rāmāyaṇa* text, embellishing it with verses that usually then become part of the corpus. Lamb traces this process, showing how the Rāmnāmīs began by viewing the *Mānas* as inviolate but gradually came, self-consciously, to cull the text for material consonant with their own beliefs. His research and that of Lutgendorf attest to another kind of fluidity within the *Rāmāyaṇa* tradition, showing how even a single, apparently fixed text can be refashioned and thus appropriated to diverse ends.

SOME IMPLICATIONS OF OUR ANALYSES

In the essays that follow we make no pretense of giving an exhaustive survey of all the *Rāmāyaṇas* in India nor do we believe that such is feasible. We thus acknowledge that many significant tellings of Rāma's story—such as the *Śakta Rāmāyaṇas*, in which Sītā slays Rāvaṇa, or the South Asian Persian *Rāmāyaṇas*—go unrepresented here. Our goal has been to be suggestive, rather than comprehensive. Nor have we attempted an analysis of the *Rāmāyaṇas* of each major region in India.[27] Rather, our aim has been to elucidate the compelling logic of a number of intriguing *Rāmāyaṇas*, delineate their context, and juxtapose telling with telling to reveal wider patterns within the *Rāmāyaṇa* tradition.

Clearly, each contributor to this volume adds to our knowledge of specific *Rāmāyaṇas* in India and Thailand. For example, Shulman shows how the portrayal of Rāma's repudiation of Sītā in the *Irāmāvatāram* has been shaped by the assumptions of Tamil *bhakti*; Lutgendorf considers why scholars have neglected *rasik* tradition; Blackburn points out that the Kerala puppet plays include an antiheroic interpretation of certain events in Rāma's story; Reynolds identifies both Hindu and Buddhist elements in the *Ramakien*. In addition to reflecting specifically on individual tellings of the story, moreover, these essays reveal certain patterns across *Rāmāyaṇas*.

The essays collected here also testify to the validity of Ramanujan's claims about the *Rāmāyaṇa* tradition. Ramanujan argues that the *Rāmāyaṇa* has become "a second language of a whole culture area," and we have found it to be an extraordinarily eloquent language. The *Rāmāyaṇa* provides Kampaṉ with the language to express the complex relationship between god and devotee; it furnishes the Rāmnāmīs with quotations to use in sophisticated debate; it lends Dutt the ability to articulate the colonial dilemma of cultural ambivalence; it provides Thai kings with the vocabulary of political legitimacy. Sītā's trials give Telugu Brahmin women a way to talk about a husband's neglect, while Rāvaṇa's situation enables E. V. Ramasami to polemicize about Tamil separatism. Theological, sexual, and political discourse: all emerge from the great pool of *Rāmāyaṇa* tradition.

The cultural uses of the *Rāmāyaṇa* are manifold and ever changing. Particular groups at particular times in history develop an elective affinity for specific characters. Vālmīki currently attracts the affection of certain *jātis* of sanitation workers,[28] Sītā has traditionally elicited the empathy of long-suffering wives,[29] and the proponents of a separate Tamil state have identified with Rāvaṇa. Clearly, the significance of the *Rāmāyaṇa* goes beyond specific texts to encompass twin processes that lie at the heart of culture. Thus some tellings of the *Rāmāyaṇa* affirm the hierarchy found in social, political, and religious relations, while other tellings contest that hierarchy.

Contesting often coalesces around the figure of Rāvaṇa. Seely reveals how Dutt has glorified Rāvaṇa and his fellow *rākṣasas* (demons), presenting them in a sympathetic way, while simultaneously portraying Rāma and his followers in a poor light.[30] The same elevation of Rāvaṇa predominates in the telling of the *Rāmāyaṇa* assumed in E. V. Ramasami's interpretation, but within a political context. There Rāvaṇa stands as a paragon of South Indian virtue.

Even if Dutt and Ramasami were the only ones who presented Rāvaṇa in this way, their telling would be significant. But they are not. Many "non-mainstream" groups have laid claim to Rāvaṇa at different times in history and in different parts of India. Ramanujan's essay outlines how certain Jain *Rāmāyaṇas* portray the story from Rāvaṇa's perspective. The Dalits, a group of militant Mahars (considered Untouchables by higher *jātis*) in Maharashtra, have embraced Rāvaṇa as one of their heroes.[31] The Nadars, a low *jāti* that was composed primarily of impoverished toddy-tappers until some of its members converted to Christianity, claimed Mahodara (Rāvaṇa's prime minister) as their ancestor.[32] A number of Dravidian tribals and lower *jātis* of southern and central India have caste traditions that connect them with Rāvaṇa and/or Lanka.[33]

Our conclusions about Rāvaṇa suggest ways of looking at other *Rāmāyaṇa* characters as well. In a male-dominated society, Telugu Brahmin women's songs present Sītā as finally victorious over Rāma. The same songs also tell of Śūrpaṇakhā's revenge on Rāma. Perhaps someday Śūrpaṇakhā will be claimed as a symbol of the physical violence that has been unjustly perpetrated upon women who seek independence from constraining social norms. Similarly, several characters in the Kerala puppet play express the anger of those low in the social hierarchy against those in positions of power and decision making. In the oppositional tellings of the *Rāmāyaṇa*, then, we encounter the traditions of those set apart from the mainstream by religious persuasion, social location, or gender, who struggle against an understanding of themselves as presented through the lens of a religious text. Non-Hindu males, men labeled "low-caste," and women of many communities have created and maintained counter-*Rāmāyaṇas*. These groups take the story of Rāma and use it to express their own perception of "the way things are."

In addition to resistance expressed through nontraditional perspectives on characterization, other groups have contested dominant *Rāmāyaṇa* traditions by selectively dismembering particular tellings of the story of Rāma. In such cases, less is often more. When, for their own reasons, particular groups metonymize, appropriate, or abridge parts of the Rāma story, these incidents gain power and richness. For these groups, to use the *Rāmāyaṇa* is to claim specific portions of the story as expressing the essence of their ultimate concerns.

A most concise kind of reduction emerges from metonymy, the selection of one small part of the text as representing the essence of the whole; this is what we find among the *rasiks* analyzed by Lutgendorf.[34] For them, the dalliance of Rāma and Sītā constitutes the esoteric essence of the *Rāmāyaṇa*, their religious elaboration on this section of the text affording them rich meditative experience. The Śrīvaiṣṇava commentarial process likewise employs highly selective appropriation but yields another kind of fruit. Commentators search through the *Rāmāyaṇa*, find incidents that seem to them pregnant with theological meaning, and then assist in the birth of that meaning. These radically decontextualized incidents yield Teṉkalai writers tremendously powerful imagery for salvific instruction. When the Rāmnāmīs cull the *Rāmcaritmānas* and create personalized texts, they affirm their commitment to egalitarian ideology, gaining a power that continues to increase with their ever-growing attainment of literacy. Literacy gives them the ability to reject passages praising Brahmins and caste structure and to stress verses that assert Rāma's love for all people and the benefits of chanting Rāma's name. The Rāmnāmī abridgment of the *Mānas* is yet one more example of the process of recasting the story in consonance with a particular worldview.

The essays in this volume have highlighted that recasting process again and again—the manner in which particular authors, performers, commentators, and communities have embraced the Rāma story but have told it in distinctive ways in order to make it their own. Together, the essays in this volume bear witness to the plurality of *Rāmāyaṇa* tradition. It is a multivoiced entity, encompassing tellings of the Rāma story that vary according to historical period, regional literary tradition, religious affiliation, genre, intended audience, social location, gender, and political context. The *Rāmāyaṇa* tradition can be seen as indicative of the range and complexity of narrative traditions from South Asian culture, both in India proper and in spheres of Indian cultural influence. We hope we have revealed something of South Asian culture's diversity, and emphasized its richness and power, through our study of many *Rāmāyaṇas*.

NOTES

In working out the ideas for this introduction I received invaluable aid from many individuals. I am grateful to Wendy Doniger, Michael Fisher, Rich Freeman, Sandria Freitag, Charles Hallisey, Philip Lutgendorf, Patricia Mathews, Sheldon Pollock, Sumathi Ramaswamy, Clinton Seely, David Shulman, H. Daniel Smith, and Sandra Zagarell for their comments and suggestions.

1. While an article in *India Today* titled "Epic Spin-offs" (15 July 1988, 72) men-

tions an audience of sixty million, other sources give the higher number cited here. It is difficult to obtain exact figures, because in the case of very popular programs like the *Rāmāyaṇa*, the number of viewers watching a single television set appears to increase dramatically. See the *Illustrated Weekly of India*'s article titled "The Ramayan" (8 November 1987), 9.

2. This book includes an account of Sītā's stay at Vālmīki's forest hermitage, after she is banished by Rāma. According to one tradition, Vālmīki is said to have been an outcaste; several North Indian *jātis* of street sweepers (usually referred to by the euphemistic title "sanitation workers") claim descent from him. The possibility that the television *Rāmāyaṇa* might conclude without portraying the episodes dealing with Sītā and their purported ancestor upset a number of sanitation workers greatly. For an account of this incident and the political factors that led to the continuation of the serial, see "The Second Coming," *India Today* (31 August 1988), 81.

3. Philip Lutgendorf, "Ramayan: The Video," *The Drama Review* 34, no. 2 (Summer 1990): 128.

4. Romila Thapar, "The Ramayana Syndrome," *Seminar*, no. 353 (January 1989), 74.

5. For a historical discussion of *Rāmāyaṇa* patronage, see Philip Lutgendorf, "Ram's Story in Shiva's City: Public Arenas and Private Patronage" in *Culture and Power in Banaras: Community, Performance, and Environment, 1800–1980*, ed. Sandria B. Freitag (Berkeley and Los Angeles: University of California Press, 1989), 34–61.

6. Thapar, "The Ramayana Syndrome," 72.

7. Ibid.

8. For an account of the extraordinary new market for books on the *Rāmāyaṇa* created by the television serial, see "Epic Spin-offs," 73. In addition, Lutgendorf notes a scholarly trend to pay more attention to Rāma, who was earlier neglected in favor of studies on Kṛṣṇa. See pp. 217–18, this volume.

9. The phrase "the *Rāmāyaṇa* tradition" is used in this essay to refer to the many tellings of the Rāma story as a whole, rather than to Vālmīki's telling or some other specific telling limited to a particular region or particular time.

10. As Robert P. Goldman, general editor of a new English translation of Vālmīki's *Rāmāyaṇa*, says, "Few works of literature produced in any place at any time have been as popular, influential, imitated, and successful as the great and ancient Sanskrit epic poem, the Vālmīki *Rāmāyaṇa*" (*The Rāmāyaṇa of Vālmīki*, vol. 1: *Bālakāṇḍa* [Princeton: Princeton University Press, 1984], x). For an up-to-date overview of the history of Vālmīki's text and the scholarship concerning it, consult the introductory essays to this seven-volume translation (vol. 1: *Bālakāṇḍa*, trans. Robert P. Goldman, 1984; vol. 2: *Ayodhyākāṇḍa*, trans. Sheldon I. Pollock, 1986; vol. 3: *Araṇyakāṇḍa*, trans. Sheldon I. Pollock, 1991; remaining four volumes, forthcoming).

11. The reader who immediately wants to learn about a competing telling of Rāma's story that differs in religious affiliation, literary form, characterization, and overall message should turn ahead to the essay by Frank Reynolds, which discusses the Pali *Dasaratha Jātaka*, an early Buddhist telling of the story of Rāma. Although less popular than Vālmīki in South Asia, this telling has had substantial influence on the *Rāmāyaṇa* tradition in Southeast Asia. For an English translation of this telling, see E. B. Cowell, ed., *The Jātaka; or, Stories of the Buddha's Former Births*, 7 vols. (1895–1913; repr. London: Luzac and Co. for the Pali Text Society, 1956), 4:78–82. See also

Richard Gombrich, "The Vessantara Jātaka, the Rāmāyaṇa and the Dasaratha Jātaka," *Journal of the American Oriental Society* 105, no. 3 (July–September 1985): 427–37.

12. Shulman describes Kampaṉ's *Irāmāvatāram* thus: "Perhaps the supreme achievement of Tamil letters, and certainly one of the great works of the world's religious literature, is Kampaṉ's version of the Hindu epic, the *Rāmāyaṇa*. No creation of Tamil poets has ever been so passionately loved as Kampaṉ's *Irāmāvatāram*." See "The Cliché as Ritual and Instrument: Iconic Puns in Kampaṉ's *Irāmāvatāram*," *Numen* 25, no. 2 (August 1978): 135. For a recent English translation of the *Araṇyakāṇḍa* of Kampaṉ's poem, see George L. Hart and Hank Heifetz, trans., *The Forest Book of the Rāmāyaṇa of Kampaṉ* (Berkeley and Los Angeles: University of California Press, 1988), which also contains an introductory essay that includes a comparison of Vālmīki and Kampaṉ. For studies of the uniqueness of Kampaṉ's rendition of the story, see David Shulman, "The Cliché as Ritual and Instrument"; "The Crossing of the Wilderness: Landscape and Myth in the Tamil Story of Rāma," *Acta Orientalia* 42 (1981): 21–54; and "The Anthropology of the Avatār in Kampaṉ's *Irāmāvatāram*," in *Gilgul: Essays on Transformation, Revolution, and Permanence in the History of Religions*, ed. Shaul Shaked, David Shulman, and Gedaliahu Stroumsa (Leiden: E. J. Brill, 1987), 270–87.

13. There are many studies of Jain *Rāmāyaṇas*, among which the following are especially helpful: V. M. Kulkarni, "The Origin and Development of the Rama Story in Jaina Literature," *Journal of the Oriental Institute of Baroda* 9, no. 2 (December 1959): 189–204, and no. 3 (March 1960): 284–304; K. R. Chandra, *A Critical Study of Paumacariyaṁ* (Muzaffarpur: Research Institute of Prakrit, Jainology and Ahimsa, 1970); and D. L. Narasimhachar, "Jaina Ramayanas," *Indian Historical Quarterly* 15, no. 4 (December 1939): 575–94.

14. For other studies of the *Rāmāyaṇa* tradition that use the psychoanalytic method, see J. Moussaieff Masson, "Fratricide among the Monkeys: Psychoanalytic Observations on an Episode in the Vālmīkirāmāyaṇam," *Journal of the American Oriental Society* 95, no. 4 (October–December 1975): 672–78; "Hanumān as an Imaginary Companion," *Journal of the American Oriental Society* 101, no. 3 (July–September 1981): 355–60.

15. For a discussion of the geography—physical and emotional—of classical Tamil poetry, see A. K. Ramanujan, *The Interior Landscape* (Bloomington: Indiana University Press, 1967).

16. Especially noteworthy is the research of V. Raghavan, whose commitment to exploring the many *Rāmāyaṇas* in Asia led to a number of works including *The Greater Ramayana* (Varanasi: All-India Kashiraj Trust, 1973); *The Ramayana in Greater India* (Surat: South Gujarat University, 1975); and *Some Old Lost Rama Plays* (Annamalainagar: Annamalai University, 1961).

It is understandably beyond the scope of this essay to give a complete bibliography of works that analyze the *Rāmāyaṇa* tradition, but especially useful are: Romila Thapar, *Exile and the Kingdom: Some Thoughts on the Ramayana* (Bangalore: The Mythic Society, 1978); V. Raghavan, ed., *The Ramayana Tradition in Asia* (Delhi: Sahitya Akademi, 1980); K. R. Srinivasa Iyengar, ed., *Asian Variations on the Ramayana* (New Delhi: Sahitya Akademi, 1980); J. L. Brockington, *Righteous Rāma: The Evolution of an Epic* (Delhi: Oxford University Press, 1984); P. Banerjee, *Rama in Indian Literature, Art and Thought*, 2 vols. (Delhi: Sundeep Prakashan, 1986); Amal Sarkar, *A Study on the Rāmāyaṇas* (Calcutta: Rddhi-India, 1987).

Recent work includes Joyce Burkhalter Flueckiger and Laurie Sears, eds., *The Boundaries of Tradition: Ramayana and Mahabharata Performances in South and Southeast Asia* (Ann Arbor: University of Michigan Center for South and Southeast Asian Studies, 1990); Monika Thiel-Horstmann, ed., *Contemporary Rāmāyaṇa Traditions: Written, Oral, and Performed* (Wiesbaden: Otto Harrassowitz, 1991); Brenda E. F. Beck, "Core Triangles in the Folk Epics of India," and John D. Smith, "Scapegoats of the Gods: The Ideology of the Indian Epics," both in Stuart H. Blackburn et al., eds., *Oral Epics in India* (Berkeley and Los Angeles: University of California Press, 1989), 155–75 and 176–94.

For bibliographies, see N. A. Gore, *Bibliography of the Ramayana* (Poona: By the author, 1943); H. Daniel Smith, *Reading the Rāmāyaṇa: A Bibliographic Guide for Students and College Teachers—Indian Variants on the Rāma-Theme in English Translations*, Foreign and Comparative Studies, South Asian special publications no. 4 (Syracuse: Maxwell School of Citizenship and Public Affairs, Syracuse University, 1983); H. Daniel Smith, *Select Bibliography of Rāmāyaṇa-related Studies*, Ananthacharya Indological Series, no. 21 (Bombay, 1989); and Sudha Varma, *Tulsidas Bibliography* (forthcoming).

17. See Goldman, trans., *The Rāmāyaṇa of Vālmīki*, vol. 1: *Bālakāṇḍa*, 14–29, for an overview of this scholarship.

18. Both Ramanujan, in his essay for this volume, and Kamil Zvelebil, in the introduction to his *Two Tamil Folktales: The Story of King Mataṉakāma and the Story of Peacock Rāvaṇa* (Delhi: Motilal Banarsidass, 1987), suggest a set of motifs that appear only in the southern versions. In addition, it is important to remember that Vālmīki's "version" is itself many versions.

19. Recent scholarship on the Rām Līlā of Banaras has demonstrated the vitality and social significance of performance traditions in North India. See, among others, Linda Hess and Richard Schechner, "The Ramlila of Ramnagar," *The Drama Review* 21, no. 3 (September 1977): 51–82; Philip Lutgendorf, *The Life of a Text: Performing the Rāmcaritmānas of Tulsidas* (Berkeley and Los Angeles: University of California Press, 1991); Anuradha Kapur, "The Ram Lila at Ramnagar: A North Indian Drama" (Ph.D. diss., University of Leeds, 1980). For an analysis of variety within the *Rāmāyaṇa* performance tradition, see the discussion of the Nakkatayya festival, a rambunctious festival in Banaras based upon Śūrpaṇakhā's mutilation, in the section entitled "Cutting Off of the Nose" in Nita Kumar, "Popular Culture in Urban India: The Artisans of Banaras, c. 1884–1984" (Ph.D. diss., University of Chicago, 1984), 261–94; Sandria Freitag, "Behavior as Text: Popular Participation in the Story of Ram," presentation to the Society for Cultural Anthropology, Santa Monica, California, May 1990.

20. Rāma's role as exemplar is especially evident in the *Ayodhyākāṇḍa* of Vālmīki's *Rāmāyaṇa*. Pollock shows that Vālmīki portrays Rāma as a moral paradigm rather than a developing character whose actions are a mixture of good and bad: "Rāma and the others are evidently designed to be monovalent paradigms of conduct." See Sheldon I. Pollock, trans., *The Rāmāyaṇa of Vālmīki*, vol. 2: *Ayodhyākāṇḍa*, 50–51. As if to attest to the success of Vālmīki's efforts, readings that attempt to rationalize away

Rāma's moral rough spots recur frequently in devotional, apologetic, and scholarly writing. V. Raghavan himself wrote a devotional treatise extolling the virtues of Rāma and vilifying Rāvaṇa for his lust and greed: see his *The Two Brothers: Rama and Lakshmana* (Madras: Ramayana Printing Works, 1976). In this slim book, which differs from many of his other writings in its personal quality, he discusses Rāma's deeds entirely in terms of his absolute adherence to dharma, never once even referring to Rāma's killing of Vālin. Consider, as well, the way another author contrives to maintain Rāma's reputation.

> But this episode [the killing of Vālin] has another redeeming side. . . . The very fact that this one incident has raised such a huge cry of criticism is itself an acknowledgement of Rāma's superhuman excellence in all other respects. Therefore, this one stain only adds to the beauty of the portrait as the *śrīvatsa* mark [chest ornament] on the person of Viṣṇu.

See Swami Siddhinathananda, "Śrī Rāma—Dharma Personified," *Prabuddha Bharata* 77, no. 8 (September 1972), 395. Also see Frank Whaling, *The Rise of the Religious Significance of Rāma* (Delhi: Motilal Banarsidass, 1980), 39–48.

21. In "Divine Order and Divine Evil in the Tamil Tale of Rāma" (*Journal of Asian Studies* 38, no. 4 [August 1979]: 653), David Shulman assesses one of the most notorious of the morally ambiguous actions performed by Rāma, namely, his murder of Vālin.

22. For a discussion of how scholars have often overlooked the ambiguity of Sītā's behavior, see Sally J. Sutherland, "Sītā and Draupadī: Aggressive Behavior and Female Role-Models in the Sanskrit Epics," *Journal of the American Oriental Society* 109, no. 1 (January–March 1989): 63.

23. Gloria Goodwin Raheja, "Subversion and Moral Evaluation in North Indian Women's Songs" (paper presented at the 41st annual meeting of the Association for Asian Studies, Washington, D.C., March 1989), 2.

24. Ashis Nandy, *The Intimate Enemy: Loss and Recovery of Self Under Colonialism* (Delhi: Oxford University Press, 1983), 20.

25. Philip Lutgendorf, "The View from the Ghats: Traditional Exegesis of a Hindu Epic," *Journal of Asian Studies* 48, no. 2 (May 1989): 272–88.

26. It is intriguing that E. V. Ramasami produced this decidedly regional interpretation at the same time that another Madrasi, C. Rajagopalachari, broadcast his telling of the *Rāmāyaṇa* as a "national epic." See Joanne Punzo Waghorne, *Images of Dharma: The Epic World of C. Rajagopalachari* (Delhi: Chanakya Publications, 1985), 133–55. Perhaps the two—the regional and the national—help to constitute each other. Arjun Appadurai notes their interrelatedness in his recent article entitled "How to Make a National Cuisine: Cookbooks in Contemporary India" (*Comparative Studies in Society and History* 30, no. 1 [January 1988]: 3–24): "The idea of an 'Indian' cuisine has emerged because of, rather than despite, the increasing articulation of regional and ethnic cuisines" (21). I am indebted to Charles Hallisey for pointing out this parallel to me.

27. That enormous task has barely been begun, but W. L. Smith has made a major contribution for Bengali, Oriya, and Assamese *Rāmāyaṇas*: see his *Rāmāyaṇa Traditions in Eastern India: Assam, Bengal, and Orissa* (Stockholm: Department of Indology, University of Stockholm, 1988). See also Asit K. Banerjee, ed., *The Ramayana in*

Eastern India (Calcutta: Prajna, 1983). Other regional studies include C. R. Sharma, *The Ramayana in Telugu and Tamil: A Comparative Study* (Madras: Lakshminarayana Granthamala, 1973); A. Pandurangam, "Ramayana Versions in Tamil," *Journal of Tamil Studies* 21 (June 1982): 58–67.

28. See Mark Juergensmeyer, *Religion as Social Vision* (Berkeley and Los Angeles: University of California Press, 1982), 169–80.

29. Although Narayana Rao's article in this volume deals only with Telugu women's songs, the emphases and perspectives characteristic of these songs seem to occur elsewhere in Indian women's *Rāmāyaṇa* traditions. For example, some of the same emphasis on Rāma's neglect of Sītā and the importance of her twin sons is found among Maharashtran women: see Indira Junghare, "The Ramayana in Maharashtran Women's Folk Songs," *Man in India* 56, no. 4 (October–December 1976): 285–305. See especially the songs translated on pp. 297–301 of this article.

30. Nirad C. Chaudhuri, *The Autobiography of an Unknown Indian* (New York: Macmillan, 1951), 188.

31. V. T. Rajshekar, *Aggression on Indian Culture: Cultural Identity of Dalits and the Dominant Tradition of India* (Bangalore: Dalit Sahitya Akademy, 1988), 13.

32. Robert Caldwell, *The Tinnevelly Shanars: A Sketch of Their Religion and Their Moral Condition and Characteristics as a Caste* (Madras: Christian Knowledge Society Press, 1849), 27–28. According to Bishop Caldwell's account, the Nadars celebrated the day on which Rāvaṇa carried Sītā to Lanka as one of their religious festivals.

33. James Ryan, "Rāvaṇa, Tirukkuṟaḷ, and the Historical Roots of the Philosophy of Periyār" (paper presented at the 11th Annual Conference on South Asia, Madison, Wisconsin, November 1982).

34. Goldman likewise calls attention to the tradition of producing abridged (*saṃkṣipta*) versions of Vālmīki's text: *The Rāmāyaṇa of Vālmīki*, vol. 1: *Bālakāṇḍa*, 6, n. 10; 274.

TWO

Three Hundred *Rāmāyaṇas*: Five Examples and Three Thoughts on Translation

A. K. Ramanujan

How many *Rāmāyaṇas*? Three hundred? Three thousand? At the end of some *Rāmāyaṇas*, a question is sometimes asked: How many *Rāmāyaṇas* have there been? And there are stories that answer the question. Here is one.

One day when Rāma was sitting on his throne, his ring fell off. When it touched the earth, it made a hole in the ground and disappeared into it. It was gone. His trusty henchman, Hanumān, was at his feet. Rāma said to Hanumān, "Look, my ring is lost. Find it for me."

Now Hanumān can enter any hole, no matter how tiny. He had the power to become the smallest of the small and larger than the largest thing. So he took on a tiny form and went down the hole.

He went and went and went and suddenly fell into the netherworld. There were women down there. "Look, a tiny monkey! It's fallen from above!" Then they caught him and placed him on a platter (*thāli*). The King of Spirits (*bhūt*), who lives in the netherworld, likes to eat animals. So Hanumān was sent to him as part of his dinner, along with his vegetables. Hanumān sat on the platter, wondering what to do.

While this was going on in the netherworld, Rāma sat on his throne on the earth above. The sage Vasiṣṭha and the god Brahmā came to see him. They said to Rāma, "We want to talk privately with you. We don't want anyone to hear what we say or interrupt it. Do we agree?"

"All right," said Rāma, "we'll talk."

Then they said, "Lay down a rule. If anyone comes in as we are talking, his head should be cut off."

"It will be done," said Rāma.

Who would be the most trustworthy person to guard the door? Hanumān had gone down to fetch the ring. Rāma trusted no one more than Lakṣmaṇa, so he asked Lakṣmaṇa to stand by the door. "Don't allow anyone to enter," he ordered.

Lakṣmaṇa was standing at the door when the sage Viśvāmitra appeared and said, "I need to see Rāma at once. It's urgent. Tell me, where is Rāma?"

Lakṣmaṇa said, "Don't go in now. He is talking to some people. It's important."

"What is there that Rāma would hide from me?" said Viśvāmitra. "I must go in, right now."

Lakṣmaṇa said, "I'll have to ask his permission before I can let you in."

"Go in and ask then."

"I can't go in till Rāma comes out. You'll have to wait."

"If you don't go in and announce my presence, I'll burn the entire kingdom of Ayodhya with a curse," said Viśvāmitra.

Lakṣmaṇa thought, "If I go in now, I'll die. But if I don't go, this hotheaded man will burn down the kingdom. All the subjects, all things living in it, will die. It's better that I alone should die."

So he went right in.

Rāma asked him, "What's the matter?"

"Viśvāmitra is here."

"Send him in."

So Viśvāmitra went in. The private talk had already come to an end. Brahmā and Vasiṣṭha had come to see Rāma and say to him, "Your work in the world of human beings is over. Your incarnation as Rāma must now be given up. Leave this body, come up, and rejoin the gods." That's all they wanted to say.

Lakṣmaṇa said to Rāma, "Brother, you should cut off my head."

Rāma said, "Why? We had nothing more to say. Nothing was left. So why should I cut off your head?"

Lakṣmaṇa said, "You can't do that. You can't let me off because I'm your brother. There'll be a blot on Rāma's name. You didn't spare your wife. You sent her to the jungle. I must be punished. I will leave."

Lakṣmaṇa was an avatar of Śeṣa, the serpent on whom Viṣṇu sleeps. His time was up too. He went directly to the river Sarayū and disappeared in the flowing waters.

When Lakṣmaṇa relinquished his body, Rāma summoned all his followers, Vibhīṣaṇa, Sugrīva, and others, and arranged for the coronation of his twin sons, Lava and Kuśa. Then Rāma too entered the river Sarayū.

All this while, Hanumān was in the netherworld. When he was finally taken to the King of Spirits, he kept repeating the name of Rāma. "Rāma Rāma Rāma . . ."

Then the King of Spirits asked, "Who are you?"

"Hanumān."

"Hanumān? Why have you come here?"

"Rāma's ring fell into a hole. I've come to fetch it."

The king looked around and showed him a platter. On it were thousands of rings. They were all Rāma's rings. The king brought the platter to Hanumān, set it down, and said, "Pick out your Rāma's ring and take it."

They were all exactly the same. "I don't know which one it is," said Hanumān, shaking his head.

The King of Spirits said, "There have been as many Rāmas as there are rings on this platter. When you return to earth, you will not find Rāma. This incarnation of Rāma is now over. Whenever an incarnation of Rāma is about to be over, his ring falls down. I collect them and keep them. Now you can go."

So Hanumān left.

This story is usually told to suggest that for every such Rāma there is a *Rāmāyaṇa*.[1] The number of *Rāmāyaṇas* and the range of their influence in South and Southeast Asia over the past twenty-five hundred years or more are astonishing. Just a list of languages in which the Rāma story is found makes one gasp: Annamese, Balinese, Bengali, Cambodian, Chinese, Gujarati, Javanese, Kannada, Kashmiri, Khotanese, Laotian, Malaysian, Marathi, Oriya, Prakrit, Sanskrit, Santali, Sinhalese, Tamil, Telugu, Thai, Tibetan—to say nothing of Western languages. Through the centuries, some of these languages have hosted more than one telling of the Rāma story. Sanskrit alone contains some twenty-five or more tellings belonging to various narrative genres (epics, *kāvyas* or ornate poetic compositions, *purāṇas* or old mythological stories, and so forth). If we add plays, dance-dramas, and other performances, in both the classical and folk traditions, the number of *Rāmāyaṇas* grows even larger. To these must be added sculpture and bas-reliefs, mask plays, puppet plays and shadow plays, in all the many South and Southeast Asian cultures.[2] Camille Bulcke, a student of the *Rāmāyaṇa*, counted three hundred tellings.[3] It's no wonder that even as long ago as the fourteenth century, Kumāravyāsa, a Kannada poet, chose to write a *Mahābhārata*, because he heard the cosmic serpent which upholds the earth groaning under the burden of *Rāmāyaṇa* poets (*tiṇikidanu phaṇirāya rāmāyaṇada kavigaḷa bhāradali*). In this paper, indebted for its data to numerous previous translators and scholars, I would like to sort out for myself, and I hope for others, how these hundreds of tellings of a story in different cultures, languages, and religious traditions relate to each other: what gets translated, transplanted, transposed.

VĀLMĪKI AND KAMPAṈ: TWO AHALYĀS

Obviously, these hundreds of tellings differ from one another. I have come to prefer the word *tellings* to the usual terms *versions* or *variants* because the latter terms can and typically do imply that there is an invariant, an original or

Ur-text—usually Vālmīki's Sanskrit *Rāmāyaṇa*, the earliest and most prestigious of them all. But as we shall see, it is not always Vālmīki's narrative that is carried from one language to another.

It would be useful to make some distinctions before we begin. The tradition itself distinguishes between the Rāma story (*rāmakathā*) and texts composed by a specific person—Vālmīki, Kampaṉ, or Kṛttivāsa, for example. Though many of the latter are popularly called *Rāmāyaṇas* (like *Kamparāmāyaṇam*), few texts actually bear the title *Rāmāyaṇa*; they are given titles like *Irāmāvatāram* (The Incarnation of Rāma), *Rāmcaritmānas* (The Lake of the Acts of Rāma), *Ramakien* (The Story of Rāma), and so on. Their relations to the Rāma story as told by Vālmīki also vary. This traditional distinction between *kathā* (story) and *kāvya* (poem) parallels the French one between *sujet* and *récit*, or the English one between story and discourse.[4] It is also analogous to the distinction between a sentence and a speech act. The story may be the same in two tellings, but the discourse may be vastly different. Even the structure and sequence of events may be the same, but the style, details, tone, and texture—and therefore the import—may be vastly different.

Here are two tellings of the "same" episode, which occur at the same point in the sequence of the narrative. The first is from the first book (*Bālakāṇḍa*) of Vālmīki's Sanskrit *Rāmāyaṇa*; the second from the first canto (*Pālakāṇṭam*) of Kampaṉ's *Irāmāvatāram* in Tamil. Both narrate the story of Ahalyā.

The Ahalyā Episode: Vālmīki

Seeing Mithilā, Janaka's white
  and dazzling city, all the sages
cried out in praise, "Wonderful!
  How wonderful!"

Rāghava, sighting on the outskirts
  of Mithilā an ashram, ancient,
unpeopled, and lovely, asked the sage,
  "What is this holy place,

so like an ashram but without a hermit?
  Master, I'd like to hear: whose was it?"
Hearing Rāghava's words, the great sage
  Viśvāmitra, man of fire,

expert in words answered, "Listen,
  Rāghava, I'll tell you whose ashram
this was and how it was cursed
  by a great man in anger.

It was great Gautama's, this ashram
  that reminds you of heaven, worshiped
even by the gods. Long ago, with Ahalyā
  he practiced *tapas*[5] here

for countless years. Once, knowing that Gautama
was away, Indra (called Thousand Eyes),
Śacī's husband, took on the likeness
of the sage, and said to Ahalyā:

'Men pursuing their desire do not wait
for the proper season, O you who
have a perfect body. Making love
with you: that's what I want.
That waist of yours is lovely.'

She knew it was Indra of the Thousand Eyes
in the guise of the sage. Yet she,
wrongheaded woman, made up her mind,
excited, curious about the king
of the gods.

And then, her inner being satisfied,
she said to the god, 'I'm satisfied, king
of the gods. Go quickly from here.
O giver of honor, lover, protect
yourself and me.'

And Indra smiled and said to Ahalyā,
'Woman of lovely hips, I am
very content. I'll go the way I came.'
Thus after making love, he came out
of the hut made of leaves.

And, O Rāma, as he hurried away,
nervous about Gautama and flustered,
he caught sight of Gautama coming in,
the great sage, unassailable
by gods and antigods,

empowered by his *tapas*, still wet
with the water of the river
he'd bathed in, blazing like fire,
with *kuśa* grass and kindling
in his hands.

Seeing him, the king of the gods was
terror-struck, his face drained of color.
The sage, facing Thousand Eyes now dressed
as the sage, the one rich in virtue
and the other with none,

spoke to him in anger: 'You took my form,
you fool, and did this that should never
be done. Therefore you will lose your testicles.'
At once, they fell to the ground, they fell
even as the great sage spoke

his words in anger to Thousand Eyes.
Having cursed Indra, he then cursed
Ahalyā: 'You, you will dwell here
many thousands of years, eating the air,
without food, rolling in ash,

and burning invisible to all creatures.
When Rāma, unassailable son
of Daśaratha, comes to this terrible
wilderness, you will become pure,
you woman of no virtue,

you will be cleansed of lust and confusion.
Filled then with joy, you'll wear again
your form in my presence.' And saying
this to that woman of bad conduct,
blazing Gautama abandoned

the ashram, and did his *tapas*
on a beautiful Himalayan peak,
haunt of celestial singers and
perfected beings.

Emasculated Indra then
spoke to the gods led by Agni
attended by the sages
and the celestial singers.

'I've only done this work on behalf
of the gods, putting great Gautama
in a rage, blocking his *tapas*.
He has emasculated me

and rejected her in anger.
Through this great outburst
of curses, I've robbed him
of his *tapas*. Therefore,

great gods, sages, and celestial singers,
help me, helper of the gods,
to regain my testicles.' And the gods,
led by Agni, listened to Indra

of the Hundred Sacrifices and went
with the Marut hosts
to the divine ancestors, and said,
'Some time ago, Indra, infatuated,

ravished the sage's wife
and was then emasculated
by the sage's curse. Indra,
king of gods, destroyer of cities,

is now angry with the gods.
This ram has testicles
but great Indra has lost his.
So take the ram's testicles

and quickly graft them on to Indra.
A castrated ram will give you
supreme satisfaction and will be
a source of pleasure.

People who offer it
will have endless fruit.
You will give them your plenty.'
Having heard Agni's words,

the Ancestors got together
and ripped off the ram's testicles
and applied them then to Indra
of the Thousand Eyes.

Since then, the divine Ancestors
eat these castrated rams
and Indra has the testicles
of the beast through the power
of great Gautama's *tapas*.

Come then, Rāma, to the ashram
of the holy sage and save Ahalyā
who has the beauty of a goddess."
Rāghava heard Viśvāmitra's words

and followed him into the ashram
with Lakṣmaṇa: there he saw
Ahalyā, shining with an inner light
earned through her penances,

blazing yet hidden from the eyes
of passersby, even gods and antigods.[6]

The Ahalyā Episode: Kampaṉ

They came to many-towered Mithilā
and stood outside the fortress.
On the towers were many flags.

There, high on an open field,
stood a black rock
that was once Ahalyā,

the great sage's wife who fell
because she lost her chastity,
the mark of marriage in a house. 547

Rāma's eyes fell on the rock,
the dust of his feet
wafted on it.

Like one unconscious
coming to,
cutting through ignorance,

changing his dark carcass
for true form
as he reaches the Lord's feet,

so did she stand alive
formed and colored
again as she once was. 548

In 550, Rāma asks Viśvāmitra why this lovely woman had been turned to stone. Viśvāmitra replies:

"Listen. Once Indra,
Lord of the Diamond Axe,
waited on the absence

of Gautama, a sage all spirit,

meaning to reach out
for the lovely breast
of doe-eyed Ahalyā, his wife. 551

Hurt by love's arrows,
hurt by the look in her eyes
that pierced him like a spear, Indra
writhed and cast about
for stratagems;

one day, overwhelmed
and mindless, he isolated
the sage; and sneaked
into the hermitage
wearing the exact body of Gautama

whose heart knew no falsehoods. 552

Sneaking in, he joined Ahalyā;
coupled, they drank deep
of the clear new wine
of first-night weddings;

and she knew.

Yet unable
to put aside what was not hers,
she dallied in her joy,
but the sage did not tarry,
he came back, a very Śiva
with three eyes in his head. 553

Gautama, who used no arrows
from bows, could use more inescapable
powers of curse and blessing.

When he arrived, Ahalyā stood there,
stunned, bearing the shame of a deed
that will not end in this endless world.

Indra shook in terror,
started to move away
in the likeness of a cat. 554

Eyes dropping fire, Gautama
saw what was done,
and his words flew
like the burning arrows
at your hand:

'May you be covered
by the vaginas
of a thousand women!'
In the twinkle of an eye
they came and covered him. 555

Covered with shame,
laughingstock of the world,
Indra left.

The sage turned
to his tender wife
and cursed:

'O bought woman!
May you turn to stone!'
and she fell at once

a rough thing
of black rock. 556

Yet as she fell she begged:
'To bear and forgive wrongs
is also the way of elders.
O Śiva-like lord of mine,
set some limit to your curse!'

So he said: 'Rāma
will come, wearing garlands that bring
the hum of bees with them.
When the dust of his feet falls on you,
you will be released from the body of stone.' 557

The immortals looked at their king
and came down at once to Gautama
in a delegation led by Brahmā
and begged of Gautama to relent.

Gautama's mind had changed
and cooled. He changed
the marks on Indra to a thousand eyes
and the gods went back to their worlds,
while she lay there, a thing of stone. 558

That was the way it was.
From now on, no more misery,
only release, for all things
in this world.

O cloud-dark lord

who battled with that ogress,
black as soot, I saw there
the virtue of your hands
and here the virtue of your feet."[7] 559

Let me rapidly suggest a few differences between the two tellings. In Vālmīki, Indra seduces a willing Ahalyā. In Kampaṉ, Ahalyā realizes she is doing wrong but cannot let go of the forbidden joy; the poem has also suggested earlier that her sage-husband is all spirit, details which together add a certain psychological subtlety to the seduction. Indra tries to steal away in the shape of a cat, clearly a folklore motif (also found, for example, in the *Kathāsaritsāgara*, an eleventh-century Sanskrit compendium of folktales).[8] He is cursed with a thousand vaginas which are later changed into eyes, and Ahalyā is changed into frigid stone. The poetic justice wreaked on both offenders is fitted to their wrongdoing. Indra bears the mark of what he lusted for, while Ahalyā is rendered incapable of responding to anything. These motifs, not found in Vālmīki, are attested in South Indian folklore and other southern Rāma stories, in inscriptions and earlier Tamil poems, as well as in non-Tamil sources. Kampaṉ, here and elsewhere, not only makes full use of his predecessor Vālmīki's materials but folds in many regional folk traditions. It is often through him that they then become part of other *Rāmāyaṇas*.

In technique, Kampaṉ is also more dramatic than Vālmīki. Rāma's feet transmute the black stone into Ahalyā first; only afterward is her story told. The black stone standing on a high place, waiting for Rāma, is itself a very effective, vivid symbol. Ahalyā's revival, her waking from cold stone to fleshly human warmth, becomes an occasion for a moving *bhakti* (devotional) meditation on the soul waking to its form in god.

Finally, the Ahalyā episode is related to previous episodes in the poem such as that in which Rāma destroys the demoness Tāṭakā. There he was the destroyer of evil, the bringer of sterility and the ashes of death to his enemies. Here, as the reviver of Ahalyā, he is a cloud-dark god of fertility. Throughout

Kampaṉ's poem, Rāma is a Tamil hero, a generous giver and a ruthless destroyer of foes. And the *bhakti* vision makes the release of Ahalyā from her rock-bound sin a paradigm of Rāma's incarnatory mission to release all souls from world-bound misery.

In Vālmīki, Rāma's character is that not of a god but of a god-man who has to live within the limits of a human form with all its vicissitudes. Some argue that the references to Rāma's divinity and his incarnation for the purpose of destroying Rāvaṇa, and the first and last books of the epic, in which Rāma is clearly described as a god with such a mission, are later additions.[9] Be that as it may, in Kampaṉ he is clearly a god. Hence a passage like the above is dense with religious feeling and theological images. Kampaṉ, writing in the twelfth century, composed his poem under the influence of Tamil *bhakti*. He had for his master Nammāḻvār (9th C.?), the most eminent of the Śrīvaiṣṇava saints. So, for Kampaṉ, Rāma is a god who is on a mission to root out evil, sustain the good, and bring release to all living beings. The encounter with Ahalyā is only the first in a series, ending with Rāma's encounter with Rāvaṇa the demon himself. For Nammāḻvār, Rāma is a savior of *all* beings, from the lowly grass to the great gods:

By Rāma's Grace

Why would anyone want
  to learn anything but Rāma?

Beginning with the low grass
  and the creeping ant
with nothing
  whatever,

he took everything in his city,
  everything moving,
  everything still,

he took everything,
  everything born
of the lord
  of four faces,

he took them all
  to the very best of states.

Nammāḻvār 7.5.1[10]

Kampaṉ's epic poem enacts in detail and with passion Nammāḻvār's vision of Rāma.

Thus the Ahalyā episode is essentially the same, but the weave, the texture, the colors are very different. Part of the aesthetic pleasure in the later poet's telling derives from its artistic use of its predecessor's work, from ringing changes on it. To some extent all later *Rāmāyaṇas* play on the knowledge of previous tellings: they are meta-*Rāmāyaṇas*. I cannot resist repeating my favorite example. In several of the later *Rāmāyaṇas* (such as the *Adhyātma Rāmāyaṇa*, 16th C.), when Rāma is exiled, he does not want Sītā to go with him into the forest. Sītā argues with him. At first she uses the usual arguments: she is his wife, she should share his sufferings, exile herself in his exile, and so on. When he still resists the idea, she is furious. She bursts out, "Countless *Rāmāyaṇas* have been composed before this. Do you know of one where Sītā doesn't go with Rāma to the forest?" That clinches the argument, and she goes with him.[11] And as nothing in India occurs uniquely, even this motif appears in more than one *Rāmāyaṇa*.

Now the Tamil *Rāmāyaṇa* of Kampaṉ generates its own offspring, its own special sphere of influence. Read in Telugu characters in Telugu country, played as drama in the Malayalam area as part of temple ritual, it is also an important link in the transmission of the Rāma story to Southeast Asia. It has been convincingly shown that the eighteenth-century Thai *Ramakien* owes much to the Tamil epic. For instance, the names of many characters in the Thai work are not Sanskrit names, but clearly Tamil names (for example, Ṛśyaśṛṅga in Sanskrit but Kalaikkōṭu in Tamil, the latter borrowed into Thai). Tulsī's Hindi *Rāmcaritmānas* and the Malaysian *Hikayat Seri Ram* too owe many details to the Kampaṉ poem.[12]

Thus obviously transplantations take place through several routes. In some languages the word for tea is derived from a northern Chinese dialect and in others from a southern dialect; thus some languages, like English and French, have some form of the word *tea*, while others, like Hindi and Russian, have some form of the word *chā(y)*. Similarly, the Rāma story seems to have traveled along three routes, according to Santosh Desai: "By land, the northern route took the story from the Punjab and Kashmir into China, Tibet, and East Turkestan; by sea, the southern route carried the story from Gujarat and South India into Java, Sumatra, and Malaya; and again by land, the eastern route delivered the story from Bengal into Burma, Thailand, and Laos. Vietnam and Cambodia obtained their stories partly from Java and partly from India via the eastern route."[13]

JAINA TELLINGS

When we enter the world of Jaina tellings, the Rāma story no longer carries Hindu values. Indeed the Jaina texts express the feeling that the Hindus, especially the Brahmins, have maligned Rāvaṇa, made him into a villain. Here is a set of questions that a Jaina text begins by asking: "How can monkeys vanquish the powerful *rākṣasa* warriors like Rāvaṇa? How can noble men and Jaina worthies like Rāvaṇa eat flesh and drink blood? How can Kumbhakarṇa sleep through six months of the year, and never wake up even though boiling oil was poured into his ears, elephants were made to trample over him, and war trumpets and conches blow around him? They also say that Rāvaṇa captured Indra and dragged him handcuffed into Lanka. Who can do that to Indra? All this looks a bit fantastic and extreme. They are lies and contrary to reason." With these questions in mind King Śreṇika goes to sage Gautama to have him tell the true story and clear his doubts. Gautama says to him, "I'll tell you what Jaina wise men say. Rāvaṇa is not a demon, he is not a cannibal and a flesh eater. Wrong-thinking poetasters and fools tell these lies." He then begins to tell his own version of the story.[14] Obviously, the Jaina *Rāmāyaṇa* of Vimalasūri, called *Paumacariya* (Prakrit for the Sanskrit *Padmacarita*), knows its Vālmīki and proceeds to correct its errors and Hindu extravagances. Like other Jaina *purāṇas*, this too is a *pratipurāṇa*, an anti- or counter-*purāṇa*. The prefix *prati*, meaning "anti-" or "counter-," is a favorite Jaina affix.

Vimalasūri the Jaina opens the story not with Rāma's genealogy and greatness, but with Rāvaṇa's. Rāvaṇa is one of the sixty-three leaders or *śalākāpuruṣas* of the Jaina tradition. He is noble, learned, earns all his magical powers and weapons through austerities (*tapas*), and is a devotee of Jaina masters. To please one of them, he even takes a vow that he will not touch any unwilling woman. In one memorable incident, he lays siege to an impregnable fort. The queen of that kingdom is in love with him and sends him her messenger; he uses her knowledge of the fort to breach it and defeat the king. But, as soon as he conquers it, he returns the kingdom to the king and advises the queen to return to her husband. Later, he is shaken to his roots when he hears from soothsayers that he will meet his end through a woman, Sītā. It is such a Rāvaṇa who falls in love with Sītā's beauty, abducts her, tries to win her favors in vain, watches himself fall, and finally dies on the battlefield. In these tellings, he is a great man undone by a passion that he has vowed against but that he cannot resist. In another tradition of the Jaina *Rāmāyaṇas*, Sītā is his daughter, although he does not know it: the dice of tragedy are loaded against him further by this oedipal situation. I shall say more about Sītā's birth in the next section.

In fact, to our modern eyes, this Rāvaṇa is a tragic figure; we are moved to admiration and pity for Rāvaṇa when the Jainas tell the story. I should mention one more motif: according to the Jaina way of thinking, a pair of antagonists, Vāsudeva and Prativāsudeva—a hero and an antihero, almost like self and Other—are destined to fight in life after life. Lakṣmaṇa and Rāvaṇa are the eighth incarnations of this pair. They are born in age after age, meet each other in battle after many vicissitudes, and in every encounter Vāsudeva inevitably kills his counterpart, his *prati*. Rāvaṇa learns at the end that Lakṣmaṇa is such a Vāsudeva come to take his life. Still, overcoming his despair after a last unsuccessful attempt at peace, he faces his destined enemy in battle with his most powerful magic weapons. When finally he hurls his discus (*cakra*), it doesn't work for him. Recognizing Lakṣmaṇa as a Vāsudeva, it does not behead him but gives itself over to his hand. Thus Lakṣmaṇa slays Rāvaṇa with his own cherished weapon.

Here Rāma does not even kill Rāvaṇa, as he does in the Hindu *Rāmāyaṇas*. For Rāma is an evolved Jaina soul who has conquered his passions; this is his last birth, so he is loath to kill anything. It is left to Lakṣmaṇa to kill enemies, and according to inexorable Jaina logic it is Lakṣmaṇa who goes to hell while Rāma finds release (*kaivalya*).

One hardly need add that the *Paumacariya* is filled with references to Jaina places of pilgrimage, stories about Jaina monks, and Jaina homilies and legends. Furthermore, since the Jainas consider themselves rationalists—unlike the Hindus, who, according to them, are given to exorbitant and often bloodthirsty fancies and rituals—they systematically avoid episodes involving miraculous births (Rāma and his brothers are born in the normal way), blood sacrifices, and the like. They even rationalize the conception of Rāvaṇa as the Ten-headed Demon. When he was born, his mother was given a necklace of nine gems, which she put around his neck. She saw his face reflected in them ninefold and so called him Daśamukha, or the Ten-faced One. The monkeys too are not monkeys but a clan of celestials (*vidyādharas*) actually related to Rāvaṇa and his family through their great grandfathers. They have monkeys as emblems on their flags: hence the name Vānaras or "monkeys."

FROM WRITTEN TO ORAL

Let's look at one of the South Indian folk *Rāmāyaṇas*. In these, the story usually occurs in bits and pieces. For instance, in Kannada, we are given separate narrative poems on Sītā's birth, her wedding, her chastity test, her exile, the birth of Lava and Kuśa, their war with their father Rāma, and so on. But we do have one complete telling of the Rāma story by traditional bards (*tambūri dāsayyas*), sung with a refrain repeated every two lines by a chorus. For the following discussion, I am indebted to the transcription by Rāmē Gowḍa, P. K. Rājaśēkara, and S. Basavaiah.[15]

This folk narrative, sung by an Untouchable bard, opens with Rāvaṇa (here called Ravuḷa) and his queen Manḍodari. They are unhappy and childless. So Rāvaṇa or Ravuḷa goes to the forest, performs all sorts of self-mortifications like rolling on the ground till blood runs from his back, and meets a *jōgi*, or holy mendicant, who is none other than Śiva. Śiva gives him a magic mango and asks him how he would share it with his wife. Ravuḷa says, "Of course, I'll give her the sweet flesh of the fruit and I'll lick the mango seed." The *jōgi* is skeptical. He says to Ravuḷa, "You say one thing to me. You have poison in your belly. You're giving me butter to eat, but you mean something else. If you lie to me, you'll eat the fruit of your actions yourself."

Ravuḷa has one thing in his dreams and another in his waking world, says the poet. When he brings the mango home, with all sorts of flowers and incense for the ceremonial *pūjā*, Maṇḍodari is very happy. After a ritual *pūjā* and prayers to Śiva, Rāvaṇa is ready to share the mango. But he thinks, "If I give her the fruit, I'll be hungry, she'll be full," and quickly gobbles up the flesh of the fruit, giving her only the seed to lick. When she throws it in the yard, it sprouts and grows into a tall mango tree. Meanwhile, Ravuḷa himself becomes pregnant, his pregnancy advancing a month each day.

> In one day, it was a month, O Śiva.
> In the second, it was the second month,
> and cravings began for him, O Śiva.
> How shall I show my face to the world of men, O Śiva.
> On the third day, it was the third month,
> How shall I show my face to the world, O Śiva.
> On the fourth day, it was the fourth month.
> How can I bear this, O Śiva.
> Five days, and it was five months,
> O lord, you've given me trouble, O Śiva.
> I can't bear it, I can't bear it, O Śiva.
> How will I live, cries Ravuḷa in misery.
> Six days, and he is six months gone, O mother,
> in seven days it was seven months.
> O what shame, Ravuḷa in his seventh month,
> and soon came the eighth, O Śiva.
> Ravuḷa was in his ninth full month.
> When he was round and ready, she's born, the dear,
> Sītā is born through his nose.
> When he sneezes, Sītamma is born,
> And Ravuḷa names her Sītamma.[16]

In Kannada, the word *sīta* means "he sneezed": he calls her Sītā because she is born from a sneeze. Her name is thus given a Kannada folk etymology, as in the Sanskrit texts it has a Sanskrit one: there she is named Sītā, because King Janaka finds her in a furrow (*sītā*). Then Ravuḷa goes to astrologers, who tell him he is being punished for not keeping his word to Śiva and for eating the flesh of the fruit instead of giving it to his wife. They advise him to feed and dress the child, and leave her some place where she will be found and brought up by some couple. He puts her in a box and leaves her in Janaka's field.

It is only after this story of Sītā's birth that the poet sings of the birth and adventures of Rāma and Lakṣmaṇa. Then comes a long section on Sītā's marriage contest, where Ravuḷa appears and is humiliated when he falls under the heavy bow he has to lift. Rāma lifts it and marries Sītā. After that she is abducted by Rāvaṇa. Rāma lays siege to Lanka with his monkey allies, and (in a brief section) recovers Sītā and is crowned king. The poet then returns to the theme of Sītā's trials. She is slandered and exiled, but gives birth to twins who grow up to be warriors. They tie up Rāma's sacrificial horse, defeat the armies sent to guard the horse, and finally unite their parents, this time for good.

One sees here not only a different texture and emphasis: the teller is everywhere eager to return to Sītā—her life, her birth, her adoption, her wedding, her abduction and recovery. Whole sections, equal in length to those on Rāma and Lakṣmaṇa's birth, exile, and war against Rāvaṇa, are devoted to her banishment, pregnancy, and reunion with her husband. Furthermore, her abnormal birth as the daughter born directly to the male Rāvaṇa brings to the story a new range of suggestions: the male envy of womb and childbirth, which is a frequent theme in Indian literature, and an Indian oedipal theme of fathers pursuing daughters and, in this case, a daughter causing the death of her incestuous father.[17] The motif of Sītā as Rāvaṇa's daughter is not unknown elsewhere. It occurs in one tradition of the Jaina stories (for example, in the *Vasudevahiṁḍi*) and in folk traditions of Kannada and Telugu, as well as in several Southeast Asian *Rāmāyaṇas*. In some, Rāvaṇa in his lusty youth molests a young woman, who vows vengeance and is reborn as his daughter to destroy him. Thus the oral traditions seem to partake of yet another set of themes unknown in Vālmīki.

A SOUTHEAST ASIAN EXAMPLE

When we go outside India to Southeast Asia, we meet with a variety of tellings of the Rāma story in Tibet, Thailand, Burma, Laos, Cambodia, Malaysia, Java, and Indonesia. Here we shall look at only one example, the Thai *Ramakirti*. According to Santosh Desai, nothing else of Hindu origin has affected the tone of Thai life more than the Rāma story.[18] The bas-reliefs and paintings on the walls of their Buddhist temples, the plays enacted in town and village, their ballets—all of them rework the Rāma story. In succession several kings with the name "King Rama" wrote *Rāmāyaṇa* episodes in Thai: King Rama I composed a telling of the *Rāmāyaṇa* in fifty thousand verses, Rama II composed new episodes for dance, and Rama VI added another set of episodes, most taken from Vālmīki. Places in Thailand, such as Lopburi (Skt. Lavapuri), Khidkin (Skt. Kiṣkindhā), and Ayuthia (Skt. Ayodhyā) with its ruins of Khmer and Thai art, are associated with Rāma legends.

The Thai *Ramakirti* (Rāma's glory) or *Ramakien* (Rāma's story) opens with an account of the origins of the three kinds of characters in the story, the human, the demonic, and the simian. The second part describes the brothers' first encounters with the demons, Rāma's marriage and banishment, the abduction of Sītā, and Rāma's meeting with the monkey clan. It also describes the preparations for the war, Hanumān's visit to Lanka and his burning of it, the building of the bridge, the siege of Lanka, the fall of Rāvaṇa, and Rāma's reunion with Sītā. The third part describes an insurrection in Lanka, which Rāma deputes his two youngest brothers to quell. This part also describes the banishment of Sītā, the birth of her sons, their war with Rāma, Sītā's descent into the earth, and the appearance of the gods to reunite Rāma and Sītā. Though many incidents look the same as they do in Vālmīki, many things look different as well. For instance, as in the South Indian folk *Rāmāyaṇas* (as also in some Jaina, Bengali, and Kashmiri ones), the banishment of Sītā is given a dramatic new rationale. The daughter of Śūrpaṇakhā (the demoness whom Rāma and Lakṣmaṇa had mutilated years earlier in the forest) is waiting in the wings to take revenge on Sītā, whom she views as finally responsible for her mother's disfigurement. She comes to Ayodhya, enters Sītā's service as a maid, and induces her to draw a picture of Rāvaṇa. The drawing is rendered indelible (in some tellings, it comes to life in her bedroom) and forces itself on Rāma's attention. In a jealous rage, he orders Sītā killed. The compassionate Lakṣmaṇa leaves her alive in the forest, though, and brings back the heart of a deer as witness to the execution.

The reunion between Rāma and Sītā is also different. When Rāma finds out she is still alive, he recalls Sītā to his palace by sending her word that he is dead. She rushes to see him but flies into a rage when she finds she has been tricked. So, in a fit of helpless anger, she calls upon Mother Earth to take her. Hanumān is sent to subterranean regions to bring her back, but she refuses to return. It takes the power of Śiva to reunite them.

Again as in the Jaina instances and the South Indian folk poems, the account of Sītā's birth is different from that given in Vālmīki. When Daśaratha performs his sacrifice, he receives a rice ball, not the rice porridge (*pāyasa*) mentioned in Vālmīki. A crow steals some of the rice and takes it to Rāvaṇa's wife, who eats it and gives birth to Sītā. A prophecy that his daughter will cause his death makes Rāvaṇa throw Sītā into the sea, where the sea goddess protects her and takes her to Janaka.

Furthermore, though Rāma is an incarnation of Viṣṇu, in Thailand he is subordinate to Śiva. By and large he is seen as a human hero, and the *Ramakirti* is not regarded as a religious work or even as an exemplary work on which men and women may pattern themselves. The Thais enjoy most the sections about the abduction of Sītā and the war. Partings and reunions, which are the heart of the Hindu *Rāmāyaṇas*, are not as important as the excitement and the details of war, the techniques, the fabulous weapons. The *Yuddhakāṇḍa* or the War Book is more elaborate than in any other telling, whereas it is of minor importance in the Kannada folk telling. Desai says this Thai emphasis on war is significant: early Thai history is full of wars; their concern was survival. The focus in the *Ramakien* is not on family values and spirituality. Thai audiences are more fond of Hanumān than of Rāma.

Neither celibate nor devout, as in the Hindu *Rāmāyaṇas*, here Hanumān is quite a ladies' man, who doesn't at all mind looking into the bedrooms of Lanka and doesn't consider seeing another man's sleeping wife anything immoral, as Vālmīki's or Kampaṉ's Hanumān does.

Rāvaṇa too is different here. The *Ramakirti* admires Rāvaṇa's resourcefulness and learning; his abduction of Sītā is seen as an act of love and is viewed with sympathy. The Thais are moved by Rāvaṇa's sacrifice of family, kingdom, and life itself for the sake of a woman. His dying words later provide the theme of a famous love poem of the nineteenth century, an inscription of a Wat of Bangkok.[19] Unlike Vālmīki's characters, the Thai ones are a fallible, human mixture of good and evil. The fall of Rāvaṇa here makes one sad. It is not an occasion for unambiguous rejoicing, as it is in Vālmīki.

PATTERNS OF DIFFERENCE

Thus, not only do we have one story told by Vālmīki in Sanskrit, we have a variety of Rāma tales told by others, with radical differences among them. Let me outline a few of the differences we have not yet encountered. For instance, in Sanskrit and in the other Indian languages, there are two endings to the story. One ends with the return of Rāma and Sītā to Ayodhya, their capital, to be crowned king and queen of the ideal kingdom. In another ending, often considered a later addition in Vālmīki and in Kampaṉ, Rāma hears Sītā slandered as a woman who lived in Rāvaṇa's grove, and in the name of his reputation as a king (we would call it credibility, I suppose) he banishes her to the forest, where she gives birth to twins. They grow up in Vālmīki's hermitage, learn the *Rāmāyaṇa* as well as the arts of war from him, win a war over Rāma's army, and in a poignant scene sing the *Rāmāyaṇa* to their own father when he doesn't quite know who they are. Each of these two endings gives the whole work a different cast. The first one celebrates the return of the royal exiles and rounds out the tale with reunion, coronation, and peace. In the second one, their happiness is brief, and they are separated again, making separation of loved ones (*vipralambha*) the central mood of the whole work. It can even be called tragic, for Sītā finally cannot bear it any more and enters a fissure in the earth, the mother from whom she had originally come—as we saw earlier, her name means "furrow," which is where she was originally found by Janaka. It also enacts, in the rise of Sītā from the furrow and her return to the earth, a shadow of a Proserpine-like myth, a vegetation cycle: Sītā is like the seed and Rāma with his cloud-dark body the rain; Rāvaṇa in the South is the Pluto-like abductor into dark regions (the south is the abode of death); Sītā reappears in purity and glory for a brief period before she returns again to the earth. Such a myth, while it should not be blatantly pressed into some rigid allegory, resonates in the shadows of the tale in many details. Note the many references to fertility and rain, Rāma's opposition to Śiva-like ascetic figures (made explicit by Kampan̲ in the Ahalyā story), his ancestor bringing the river Ganges into the plains of the kingdom to water and revive the ashes of the dead. Relevant also is the story of Ṛśyaśṛṅga, the sexually naive ascetic who is seduced by the beauty of a woman and thereby brings rain to Lomapāda's kingdom, and who later officiates at the ritual which fills Daśaratha's queens' wombs with children. Such a mythic groundswell also makes us hear other tones in the continual references to nature, the potent presence of birds and animals as the devoted friends of Rāma in his search for his Sītā. Birds and monkeys are a real presence and a poetic necessity in the Vālmīki *Rāmāyaṇa*, as much as they are excrescences in the Jaina view. With each ending, different effects of the story are highlighted, and the whole telling alters its poetic stance.

One could say similar things about the different beginnings. Vālmīki opens with a frame story about Vālmīki himself. He sees a hunter aim an arrow and kill one of a happy pair of lovebirds. The female circles its dead mate and cries over it. The scene so moves the poet and sage Vālmīki that he curses the hunter. A moment later, he realizes that his curse has taken the form of a line of verse—in a famous play on words, the rhythm of his grief (*śoka*) has given rise to a metrical form (*śloka*). He decides to write the whole epic of Rāma's adventures in that meter. This incident becomes, in later poetics, the parable of all poetic utterance: out of the stress of natural feeling (*bhāva*), an artistic form has to be found or fashioned, a form which will generalize and capture the essence (*rasa*) of that feeling. This incident at the beginning of Vālmīki gives the work an aesthetic self-awareness. One may go further: the incident of the death of a bird and the separation of loved ones becomes a leitmotif for this telling of the Rāma story. One notes a certain rhythmic recurrence of an animal killed at many of the critical moments: when Daśaratha shoots an arrow to kill what he thinks is an elephant but instead kills a young ascetic filling his pitcher with water (making noises like an elephant drinking at a water hole), he earns a curse that later leads to the exile of Rāma and the separation of father and son. When Rāma pursues a magical golden deer (really a demon in disguise) and kills it, with its last breath it calls out to Lakṣmaṇa in Rāma's voice, which in turn leads to his leaving Sītā unprotected; this allows Rāvaṇa to abduct Sītā. Even as Rāvaṇa carries her off, he is opposed by an ancient bird which he slays with his sword. Furthermore, the death of the bird, in the opening section, and the cry of the surviving mate set the tone for the many separations throughout the work, of brother and brother, mothers and fathers and sons, wives and husbands.

Thus the opening sections of each major work set into motion the harmonics of the whole poem, presaging themes and a pattern of images. Kampan̲'s Tamil text begins very differently. One can convey it best by citing a few stanzas.

The River

The cloud, wearing white
on white like Śiva,
making beautiful the sky
on his way from the sea

grew dark

as the face of the Lord
who wears with pride
on his right the Goddess
of the scented breasts. 2

Mistaking the Himalayan dawn
for a range of gold,
the clouds let down chains
and chains of gleaming rain.

They pour like a generous giver
giving all he has,
remembering and reckoning
all he has. 15

It floods, it runs over
its continents like the fame
of a great king, upright,
infallible, reigning by the Laws
under cool royal umbrellas. 16

Concubines caressing
their lovers' hair, their lovers'
bodies, their lovers' limbs,

take away whole hills
of wealth yet keep little
in their spendthrift hands

as they move on: so too
the waters flow from the peaks
to the valleys,

beginning high and reaching low. 17

The flood carrying all before it
like merchants, caravans
loaded with gold, pearls,
peacock feathers and rows
of white tusk and fragrant woods. 18

Bending to a curve, the river,
surface colored by petals,
gold yellow pollen, honey,
the ochre flow of elephant lust,
looked much like a rainbow. 19

Ravaging hillsides, uprooting trees,
covered with fallen leaves all over,
the waters came,

like a monkey clan
facing restless seas
looking for a bridge. 20

Thick-faced proud elephants
ranged with foaming cavalier horses
filling the air with the noise of war,

raising banners,
the flood rushes
as for a battle with the sea. 22

Stream of numberless kings
in the line of the Sun,
continuous in virtue:

the river branches into deltas,
mother's milk to all lives
on the salt sea-surrounded land. 23

Scattering a robber camp on the hills
with a rain of arrows,

the sacred women beating their bellies
and gathering bow and arrow as they run,

the waters assault villages
like the armies of a king. 25

Stealing milk and buttermilk,
guzzling on warm ghee and butter
straight from the pots on the ropes,

leaning the *marutam* tree on the *kuruntam*,
carrying away the clothes and bracelets
of goatherd girls at water games,

like Kṛṣṇa dancing
on the spotted snake,
the waters are naughty. 26

Turning forest into slope,
field into wilderness,
seashore into fertile land,

changing boundaries,
exchanging landscapes,
the reckless waters

roared on like the pasts
that hurry close on the heels
of lives. 28

Born of Himalayan stone
and mingling with the seas,
it spreads, ceaselessly various,

one and many at once,

like that Original
even the measureless Vedas
cannot measure with words. 30

Through pollen-dripping groves,
clumps of champak,
lotus pools,

water places with new sands,
flowering fields cross-fenced
with creepers,

like a life filling
and emptying
a variety of bodies,

the river flows on.[20] 31

This passage is unique to Kampaṉ; it is not found in Vālmīki. It describes the waters as they are gathered by clouds from the seas and come down in rain and flow as floods of the Sarayū river down to Ayodhya, the capital of Rāma's kingdom. Through it, Kampaṉ introduces all his themes and emphases, even his characters, his concern with fertility themes (implicit in Vālmīki), the whole dynasty of Rāma's ancestors, and his vision of *bhakti* through the *Rāmāyaṇa.*

Note the variety of themes introduced through the similes and allusions, each aspect of the water symbolizing an aspect of the *Rāmāyaṇa* story itself and representing a portion of the *Rāmāyaṇa* universe (for example, monkeys), picking up as it goes along characteristic Tamil traditions not to be found anywhere else, like the five landscapes of classical Tamil poetry. The emphasis on water itself, the source of life and fertility, is also an explicit part of the Tamil literary tradition. The *Kuṟaḷ*—the so-called Bible of the Tamils, a didactic work on the ends and means of the good life—opens with a passage on God and follows it up immediately with a great ode in celebration of the rains (*Tirukkuṟaḷ* 2).

Another point of difference among *Rāmāyaṇas* is the intensity of focus on a major character. Vālmīki focuses on Rāma and his history in his opening sections; Vimalasūri's Jaina *Rāmāyaṇa* and the Thai epic focus not on Rāma but on the genealogy and adventures of Rāvaṇa; the Kannada village telling focuses on Sītā, her birth, her wedding, her trials. Some later extensions like the *Adbhuta Rāmāyaṇa* and the Tamil story of *Śatakanṭharāvaṇa* even give Sītā a heroic character: when the ten-headed Rāvaṇa is killed, another appears with a hundred heads; Rāma cannot handle this new menace, so it is Sītā who goes to war and slays the new demon.[21] The Santals, a tribe known for their extensive oral traditions, even conceive of Sītā as unfaithful—to the shock and horror of any Hindu bred on Vālmīki or Kampaṉ, she is seduced both by Rāvaṇa and by Lakṣmaṇa. In Southeast Asian texts, as we saw earlier, Hanumān is not the celibate devotee with a monkey face but a ladies' man who figures in many love episodes. In Kampaṉ and Tulsī, Rāma is a god; in the Jaina texts, he is only an evolved Jaina man who is in his last birth and so does not even kill Rāvaṇa. In the latter, Rāvaṇa is a noble hero fated by his karma to fall for Sītā and bring death upon himself, while he is in other texts an overweening demon. Thus in the conception of every major character there are radical differences, so different indeed that one conception is quite abhorrent to those who hold another. We may add to these many more: elaborations on the reason why Sītā is banished, the miraculous creation of Sītā's second son, and the final reunion of Rāma and Sītā. Every one of these occurs in more than one text, in more than one textual community (Hindu, Jaina, or Buddhist), in more than one region.

Now, is there a common core to the Rāma stories, except the most skeletal set of relations like that of Rāma, his brother, his wife, and the antagonist Rāvaṇa who abducts her? Are the stories bound together only by certain family resemblances, as Wittgenstein might say? Or is it like Aristotle's jack knife? When the philosopher asked an old carpenter how long he had had his knife, the latter said, "Oh, I've had it for thirty years. I've changed the blade a few times and the handle a few times, but it's the same knife." Some shadow of a relational structure claims the name of *Rāmāyaṇa* for all these tellings, but on closer look one is not necessarily all that like another. Like a collection of people with the same proper name, they make a class in name alone.

THOUGHTS ON TRANSLATION

That may be too extreme a way of putting it. Let me back up and say it differently, in a way that covers more adequately the differences between the texts and their relations to each other, for they *are* related. One might think of them as a series of translations clustering around one or another in a family of texts: a number of them cluster around Vālmīki, another set around the Jaina Vimalasūri, and so on.

Or these translation-relations between texts could be thought of in Peircean terms, at least in three ways.

Where Text 1 and Text 2 have a geometrical resemblance to each other, as one triangle to another (whatever the angles, sizes, or colors of the lines), we call such a relation *iconic.*[22] In the West, we generally expect translations to be "faithful," i.e. iconic. Thus, when Chapman translates Homer, he not only preserves basic textual features such as characters, imagery, and order of incidents, but tries to reproduce a hexameter and retain the same number of lines as in the original Greek—only the language is English and the idiom Elizabethan. When Kampaṉ retells Vālmīki's *Rāmāyaṇa* in Tamil, he is largely faithful in keeping to the order and sequence of episodes, the structural relations between the characters of father, son, brothers, wives, friends, and enemies. But the iconicity is limited to such structural relations. His work is much longer than Vālmīki's, for example, and it is composed in more than twenty different kinds of Tamil meters, while Vālmīki's is mostly in the *śloka* meter.

Very often, although Text 2 stands in an iconic relationship to Text 1 in terms of basic elements such as plot, it is filled with local detail, folklore, poetic traditions, imagery, and so forth—as in Kampaṉ's telling or that of the Bengali Kṛttivāsa. In the Bengali *Rāmāyaṇa*, Rāma's wedding is very much a Bengali wedding, with Bengali customs and Bengali cuisine.[23] We may call such a text *indexical*: the text is embedded in a locale, a context, refers to it, even signifies it, and would not make much sense without it. Here, one may say, the *Rāmāyaṇa* is not merely a set of individual texts, but a genre with a variety of instances.

Now and then, as we have seen, Text 2 uses the plot and characters and names of Text 1 minimally and uses them to say entirely new things, often in an effort to subvert the predecessor by producing a countertext. We may call such a translation *symbolic*. The word *translation* itself here acquires a somewhat mathematical sense, of mapping a structure of relations onto another plane or another symbolic system. When this happens, the Rāma story has become almost a second language of the whole culture area, a shared core of names, characters, incidents, and motifs, with a narrative language in which Text 1 can say one thing and Text 2 something else, even the exact opposite. Vālmīki's Hindu and Vimalasūri's Jaina texts in India—or the Thai *Ramakirti* in Southeast Asia—are such symbolic translations of each other.

One must not forget that to some extent all translations, even the so-called faithful iconic ones, inevitably have all three kinds of elements. When Goldman and his group of scholars produce a modern translation of Vālmīki's *Rāmāyaṇa*, they are iconic in the transliteration of Sanskrit names, the number and sequence of verses, the order of the episodes, and so forth.[24] But they are also indexical, in that the translation is in English idiom and comes equipped with introductions and explanatory footnotes, which inevitably contain twentieth-century attitudes and misprisions; and symbolic, in that they cannot avoid conveying through this translation modern understandings proper to their reading of the text. But the proportions between the three kinds of relations differ vastly between Kampaṉ and Goldman. And we accordingly read them for different reasons and with different aesthetic expectations. We read the scholarly modern English translation largely to gain a sense of the original Vālmīki, and we consider it successful to the extent that it resembles the original. We read Kampaṉ to read Kampaṉ, and we judge him on his own terms—not by his resemblance to Vālmīki but, if anything, by the extent that he differs from Vālmīki. In the one, we rejoice in the similarity; in the other, we cherish and savor the differences.

One may go further and say that the cultural area in which *Rāmāyaṇas* are endemic has a pool of signifiers (like a gene pool), signifiers that include plots, characters, names, geography, incidents, and relationships. Oral, written, and performance traditions, phrases, proverbs, and even sneers carry allusions to the Rāma story. When someone is carrying on, you say, "What's this *Rāmāyaṇa* now? Enough." In Tamil, a narrow room is called a *kiṣkindhā*; a proverb about a dim-witted person says, "After hearing the *Rāmāyaṇa* all night, he asks how Rāma is related to Sītā"; in a Bengali arithmetic textbook, children are asked to figure the dimensions of what is left of a wall that Hanumān built, after he has broken down part of it in mischief. And to these must be added marriage songs, narrative poems, place legends, temple myths, paintings, sculpture, and the many performing arts.

These various texts not only relate to prior texts directly, to borrow or refute, but they relate to each other through this common code or common pool. Every author, if one may hazard a metaphor, dips into it and brings out a unique crystallization, a new text with a unique texture and a fresh context. The great texts rework the small ones, for "lions are made of sheep," as Valéry said. And sheep are made of lions, too: a folk legend says that Hanumān wrote the original *Rāmāyaṇa* on a mountaintop, after the great war, and scattered the manuscript; it was many times larger than what we have now. Vālmīki is said to have captured only a fragment of it.[25] In this sense, no text is original, yet no telling is a mere retelling—and the story has no closure, although it may be enclosed in a text. In India and in Southeast Asia, no one ever reads the *Rāmāyaṇa* or the *Mahābhārata* for the first time. The stories are there, "always already."

WHAT HAPPENS WHEN YOU LISTEN

This essay opened with a folktale about the many *Rāmāyaṇas*. Before we close, it may be appropriate to tell another tale about Hanumān and Rāma's ring.[26] But this story is about the power of the *Rāmāyaṇa*, about what happens when you really listen to this potent story. Even a fool cannot resist it; he is entranced and caught up in the action. The listener can no longer bear to be a bystander but feels compelled to enter the world of the epic: the line between fiction and reality is erased.

A villager who had no sense of culture and no interest in it was married to a woman who was very cultured. She tried various ways to cultivate his taste for the higher things in life but he just wasn't interested.

One day a great reciter of that grand epic the *Rāmāyaṇa* came to the village. Every evening he would sing, recite, and explain the verses of the epic. The whole village went to this one-man performance as if it were a rare feast.

The woman who was married to the uncultured dolt tried to interest him in the performance. She nagged him and nagged him, trying to force him to go and listen. This time, he grumbled as usual but decided to humor her. So he went in the evening and sat at the back. It was an all-night performance, and he just couldn't keep awake. He slept through the night. Early in the morning, when a canto had ended and the reciter sang the closing verses for the day, sweets were distributed according to custom. Someone put some sweets into the mouth of the sleeping man. He woke up soon after and went home. His wife was delighted that her husband had stayed through the night and asked him eagerly how he enjoyed the *Rāmāyaṇa*. He said, "It was very sweet." The wife was happy to hear it.

The next day too his wife insisted on his listening to the epic. So he went to the enclosure where the reciter was performing, sat against a wall, and before long fell fast asleep. The place was crowded and a young boy sat on his shoulder, made himself comfortable, and listened open-mouthed to the fascinating story. In the morning, when the night's portion of the story came to an end, everyone got up and so did the husband. The boy had left earlier, but the man felt aches and pains from the weight he had borne all night. When he went home and his wife asked him eagerly how it was, he said, "It got heavier and heavier by morning." The wife said, "That's the way the story is." She was happy that her husband was at last beginning to feel the emotions and the greatness of the epic.

On the third day, he sat at the edge of the crowd and was so sleepy that he lay down on the floor and even snored. Early in the morning, a dog came that way and pissed into his mouth a little before he woke up and went home. When his wife asked him how it was, he moved his mouth this way and that, made a face and said, "Terrible. It was so salty." His wife knew something was wrong. She asked him what exactly was happening and didn't let up till he finally told her how he had been sleeping through the performance every night.

On the fourth day, his wife went with him, sat him down in the very first row, and told him sternly that he should keep awake no matter what might happen. So he sat dutifully in the front row and began to listen. Very soon, he was caught up in the adventures and the characters of the great epic story. On that day, the reciter was enchanting the audience with a description of how Hanumān the monkey had to leap across the ocean to take Rāma's signet ring to Sītā. When Hanumān was leaping across the ocean, the signet ring slipped from his hand and fell into the ocean. Hanumān didn't know what to do. He had to get the ring back quickly and take it to Sītā in the demon's kingdom. While he was wringing his hands, the husband who was listening with rapt attention in the first row said, "Hanumān, don't worry. I'll get it for you." Then he jumped up and dived into the ocean, found the ring in the ocean floor, brought it back, and gave it to Hanumān.

Everyone was astonished. They thought this man was someone special, really blessed by Rāma and Hanumān. Ever since, he has been respected in the village as a wise elder, and he has also behaved like one. That's what happens when you really listen to a story, especially to the *Rāmāyaṇa*.

NOTES

This paper was originally written for the Conference on Comparison of Civilizations at the University of Pittsburgh, February 1987. I am indebted to the organizers of the conference for the opportunity to write and present it and to various colleagues who have commented on it, especially V. Narayana Rao, David Shulman, and Paula Richman.

1. I owe this Hindi folktale to Kirin Narayan of the University of Wisconsin.

2. Several works and collections of essays have appeared over the years on the many *Rāmāyaṇas* of South and Southeast Asia. I shall mention here only a few which were directly useful to me: Asit K. Banerjee, ed., *The Ramayana in Eastern India* (Calcutta: Prajna, 1983); P. Banerjee, *Rama in Indian Literature, Art and Thought*, 2 vols. (Delhi: Sundeep Prakashan, 1986); J. L. Brockington, *Righteous Rāma: The Evolution of an Epic* (Delhi: Oxford University Press, 1984); V. Raghavan, *The Greater Ramayana* (Varanasi: All-India Kashiraj Trust, 1973); V. Raghavan, *The Ramayana in Greater India* (Surat: South Gujarat University, 1975); V. Raghavan, ed., *The Ramayana Tradition in Asia* (Delhi: Sahitya Akademi, 1980); C. R. Sharma, *The Ramayana in Telugu and Tamil: A Comparative Study* (Madras: Lakshminarayana Granthamala, 1973); Dineshchandra Sen, *The Bengali Ramayanas* (Calcutta: University of Calcutta, 1920); S. Singaravelu, "A Comparative Study of the Sanskrit, Tamil, Thai and Malay Versions of the Story of Rāma with special reference to the Process of Acculturation in the Southeast Asian Versions," *Journal of the Siam Society* 56, pt. 2 (July 1968): 137–85.

3. Camille Bulcke, *Rāmkathā: Utpatti aur Vikās* (The Rāma story: Origin and development; Prayāg: Hindī Pariṣad Prakāśan, 1950; in Hindi). When I mentioned Bulcke's count of three hundred *Rāmāyaṇas* to a Kannada scholar, he said that he had recently counted over a thousand in Kannada alone; a Telugu scholar also mentioned a thousand in Telugu. Both counts included Rāma stories in various genres. So the title of this paper is not to be taken literally.

4. See Seymour Chatman, *Story and Discourse: Narrative Structure in Fiction and Film* (Ithaca, N.Y.: Cornell University Press, 1978).

5. Through the practice of *tapas*—usually translated "austerities" or "penances" —a sage builds up a reserve of spiritual power, often to the point where his potency poses a threat to the gods (notably Indra). Anger or lust, however, immediately negates this power; hence Indra's subsequent claim that by angering Gautama he was doing the gods a favor.

6. *Śrīmad Vālmīkirāmāyaṇa*, ed. by K. Chinnaswami Sastrigal and V. H. Subrahmanya Sastri (Madras: N. Ramaratnam, 1958), I.47–48; translation by David Shulman and A. K. Ramanujan.

7. The translation in the body of this article contains selected verses from I.9, the section known in Tamil as *akalikaippaṭalam*. The edition I cite is *Kampar Iyaṟṟiya Irāmāyaṇam* (Aṇṇāmalai: Aṇṇāmalai Palkalaikkaḻakam, 1957), vol. 1.

8. C. H. Tawney, trans., N. M. Penzer, ed., *The Ocean of Story*, 10 vols. (rev. ed. 1927; repr. Delhi: Motilal Banarsidass, 1968), 2:45–46.

9. See, for example, the discussion of such views as summarized in Robert P. Goldman, trans., *The Rāmāyaṇa of Vālmīki*, vol. 1: *Bālakāṇḍa* (Princeton: Princeton University Press, 1984), 15. For a dissenting view, see Sheldon I. Pollock, "The Divine King in the Indian Epic," *Journal of the American Oriental Society* 104, no. 3 (July–September 1984): 505–28.

10. A. K. Ramanujan, trans., *Hymns for the Drowning: Poems for Viṣṇu by Nammāḻvār* (Princeton: Princeton University Press, 1981), 47.

11. *Adhyātma Rāmāyaṇa*, II.4.77–78. See Rai Bahadur Lala Baij Nath, trans., *The Adhyatma Ramayana* (Allahabad: The Panini Office, 1913; reprinted as extra volume 1 in the *Sacred Books of the Hindus*, New York: AMS Press, 1974), 39.

12. See S. Singaravelu, "A Comparative Study of the Sanskrit, Tamil, Thai and Malay Versions of the Story of Rāma."

13. Santosh N. Desai, "Rāmāyaṇa—An Instrument of Historical Contact and Cultural Transmission Between India and Asia," *Journal of Asian Studies* 30, no. 1 (November 1970): 5.

14. K. R. Chandra, *A Critical Study of Paumacariyaṁ* (Muzaffarpur: Research Institute of Prakrit, Jainology and Ahimsa, 1970), 234.

15. Rāmē Gowḍa, P. K. Rājaśēkara, and S. Basavaiah, eds., *Janapada Rāmāyaṇa* (Folk Ramayanas) (Mysore: n.p., 1973; in Kannada).

16. Rāmē Gowḍa et al., *Janapada Rāmāyaṇa*, 150–51; my translation.

17. See A. K. Ramanujan, "The Indian Oedipus," in *Oedipus: A Folklore Casebook*, ed. Alan Dundes and Lowell Edmunds (New York: Garland, 1983), 234–61.

18. Santosh N. Desai, *Hinduism in Thai Life* (Bombay: Popular Prakashan, 1980), 63. In the discussion of the *Ramakirti* to follow, I am indebted to the work of Desai and Singaravelu. For a translation of the Thai Ramayana, see Swami Satyananda Puri and Chhaoen Sarahiran, trans., *The Ramakirti or Ramakien: The Thai Version of the Ramayana* (Bangkok: Thai Bharat Cultural Lodge and Satyanand Puri Foundation, 1949).

19. Desai, *Hinduism in Thai Life*, 85.

20. *Kampar Iyaṟṟiya Irāmāyaṇam*, vol. 1, selected verses from I.1, in the section known as *nāṭṭuppaṭalam*.

21. See David Shulman, "Sītā and Śatakaṇṭharāvaṇa in a Tamil Folk Narrative," *Journal of Indian Folkloristics* 2, nos. 3/4 (1979): 1–26.

22. One source for Peirce's semiotic terminology is his "Logic as Semiotic," in Charles Sanders Peirce, *Philosophical Writings of Peirce*, ed. by Justus Buchler (1940; repr. New York: Dover, 1955), 88–119.

23. Dineshchandra Sen, *Bengali Ramayanas*.

24. Robert P. Goldman, ed., *The Rāmāyaṇa of Vālmīki*, 7 vols. (Princeton: Princeton University Press, 1984–).

25. Personal communication from V. Narayana Rao.

26. I heard the Telugu tale to follow in Hyderabad in July 1988, and I have collected versions in Kannada and Tamil as well. For more examples of tales around the *Rāmāyaṇa*, see A. K. Ramanujan, "Two Realms of Kannada Folklore," in *Another Harmony: New Essays on the Folklore of India*, ed. Stuart H. Blackburn and A. K. Ramanujan (Berkeley and Los Angeles: University of California Press, 1986), 41–75.

THREE

Rāmāyaṇa, *Rāma Jātaka*, and *Ramakien*: A Comparative Study of Hindu and Buddhist Traditions

Frank E. Reynolds

In the history and literature of religions few stories have been told as many different times in as many different ways as the story of Rāma. For at least two thousand years—and probably longer—various versions of the story have been told in India and Sri Lanka; for over a thousand years—and probably much longer still—these and other versions have been told in Central and Southeast Asia, in China and Japan. Now, increasingly, the story is being told in the West as well.[1]

The story of Rāma has been recited, sung, and commented on by bards, priests, and monks. It has been dramatized and danced in royal courts and in rustic villages. It has been depicted in the sculpture and art of innumerable temples in capital cities and faraway provinces. Its characters have been the subjects of worship, and the events that the story recounts have been associated with famous places that mark the geography of various locales.

What is more, certain episodes in the story have been singled out, taking on special significance in particular contexts. Segments of the story have been presented in order to evoke religious devotion, to glorify royal sponsors (often in direct opposition to other royal competitors), to inculcate moral values, to express and cultivate aesthetic sensitivities, and—perhaps most of all—simply to provide popular entertainment. Particular segments of the story have also been performed for other less obviously related purposes. For example, in certain very popular rituals in southern Thailand the enactment of certain episodes from the Rāma story (most notably that in which Rāma kills Rāvaṇa) serves as a substitute for the performance of animal sacrifice.[2]

For the most part the story of Rāma has been presented and interpreted as a Hindu story told primarily in Hindu contexts. And there is some justification for this emphasis. Certainly it is within Hinduism that the Rāma story has had its most elaborated and sophisticated tellings and has exercised its greatest popular appeal. This emphasis, however, tends to throw into the shadows the possibility, already raised in Ramanujan's essay, that the story of Rāma is better understood as an Indian/Southeast Asian story that has been crystallized (to use his image) in the context of a variety of religious traditions including, but not limited to, Hinduism.[3]

I propose here to consider the religious structure of the classical Rāma stories belonging to the Hindu tradition, and the parallel but contrasting religious structure of the classical Rāma stories that belong to the tradition of Theravāda Buddhism.[4] With this background established, I will go on to raise a fundamental question concerning the great tradition of Rāma narratives that has been prominent in Thailand at least since the late eighteenth century. Is this so-called *Ramakien* (Glory of Rāma) tradition essentially Hindu in character, as many scholars have presumed? Or is it—as one might expect given its *sitz im leben* in Thailand—essentially Buddhist? It is my hope that by exploring this question we will gain a better understanding not only of the relevant literary texts but of the correlated forms of dance, sculpture, and painting as well.[5]

RĀMA TRADITIONS IN HINDUISM

Although the Rāma story is not, as such, a Hindu story, Hindu versions are very ancient. They have been a prominent element in Hindu religious life over the centuries and continue to play a prominent role in contemporary Hinduism. Moreover, certain dominant features in many Rāma traditions—both in India and in Southeast Asia—can be clearly identified as Hindu.

Most of the literary versions of the classical Hindu Rāma story are attributed to an author recognized as a religiously inspired sage or poet. In some cases the reputed author (for example, Vālmīki) seems from our perspective more or less a mythic figure. In other cases the reputed author is a relatively identifiable historical personage (for example, Tulsīdās). Either way, the author is considered to be a Hindu virtuoso possessing special religious insight and poetic inspiration.

For the most part, these Hindu crystallizations set the story of Rāma in a primordial time situated at or near the beginning of the present eon when the gods are very much involved in human affairs and the character of the world as we know it is just being established.[6] At a certain moment, the proper order in the cosmos and society is challenged by a countervailing force that threatens to disrupt the world with injustice and disharmony. In order to prevent this situation from getting out of hand, a prominent god (usually Viṣṇu) becomes incarnate in the person of Rāma, a prince of a northern kingdom usually identified with the city of Ayodhya in northeastern India. In his incarnation as Rāma Viṣṇu is surrounded by a host of companions and helpers, many of whom are themselves the embodiments or descendants of members of the Hindu pantheon—although the particular deities and the relationships involved vary significantly from one account to another. In some Hindu versions Rāma and his companions are presented in a way that highlights Rāma's divinity and thus evokes devotion directed toward him. In other versions Rāma and his companions are depicted as semidivine exemplars who embody the virtues that Hindus are expected to cultivate. In still other versions a greater degree of moral ambiguity is evident.

In most classical Hindu accounts Rāma is denied his rightful succession to the throne through the machinations of one of his father's wives, who seeks the throne for her own son. But the primary opponent of Rāma and his illustrious companions—the figure around whom the forces of disorder are most fully marshalled—is Rāvaṇa, the ruler of the kingdom of Lanka in the south. Like most of the major characters in the story, Rāvaṇa is usually depicted as the embodiment, descendant, or assistant of one of the Hindu gods, generally one not in particularly good favor with the tellers of the tale. As for Rāvaṇa himself, he is a more or less demonic figure who acts in ways that generate disorder in the cosmos and turbulence in society. In some tellings of the tale Rāvaṇa is presented as a thoroughly evil character with no redeeming virtues. In others he is more a kind of flawed hero whose demise, though necessary and appropriate, is not devoid of truly tragic dimensions.

According to most classical Hindu versions, the battle between the forces of order and disorder, between Rāma and his companions on the one hand, and Rāvaṇa and his allies on the other, is fully joined when Rāvaṇa becomes desirous of Rāma's wife, Sītā, and kidnaps her. But, after winning the initial round of his battle with Rāma, Rāvaṇa is twice defeated—first by Sītā, who, despite her position as a powerless captive, rebuffs his advances, and then by Rāma, who invades Rāvaṇa's capital, overcomes his armies, and finally kills him in personal combat. Thus the forces of disorder and injustice that were threatening the cosmos and society are destroyed. With his mission accomplished, Rāma returns to Ayodhya with Sītā at his side and takes the throne that is rightfully his.

RĀMA TRADITIONS IN THERAVĀDA BUDDHISM

Like the Hindus, Theravāda Buddhists have, over the centuries, crystallized their own classical versions of the Rāma story, ones whose religious structure clearly establishes their Buddhist identity.[7] The basic components of this Buddhist structure parallel the basic components of the Hindu pattern, but they differ in fundamental respects.

Within the Buddhist context there are two classical crystallizations of the Rāma story that need to be considered. The first is the *Dasaratha Jātaka*, a relatively well known text. Some scholars have argued that this text (which they date to the pre-Christian era) is actually the first crystallization of the

Rāma story that we possess; others contend that it was written after Vālmīki's version. Either way—and my own view is that the evidence is not conclusive—there is general agreement that the *Dasaratha Jātaka* is a very ancient Buddhist crystallization of the Rāma story.[8]

The second Buddhist-oriented Rāma tradition is much more complex and in many respects much more interesting, though far less widely known and studied than the *Dasaratha Jātaka*. Dating from medieval times, this Buddhist Rāma tradition has had a widespread distribution through an area we might call greater Laos, from Yunan in the north through Laos and northeastern Thailand to the borders of Cambodia in the south. The most extensive text that we now possess is the Laotian *Phra Lak/Phra Lam* (the Laotian names for Lakṣmaṇa and Rāma) which has been published in a two-volume edited version that runs to more than nine hundred pages.[9] In addition, there are a number of "sister texts" that are clearly a part of this same classical tradition.[10]

Within Buddhist tradition, the author to whom the various literary crystallizations of the Rāma story are attributed does not vary from text to text. In each instance the "author," in the sense of the first teller of the tale, is said to be the Buddha himself. The *Dasaratha Jātaka* is included in a lengthy *jātaka* commentary that presents itself as a collection of *jātaka* stories (stories of events in the previous lives of the Buddha) that the Buddha preached during his stay at the Jetavana monastery. The classical Rāma texts of the Laotian tradition are not included in any of the collections traditionally attributed to the founder. However, each of these independent texts quite explicitly presents itself as a sermon preached by the Buddha during the course of his ministry.

Like the classical Hindu versions, the various Buddhist crystallizations are situated in a special time that is clearly set apart from the present day. In both the *Dasaratha Jātaka* and the Laotian tradition, this time is located in the distant past, when the Buddha was living one of his more eventful previous lives. The Laotian texts also make clear that these previous lives took place at or near the beginning of the present cosmic epoch, at a time when the gods were closely involved in human affairs and the conditions of our present existence were being established. Their account draws heavily on the classical Theravāda cosmogony that appears in the Pali Tipiṭaka, most fully in the Aggañña Sutta.[11]

The *Phra Lak/Phra Lam* cosmogony begins with the descent of two *brahma* deities, a male and a female, from the heavens (where they had escaped the destruction of the old world) to the new earth that is taking shape out of the waters.[12] Having been tempted into tasting the "savor of the material world," the two *brahma* deities lose their divine powers and are unable to return to the heavenly realm. Living now on earth, they found the city of Inthapatha on the banks of the Mekong River and establish a dynastic succession that divides into two lines. One line—which continues to rule in the original kingdom of Inthapatha—runs from the original divine couple to a great grandson named Rāvaṇa. The other line—which founds its own royal city further to the north on the site of the present Laotian capital of Vientienne—runs from the original divine couple to two other great grandsons named Phra Lak and Phra Lam.

In this cosmogonic account Indra, who is an especially important deity within the Theravāda tradition, plays a very significant role. Specifically, he facilitates the rebirth processes that result in the birth of Rāvaṇa as Rāvaṇa and of Rāma as Rāma. Having been impressed with the intellectual erudition of a deformed child, Indra sees to it that the child's physical deformity is healed and that he is ultimately reborn as Rāvaṇa. Later, as Indra becomes aware of the threat to the proper order that Rāvaṇa's activities are posing, he sees to it that a *bodhisatta* (a future Buddha) is reborn as Rāma.[13]

As one might expect, virtually all the Buddhist crystallizations of the story identify Rāma and his companions as the rebirth precursors of the Buddha and his family or faithful disciples.[14] In the *Dasaratha Jātaka* this is the only source for the sacrality of the major figures in the story, whereas in the *Phra Lak/Phra Lam* tradition the leading figures often simultaneously participate in the sacrality associated with divinities central to Buddhist cosmology. Even here, however, the primary emphasis is placed on the rebirth connection between Rāma and his companions on the one hand and the Buddha and his companions on the other.[15]

These two Theravāda Buddhist traditions also interpret the exact identity of the disrupting forces that Rāma must overcome rather differently. In the *Dasaratha Jātaka* the enemy is not personified, and the "victory" is purely spiritual. In this distinctive crystallization of the Rāma story, the enemy is the kind of desirous attachment that binds persons to this-worldly life; and the victory comes when the exiled Rāma confronts the news of his father's untimely death with an appropriately Buddhist attitude of equanimity and an appropriately Buddhist commitment to compassionate activity. In the later *Phra Lak/Phra Lam* tradition, the enemy appears in his familiar guise as Rāvaṇa, and the narrative shares with the Hindu versions many key episodes of encounter and conflict.[16] But in the *Phra Lak/Phra Lam* context, Rāvaṇa, like the companions of Rāma, is closely associated with a figure who plays a role in the life of the Buddha. In some cases Rāvaṇa is identified as an earlier form of Māra, the personalized embodiment of desire and death whom the Buddha defeats again and again during the course of his final life as Gotama. In other cases he is identified as the rebirth precursor of Devadatta, the Buddha's angry and desire-driven cousin and archenemy who repeatedly challenges him but finally succumbs in the face of the Buddha's superior wisdom and compassion.[17]

Finally, both tellings culminate with the triumphant return of Rāma to his own country and his installation as the legitimate successor to his father. In religious terms, proper order is restored, and a ruler imbued with Buddhist virtues reclaims the throne. In the *Dasaratha Jātaka* Rāma returns to Banaras, where his father had been king, and establishes his wise and benevolent rule. In the *Phra Lak/Phra Lam* tradition Rāma returns to and establishes his wise and benevolent rule in the Laotian city of his birth. In both instances, the basic theme is the same: a dynasty that embodies and supports Buddhist values has carried the day and is now firmly in charge.

RĀMA TRADITIONS IN THAILAND: THE TEXTS

Thus far, we have characterized two quite distinctive classical Rāma traditions, one clearly Hindu and one clearly Buddhist. With that background in mind, we can now turn to our question concerning the *Ramakien* tradition established in Thailand in the late eighteenth century. Is it Hindu or Buddhist? Or is it a new kind of crystallization that combines elements of both?

Although modern Thai versions of the Rāma story show definite affinities with South Indian, Javanese, and Khmer (Cambodian) versions, there is simply no basis for determining with any degree of precision when, from where, or in what form the story was introduced into the central Thai context.[18] The fact that certain episodes of the Rāma story have been geographically localized at sacred sites around the city of Lopburi suggests that the Rāma story may have been prominent there during the late centuries of the first millennium C.E., when Lopburi was the capital of a major Mon kingdom, and/or during the first centuries of the second millennium C.E., when it was a major provincial center of the Khmer empire ruled from Angkor.

The fact that the most important ruler of the early Thai kingdom of Sukothai took the name Ramkemheng (Rāma the Strong) indicates that by the late thirteenth century some form of the Rāma story was well established in the area, and that it had already been taken up by the Thai. And it is certain that a classical version of the Rāma story played a significant role in the religion and culture of the Thai kingdom that dominated central Thailand from the fourteenth to the late eighteenth centuries. It is not by chance that the capital of this kingdom was named Ayudhya (the Thai name for the city of Rāma) and that several of the kings who ruled there took names that included the name of Rāma. But the destruction and sacking of Ayudhya in the mid eighteenth century has made it impossible to reconstruct the premodern tradition in any detail.[19]

When, in the late eighteenth century, a stable new dynasty was established with its capital at Bangkok, one of the prime concerns of King Rama I was to reconstruct the religious and cultural life of the country. One of the major components in that reconstructive effort was his own specifically ordered and personally supervised composition of a new crystallization of the Rāma story called the *Ramakien*. This classic text was then supplemented by episodes written by King Rama II (reigned 1809–1824) and by King Rama VI (reigned 1925–1935).[20]

Any reader of these *Ramakien* texts will be immediately impressed by the Hindu character of the narrative. From the outset the Hindu gods dominate the scene. In the background is Śiva as the preeminent deity, the creator of the world, and the continuing presence under whose aegis the narrative unfolds. More in the foreground of the action is Viṣṇu, who at Śiva's behest becomes incarnate in the person of Rāma in order to save the world from the threat of social and cosmic disorder. The Hindu gods continue to play a role throughout the narrative, and Hindu figures continue to dominate the action.

Conversely, the most crucial elements of the earlier Buddhist versions of the story are simply not present. There is no suggestion whatsoever that the Buddha was the original teller of the tale, and, although there is a clear cosmogonic dimension to the narrative, there are no indications that a distinctively Buddhist version of the cosmogony had any influence on the presentation. And—what is certainly most important—the story is not presented as an incident in a previous life of the Buddha.

But before we jump to the seemingly obvious conclusion that we are dealing with an unambiguously Hindu crystallization of the story, several additional factors need to be taken into account. First, the primary *Ramakien* text was produced by (and widely associated with) an "author" who was not only a Buddhist king but one especially noted for his support of Buddhism. Second, during the period when the principal *Ramakien* text was being composed, Thai Buddhists were actively engaged in encompassing and assimilating Hindu elements. This was the period, for example, when authoritative Buddhist texts were being written in which Śiva and Viṣṇu were explicitly included among the deities who populate the three worlds of the Buddhist cosmos.[21] Third, since various hierarchical, brahmanical, and dualistic elements that characterize some Hindu versions of the story are not prominent in the *Ramakien*, much of the narrative is quite compatible with Buddhist sensibilities. Fourth, a careful reading discerns distinctively Buddhist emphases in the text. For example, Indra plays a more prominent role than in most Hindu tellings, karmic explanations are more common, and Buddhist attitudes toward life are given greater play.[22]

But the strongest argument against viewing the *Ramakien* as an unambiguously Hindu text (or perhaps even a Hindu text at all) comes from the epilogue attached to the original composition by King Rama I himself. "The writing of the *Ramakien*," he asserts, "was done in accordance with a traditional tale. It is not of abiding importance; rather, it has been written to be used on celebrative occasions. Those who hear it and see it performed should not be deluded. Rather, they should be mindful of impermanence."[23] The Thai word that Rama I uses to convey the notion of delusion is *lailong*—a direct translation of the Pali *moha*, a technical term that refers to one of the three preeminent Buddhist vices (delusion, anger, and greed); and the word that he uses when he urges his readers to be mindful of impermanence is *anitchang*—the Thai transliteration of the Pali technical term *anicca* (impermanence). Thus in his epilogue Rama I very explicitly highlights his own conviction that those who participate in the *Ramakien* tradition can and should approach the *Ramakien* story in a way consistent with Buddhist teachings and insight.[24]

It is clear that both during and after the time of Rama I some participants in the *Ramakien* tradition were—in his terms—"deluded" by the story and "unmindful" concerning the reality of impermanence. During Rama I's own reign *Ramakien* performances that pitted dancers associated with Rama I (representing Rāma) against those associated with his brother who held the position of "second king" (representing Rāvaṇa) occasionally led to pitched battles that resulted in the deaths of some of the participants.[25] It is also true that many participants in the *Ramakien* tradition, especially in more recent times, have adopted a skeptical attitude toward the Hindu structure of the story, but on the basis of their secular, rather than Buddhist, orientation. However Rama I's notion that the *Ramakien* is a rendition of a traditional tale that can and should be approached with specifically Buddhist sensibilities has never been totally forgotten.[26]

RĀMA TRADITIONS IN THAILAND: THE DYNASTIC CULT

Like other classical versions of the Rāma story, the *Ramakien* tradition has been expressed not only in literature and artistic performance but in sculpture and in painting as well. These visual representations of the tale have almost always existed in temple settings, and it is probable that most of them had, at one time or another, specific associations with cultic practice. Insofar as these practices are historically remote, the character of the relevant cult is impossible to reconstruct. In the case of the *Ramakien* tradition, however, we are dealing with a relatively recent cult established by Rama I, the same king who sponsored the primary *Ramakien* text. And, like that text, it remains a vital part of religious and cultural life in contemporary Thailand.

For our purposes the most important iconic expression of the *Ramakien* tradition is one intimately associated with the so-called Holy Emerald Jewel or Emerald Buddha that King Rama I brought to Bangkok from the Laotian capital of Vientienne, and with the closely related dynastic practices that he subsequently established when he became king and built his new capital at Bangkok.[27] Although there had almost certainly been similar images and dynastic cults in the old central Thai capital of Ayudhya, Rama I bypassed any Ayudhyan precedents and drew on the heritage of another region, ultimately founding a tradition distinctive to the Bangkok kingdom and its Chakri rulers.

Evidence strongly suggests that the image of the Emerald Buddha and the rituals associated with it in Vientienne were Buddhist transformations of a Śaivite "Holy Jewel" and corresponding dynastic cult established in the ancient Khmer capital of Angkor in the early centuries of the second millennium C.E. Through a long and fascinating process, this originally Śaivite tradition was appropriated and transformed by the Theravāda Buddhist reformers who subsequently came to dominate the religious life of the area.[28] Although the early phases of this process are hard to trace in any detail, it is certain that thoroughly Buddhized forms of the image and its cult were well established in the northern Thai kingdom of Lannathai by the late fifteenth century. They were transported to the Laotian capital of Luang Prabang in the middle of the sixteenth century and a few years later taken to the Laotian capital of Vientienne.

During this northern Thai-Laotian period, the image and the practices associated with it were closely affiliated with different Buddhist dynasties. There is strong evidence that the image itself served as the palladium of Buddhist kings in each of the three capitals mentioned above, and that the cult was a central element in the ritual structure that legitimated their rule. There is also strong evidence that the stories told about the image and the activities surrounding it involved a wide variety of Buddhist symbols that signified various aspects of royal authority and power. These include notions of the king as a *cakkavatti*, as an Indra, as a *bodhisatta*, and (though in proper Theravāda fashion this always remained ambiguous) as a Buddha.

When Rama I installed the Emerald Buddha in his new royal temple in Bangkok, the image became the palladium of his dynasty and kingdom, the cultic activities associated with it were regularly performed, and all the earlier associations with Buddhist notions of royal power and authority were retained. But what is especially interesting for our purposes is that Rama I added an important component which, as far as I have been able to discover, had not previously been connected with the image.[29] Along the galleries surrounding the central altar of the royal temple, Rama I commissioned the painting of a set of murals that depicted episodes from the *Ramakien*. When celebrations associated with the image of the Emerald Buddha were held, he saw to it that performances of episodes from the *Ramakien* story were included. In visual and ritual terms a clear message was being sent. The "Glory of Rāma" had now been incorporated into the Buddhist ideal of royal power and authority manifested in the Emerald Buddha on the one hand and in the reigning dynasty on the other.

As in the literary and performance strand of the *Ramakien* tradition, so in the iconographic and ritual strand: the pattern established by King Rama I has persisted to the present day. The Emerald Buddha has continued to serve as the palladium of the kingdom; the Buddhist cult associated with the image has continued to legitimate the rule of the Chakri dynasty; and the iconic version of the *Ramakien* story has continued to play a central symbolic role. Thus, to celebrate the fiftieth anniversary of the founding of the dynasty, the *Ramakien* murals painted on the walls of the gallery in the Temple of the Emerald Buddha were refurbished by King Rama III.[30] On the one hundredth anniversary they were refurbished by King Rama V, and on the one hundred and fiftieth anniversary by King Rama VII. During the 1980s, to mark the two hundredth anniversary, they were refurbished once again, this time by the present monarch, King Rama IX.

CONCLUDING COMMENTS

When the literary, performative, iconic, and cultic aspects of the *Ramakien* tradition are all taken fully into account, it is necessary to conclude that this rendition of the Rāma story—at least since its reformulation in the late eighteenth century—tilts more toward Buddhism than Hinduism. In fact, I would go still further and claim that the *Ramakien* crystallizations generated by King Rama I and his successors represent a third classical type of Buddhist-oriented Rāma story that should be considered alongside the first type presented in the *Dasaratha Jātaka* and the second type represented by the *Phra Lak/Phra Lam* tradition.

To be sure, the *Ramakien* versions of the Rāma story do not exhibit the full-fledged Buddhist structure characteristic of earlier Buddhist tellings. Nowhere is the story attributed to the Buddha or presented as an account of events associated with one of his previous lives, nor does it occur in the kind of cosmogonic context that Buddhists traditionally affirm.[31] However, it *is* a tradition which self-consciously sets the Rāma story in explicitly Buddhist contexts, thereby giving it an explicitly Buddhist significance. In the literary and performative strand of the tradition, the Buddhist significance remains relatively muted and largely audience-dependent. In the iconic and cultic strand, the vision of Rāma as a royal hero who embodies Buddhist values is vividly portrayed for all to see. Coexisting and subtly interacting, these two strands of the *Ramakien* tradition have, over the past two centuries, maintained the story of Rāma as an integral, Buddhist-oriented component in Thai religion, culture, and politics.

NOTES

I would like to thank Mani Reynolds for her assistance in locating and interpreting Thai texts and materials. Charles Hallisey has, as always, proved a superb critic, offering numerous corrections and suggestions. All have been appreciated, and most have been incorporated into the text.

1. In this connection, I might note that this paper was originally written as the

inaugural lecture for a three-day Brown Symposium held at Southwestern University (Georgetown, Texas) in October 1988. The symposium was devoted to the Thai version of the Rāma story and was supplemented by the performance of major segments of the story by a dance troupe from Thailand.

2. For a description of these *kae bon* ("releasing from the promise") rituals, see Chantat Tongchuay, *Ramakien kap Wanakam Thongton Pak Tai* (research paper no. 8, Institute for the Dissemination of Scientific Knowledge, Sinakharintharavirot University, Songkhla, Thailand, 1979; in Thai), 27–31.

3. The tendency unduly to privilege Hindu versions in general, and certain Hindu versions in particular, is evidenced by the common practice of referring to the various tellings of the Rāma story by the essentially Hindu term *Rāmāyaṇa*. The practical advantages of following this convention are obvious, but the fact that it implicitly privileges some versions over others should not be ignored.

4. I do not wish to imply here any radical dichotomy between classical and popular traditions. I use the term *classical* simply to signal the fact that the tellings of the Rāma story that I will consider in this paper are fully developed Rāma traditions that have been continuously transmitted over the course of many generations. Although these traditions are associated with particular literary texts, they have also been expressed in a variety of other media including, especially, dance and iconography.

5. A great amount of work has been done comparing various versions of the Rāma story. Generally, however, the emphasis has been on literary elements of style and narrative detail rather than on differences in religious structure. So far as I am aware, the only wide-ranging attempt to compare Hindu and Buddhist versions that shows any significant concern for their religious structure is Harry Buck's now seriously dated essay, "The Figure of Rāma in Asian Cultures," *Asian Profile* 1, no. 1 (August 1973): 133–58.

6. In dance performances and iconographic representations that lack introductory narratives to set the scene, the sense that the story is occurring in a primordial time is often evoked through the use or representation of masks charged with sacral significance.

7. In the remainder of this article, unless otherwise specified "Buddhism" refers to the Theravāda tradition. The Rāma story has, of course, had significant crystallizations in other Buddhist environments, and the Buddhist structure delineated below is to a considerable extent discernible in many of those other contexts as well. However, I have chosen to focus the discussion on Theravāda materials. So far as I am aware, the full range of classical crystallizations of the Rāma story within the Theravāda tradition has never been seriously treated by a Theravāda scholar. In part, this serious lacuna in Theravāda scholarship can be traced to some very influential Buddhologists, who have concluded from the seeming paucity of classical Rāma traditions in Sri Lanka that these traditions do not play a significant role in Theravāda culture as a whole. For an example of this kind of over-generalization from the Sinhalese situation, see Richard Gombrich, "The Vessantara Jātaka, the Rāmāyaṇa and the Dasaratha Jātaka" in *Journal of the American Oriental Society* 105, no. 3 (July–September 1985), 427–37. For a very brief but much more accurate assessment of the presence and role of the Rāma story, both in Sri Lanka and in the Theravāda countries of Southeast Asia, see Heinz Bechert, "On the Popular Religion of the Sinhalese" in *Buddhism in Ceylon and Studies on Religious Syncretism in Buddhist Countries*, ed. Heinz Bechert (Göttingen: Vandenhoeck & Ruprecht, 1978), 230–31.

8. In the article cited in note 7, Richard Gombrich argues that the *Dasaratha Jātaka* is a self-conscious "parody" of the Hindu *Rāmāyaṇa*. In my judgment his argument, which seriously underplays some of the most distinctive characteristics of the *Dasaratha Jātaka* that I will discuss, is not convincing.

9. *The Phra Lak Phra Lam or the Phra Lam Sadok*, 2 vols. (New Delhi: Indian Council for Cultural Relations, 1973). For a discussion of this text, which was found in the Laotian capital of Vientienne, see Vọ Thu Tinh, *Phra Lak/Phra Lam: Version Lao du Ramayana indien et les fresques murales du Vat Wat Oup Moung, Vientienne*, vol. 1 of *Littérature Lao* (Vientienne: Vithanga, 1972).

10. Among the "sister texts" that have thus far been identified, there is a north Laotian version known as the *P'ommachak* (see the reference in Vo Thu Tinh, *Phra Lak/Phra Lam*) and a fascinating variant called *Gvāy Dvóṟahbī* (see Sachchidanand Sahai, *The Ramayana in Laos: A Study in the Gvāy Dvóṟahbī* [Delhi: B. R. Publishing, 1976]). This latter text, based on the Dundubhi episode in the Rāma story, involves the killing of a buffalo, which suggests that this telling of the tale may have served as a correlate or substitute for the buffalo sacrifices that have, in the past, been ubiquitous in Laos. At this point, however, this remains a topic for further research.

11. For a Southeast Asian rendition of Theravāda cosmology and correlated cosmogony based directly on the Pali Tipiṭaka (Skt. Tripiṭaka) and early Pali commentaries, see chapter 10 of Frank E. Reynolds and Mani B. Reynolds, *Three Worlds According to King Ruang*, University of California Buddhist Research Series no. 4 (Berkeley: Asian Humanities Press, 1982).

12. When details vary from text to text, I follow the Vientienne version.

13. Given that Śiva is the preeminent god in the literary *Ramakien* tradition that was associated with the kings of Thailand in the Bangkok period, and probably in the earlier Ayudhya period as well, it is interesting to note the way he is portrayed in the Laotian tellings of the story. In the Vientienne text, Śiva (Lao: Aysouane) is a second name that Indra gives to a Buddhist-type *brahma* deity, the only son of the original pair of *brahma* deities who came down to earth and established the city of Inthapatha. In the *P'ommachak* account from northern Laos, Śiva is presented as a relatively minor deity who once became inebriated and as a result fell from heaven to earth. The fallen Śiva becomes an ally of Rāvaṇa's father and an enemy of Indra and Daśaratha, the father of Rāma. According to the story, a battle is fought and Śiva and Rāvaṇa are defeated. (The *P'ommachak* version is summarized in Vo Thu Tinh, *Phra Lak/Phra Lam*, 87.) Though corroborating evidence is not available, it is very tempting to see in these accounts a political polemic in which the Thai monarchs are being "situated" within the Laotian world.

14. The one exception to this that I know of is the Laotian *Gvāy Dvóṟahbī* text mentioned in note 10. In this text the story *is* presented as a sermon of the Buddha, but it does *not* (at least explicitly) take the form of a *jātaka* story.

15. Within the broader Buddhist context an interesting variant was discovered by H. W. Bailey, which he discussed in his "The Rāma Story in Khotanese," *Journal of the American Oriental Society* 59 (1939): 460–68. In this Khotanese version, Lakṣmaṇa rather than Rāma plays the leading role: the Gotama Buddha who tells the story identifies Lakṣmaṇa as himself in a previous life, while Rāma is identified as one who will be reborn as Metteya (Skt. Maitreya), the Buddha of the future who will appear at the end of the present age. Given the importance of non-Theravāda, Sanskrit traditions in the history of the greater Laos area, it is perhaps interesting to note the

primacy seemingly given to Lakṣmaṇa in the naming (though not in the content) of the *Phra Lak/Phra Lam* tradition.

16. The *Phra Lak/Phra Lam* narratives exhibit the general Buddhist tendency not to radicalize the distinction between good and evil. As in some (though by no means all) of the Hindu versions, Rāvaṇa is presented as a figure who evokes a considerable amount of admiration and sympathy.

17. Given that the Vientienne version of the *Phra Lak/Phra Lam* account identifies Rāma and Rāvaṇa as the rebirth precursors of the Buddha and Devadatta, it is not surprising that Rāma and Rāvaṇa are (like the Buddha and Devadatta) depicted as cousins. In this same text the deformed child who was the rebirth precursor of Rāvaṇa demonstrates unmatched religious erudition by solving a set of riddles presented to him by Indra. Could it be that the text intends to highlight, in the figure of Rāvaṇa, the insufficiency of such religious erudition in the absence of proper attitudes and behavior? Certainly this combination of religious virtuosity with improper attitudes and behavior would make the parallel between Rāvaṇa and Devadatta very close indeed: according to the Buddhist tradition, Devadatta was an extremely erudite religious virtuoso who nonetheless harbored a degree of jealousy and anger that caused him to seek the Buddha's death.

18. Up to this point the most detailed research has focused on the literary and episodic connections between the modern *Ramakien* (which presumably preserves the characteristics of earlier Thai versions) and Tamil traditions. See, for example, S. Singaravelu, "A Comparative Study of the Sanskrit, Tamil, Thai and Malay Versions of the Story of Rāma," *Journal of the Siam Society* 56, pt. 2 (July 1968): 137–85; "The Rāma Story in the Thai Cultural Tradition," *Journal of the Siam Society* 70, pts. 1 and 2 (July 1982): 215–25 (repr. in *Asian Folklore Studies* 44, no. 2 [1985]: 269–79); and "The Episode of Maiyarāb in the Thai Rāmakien and Its Possible Relation to Tamil Folklore," *Indologica Taurinensia* 13 (1985–86): 297–312.

19. For a discussion of the available evidence, see P. Schweisguth, *Etude sur la littérature siamois* (Paris: Imprimerie Nationale, 1951).

20. Although the founder and early kings of the Chakri dynasty that founded the present Bangkok kingdom associated themselves closely with the figure of Rāma, the now extremely common practice of designating them and their successors as Rama I, Rama II, and so on was not established until the time of Rama VI.

21. See, for example, *Traiphum lok winitchai, chamlong chak chabap luang* (Bangkok, 1913), which describes the Buddhist cosmos, including the various heavenly realms and their occupants.

22. The distinctively Buddhist elements are highlighted by Srisurang Poolthupya and Sumalaya Bangloy in *Phrutikam Kong Tua Nai Rueng Ramakien Thai Prieb Tieb Kab Tua Lakhon Nai Mahakap Ramayana*" (Research Document no. 12, Institute for Thai Studies, Thammasat University, Bangkok, 1981); and by Sathian Koset [Phaya Anuman Rajadhon], *Uppakon Ramakien* (Bangkok: Bannakan Press, 1972).

23. King Rama I, *Ramakien*, 2 vols. (Bangkok: Sinlapa Bannakhan, 1967), 1068. The rationalistic, skeptical attitude expressed toward Hindu mythology in this passage provides important confirmation of David Wyatt's thesis that the modernist orientation evident in the Buddhist reform movement led by Rama IV in the middle decades of the nineteenth century was prefigured in the workings and actions of Rama I. See Wyatt, "The 'Subtle Revolution' of King Rama I of Siam," in *Moral Order and*

the Question of Change: Essays on Southeast Asian Thought, ed. David Wyatt and Alexander Woodside (Monograph series no. 24, Yale University Southeast Asia Studies, New Haven, 1982), 9–52.

24. Whether or not Rama I was aware of earlier Buddhist tellings of the Rāma story, he was in fact following a Buddhist tradition in using an epilogue to indicate the significance of the story he had told. In the *Dasaratha Jātaka* and the *Phra Lak/Phra Lam* tellings of the tale, the crucial point that most explicitly reveals the Buddhist significance of the story (namely Rāma's identity as a rebirth precursor of the Buddha and the identities of the other characters as rebirth precursors of the Buddha's "supporting cast") is always revealed in an epilogue.

25. See Mattani Rutnin, "The Modernization of Thai Dance-Drama, with Special Reference to the Reign of King Chulalongkorn" (Doctoral diss., School of Oriental and African Studies, University of London, 1978), 1:14–15.

26. This point was strongly confirmed by the *Ramakien* musicians and dancers who performed at the Brown Symposium at which the original version of this paper was presented.

27. Another important iconic telling of the *Ramakien* story is the set of sculptures now located in Wat Jetupom in Bangkok. Although this set of sculptures is of great artistic interest, it has not—in recent years at least—had a significant cultic function.

28. For an extended account of this process, see my essay "The Holy Emerald Jewel" in *Religion and the Legitimation of Power in Thailand, Laos and Burma*, ed. Bardwell Smith (Chambersburg, Penn.: Anima Books, 1978), 175–93.

29. Northern Thai texts contain accounts of processions of the Emerald Buddha image in which unspecified *jātakas* were chanted, a practice that clearly highlights the association of the image with *bodhisatta*-hood and Buddhahood. It is theoretically possible that a *Rama Jātaka* was among those *jātakas*, but I am not aware of any evidence to support this conjecture.

30. Unlike his two predecessors and most of his successors, Rama III followed a school of opinion that considered literary and performance renditions of the Rāma story too frivolous to deserve the attention of a serious Buddhist. However, his convictions did not inhibit his interest in refurbishing the iconic presentation of the story that was an integral component of the cult supporting the legitimacy of his dynasty.

31. The setting of the *Ramakien* murals on the walls of the galleries around the central altar on which the Emerald Buddha is installed, especially when taken in conjunction with the fact that the chanting of *jātakas* is a common practice in the cult, is clearly intended to hint that Rāma might be a rebirth precursor of the Buddha. There is, however, no evidence that this intimation has ever been explicitly formulated.

PART TWO

Tellings as Refashioning and Opposition

FOUR

The Mutilation of Śūrpaṇakhā

Kathleen M. Erndl

The Rāma story, more than any other sacred story in India, has been interpreted as a blueprint for right human action. Although the *Rāmāyaṇa* is a myth that can be approached on many levels, it is the human level that has had the most profound effect on the Indian people.[1] Certainly Rāma, much more so than Kṛṣṇa, Śiva, Durgā, or other popular Hindu deities, has been held up as the exemplary ethical deity, as dharma personified.

Nonetheless, Western scholars of Indian mythology have until fairly recently neglected to examine the ethical implications even of those texts which cry out for such examination, as Jeffrey Masson has pointed out, chiding them for their detached and impersonal approach to Sanskrit texts.[2] Members of the Indian interpretive tradition—authors of *Rāmāyaṇa* texts and commentators on them—have not been nearly so squeamish and have found fault with Rāma's behavior in several episodes. Or rather one might say that they have been sufficiently uncomfortable with these episodes as to feel the need to explain them, usually in order to make them fit in with the picture of Rāma as a dharmic character. Two frequently cited examples are Rāma's killing of the monkey-king Vālin in an unchivalrous manner from behind his back (*Kiṣkindhakāṇḍa*) and his repudiation of Sītā (both in the fire ordeal of the *Yuddhakāṇḍa* and in the banishment of the *Uttarakāṇḍa*).[3]

A third such episode, the subject of this essay, is the mutilation of Rāvaṇa's sister, Śūrpaṇakhā, in most tellings carried out by Lakṣmaṇa at Rāma's behest, after she has proclaimed her love and made sexual advances to Rāma at Pañcavatī (*Araṇyakāṇḍa*).[4] From a narrative point of view, this episode proves a crucial turning point in the story, the catalyst which sets off a chain of events, notably Rāvaṇa's abduction of Sītā, around which the remainder of the epic in turn revolves. It is also crucial from an ethical point of view, for it sheds light on Rāma's character and on attitudes toward female sexuality in Indian culture. The authors and commentators of various *Rāmāyaṇas* have handled the episode in various ways, reflecting a deep ambivalence in the tradition concerning the actions of Rāma, Lakṣmaṇa, and Śūrpaṇakhā herself. On the one hand, there is the desire to show Rāma as a fair, chivalrous protector of women and other weak members of society. On the other hand, there is a deep suspicion of women's power and sexuality when unchecked by male control. On the one hand, there is an effort to evade the question of whether Rāma's behavior in teasing and goading Śūrpaṇakhā before having her mutilated was appropriate. On the other, there is in many tellings the not-so-subtle suggestion that Śūrpaṇakhā, as an immodest would-be adulteress, deserves whatever treatment she receives.

At this point I feel compelled to take up Masson's challenge and state that my approach to the Śūrpaṇakhā episode does not reflect mere antiquarian curiosity. Nor do I aspire to complete objectivity. I became fascinated with Śūrpaṇakhā when first reading Vālmīki's *Rāmāyaṇa*, feeling both sympathy for her plight and admiration for her forthrightness and independence. It seemed to me that she, like Rāma's stepmother Kaikeyī, had gotten a raw deal in a world where the rules were made by men.[5] I wondered how other *Rāmāyaṇas* depicted the episode and began to collect various tellings. The more I collected, the more ambiguity I saw, an ambiguity which also surrounds many of the dichotomies critical to Indian culture, such as the opposition of good and evil, pure and impure, auspicious and inauspicious, divine and human, male and female.

I will discuss the implications of this episode in several versions of the *Rāmāyaṇa*, allowing each version to shed light on the others so that common patterns can emerge. I have chosen to focus mainly on selected Hindu *Rāmāyaṇas* from the epic (*itihāsa*) and devotional (*bhakti*) traditions. These are:

Rāmāyaṇa (Vālmīki), in Sanskrit (roughly 2nd C. B.C.E.–2nd C. C.E.)
Irāmāvatāram (Kampaṉ), in Tamil (12th C.)
Adhyātma Rāmāyaṇa, in Sanskrit (15th C.)
Rāmcaritmānas (Tulsīdās), in Avadhi or "Old Hindi" (16th C.)
Rādheśyām Rāmāyaṇ, in modern Hindi (20th C.)

Following Lévi-Strauss, I will treat all tellings and interpretations of the story as equally valid; unlike an orthodox structuralist, however, I will take into account not only the structural features of the stories but also their content and the ideological positions explicitly taken by the authors.[6] Although I begin by summarizing the episode as it occurs in the Vālmīki *Rāmāyaṇa* and use it as a basis for the subsequent discussion, I do so only because it is the earliest complete literary version, one with which the composers of the other versions were surely familiar. My intention is not to privilege it as the normative or *Ur*-text: authors of the later literary versions, though drawing on the Vālmīki *Rāmāyaṇa*, also drew on their own local oral traditions, as well as on their creativity and personal ideologies. As A. K. Ramanujan so delightfully illustrates in chapter 2 of this volume, the Rāma story constitutes a universe so vast that it cannot be defined by a single text or even by a group of texts. Because of this, every interpretation is also a telling, and every telling also an interpretation.

THE ŚŪRPAṆAKHĀ EPISODE

Vālmīki Rāmāyaṇa (*Araṇyakāṇḍa* 16–17)

The Vālmīki *Rāmāyaṇa* is so famous that it needs no introduction here. Scholars generally concur that the bulk of the text, including the *Araṇyakāṇḍa*, portrays Rāma as an epic hero with human rather than divine status.

The scene in which Śūrpaṇakhā is mutilated opens with Rāma, Lakṣmaṇa, and Sītā living an idyllic existence in exile at Pañcavaṭī, practicing austerities and telling stories. One day a *rākṣasī* named Śūrpaṇakhā, the sister of Rāvaṇa, happens to pass by. Seeing Rāma's beauty, she is instantly infatuated. The poet contrasts her appearance with Rāma's:

> His face was beautiful; hers was ugly. His waist was slender; hers was bloated. His eyes were wide; hers were deformed. His hair was beautifully black; hers was copper-colored. His voice was pleasant; hers was frightful. He was a tender youth; she was a dreadful old hag. He was well spoken; she was coarse of speech. His conduct was lawful; hers was evil. His countenance was pleasing; hers was repellent. (16.8–9)[7]

Seized with desire, Śūrpaṇakhā approaches Rāma, saying, "Why have you, while in the guise of an ascetic wearing matted locks, accompanied by a wife and bearing bow and arrows, come to this spot which is frequented by *rākṣasas*?" (16.11). In response, Rāma introduces himself, his brother, and his wife. He then asks her about herself, adding, in some versions of the text (though not the Critical Edition), "You have such a charming body that you appear to be a *rākṣasī*."[8] She replies that she is a *rākṣasī* named Śūrpaṇakhā, able to change her form at will (*kāmarūpiṇī*), and has been roaming the Daṇḍaka forest alone, frightening all living beings.

This exchange raises many questions. How did Śūrpaṇakhā really appear to Rāma? Was she beautiful or ugly?[9] If, as a *rākṣasī*, she was able to take on any form she pleased, why did she appear ugly? Was Vālmīki describing her "true" form rather than her "apparent" form? If Rāma did in fact comment on her beauty, was his comment serious or sarcastic? As we shall see, other versions have tried to clarify or otherwise interpret this ambiguity, in some cases adding to it.

Śūrpaṇakhā goes on to describe her brothers, King Rāvaṇa, the hibernating Kumbhakarṇa, the virtuous Vibhīṣaṇa, and the heroic Khara and his general, Dūṣaṇa, saying that she could overcome all of them.[10] She then declares her love to Rāma and invites him to become her husband, offering first to devour Sītā, that "ugly, unfaithful, hideous, potbellied" woman, and then Lakṣmaṇa. With those two out of the way, she argues, they could wander the Daṇḍaka forest together forever, taking in all the sights. Rāma laughs and says:

> I am married, O lady, and cherish my wife. For women like you, the presence of a co-wife would be unbearable. Here is my brother Lakṣmaṇa, virtuous, good-looking, gentlemanly, and virile. He is unmarried. Not having a wife, he is eager [for marriage], and since he is so handsome, he will make an appropriate match for one of your beauty. So, O wide-eyed, shapely one, attend upon him unencumbered by a co-wife, as the sunlight upon Mount Meru. (17.2–5)

Commentators have debated the significance of these lines at great length. If, as is said, Rāma never tells a lie, then why does he say that Lakṣmaṇa is a bachelor? The simplest explanation would seem to be that what is spoken in jest cannot be considered a lie, but the reading in the Critical Edition indicating that he spoke in jest (*svecchayā*) is uncertain.[11] Moreover, given that the word *svecchayā* can connote self-indulgence, one wonders as to the purpose of such a potentially cruel jest. Was he taunting his brother affectionately, or was he having fun at Śūrpaṇakhā's expense? In contrast, some text-historical critics have taken Rāma's statement seriously, using it as one argument among others to prove that the *Bālakāṇḍa*—in which Lakṣmaṇa is married to Sītā's sister, Ūrmilā—is an interpolated book.[12]

A third, and by far the most ingenious, interpretation has been advanced by P. S. Subramanya Sastri in an essay entitled "Telling a Lie or Otherwise by Rama at Panchavati." He argues that the word *akṛtadāra* ("unmarried") can also mean "one whose wife is not with him" or "one who is not using his wife." He also says that the verses following that statement are a double entendre (*śleṣa*) which can be read simultaneously to mean that Lakṣmaṇa has had no opportunity to enjoy conjugal pleasures and thus needs Śūrpaṇakhā, or that Lakṣmaṇa has shown unprecedented behavior in leaving his wife to suffer pangs of separation in the prime of youth.[13] If there is indeed a play on words, it is a very strained one. My point, however, in citing this argument is not to quibble over Sanskrit tropes but rather to illustrate another way in which the problematic nature of this and similar verses has spawned attempts at reconciliation.

The story continues with Śūrpaṇakhā making a similar proposal to Lakṣmaṇa, who smiles and says that as he is Rāma's slave, he cannot be a suitable husband for her, and that she should instead turn to Rāma and become his junior wife. Soon, he argues, Rāma will abandon that "ugly, unfaithful, hideous, potbellied old" wife and attend upon her alone. Śūrpaṇakhā takes Lakṣmaṇa's words at face value, "not being aware of the joke," and says that she will devour Sītā on the spot to be rid of her rival.

Note that Lakṣmaṇa, mockingly engaging in a joke at Śūrpaṇakhā's expense, uses the same adjectives to describe Sītā that Śūrpaṇakhā herself used earlier. Reading additional meaning into the statement, presumably in an effort to redeem Lakṣmaṇa's character, a note to the Hindi translation of the Gita Press edition again suggests a double entendre:

> The meaning from Śūrpaṇakhā's point of view has been given above [in the Hindi translation of the Sanskrit text], but from Lakṣmaṇa's point of view, these adjectives are not critical but laudatory. Thus, *virūpā* (ugly, deformed) means one with a *viśiṣṭa rūpa* (distinguished form); *asatī* (unfaithful, unvirtuous) means one who is unsurpassed in virtue; *karālā* (hideous, horrible) means one whose limbs are high and low with respect to body structure; *nīrṇatodarī* (pot-bellied) means thin-waisted; *vṛddhā* (old) means advanced in wisdom. Thus, the verse could also read as, "Having gotten rid of you, he will attend upon Sītā [who has said qualities]."[14]

The argument here is similar to that of P. S. Subramanya Sastri noted above.

Another scholar, K. Ramaswami Sastri, in an essay entitled "The Riddle of Surpanakha," offers the following commentary:

> The Surpanakha episode is one of the many examples of the wonderfully creative inventiveness of Valmiki's imagination. The story of her lasciviousness is a cleverly contrived prelude to the story of the lustful abduction of Sita by Ravana and gives ample scope to the poet to make the best of a situation which could afford him an ample opportunity for comic portrayal. Rama and Laksmana crack jokes at her expense. The poet says there is no humour in her mental composition (parihasavicaksana). He probably suggests that the cruel and egoistic Rakshasas were not capable of humour.[15]

The suggestion here is that Śūrpaṇakhā had no sense of humor because she was a *rākṣasī* rather than a human female, not because she was a woman blinded by infatuation—although one wonders whether Śūrpaṇakhā would have found the joke funny in any case. The construction of Śūrpaṇakhā as "other," as nonhuman, is particularly appropriate, since she really *is* other than human. Indeed, one purpose for Rāma's presence in the forest is to rid it of the *rākṣasas* who torment the human ascetics.

To continue with Vālmīki's account: Śūrpaṇakhā then prepares to pounce on a frightened Sītā, whereupon Rāma angrily grabs Śūrpaṇakhā, saying to Lakṣmaṇa, "One should never joke with cruel, ignoble people. . . . Mutilate this ugly, unvirtuous, extremely ruttish, great-bellied *rākṣasī*" (17.19–20). At this, Lakṣmaṇa cuts off Śūrpaṇakhā's nose and ears with his sword. Screaming loudly and bleeding profusely, she runs to her brother Khara and tells him what happened. Intending to avenge the insult, Khara, Dūṣaṇa, and Triśiras wage battle against Rāma, who defeats them singlehandedly. Rāvaṇa is first informed of these events by his minister, then by Śūrpaṇakhā herself. Hearing of Sītā's beauty, Rāvaṇa decides to gain revenge by abducting her.

The immediate reason for Śūrpaṇakhā's disfigurement thus seems to be her attempt to devour Sītā. However, the implied reason is her attempt at adultery, which, as we shall see, is made more explicit in other tellings. Disfigurement of a woman is not unknown elsewhere in Vālmīki's text. In the *Bālakāṇḍa* (26.18), Rāma kills the *rākṣasī* Tāṭakā for her crimes against the sage Viśvāmitra, after Lakṣmaṇa first cuts off her hands, nose, and ears as punishment. Similarly, there is a multiform of the Śūrpaṇakhā episode later in the *Araṇyakāṇḍa* (69.17), in which Lakṣmaṇa kills the *rākṣasī* Ayomukhī for making lustful advances toward him.

Modern Indian students of the *Rāmāyaṇa*, like the traditional commentators, have been faced with the problem of reconciling episodes such as the mutilation of Śūrpaṇakhā with the concept of Rāma as the perfect human being or as an incarnation of Viṣṇu. Some argue that the inclusion of such episodes "proves" the historicity of the text, for why would Vālmīki report an unflattering deed of the hero if it were not true?[16] Another approach is the apologetic, inspired by pious devotionalism (*bhakti*), often in reaction to what is perceived as antireligious criticism. Thus C. Rajagopalachari remarks in a footnote to his retelling of the Vālmīki *Rāmāyaṇa*:

> There are some people who pose as critics of our holy books and traditions, saying "This hero killed a woman. He insulted and injured a woman who offered him her love. He killed Vaali from behind. . . . He unjustly banished Sita. . . ." All such criticisms are based on a mentality of hatred. We have unfortunately plenty of barren, heartless cleverness, devoid of true understanding. Let those who find faults in Rama see faults, and if these critics faultlessly pursue *dharma* and avoid in their own lives the flaws they discover in Rama, the *bhaktas* [devotees] of Sri Rama will indeed welcome it with joy.[17]

In the *Uttarakāṇḍa* (23–24), which is considered to be of later composition, more information is given concerning Śūrpaṇakhā's background. She is said to have been the hideous daughter of Viśravas, the grandson of Brahmā, and the *rākṣasī* Kaikasī. Her brother Rāvaṇa is said to have married her to Vidyujjihva, the king of the Kālakas, but Rāvaṇa then killed her husband accidentally in Aśmanagara while conquering the netherworld. Śūrpaṇakhā came to him and censured him, whereupon he sent her to live in the Daṇḍaka forest with her brother Khara and his general Dūṣaṇa. Although Śūrpaṇakhā's status as a widow does not figure at the forefront of Vālmīki's tale, it is prominent in other tellings, as we shall see.

Irāmāvatāram (*paṭalam* 5)

Kampaṉ's *Rāmāyaṇa*, written in Tamil in the twelfth century, is a poetic work renowned for both its aesthetic and religious merit.[18] That it was greatly influenced by Vaiṣṇava devotional (*bhakti*) movements is evident even from its Tamil title, *Irāmāvatāram*, which means "Rāma, the incarnation [of Viṣṇu]." There are a great many differences between Vālmīki's and Kampaṉ's tellings of the Rāma story, and not surprisingly the Śūrpaṇakhā episode is no exception. In fact, Kampaṉ's portrayal of Śūrpaṇakhā is unique among Hindu *Rāmāyaṇas*. It is so compelling that Rajagopalachari, while largely following Vālmīki in his English retelling, chose to append Kampaṉ's version of this particular episode as well. One immediately striking difference between the Sanskrit and Tamil tellings is that while in Vālmīki the episode is a single encounter related in 51 *ślokas*, Kampaṉ dwells lovingly upon the scene, which now extends over a two-day period, in 143 verses of various metres. Unlike Vālmīki, Kampaṉ not only describes Śūrpaṇakhā's appearance as beautiful but expresses considerable sympathy for her plight. I cannot hope to reproduce the beauty of his language here, but will be content to provide a summary with occasional quotations from the excellent translation by George Hart and Hank Heifetz.

The episode begins with a description of Rāma, Sītā, and Lakṣmaṇa settling in the beautiful Pañcavaṭī grove near the Godāvarī river. Into this idyllic scene wanders Śūrpaṇakhā, whom the poet describes immediately as the one fated to bring about Rāvaṇa's destruction. Seeing Rāma alone, she falls in love with him at once, captivated by his beauty, and wonders how to approach him.

> As the love in her heart swelled higher than a flooding river or even the ocean, as her wisdom disappeared, her purity waned like the fame of a man who hoards up wealth and gives nothing with love as his reward for praise! (26.2854)[19]

Purity (*kaṟpu*, also translated "chastity") is a significant quality for the Tamils, for it is believed to provide women with great power.[20] Kampaṉ's introduction of the concept here reinforces the foreshadowing he has already employed: if Śūrpaṇakhā lacks purity, then all her other powers will ultimately fail.

Knowing her own appearance to be forbidding, Śūrpaṇakhā visualizes the goddess Śrī seated on a lotus, utters a magic spell (*mantra*), and becomes a radiantly beautiful woman:

> Beautiful as Śrī on her flower flowing gold,
>   like a streak of lightning
> fallen, never to vanish, out of the sky,
>   with her jewelled chariot
> fresh as that of a young girl
>   and softly clothed,
> and her shining face, the swords of her eyes,
>   like a lovely myna bird, (32.2860)
> she came as if a peacock were coming,
>   with eyes like a deer,
> of a sweet, abundant beauty, with a perfumed
>   honey of words

that would draw out desire for her who had taken
a body just like the vaḷḷi,
glowing vine of heaven, given its life by the tall
and fragrant Wish-Granting Tree. (33.2861)[21]

In this beautiful form she introduces herself to Rāma as the virgin Kāmavaḷḷi, granddaughter of Brahmā and sister of Kubera and Rāvaṇa, whereupon Rāma asks her how she can have such a form even though she is a demoness and why she has come there alone. She replies that her beauty was a result of her good character and penances and that she has spurned the company of unvirtuous *rākṣasas*. She then proposes marriage to Rāma, who meets her proposal with several objections. First, he argues, a Brahmin woman cannot marry a Kṣatriya, to which she replies that she is not really a Brahmin, since her mother is of royal descent. Deciding to have some fun, Rāma says that it was not fitting for a human man to marry a *rākṣasī*. She replies that she has managed to cast off that unfortunate birth. Rāma then says that he will take her only if her brothers will give her to him in marriage, but she insists that they have a *gandharva* rite, as is prescribed by the Vedas when a man and woman fall in love. Her brother will assent after it has taken place, she tells Rāma, adding that with her as his wife, he will no longer need to fear harassment from the *rākṣasas*. Rāma laughs, saying that would be a blessing indeed.

At that moment Sītā returns from her bath. Śūrpaṇakhā, seeing Sītā's beauty and not thinking that Rāma, in his ascetic garb, would be accompanied by a wife, wonders who she is and warns Rāma that Sītā must be a shape-shifting *rākṣasī* who has come to deceive him. Rāma teasingly agrees. When Sītā becomes frightened, Rāma senses danger and, sending Śūrpaṇakhā away, enters the hut with Sītā.

Śūrpaṇakhā spends the night pining for Rāma, almost dying with the intensity of her love:

When the water she bathed in began boiling, she was terrified
in fear of the flames burning away her life and
the body that she so cherished and she thought,
"Where can I hide from the roaring ocean
or the cruel arrows of love?" (79.2907)[22]

Wondering how her suffering will ever vanish, she contrasts herself with Sītā: "Would he look at me as well, I who am so impure? . . . That woman is all purity, she is beautiful, and she is the mistress of his broad chest" (87.2915–88.2916).[23] In the morning, seeing Sītā alone, she approaches her with the idea of snatching her, hiding her away somewhere, and taking on her form, but Lakṣmaṇa, who did not witness the previous day's exchange, pushes her down and cuts off her nose, ears, and nipples. As Śūrpaṇakhā lies writhing in pain, crying out to her brothers to take revenge, Rāma appears and asks who she is. She says that she is the same woman who appeared the day before, but "when a woman has lost her nipples, her ears with their earrings, her nose like a vine, . . . isn't her beauty destroyed?" (119.2947).[24] When Lakṣmaṇa explains that she was about to attack Sītā, Rāma orders her to leave.

Śūrpaṇakhā still does not give up, saying that if she were to tell her brother what had happened he would destroy Rāma and his race, but that she will save him from this fate if he accepts her. She argues that a strong woman like herself, who could protect him in battle, is better than the delicate Sītā. She also accuses Rāma of having her nose cut off to make her undesirable to other suitors, but offers to create it again, if he wishes. Rāma replies that he and his brother are capable of slaying the *rākṣasas* without her help. He tells her to leave, but she persists until Lakṣmaṇa asks Rāma for permission to kill her. At this point she goes to find Khara.

The attack of Khara and Dūṣaṇa proceeds as in the Vālmīki *Rāmāyaṇa*. However, even after their defeat, Śūrpaṇakhā cannot rid herself of her love for Rāma. She goes to Rāvaṇa and describes Sītā's beauty in such detail that he hallucinates an image of her and falls in love with her. Śūrpaṇakhā confesses her love for Rama to her brother, saying that when Rāvaṇa takes Sītā as a wife, she will have Rāma to herself.

Besides the differences in tone mentioned above, there are a few details of plot on which Kampaṉ's *Rāmāyaṇa* differs from Vālmīki's. In this version, although Rāma still jokes with Śūrpaṇakhā, he does so in a gentler and more urbane fashion. He does not crudely suggest that she approach Lakṣmaṇa, as he does in Vālmīki's telling. Furthermore, Lakṣmaṇa bears full responsibility for her mutilation: Rāma only finds out about it afterward. All this is in keeping with Kampaṉ's generally more "chivalrous" approach to Sītā's abduction, in which Rāvaṇa picks up the earth around her rather than subject her to the indignity of having her body touched. On the other hand, Lakṣmaṇa cuts off her nipples as well as her nose and ears. In Tamil culture, the breasts are symbolic of a woman's power, so mutilation of them is a harsh indignity.[25] On the whole, then, Śūrpaṇakhā, like Rāvaṇa, is portrayed in a far more sympathetic light than in Vālmīki, even though the tactics she employs are far more devious.

Adhyātma Rāmāyaṇa (*Araṇyakāṇḍa* 5)

The *Adhyātma* (or "spiritual") *Rāmāyaṇa*, a Sanskrit text dating from the fourteenth or fifteenth century, is an important document in the development of the Rāma cult in North India and is the sacred scripture of the Rāmānandī sect.[26] Integrating various Vedāntic, Purāṇic, and Tantric elements, it tends to view the human events and characters of the Rāma story as divine allegory. Thus, Rāma is an incarnation of Viṣṇu, Lakṣmaṇa is the cosmic serpent Śeṣa, and Sītā the goddess Lakṣmī.

The Śūrpaṇakhā episode follows the basic pattern of the Vālmīki telling but is much briefer and has some differences in emphasis. Śūrpaṇakhā is not described as ugly, as in the Vālmīki version, nor is she said to take on a beautiful form, as in the Kampaṉ version: she is merely said to be capable of assuming diverse forms at will. She falls in love with Rāma when she sees his footprints in the earth, which bear the divine marks of the lotus, thunderbolt, and goad. She approaches him but he directs her to Lakṣmaṇa, saying only that she would not want Sītā as a co-wife: he does not say that Lakṣmaṇa is unmarried. She turns to Lakṣmaṇa, who argues that as he is Rāma's devoted slave, he is not fit to take a wife and that she should turn to Rāma, "the Lord of all." Angry at being sent back and forth, Śūrpaṇakhā says she will eat Sītā up. The story proceeds as in the Vālmīki *Rāmāyaṇa*, with Lakṣmaṇa cutting off her nose and ears. She appeals to Khara and Dūṣaṇa, who fight Rāma and are defeated. She then goes to Rāvaṇa, saying that she was mutilated when she attempted to bring Sītā to him to be his wife. Rāvaṇa realizes that Rāma is not merely a man but decides: "If I am killed by the Supreme Lord, I shall enjoy the kingdom of heaven. Otherwise, I shall enjoy the sovereignty of the *rākṣasas*. I shall therefore approach Rāma."

Although the narrative is similar to that of the Vālmīki *Rāmāyaṇa*, the events are given a context very different from that of the heroic epic. Thus the perspective is changed: what was a battle between two opposing forces becomes a search for salvation through death. In the *bhakti* tradition, any intense emotion directed toward God is a form of devotion, and so, as Rāvaṇa understands, being killed in battle by God is a sure way to attain salvation. There is also an aura of playfulness (*līlā*), events being enacted according to a predetermined divine plan with everything coming out all right in the end. This playful quality allows many of the moral questions to be glossed over. Thus, in this version, it is only a phantom (*māyā*) Sītā who is abducted, not the real Sītā, and Rāma is aware of the outcome of everything beforehand. In fact, in the *Bālakāṇḍa* portion of the *Adhyātma Rāmāyaṇa*, Rāma is depicted as a playful and mischievous child, much like the child Kṛṣṇa. In this context, the Śūrpaṇakhā episode can be seen as a childish prank, ultimately imbued with grace, as is all divine play.

Rāmcaritmānas (*Araṇyakāṇḍa* 16–18)

The *Rāmcaritmānas*, which means "The Lake of the Acts of Rāma," was written by Tulsīdās in the old Hindi dialect of Avadhi in the sixteenth century.[27] It is the most popular form of the *Rāmāyaṇa* in North India, to the point that in Hindi-speaking regions the term *Rāmāyaṇa* is synonymous with the Tulsīdās version. It is first and foremost a *bhakti* text, full of discourses on devotion to Lord Rāma.

The Śūrpaṇakhā episode more or less follows that of the Vālmīki and *Adhyātma Rāmāyaṇas*, but the rhythm of the narrative emphasizes certain points and the extensive interpretive comments give it a flavor of pious didacticism that is absent in other versions. This portion of the story is narrated by Kāk Bhuśuṇḍī, the devotee crow, to Garuḍa, the giant bird who is Viṣṇu's mount. I summarize it as follows:

Rāma spends his days at Pañcavaṭī preaching discourses to Lakṣmaṇa on the nature of disinterested devotion. One day Rāvaṇa's sister Śūrpaṇakhā, "foul-mouthed and cruel as a serpent," happens by and falls in love with both Rāma and Lakṣmaṇa. At this point the narrator interjects, "At the sight of a handsome man, be he her own brother, father, or son, O Garuḍa, a woman gets excited and cannot restrain her passion, even as the sun-stone emits fire when it is brought before the sun" (16.3).[28]

This interjection sets the tone for the rest of the episode, in which the emphasis is placed not so much on Śūrpaṇakhā's *rākṣasa* nature as on her female nature. She has fallen in love with both brothers, since they are both handsome, not just Rāma: like all women, she lacks self-control.[29]

As the story continues, she assumes a charming form and proposes to Rāma, saying that there is no other man like him and no other woman like her, that theirs is a match made in heaven, and that she has remained a virgin just for him. The Lord casts a glance at Sītā and says only, "My brother is a bachelor" (16.6).[30] Śūrpaṇakhā then goes to Lakṣmaṇa, who, knowing her to be their enemy's sister, says that he is Rāma's slave and sends her back to Rāma. Rāma sends her again to Lakṣmaṇa, who remarks, "He alone will wed you who deliberately casts all shame to the winds" (16.9).[31] She then reveals her true form, frightening Sītā. Lakṣmaṇa cuts off her nose and ears, "thereby inviting Rāvaṇa to a contest through her as it were" (17.0).[32] She flees to Khara and Dūṣaṇa, who challenge Rāma and are defeated, attaining eternal bliss by crying out his name at death. Śūrpaṇakhā then goes to Rāvaṇa, scolds him for allowing this to happen, and describes Sītā's beauty. Deciding that the easiest way to "cross the ocean of mundane existence" is to be killed by Rāma, Rāvaṇa abducts Sītā—actually a phantom, the real Sītā waiting in a sacrificial fire.

The comments made about the allegorical aspects of the *Adhyātma Rāmāyaṇa* apply here as well, where the devotional overtones are even more pronounced. Rāma and Lakṣmaṇa do not even go through the motions of asking Śūrpaṇakhā who she is, for, being divine, they already know. Thus, although the goading of Śūrpaṇakhā is retained as the essential catalyst of the story, it is less extravagant and, as is implied by Rāma's glance at Sītā, who is present the whole time, Sītā is let in on the joke. While an atmosphere of divine play again pervades the episode, Tulsīdās has also attempted to justify the brothers' actions on ethical grounds, Lakṣmaṇa's moralizing reaching a degree unprecedented in any of the previously mentioned versions. However, not all commentators on the *Rāmcaritmānas* are convinced by such moral justifications. Hindi literary scholar Mataprasad Gupta, for example, resorts to an aesthetic interpretation of Rāma's actions:

> There are two episodes that do not fit with the greatness of this character: (1) disfiguring Śūrpaṇakhā and (2) killing Bālī with deceit. But some people try to justify both actions completely. However, it is perhaps necessary to point out that the objections raised in these connections are from the point of view of morality, while we are concerned with these actions from a literary point of view, too, that is how far do these blemishes prove helpful in enhancing the beauty of this poem.[33]

Two additional points: Śūrpaṇakhā, as in Kampaṉ but not the other versions, states that she is a virgin. Also, she is sent back and forth between the brothers an extra time.

Rādheśyām Rāmāyaṇ (*saṅkhyā* 10)

The *Rādheśyām Rāmāyaṇ* was composed in the mid twentieth century in simple modern Hindi verse.[34] Written in a lively, colloquial tone, it is available in cheap editions and is much easier for the average Hindi speaker to read than the *Rāmcaritmānas*, which is written in a more archaic and flowery language. Interspersed with songs, the *Rādheśyām Rāmāyaṇ* is also a major source for the Rām Līlā performances in some towns in North India.

The story begins, as in other tellings, with Śūrpaṇakhā falling desperately in love with Rāma after happening upon the pleasant abode where he dwells with Sītā and Lakṣmaṇa. I translate the rest of the episode as follows:

> She said, "In the midst of the world, there is no other woman as beautiful as I, nor is there a beautiful man like you anywhere. Our mutual beauty is as if the Creator had planned it. The maker of the moon has also made the sun. Give me shelter, O Forest-dweller; fulfill the aspiration of the Creator. I command you to marry me in the *gandharva* fashion."
>
> Sītā thought, "Let my heart not be shattered. If the sun and the moon have truly met, then for me there is complete darkness." Smiling to himself, the husband of Sītā said, "Forgive me, desirable one, you cannot be with me. I am not a bachelor, but am married and vow to remain faithful to one woman. Forget about me. I consider all other women to be mothers and sisters. Therefore, I can never accede to your request. I am a noble man and can never break the code of honor."
>
> The demoness listened, and when he had stopped talking, she turned from him and cast her eyes on Lakṣmaṇa. She said to Lakṣmaṇa, "Why are you looking at me and quietly snickering? He is married, but you seem to be a bachelor. Well then, don't give me a harsh answer as he did. If you are willing, and I am willing, then there is nothing wrong with our union."
>
> Lakṣmaṇa had always had a somewhat fierce nature. He could not bear the demoness's behavior. He said, "Aren't you ashamed to say these things? You should have died before saying these things, O sinful one! This is the first time in my life I have ever seen such shamelessness! Because I have seen

such shamelessness, this is an inauspicious day. O demoness, O disgracer of your family! If you have not yet been married, then tell your guardian to get you married somewhere. Marriage should be noble, performed according to righteous means. Don't consider it a bargain in the marketplace. Its proper goal is not the fulfillment of pleasure, but rather the fulfillment of duty. If you have already been married, then serve your own husband! He is your god and should be worshiped. Wish only for his happiness. But if you are a widow, then be a renunciant for the sake of your own husband. Become a true ascetic for the purpose of serving your family, caste, and country. Work toward instructing and improving your own sisters; this is your proper course of action. Remain steadfast in this way, in the midst of the world, remembering your own dear husband. Why do you bring shame upon yourself, uselessly going here and there in this way? O adulteress, you are drowning the good name of your father and husband."

Lakṣmaṇa's tirade in this version makes his moralizing in the *Rāmcaritmānas* seem mild. His message is clear: For a woman, there are three possible statuses, unmarried daughter, wife, or widow—and none of these permit a woman to go about choosing her own sexual partners. A family's honor is invested in the chastity of its women. There is a very modern tone to this passage, reflecting the concern of conservatives in a rapidly changing twentieth century India. The poet seems to be telling his audience that he does not approve of the recent fashion of "love marriages," lest someone think they are permissible as the modern equivalent of the ancient *gandharva* rite. (His remark about the marketplace is unintentionally ironic, since in fact many modern arranged marriages are driven by pecuniary considerations.) Similarly, he reiterates the traditional ideal that a wife should worship her husband as a god, attaining salvation only through him. His remarks about widows have a modern application, since widow remarriage among the upper castes is still a controversial issue, in spite of a relaxation of the ban in some communities. The references to serving one's country and to the educational uplift of women also have a modern, nationalistic ring to them.

The story continues:

Hearing this teaching of the forest ascetic, she was even more agitated. The pure water slid off her as off a slippery pitcher. Then she thought, "This won't work with him. He's a regular preacher and won't change his ways. Yes, the dark lotus-mouthed one seems comparatively gentle to me. But he has his wife with him. Because of her, he won't accept me. So I will assume my horrible form and eat that lovely one. In that way, I will get rid of that thorn in my path in a moment."

As she assumed a horrible form, her garland, which had been a mass of flowers, immediately became a mass of spears. She approached Sītā, but when she opened her mouth wide, Lakṣmaṇa could no longer bear her antics.

Who has the nerve to torture a mother in front of her son? How can someone harm a mistress in front of her servant? At that moment, the eyes of Lakṣmaṇa became red. At the same time, the Kṣatriya's arms became horrible weapons of death. He thought, "I will twist her neck and rid the earth of her. With my kicks and fists, I will pulverize her in a flash." When Rāma realized the fierce sentiment in Lakṣmaṇa's heart, he signaled to Lakṣmaṇa, "Don't kill her; mutilate her." Lakṣmaṇa could not ignore Rāma's order, so he immediately cut off the demoness's nose and ears.

When that evil one had left, crying in pain, the Beloved of Sītā said to Lakṣmaṇa: "You were ready to kill her, but I did not think it was right. On this occasion, I considered it appropriate not to kill a weak woman. So I had you mutilate her so that she would become ugly. Never again will she be able to make such an obscene proposition."

Lakṣmaṇa said, "You have abided by the warrior code. But even killing her would not have been a wrong action. The guru of whom we were disciples [Viśvāmitra] and who increased our zeal had us kill Tāṭakā in our childhood. He used to say, 'It is not a sin to kill a fallen woman. It is not a sin to rid the earth of heinous things.'"

Laughing, Sītā said, "You could have killed her, but your brother is an ocean of mercy and forgiveness!" Hearing the lovely one's irony, Rāma became embarrassed. Lakṣmaṇa also burst out laughing, covering his mouth with his hand.

This version is an interesting combination of black humor and didacticism. Rāma and Lakṣmaṇa do not toy with Śūrpaṇakhā in quite the same manner as in other versions. For example, Rāma does not tell Śūrpaṇakhā that Lakṣmaṇa is unmarried; she assumes it herself. Lakṣmaṇa's lecture is also an innovation, perhaps inspired by the much shorter one in *Rāmcaritmānas*. The *Rādheśyām Rāmāyaṇ* also makes it clear that the motive for mutilation is not only punishment but deterrence. Much later, in the sequel to this text, Rāma's sons Lava and Kuśa are reciting the story of Rāma. When they get to the Śūrpaṇakhā episode, they say, "Who would have thought . . . that [Rāma] would have Lakṣmaṇa cut off this woman's nose and ears? But it was really a matter of his duty to punish the wicked. He disfigured Śūrpaṇakhā in order to keep her away from sin."[35] In other words, Rāma is doing her a favor by preventing her from sinning again. After she leaves, the three of them have a good laugh over the whole thing.

The rest of the story is similar to the *Rāmcaritmānas* version. When Śūrpaṇakhā confronts Rāvaṇa with what has happened, she says, "If my nose is gone, it is gone. Now you better look after your nose." In colloquial Hindi, to lose one's nose (*nāk*) means to lose one's honor. Rāvaṇa pretends to become angry, but, as in other devotional versions, he seizes upon this chance to attain salvation.

As a counterpoint to the apologetic tone of the *Rādheśyām Rāmāyaṇ*, I present here a roughly contemporaneous critique of the mutilation of Śūrpaṇakhā, that offered by Arvind Kumar in *A Study in the Ethics of the Banishment of Sita*.[36] It was originally written as a legal defense of his poem, "Rām kā Antardvandva" (Rāma's internal conflict), which appeared in 1957 in the popular Hindi magazine *Saritā*. The poem was banned after a public uproar and could not be published in the book since the ban was still in effect.

In both the poem and the book, Kumar questions Rāma's loyalty to Sītā, broadly hinting that Rāma was attracted to Śūrpaṇakhā. Kumar describes his poem as a monologue in which Rāma looks back over the events in his life while trying to decide whether to banish Sītā. It shows Rāma doubting Sītā's faithfulness and admitting that he too was once tempted by Śūrpaṇakhā, and even now remembers her beauty. In the essay, Kumar says that Rāma has adopted many poses in his life, one of which was his treatment of Śūrpaṇakhā: "Rāma knows that he is telling a lie. Lakṣmaṇa has been married to Ūrmilā and before going to the jungle has lived with her for twelve years. Is this not a pose to say the least?"[37] He also criticizes the goading of Śūrpaṇakhā:

> The propriety of Rāma's joking in a ribald manner has also been questioned. Would an upright man, with nothing otherwise in his mind, ask a woman who has openly come to him with such an invitation, to go to his younger brother? Rāma does not refuse Śūrpaṇakhā directly. He only says, "Of course, you would not like to share me with a rival wife." Then, both Rāma and Lakṣmaṇa join in the game and make Śūrpaṇakhā fly like a shuttlecock from one end to the other.[38]

The public outrage produced by Kumar's original poem and subsequent essay defending it shows that criticism or satire involving religious figures can be just as inflammatory in Hinduism as in Christianity (the film *The Last Temptation of Christ*) or Islam (Salman Rushdie's *The Satanic Verses*). Rāma's status as moral exemplar is so central to Indian culture that to impugn his motives has become essentially an act of heresy.

MUTILATION AS A PUNISHMENT FOR WOMEN

Three interrelated themes or motifs thus seem to emerge from the Śūrpaṇakhā episode, all of which figure significantly in the broader context of Hindu mythology and culture. The first of these, mutilation as a punishment for women, is a standard feature of the Śūrpaṇakhā story. In the majority of *Rāmāyaṇa* tellings, it is Śūrpaṇakhā's nose and ears that are cut off. In some versions, it is her nose alone, whereas others add her breasts, hands, feet, or even hair.[39] As we have seen, in South India, especially Tamilnadu, the breasts are seen as a symbol of female power; thus, cutting them off is a humiliating punishment which deprives a woman of her power. The nose is a symbol of honor; in all versions of the story its removal signifies the loss of honor. In the *Rādheśyām Rāmāyaṇ*, as we have seen, this is made explicit when Śūrpaṇakhā warns Rāvaṇa that he had better watch out for his nose—meaning, of course, that his honor is at stake. Since honor is especially associated with the sexual purity of women, the cutting off of the nose has traditionally been a punishment reserved for women.

Most Indian legal texts forbid killing a woman, even as punishment for a serious crime, though the practice is not unheard of.[40] For example, in the *Bālakāṇḍa* of Vālmīki's *Rāmāyaṇa*, Rāma kills the demoness Tāṭakā at the behest of the sage Viśvāmitra, after Lakṣmaṇa first disfigures her. Generally, however, women and men receive different punishments for the same crime. Disfigurement of the woman is the most common punishment for crimes of a sexual nature, such as adultery—or even attempting to poison one's husband—and Indian mythology and folklore abound with examples of the motif.[41] Interestingly, such incidents are often presented in a humorous light.[42] Thus, in many North Indian Rām Līlā performances the Śūrpaṇakhā episode is a kind of burlesque, to which the (predominantly male) audience responds with ribald jokes and laughter, perhaps again betraying a certain male anxiety about female sexuality.[43]

SEXUALITY AND AUSTERITY IN THE FOREST

The mythologies of Śiva and of Kṛṣṇa allow a free interplay between eroticism and asceticism: though the two are in tension, full expression is given to both. In the character of Rāma, however, sexuality appears to be almost completely suppressed. There is some tension between the ascetic and the householder way of life, but the conflict is always presented in terms of dharma, that is, in terms of which duty he should fulfill, rather than in terms of the indulgence or suppression of erotic desires. According to the traditional interpretation, during his exile Rāma is a *vānaprastha*, a forest-dwelling ascetic accompanied by his wife. This stage of life is rife with complications, as it is an "unsatisfactory compromise" between two mutually exclusive modes of existence, the householder and the ascetic.[44] According to tradition, Rāma and Sītā refrained from sexual activity for the fourteen years of their exile, although Vālmīki, at least, is ambiguous on this point.

In the Sanskrit aesthetic tradition represented by Abhinavagupta, the major theme of the *Rāmāyaṇa* is summed up by the story, recounted early in Vālmīki, of a hunter sinfully killing a bird, thereby interrupting its lovemaking with its mate.[45] In the Rāma narrative proper, a somewhat similar interruption of marital bliss is created first by Śūrpaṇakhā and then, more disruptively, by Rāvaṇa. This is a common motif in Hindu mythology: when Śiva and Pārvatī were interrupted in their lovemaking, for example, disastrous consequences ensued.[46] At the same time, in keeping with the ambiguous character of the *vānaprastha* mode, the Śūrpaṇakhā episode resembles the myth of Kāma's interruption of Śiva's austerities. The Ahalyā story follows a similar pattern: Indra disrupts the marital bliss of the forest-dwelling couple Gautama and Ahalyā, but at the same time interrupts their austerities, for which both he and Ahalyā are cursed. The narration of the Śūrpaṇakhā episode generally begins with a twofold description of idyllic domesticity and the performance of austerities. Śūrpaṇakhā is punished for her display of unrepressed sexuality, which is harmful to both domesticity and asceticism.

SĪTĀ AND ŚŪRPAṆAKHĀ AS ALTER EGOS

Sītā and Śūrpaṇakhā exemplify two types of women who appear almost universally in folklore and mythology: Sītā is good, pure, light, auspicious, and subordinate, whereas Śūrpaṇakhā is evil, impure, dark, inauspicious, and insubordinate. Although male characters also divide into good and bad, the split between women is far more pronounced and is always expressed in terms of sexuality.[47] Similarly, when a woman such as Śūrpaṇakhā performs a wrong deed, it is typically ascribed to her female nature, whereas Rāvaṇa's evil deeds, for example, are never said to spring from his male nature. It is also worth noting that in the *bhakti*-oriented *Rāmāyaṇas*, in which the evil-doings of the male characters are recast as devotional acts leading to eventual salvation, Śūrpaṇakhā's salvation is not mentioned.[48]

Sītā is the chaste good woman; Śūrpaṇakhā the "loose" bad woman. The good woman is one who remains controlled, both mentally and physically, by her husband (or, in his absence, her father, brother, or son) and whose sexuality is channeled into childbearing and service to her husband. The scriptures make frequent references to a man's duty to unite himself with such a woman in order to produce sons and thereby fulfill obligations to the ancestors. According to an oft-quoted injunction, a woman must obey and be protected by her father in youth, her husband in married life, and her sons in old age; a woman should never be independent (*Manusmṛti* V.147, IX.3). The good woman, however, is far from weak and powerless. She is a source of power, *śakti*.[49] In other words, it is her auspiciousness and nurturing that keep things going, but her power must be controlled to suit the purposes of a patriarchal society. Thus Sītā comes to the forest as a companion to her husband, and she is watched over and protected every step of the way. Otherwise, she would not be allowed to set foot out of the palace.

The bad woman is one who is not subject to these controls. In contrast to Sītā, Śūrpaṇakhā is unattached and wanders about freely. In Vālmīki, she describes herself as a strong woman who goes where she likes under her own power. It is not surprising that she is said to be a widow, since widows are considered dangerous and inauspicious, circumstances having rendered them unable to bear children. Their chastity is also suspect, since they are no longer under the control of a husband, and women are believed to have insatiable sexual appetites. In Hindi, Panjabi, and other North Indian languages, the word *suhāgin* or *sumaṅgalī*, signifying auspiciousness, is used for a married woman whose husband is alive, while the word *raṇḍī* can mean both a widow and a whore.[50] Śūrpaṇakhā's unmarried state is thus the major source of her evil nature; being a *rākṣasī* is at best a contributing factor. After all, Mandodarī, also a *rākṣasī*, is praised for her virtue, chastity, and devotion to her husband, Rāvaṇa. Accordingly, it is Śūrpaṇakhā's status as an independent woman which is denounced. But the loose woman, while perceived as dangerous, also holds a certain fascination for the male imagination, which is perhaps why Rāma and Lakṣmaṇa linger a bit, egging her on rather than banishing her immediately.

It is revealing that Rāma uses Sītā as the excuse for Śūrpaṇakhā's mutilation: the "bad woman" is punished in order to protect the "good woman," or perhaps to serve as an example of what would happen to the "good woman" if she decided to go "bad"—for the division of women into two types in fact reflects a basic mistrust of all women. One could even argue that if the beautiful and virtuous Sītā is Lakṣmī, the goddess of prosperity and auspiciousness, then the ugly and unvirtuous Śūrpaṇakhā must be her sister Alakṣmī, the goddess of misfortune and inauspiciousness. In festivals honoring Lakṣmī, her sister Alakṣmī is often driven away by lighting lamps, but in a Bengali Lakṣmī festival, an image of Alakṣmī is made and ritually disfigured by cutting off its nose and ears, after which an image of Lakṣmī is installed in order to ensure good luck and prosperity in the coming year.[51] The structural similarity between this popular ritual and the Śūrpaṇakhā episode is striking.

The analysis of a single episode as it appears in selected tellings and interpretations can thus provide a telling glimpse into the dynamics of the *Rāmāyaṇa* as a whole. The mutilation of Śūrpaṇakhā is significant to the Rāma story from multiple perspectives. From a narrative point of view, it serves as the catalyst for the key events: only after Śūrpaṇakhā reports her disfigurement to Rāvaṇa does he decide to abduct Sītā. From an ethical point of view, the episode raises complex questions about Rāma's supposedly exemplary character, questions which authors and commentators have attempted to resolve in diverse ways. From a cultural perspective, the episode sheds light on Hindu attitudes toward female sexuality and its relationship to such polarities as good and evil, pure and impure, auspicious and inauspicious. However, the final word on Śūrpaṇakhā has not been voiced: her story is sure to fascinate and inspire hearers, tellers, and interpreters for generations to come.

NOTES

I wish to thank V. Narayana Rao for introducing me to the richness of the *Rāmāyaṇa* tradition, and Paula Richman for her generous attention and helpful comments on several drafts of this essay.

For the sake of consistency and readability I have, unless otherwise indicated, used the standard Sanskrit forms and transliteration system for all names, terms, and places in the *Rāmāyaṇa*.

1. As Wendy O'Flaherty has pointed out, a myth can be interpreted on several levels: the narrative, the divine, the cosmic, and the human—the last concerned with problems of human society and with the search for meaning in human life. See her *Asceticism and Eroticism in the Mythology of Śiva* (Delhi: Oxford University Press, 1973), 2. See also O'Flaherty, "Inside and Outside the Mouth of God" (*Daedalus* 109, no. 2 [Spring 1980]: 103) for a discussion of myths as "social charters." In classifying the Rāma story as a myth, I am defining a myth as a sacred story about supernatural beings and events that holds great significance for the members of a culture.

2. J. Moussaieff Masson, "Fratricide among the Monkeys: Psychoanalytic Observations on an Episode in the Vālmīkirāmāyaṇam," *Journal of the American Oriental Society* 95, no. 4 (October–December 1975), 672.

3. David Shulman has discussed both these episodes from Kampaṉ's *Rāmāyaṇa*, the first in "Divine Order and Divine Evil in the Tamil Tale of Rāma," *Journal of Asian Studies* 38, no. 4 (August 1979), 651–69; the second in his article for this volume.

4. The name Śūrpaṇakhā means literally "one who has nails (*nakha*) like a winnowing basket (*śūrpa*)." In modern Indian languages such as Hindi, it is sometimes used as an epithet to describe an ugly, pug-nosed woman.

5. In fact, the specter of Śūrpaṇakhā so haunted my imagination that, as a respite from studying for doctoral prelims, I wrote my own version of the episode (now happily consigned to oblivion) in which Sītā, recognizing her "submerged self" in Śūrpaṇakhā, leaves Rāma and flees with her to the Himalayas to join Kālī, the Great Goddess. Such is the power of the Rāma story, that it is able to transcend cultures and emerge in countless transformations.

6. Claude Lévi-Strauss, *The Savage Mind* (Chicago: University of Chicago Press, 1966).

7. I am following the Critical Edition of the *Rāmāyaṇa*, ed. by G. H. Bhatt and U. P. Shah, vol. 3: *Araṇyakāṇḍa*, ed. by P. C. Dinanji (Baroda: Oriental Institute, 1963), *sargas* 16–17. I have also consulted two other Sanskrit editions: *Śrīmadvālmīkirāmāyaṇa*, with Amṛtakataka of Mādhavayogī, ed. by N. S. Venkatanāthācārya (Mysore: University of Mysore, 1965) and *Śrīmadvālmīkiya Rāmāyaṇa*, with Hindi translation (Gorakhpur: Gītā Press, [1960]). In these two, the episode occupies *sargas* 17–18. In English translation, I have consulted volume 2 of Hari Prasad Shastri, trans., *The Ramayana of Valmiki*, 3 vols. (London: Shanti Sadan, 1957); and Sheldon I. Pollock, trans., *The Rāmāyaṇa of Vālmīki*, vol. 3: *Araṇyakāṇḍa* (Princeton: Princeton University Press, 1991). Translations are my own unless otherwise noted.

8. Sheldon Pollock quotes the Southern recension as adding a line, which the Critical Edition omits: "For with your charming body you do not look like a *rākṣasa* woman to me." As he points out, the commentators find this remark difficult to explain, although it may be correct to view it as sarcastic (note on 16.16).

9. In the Southern recension, upon which the Critical Edition relies heavily, the beauty of Rāma and the ugliness of Śūrpaṇakhā are given special emphasis, while the Bengali recension (23.18–25) clearly states that Śūrpaṇakhā takes on a beautiful form. The following versions specifically mention Śūrpaṇakhā's ugliness: *Bhāgavata Purāṇa* (9.10.9); *Garuḍa Purāṇa* (143); *Padma Purāṇa* (*Pātāla Khaṇḍa* 36 and *Uttara Khaṇḍa* 269), *Devī Bhāgavata Purāṇa* (3.28). See also Camille Bulcke, *Rāmkathā: Utpatti aur Vikās* (Prayāg: Hindī Pariṣad Prakāśan, 1950; in Hindi), 414.

10. Pollock translates *tān ahaṃ samatikrāntā* as "But I am prepared to defy them" (note to 16.21). Śūrpaṇakhā seems here to be boasting about her own power. In the Gītā Press edition the following line reads *ahaṃ prabhāvasampannā svacchandabalagāminī*, "I am powerful and able to go where I please."

11. See the note to 17.1 in Pollock.

12. See, for example, Bulcke, *Rāmkathā*, 14, and "The Ramayana: Its History and Character," *Poona Orientalist* 25, nos. 1–4 (January/October 1960), 41.

13. P. S. Subramanya Sastri, *A Critical Study of Valmiki Ramayana* (Thiruvaiyaru: [P. S. Krishnan], 1968), 26–28. The verse in question (17.4) reads:

apūrvī bhāryayā cārthī taruṇaḥ priyadarśanaḥ |
anurūpaś ca te bhartā rūpasyāsya bhaviṣyati ||

Pollock translates this as: "He has never had a woman before and is in need of a wife. He is young and handsome and will make a good husband, one suited to such beauty as yours."

14. Gītā Press edition, 538; my translation from the Hindi. The verse in question is 17.11 in the Critical Edition:

etāṃ virūpām asatīṃ karālāṃ nirṇatodarīṃ |
bhāryāṃ vṛddhāṃ parityajya tvām evaiṣa bhajiṣyati ||

15. K. Ramaswami Sastri, *Studies in Ramayana* (Baroda: State Department of Education, 1941), 100.

16. Bulcke, "The Ramayana," 58; Swami Siddhanathananda, "Śrī Rāma—Dharma Personified," *Prabuddha Bharata* 77, no. 8 (September 1972), 395.

17. C. Rajagopalachari, *Rāmāyaṇa* (Bombay: Bharatiya Vidya Bhavan, 1958), 133. In the epilogue, however, he seems to change his mind and decry the banishment of Sītā, saying that Rāma, unlike Kṛṣṇa, was unaware of his incarnation and that his divinity must have ended when he returned to Ayodhya. He also suggests that the banishment scene may be the result of a corruption in the text and his "heart rebels against it" (295–96).

18. Kampaṉ is traditionally dated to the ninth century, although most scholars consider the twelfth century more probable. I have relied on the English translation of George L. Hart and Hank Heifetz, *The Forest Book of the Rāmāyaṇa of Kampaṉ* (Berkeley and Los Angeles: University of California Press, 1988), *paṭalam* 5, from which all quotations are taken. I have also consulted "Kamban's Soorpanakha" from C. Rajagopalachari's retelling, 134–36, and S. Shankar Raju Naidu, *A Comparative Study of Kamban Ramayanam and Tulasi Ramayan* (Madras: University of Madras, 1971), 186–89 and 507–8.

19. Hart and Heifetz, *The Forest Book of the Rāmāyaṇa of Kampaṉ*, 89.

20. For a discussion of traditional notions of *kaṟpu*, see George L. Hart, *The Poems of Ancient Tamil: Their Milieu and Their Sanskrit Counterparts* (Berkeley and Los Angeles: University of California Press, 1975), 96–98. For discussions of contemporary contexts, see Susan S. Wadley, ed., *The Powers of Tamil Women*, Foreign and Comparative Studies, South Asia series no. 6 (Syracuse: Maxwell School of Citizenship and Public Affairs, Syracuse University, 1980).

21. Hart and Heifetz, *The Forest Book of the Rāmāyaṇa of Kampaṉ*, 90.

22. Ibid., 101.

23. Ibid., 102.

24. Ibid., 109.

25. Voluntary sacrifice of a breast can also have powerful effects. In the Tamil classic *Cilappatikāram*, the main character, Kaṇṇaki, tears off her own breast and throws it into the city of Madurai, bringing about the city's destruction. In another tale from Madurai, Mīnākṣī, the patron goddess of the city, loses her third breast when she first sets eyes on her future husband, Śiva. See the various articles in Wadley, ed., *Powers of Tamil Women*, for further discussion of the significance of breasts in Tamil culture.

26. See Frank Whaling, *The Rise of the Religious Significance of Rāma* (Delhi: Motilal Banarsidass, 1980), 105; Rai Bahadur Lala Baij Nath, trans., *The Adhyatma Ramayana* (Allahabad: The Panini Office, 1913; reprinted as extra volume 1 in the *Sacred Books of the Hindus*, New York: AMS Press, 1974).

27. I have used the Gītā Press edition, *Śrī Rāmcaritmānas*, which contains the Hindi text and an English translation (Gorakhpur: Gītā Press, 1968). The Śūrpaṇakhā episode is on pp. 535–38.

28. *Śrī Rāmcaritmānas*, 535.

29. A discussion of Tulsīdās's treatment of women is given by Geeta Patel, "Women, Untouchables, and Other Beasts in Tulsī Dās' *Rāmāyaṇa*" (paper presented at the 17th annual conference on South Asia, Madison, Wisconsin, November 1988).

30. *Śrī Rāmcaritmānas*, 535.

31. Ibid., 536.

32. Ibid.

33. Quoted in Arvind Kumar, *A Study in the Ethics of the Banishment of Sītā* (New Delhi: Sarita Magazine, n.d. [1975?]), 28.

34. Paṇḍit Rādheśyām Kathāvācak, *Śrīrām-kathā* (*Rādheśyām Rāmāyaṇ*) (Barelī: Śrī Rādheśyām Pustakālay, 1960), 18–24: *Araṇyakāṇḍa*, *saṅkhyā* 10 (*Pañcavatī*). The book has been reprinted many times, often in pirated editions, but was probably written shortly before or after Indian independence in 1947.

35. Madan Mohanlal Śarma, *Uttar Rāmcarit*, ed. by Paṇḍit Rādheśyām Kathāvācak (Barelī: Śrī Rādheśyām Pustakalāy, 1960), 25–26.

36. See note 33.

37. Kumar, *A Study in the Ethics of the Banishment of Sītā*, 59.

38. Ibid., 61.

39. Bulcke, *Rāmkathā*, 415, gives an extensive list of which body parts are cut off in which versions.

40. Sasanka Sekher Parui, "Punishment of Women in Ancient India," *Journal of the Oriental Institute of Baroda* 26, no. 4 (June 1977), 362–68.

41. Parui ("Punishment of Women," 366–67) gives examples from various texts,

especially the *Kathāsaritsāgara*. For other sources of the "cut-off nose" motif, see Stith Thompson and Jonas Balys, *The Oral Tales of India* (Bloomington: Indiana University Press, 1958), 327, 386, and 401.

42. For example, a Bhutanese dance troupe which recently toured the United States performed a comic interlude in which husbands cut off their wives' noses as a punishment for infidelity.

43. In the Rām Līlā of Banaras, this episode, called the Nakkatayya, is one of the most elaborate, lasting all night and featuring a procession headed by a *hijrā* (hermaphrodite) playing the role of Śūrpaṇakhā. See Nita Kumar, "Popular Culture in Urban India: The Artisans of Banaras, c. 1884–1984" (Ph.D. diss., University of Chicago, 1984), 261–94.

44. The phrase is Wendy O'Flaherty's, in *Asceticism and Eroticism in the Mythology of Śiva*.

45. Abhinavagupta, *Dhvanyāloka, kārikā* 5. The story itself is found in Vālmīki *Rāmāyaṇa*, I.2.8–18. See J. Masson, "Who Killed Cock Krauñca? Abhinavagupta's Reflections on the Origin of Aesthetic Experience," *Journal of the Oriental Institute of Baroda* 18, no. 3 (March 1969): 207–24.

46. O'Flaherty, *Asceticism and Eroticism*, 302–10.

47. Two of Daśaratha's wives, Kausalyā and Kaikeyī, are similarly dichotomized: Kausalyā is virtuous, whereas Kaikeyī is sexually attractive. See Robert P. Goldman, trans., *The Rāmāyaṇa of Vālmīki*, vol. 1: *Bālakāṇḍa* (Princeton: Princeton University Press, 1984), 54.

48. An exception is the unique account of Śūrpaṇakhā in the *Brahmavaivarta Purāṇa* (*Kṛṣṇajanmakhaṇḍa* 62), in which after her disfigurement she goes to the sacred lake Puṣkara to perform austerities: see Bulcke, *Rāmkathā*, 417. Receiving a boon from Brahmā to get Rāma as her husband in her next life, she is reborn as Kubjā, the hunchbacked woman who becomes one of the wives of Kṛṣṇa, as whom Rāma is reborn.

49. For an excellent discussion in this vein, see Cornelia Dimmitt, "Sītā: Fertility Goddess and *Śakti*," in *The Divine Consort: Rādhā and the Goddesses of India*, ed. John Stratton Hawley and Donna Marie Wulff (Berkeley: Berkeley Religious Studies Series, 1982), 210–23.

50. Even female ascetics are suspect, as are unmarried women generally, since they are not under the control of a husband.

51. David Kinsley, *Hindu Goddesses: Visions of the Divine Feminine in the Hindu Religious Tradition* (Berkeley and Los Angeles: University of California Press, 1986), 34.

FIVE

Fire and Flood: The Testing of Sītā in Kampaṉ's *Irāmāvatāram*

David Shulman

Even perfection has its problems. Especially vulnerable are those unfortunates who have to live beside or in relation to some paragon. No doubt Rāma, exemplary hero that he is in the major classical versions of the story from Vālmīki onward, attracts the love and utter loyalty of nearly everyone with whom he comes in contact, especially the members of his immediate family. As Kampaṉ, the twelfth-century author of the Tamil *Rāmāyaṇa*, puts it:

> Just as Rāma is filled with love
> of many kinds
> for all the living beings of this world,
> so, in so many ways, do they
> love him.[1]

And it is, of course, no ordinary love: elsewhere we are told—this is Sītā speaking to Lakṣmaṇa—that "those who have known him for even a single day would give their lives for him" (III.8.13). Still, statements such as these by no means exhaust the range of emotions generated by Rāma's presence. Moreover, in at least two contexts this idealized model of humanity is explicitly problematized by the *Rāmāyaṇa* tradition: first, in the painful case of his cowardly and unfair slaying of the monkey-king Vālin; and second, in his relations with Sītā after the war and her restoration to him.[2] The latter context is even, in a sense, doubled. Rāma initially rejects Sītā in Lanka, requiring her to undergo a test of fire (*agniparīkṣā*), which she passes. Only later, in the seventh book, the *Uttarakāṇḍa*, does Rāma take the more drastic and apparently final step of exiling his wife in response to continuing slanderous rumors about her faithfulness to him during her stay at Rāvaṇa's court. The Indian literary tradition has explored the tragic dimension of Rāma's action and has offered various solutions to the problems it raises—since there is no doubt that Sītā's punishment is entirely unmerited, as Rāma himself clearly knows.[3]

Modern Indological scholarship has, since Jacobi, tended to attack the problem by a characteristic act of stratigraphy: the *Uttarakāṇḍa* is declared later than the "central core" of books 2 through 6, so Rāma's final repudiation of Sītā is reduced to the status of an accretion. For reasons that I cannot develop here, I feel that this "solution" is unacceptable.[4] In any case, our present concern is with the earlier trial, in Lanka, primarily as it appears in Kampaṉ's Tamil version. In Kampaṉ this is the only such moment of overt hostility on the part of Rāma toward Sītā, for the Tamil work concludes with Rāma's happy return to Ayodhya; there is no *Uttarakāṇḍa*.[5] The Tamil poem thus achieves an outwardly pacific closure—which should not, however, mask the inherent turbulence of its emotional universe. Reading Kampaṉ, one should never be wholly taken in by surface idealizations. Still, the relationship between Rāma and his wife *is* generally idealized in the Tamil text; thus Sītā's ordeal by fire, with its bitter overtones, acquires an intriguing singularity. In many ways, this is a critical and culminating moment in the narrative.

We will study this episode as a particularly revealing illustration of certain basic themes and tensions embedded within Kampaṉ's poem, and also as a striking condensation of the cultural distinctiveness of this Tamil *Rāmāyaṇa*, especially vis-à-vis the earlier text of Vālmīki. By way of introduction, let me say merely that, however we may seek to understand Rāma's status in the Sanskrit text, there is no question that for Kampaṉ he is God in visible and earthly form. Kampaṉ rarely lets us forget this identification—though, as we shall see, its implications for the hero's own consciousness are rather different than in the case of Vālmīki's presentation of the avatar. The Tamil *Rāmāyaṇa* is a devotional *kāvya*, replete with the poses and values of Tamil *bhakti* religion and marked by the general cultural orientations of the Kaveri delta during the Chola period, when it was composed. This means, among other things, that it has the power of subtlety as well as the volatile movement of internal complexity; and that it builds, in sometimes surprising ways, on the earlier foundations of Tamil poetry with its inherited modes of classifying the world and its typical understandings of human identity and experience.

THE COST OF SELF-KNOWLEDGE: VĀLMĪKI'S VISION

We begin with an overview of the episode in Vālmīki's text. The great war is over, and Rāvaṇa slain. Vibhīṣaṇa, Rāvaṇa's righteous brother, has been crowned king of Lanka and, at Rāma's magnanimous insistence, has performed the funeral rites for his dead brother. Now Sītā, who has heard from Hanumān the happy news of her deliverance, is brought into Rāma's presence by Vibhīṣaṇa. This is the beginning of the trial. Even before any direct contact can be made between the two separated lovers, an unseemly and somewhat inauspicious commotion breaks out. Clearing a way for Sītā, Vibhīṣaṇa's servants violently push aside the curious crowd of bears, monkeys, and demons—these are, after all, the constant witnesses of Rāma's career—at which they clamor indignantly. Rāma, too, is indignant: these are *his*, Rāma's, people now, he informs Vibhīṣaṇa; they should not be injured. Moreover, there is absolutely no harm in their seeing Sītā directly, for women *can* be seen in the context of disasters, wars, a bridegroom choice, sacrifices, and weddings. There is therefore no need to protect Sītā—especially, he notes, "in my presence" (VI.117.28).[6] Hanumān, Lakṣmaṇa, and Sugrīva quite rightly detect a sinister note in this speech. They are disturbed, afraid that Rāma is somehow unhappy with Sītā; and indeed the poet-narrator has already indicated to us that Rāma is filled with conflicting emotions at this point, specifically joy, misery, and anger (*harṣo dainyaṃ ca roṣaś ca*, 117.16).

Sītā now stands before him, her eyes raised hopefully to his face. She is a little embarrassed and hides *her* face with the edge of her sari. She is weeping, repeating over and over, "My lord" (*āryaputra*). It should be a moment of joyful reunion, but to everyone's shock Rāma proceeds to speak his "innermost thought" (*hṛdayāntargataṃ bhāvam*, 118.1), articulated in a speech that is horribly cold, formal, and aloof. "So I have won you back by defeating my enemy; I have acted as a man should, wiped out the insult to my honor, revealed my prowess. Today I have fulfilled my promise and can control my life. Your misfortune in being carried off by that fickle demon, as fate (*daiva*) decreed, has been overcome by me, a mere mortal" (118.2–5). As an afterthought, he adds that the heroic feats performed by Hanumān and Sugrīva, as well as Vibhīṣaṇa's decision to abandon his wicked brother, have also been vindicated by this success.

Sītā appropriately bursts into tears at this unexpected welcome. Looking at her, Rāma becomes still angrier, like a fire fed by oblations of butter. (Some manuscripts add that he is afraid of public opinion, and that his heart is split in two.)[7] He launches into an outright attack on his wife: she should know that he fought not for her sake but simply in order to remove the insult to himself and his famous family. Now there is some doubt as to her conduct (*caritra*) during this period, and as a result she is repugnant to him, like a lamp to a person whose eyes are diseased. "Go, then, with my permission, wherever you may wish. The world is open before you; but I will have nothing to do with you, nor have I any attachment to you any more. How could I take you back, straight from Rāvaṇa's lap?"

It is a brutal outburst, perhaps calculatedly so, if we adopt the perspective that the *Rāmāyaṇa* tradition often proposes, and that Vālmīki himself may finally hint at. In any case, the listener, no doubt like Sītā herself, reels under the impact of the simile Rāma chooses for himself: he is like a man half-blind in the presence of a lamp.[8] Certainly, Rāma does appear at this point quite unable to perceive the truth. So Sītā replies, choked and weeping, in words of protest that are, at least at first, strikingly restrained: "Why are you speaking to me so harshly and inappropriately, like a common man to a common woman? I am not as you imagine me; you must believe me, I swear to you. Because of the conduct of some lowly women, you cast doubt on the entire sex. Put aside this doubt; I have been tested! I could not help it if my body was touched by another, but there was no desire involved; fate is to blame. That part of me that is wholly under my control—my heart—is always focused on you. Can I help it if the limbs of my body are ruled by others? If, after our long intimacy, you still do not know me, then I am truly cursed forever." She marshals a trenchant argument: If Rāma were determined to repudiate her, why did he bother sending Hanumān to find her when she was a prisoner? Had he so much as hinted at his intention, she would have killed herself at once, in Hanumān's presence. This would surely have saved everyone a good deal of trouble and risk! Sarcasm is creeping into her speech; it seems she is getting angry after all, to the point where she allows herself one truly biting line: "By giving in to anger like a little man, you, my lord, have made being a woman altogether preferable" (*tvayā . . . laghuneva manuṣyeṇa strītvam evaṃ puraskṛtam*, 119.14).

Rāma reacts to all this with silence, and Sītā takes command. Turning to Lakṣmaṇa, she demands that he light a pyre for her. Entering the fire is, she says, the only medicine for this illness; she will not go on living if her husband is dissatisfied with her virtue. Deeply distressed, Lakṣmaṇa looks to Rāma for a sign and gets the equivalent of a nod. So the fire is lit; Sītā quietly circumambulates her husband—who will not even raise his head to look at her—bows to the gods and Brahmins, and, calling on the fire, the witness of all that happens in the world, to protect her, leaps into the flames. The whole world, including all the gods, is watching; the monkeys and demons scream.

The moment of terror contains its own redemption. Rāma, the embodiment of dharma (*dharmātmā*), is thinking (*dadhyau*), his eyes clouded with tears. He must, in fact, have rather a lot to consider: has his life, with its unwavering commitment to dharmic ideals, inevitably brought him to this painful point? Such moments of reflection in the context of disaster are often points of transformation in the Sanskrit epics: one thinks of Yudhiṣṭhira's final act of bewildered reconsideration (*vimarśa*) in hell, where he has just discovered his brothers and his wife.[9] And Vālmīki does indeed seize upon this juncture to effect a powerful and integrative transition, which brings us back to the frame of the *Rāmāyaṇa* as a whole and to one of the central issues of the text. For, as Rāma meditates on the situation, the gods swoop down upon Lanka, crying out to him in sentences that must strike him as wholly surrealistic and confused: "How can you, who are the creator of the entire world and the most enlightened being, ignore Sītā as she is falling into the fire? Don't you know yourself, best of all the gods?" At this, Rāma, clearly unsettled, turns to the gods with an impassioned plea: "I know myself as a human being, Rāma, son of Daśaratha. Who am I really? To whom do I belong? Whence have I come? Let the Lord [Brahmā] tell me!"

The questions are by no means trivial or accidental, nor does it help to see them as the interpolations of a later generation interested in Rāma only as avatar.[10] "Who am I really?" In a way, this latent cry has pursued Rāma through the whole of his story. The *Rāmāyaṇa* is the portrait of a consciousness hidden from itself; or, one might say, of an identity obscured and only occasionally, in brilliant and poignant flashes, revealed to its owner. The problem is one of forgetting and recovery, of anamnesis: the divine hero who fails to remember that he is god comes to know himself, at least for brief moments, through hearing (always from others) his story.[11] This is what happens now: responding to his cry, Brahmā tells him the "facts" of his existence. He is none other than Nārāyaṇa, who is the imperishable Absolute; he is supreme dharma, Kṛṣṇa, the Puruṣa, Puruṣottama, the world's creator, the sacrifice, and so forth. As to the more immediate circumstances, Sītā is Lakṣmī and Rāma is Viṣṇu, who has entered into human form for the purpose of killing Rāvaṇa. Now that this has been accomplished, Rāma can return to heaven.

Note the course of development through this passage: Rāma sends for Sītā and addresses her harshly; she responds by denying his insinuations and protesting his repudiation, and jumps into the fire; the world clamors in outrage, and Rāma is led to reflect upon matters and to inquire as to his "true" identity; Brahmā then reveals the mythic and metaphysical components of his nature and the cause of his human incarnation. The sequence is carefully worked out and saturated with meaning. If one feels, as I do, that the issue of Rāma's self-awareness is basic here (as it is in related episodes, such as the scene in the *Uttarakāṇḍa* when Sītā at last returns to Rāma, only to disappear forever), then one discovers that Sītā's trial by fire is actually more a testing of Rāma than of her. By undergoing this ordeal, she precipitates the momentary switch in levels that presents the hero with his own divinity. His anamnesis proceeds directly from her suffering, the cost of his obsession with dharma as defined, rather narrowly, in wholly normative and human terms. Of course, this is only a temporary recovery of knowledge on his part—if not on ours (the listeners outside the text) or on the part of other participants in the story (within it). For now Agni, who has heard Brahmā's hymn to Rāma as Viṣṇu, can appear in visible, embodied form, holding in his hands the radiant, golden Sītā, unsinged and unscarred, even her garlands and ornaments as fresh as before. He speaks the obvious moral of this passage: Sītā is pure, totally devoted in word, thought, and sight to Rāma; she maintained this purity throughout her time in Lanka, as Rāvaṇa's prisoner, despite all threats and temptations; Rāma should take her back. He does so readily, and now he, too, breaking his silence for the first time since the revelation by Brahmā, can offer an excuse. People would have blamed him as foolish and ruled by desire (*kāmātmā*) had he taken Sītā back without purifying her (*aviśodhya*); it was all meant simply to establish her faithfulness before the eyes of the world (*pratyayārthaṃ tu lokānāṃ trayāṇām*, 121.16); he, Rāma, could no more abandon her than he could abandon his own fame (*kīrti*), for he knows that she remained true, protected by her innate radiance (*tejas*). Rāvaṇa could not touch her.

How much of this is post facto rationalization? The text gives no clear indication, although the language is, once again, eloquent: Rāma's *kīrti* is precisely what is in question, both here and in his later decision to send Sītā away. It is easy for the tradition to take at face value the hero's assertion that he was only staging a dramatic public vindication by ordeal. But however we might see this, it is clear that a reintegration has taken place—first, of the two separated lovers; then, on another plane, of their mythic counterparts, Viṣṇu and Lakṣmī, and, internally, of Rāma with his divine self. The spectators and listeners witness this as well. The whole epic drama has reached a point of (still temporary) closure, which is reinforced by the immediate aftermath to Sītā's trial. Daśaratha, Rāma's father, descends from heaven and is reunited with his sons. He expresses this sense of happy closure: "Those words uttered by Kaikeyī, which meant exile for you, have remained in my heart until now when, seeing you well and embracing you together with Lakṣmaṇa, I have been freed from sorrow, like the sun emerging from fog." Daśaratha restates the conclusion proffered earlier by Brahmā as to Rāma's mythic identity; he reminds both Lakṣmaṇa and Sītā that Rāma is the highest god and begs Sītā not to be angry because of the ordeal she has been put through, which was for her own purification. This scene of family reunion not only heals one of the bitterest wounds opened up by Rāma's story—that of Daśaratha's grief and premature death—but sets the pattern for yet another closing of the circle. When Indra, before returning to heaven, offers Rāma a boon, Rāma asks that all the monkey warriors who died for his sake in the battle of Lanka be revived. They immediately arise, as if from sleep. The *Rāmāyaṇa*, true to its ideal vision and in cogent contrast to the *Mahābhārata*, reverses death itself and leaves behind a living, restored, reintegrated world—even if the shattering tragedies of the *Uttarakāṇḍa* still lie ahead.[12]

Let us sum up the main lessons of this passage, so beautifully and carefully articulated by the Sanskrit poet. At the center lies the revelation to Rāma by the gods, with the consequent transformation of his consciousness through the momentary recovery of a lost, other self. Sītā's trial produces doubt and confusion in Rāma and outrage on the part of the world, whereupon the gods intervene with the shocking message of Rāma's mythic identity. Sītā's restoration can follow only upon this epistemic intervention. This theme relates directly to the *Rāmāyaṇa* frame story, where we find Rāma listening intently to his own story as sung by his as yet unrecognized sons, Kuśa and Lava.

We, the listeners, know Rāma as god, but he clearly lacks this knowledge, which comes to the surface only in exceptional moments of crisis and breakthrough. The basic *Rāmāyaṇa* disjunction between the text's internal and external audiences sustains this play with levels of self-awareness. Sītā's trial is one such critical moment, and thus, as we noted, the test is really more Rāma's than hers. It remains unclear just how calculated and premeditated his initial statements are; the issue of "testing" in this sense—Rāma's wish to demonstrate Sītā's faithfulness publicly and also, apparently, to purify her by passing her body through fire—is expressed but never fully resolved. Her own response to his angry words is relatively restrained, though there are flashes of sarcasm and irony as well as one impassioned assertion of women's superiority. The passage concludes with a generalized reintegration and healing: Rāma is at peace with Sītā, Daśaratha is reunited with his sons, the slain monkeys are revived. The tensions that produced the avatar and generated conflict within the cosmos have been eased, and, on this metaphysical level at least, and for the moment, harmony is restored. On all these counts, Kampaṉ's Tamil version presents us with radical contrasts.

KAMPAṈ: THE METAPHYSICS OF REUNION

"Can good fortune give rise to lunacy?" (*pākkiyam perum pittum payakkumō*, VI.37.26). This, according to Kampaṉ, is Sītā's response to Hanumān when he brings her the news of her deliverance. At first she is too moved to speak, and he is forced to ask why she is silent: is it because of an excess of joy, or does she doubt the messenger? She answers with the above question, followed by a beautiful set of verses in which she speaks of her inability to reward this messenger in any commensurate way. Note the important theme of silence because of a sensed inadequacy of language in the face of strong emotion. But Sītā's first, rhetorical question might almost serve as a motto for the entire highly charged episode to come. *Pittu*, "lunacy," is not too strong a word for the confrontational experience awaiting her, especially after the hundreds of earlier verses in which the idyllic relations between the two figures of Rāma and Sītā have been set forth. It is almost as if the orderly progression of this story, so closely linked in Kampaṉ to the examination and enactment of orthodox social ideals, had to proceed through a zone of "crazy" inversion before the end. We might also remember Kampaṉ's own proclaimed identification with this same notion of lunacy in one of the introductory verses (*avaiyaṭakkam*) to the *Irāmāvatāram*, where, as is customary, he apologizes to the connoisseurs and great Tamil poets for his supposedly flawed or inferior work:

> I would say something to those superior poets
> who have properly studied the ways of Tamil:
> who would study closely

the utterances of madmen, fools,
or of devotees?[13]

The poet, by implication, has something of all three; he is, in his own eyes, a madman and an idiot and, above all, explaining all, a devotee. His devotion breaks out of any sane limit; moreover, much of Kampaṉ's text will be devoted to exploring the operation and limitations of this same unruly, "mad" quality, based on flooding feeling, in the terrestrial career of his god.

Sītā's question sounds a note that will continue to echo through the description of her ordeal. Let us see how Kampaṉ chooses to present her situation. Here the setting, if not quite lunatic, is at least suitably lurid. Sītā is brought before her husband as he stands, still, on the battlefield—so beloved of Tamil poets—where he has generously arranged a feast of corpses to assuage the hunger of the kites, vultures, and demons (*paruntoṭu kaḻukum pēyum*, 55). Against this stark backdrop Sītā gets her first glimpse, after so many months of separation, of her husband, with his dark body, mouth red as coral, his bow in his hand. The poet reminds us first of her earlier feelings, during the period of loss and captivity: this is the same flawless woman who had thought, "My body is polluted; my life's breath has gone; there is nothing I want any more" (57). These were suicidal thoughts, born of despair; yet now, as Sītā stands before Rāma, they are strangely echoed by the metaphor the poet summons to describe her state, a metaphor grounded in the notion that the physical body alone is *always* potentially impure and subject to the inherent confusions of sensory experience:

As when the false body
that has lost the breath of life
sees it, and reaches out
to steal it back again,
she touched the ground
as she unveiled her face. (58)

By seeing Rāma, she is reclaiming, "stealing back," the life that she lost. She expresses her feeling in a single verse:

Even if I must be born again,
or if I leave forever
the great suffering of being born;
if I forget,
or if I fall and die
in some other way,
still all is well
now that I have worshiped
this husband,
this lord. (59)

She still has reason to be afraid—not only of rebirth and dying, but also, we might note, of forgetting—but at least this moment of reunion promises to relieve the cumulative burden of anxious anticipation and potential despair. The sight of her husband induces in Sītā an illusion of closure and containment. Meanwhile, he sees her too, pregnantly described as "that queen of chastity" and also "like merciful dharma that had been separated from him" (60). This is essentially all we are given before Rāma's tirade: having caught sight of her, he at once begins to abuse her, "like a snake raising its hood." Before we pursue this speech, though, let us notice the way Kampaṉ has introduced the major metaphysical and psychological themes of this section in these three simple, hard-hitting verses.

Most salient is the image of life separated from and rejoining the body. Indeed, this image may be said to condense the entire issue of union and separation, so basic to Kampaṉ's poem (as to all Tamil *bhakti*). It is not by chance that Kampaṉ opens the episode with just this simile: this moment that ends the period of separation also recalls, perhaps deliberately, the very instant of its beginning, its first intrusion into the hero's consciousness. When Rāma races back to the hut in the forest where Lakṣmaṇa has so reluctantly left Sītā alone and finds it empty—for Rāvaṇa has meanwhile abducted her, as the audience well knows—he is compared to "the breath of life that has been separated from its containing body (*kūṭu*) and has come in search of it, but cannot find it" (III.8.158).[14] If we apply the metaphor literally, in both cases Rāma is compared to the breath of life (*uyir*), while Sītā is like the body; in the forest, the *uyir* panics at the loss of its corporeal container, while in Lanka the body reaches out to recover its lost vital force (as Sītā glimpses Rāma). The separation that informs so large a part of the epic story is thus, metaphorically and also metaphysically, the shattering of a longed-for and necessary symbiosis on the level of the composition of the human individual. This symbiosis is not that of body and soul, inert matter and spiritual substance (and thus the temptation to allegoresis is easily resisted for the *Irāmāvatāram*); indeed, it is not truly dualistic at all. Rather, it reflects the interlocking relationship between two dynamic, equally living and substantial entities that together create a unity of perceived experience.

This unity of body and life-force has, in Kampaṉ, several associated characteristics and implications that are invoked at points throughout the *Irāmāvatāram* when this recurrent metaphor breaks through the text. It is, first of all, a unity based on flux, resistant to stasis and stable definition. The fluid quality that pervades the relation of life to body is nowhere clearer than in the introductory canto to the poem as a whole, the *Āṟṟuppaṭalam* or "Chapter on the River." This opening replaces the entire *Rāmāyaṇa* frame story as given in Vālmīki; in its stead, we have a striking description of water flooding down from the Himalayas, violently jumbling together the elements of hitherto distinct landscapes:

Turning forest into slope,
field into wilderness,
seashore into fertile land,

changing boundaries,
exchanging landscapes,
the reckless waters

roared on like the pasts
that hurry close on the heels
of lives.[15]

The rushing water is translated into the register of rushing lives (with their burdens of past deeds and memories), a metaphoric conjunction that becomes even more powerful as the description reaches its climax:

Like a life filling
and emptying
a variety of bodies,

the river flowed on.[16]

Uyir again, the vital breath that moves endlessly through one body after another, always seeks but then separates from these partial vessels. The life-force clearly enjoys an ontological superiority of sorts—it is the "false body" that reclaims its lost *uyir* in the verse describing Sītā's glimpse of Rāma—yet this animating power can never dispense with embodiment, even as it can never be entirely contained by it. This is the second characteristic to be stressed, one directly relevant to Sītā's situation in Lanka: the unity of life and body is always unfinished. No final integration is called for; the restless flux has no teleology beyond its own process. The body that reclaims its *uyir*, as we are told Sītā wishes to do, will doubtless lose it again. Sītā's emerging confrontation with Rāma thus fits naturally into the underlying metaphysics of flux, in which separation is no less necessary than union. A jarring narrative episode inherited from Vālmīki is integrated into a conceptual constellation specific to the Tamil literary and philosophical universe. The prevalent Tamil *bhakti* characterization of the relation between god and his human devotee as troubled, even tormented, also fits this pattern, and it is thus not surprising that in Kampaṉ, too, one "regains" Rāma only to be immediately rejected by him.

But the potential for union is also crucial to this set of images, especially insofar as it includes the dimension of loving emotion. Thus when Rāma and Sītā first catch sight of one another in Mithila, *before* they are married, they become

one breath of life
in two different bodies.
When the two lovers separated

from their bed on the dark sea
found each other again,
was there need for words? (I.10.38)

Uyir is unitary, even as it flows in and out of an endlessly fragmented series of distinct bodies; when two embodied beings feel love for one another, they experience this underlying unity of the life-force. In the case of Rāma and Sītā, there is also a mythic dimension, evident in this passage, hovering somewhere in the background of awareness—for the two lovers are Viṣṇu and Lakṣmī, who have become separated from one another and from their proper cosmic setting, the serpent-couch floating upon the "dark sea" of milk. They find one another again, in moving silence, when Rāma and Sītā fall in love.

And having found one another, they then proceed to lose each other, to experience at great length the impatient longings and confusions inherent in separation, ultimately to confront one another again, in our scene at Lanka. We begin to see why this meeting must have something of the quality of the *uyir*'s unstable meeting with the body. Dynamic flux, instability, emotional excess and imbalance, the flooding of memory, the mingling of past and present, an inner experience of potential unity, the hesitations of language—this is the range of associations that Kampaṉ calls up at the outset of Sītā's ordeal.[17] Schematically stated, this episode is made to embrace three forms of movement along a thematic continuum: an oscillation between separation and union, on the most fundamental experiential and metaphysical level; an interplay of speech and eloquent silence, on the external linguistic level; and an unfolding tension between forgetting or lack of feeling and memory or intuitive understanding, on the cognitive and epistemic level. The opening verses already bring these issues to the fore.

Now comes Rāma's speech, which is even more cruel to Sītā, and more outspoken, than in Vālmīki's text:

You took pleasure in food,
you didn't die
for all your disgrace
in the great palace of the devious demon.
You stayed there, submissive,
wholly without fear.
What thought has brought you here?
Did you imagine that *I*
could want *you*? (VI.37.62)

Kampaṉ's male heroes have the somewhat unpleasant habit, at difficult moments, of blaming their women for not dying (thus Daśaratha to Kaikeyī, II.3.222). Rāma will return to this theme, as he does to the oral obsession with which the whole diatribe begins:

You abandoned us.
All this while, you have been relishing
the flesh of living beings,
sweeter than ambrosia,
and happily drinking strong liquor.
So you tell me: what proper feasts
are in store for me now? (64)

A nice inversion: Sītā is held responsible for having "abandoned us." The kidnapping has become irrelevant, and the focus is on *her* hedonistic delight in the carnivorous cuisine of Lanka. Can a wife so corrupted ever serve the fastidious Rāma another meal? (South Indian vegetarian values have by this point superseded any dim memories of Rāma's habitual Kṣatriya diet of game!) To make things crystal clear, Rāma also informs her, as he does in Vālmīki's version, of the real reason for his campaign:

It was not to save you
that I dammed the sea,
cut off at the root
these demons with their gleaming weapons,
and overcame their enmity:
it was to redeem myself from error
that I came here, to Lanka. (63)

Pi<u>l</u>ai, "error," is also a lack or deficiency, or some more serious mistake, even a crime. Rāma speaks with the hero's egoistic concern for his own honor, and without intentionally implying that he is now enacting a mistake of greater magnitude than any previously connected with his story. His attack gathers force, becoming more and more personal and unfair: Sītā was, after all, born not in a family distinguished by goodness but, like a worm (*kīṭam pōl*), from the soil (65; here Kampa<u>n</u> has lifted a theme from Sītā's speech in Vālmīki, intensified it, and placed it in Rāma's mouth).[18] It is no wonder, then, that

womanhood, greatness,
high birth, the power
known as chastity,
right conduct,
clarity and splendor
and truth:

all have perished by the mere birth
of a single creature such as you,

like the fame of a king
who gives no gifts. (66)

Sītā has become the total antithesis to the exemplary figure Rāma had always recognized in her. Her survival alone is enough to impeach her: well-born women in her situation would have embarked on a regimen of rigorous austerities; and if disgrace (*pali*) came, they would wipe it out by wiping out their lives (67). (Again, the male complaint at his wife's refusal to disappear.) Now Rāma can conclude (again rendering Vālmīki's formulation more extreme):

> What is the point of talking?
> Your conduct has destroyed forever
> all understanding.
> The thing to do
> is to die—
> or, if you won't do that,
> then go somewhere,
> anywhere,
> away. (68)

The demand for death is Kampan's innovation, to be seized upon at once by Sītā. But this verse also introduces, for the first time in this episode, the important concept of *uṇarvu*, the intuitive, felt understanding that is the normal medium of connection between individuals and, across existential levels, between human beings and the god. It is this form of communicative understanding that Rāma claims Sītā has destroyed through her conduct; her survival is beyond his *uṇarvu*, and she should therefore die or disappear. We shall soon see how Sītā takes up this important statement and develops it in crucial and suggestive ways.

So far we notice an impressive exacerbation of the bitterness inherent in Rāma's speech as set out in Vālmīki. Rāma lashes out at Sītā with horrific accusations, ridicules her miraculous birth, and even tells her she should die. This extreme heightening of tone continues into Sītā's reply, as we shall see. But before she begins to speak, her inner state is summed up in another graphic metaphor:

> Like a deer
> on the point of death,
> tortured by terrible thirst
>   in the middle of a desert
>   thick with kites,
> who sees a lake
> just beyond reach,
> she grieved at the barrier
> that rose before her. (71)

Perhaps most striking here is Kampan's use of imagery drawn from classical Tamil love poetry, the *akam* or "inner" division structured around conventionalized landscapes with their associated emotional states. A Tamil reader immediately identifies this verse as a *pālai* or wilderness poem calling up a sense of traumatic separation.[19] The image of the predatory kite, which helps to specify the landscape, also points to something in the dramatic situation—

no doubt something in Rāma's menacing attitude and conduct. Sītā's inner reality is indeed a *pālai* experience at this moment: she has entered a wilderness zone of rejection and loss. This suggestive use of the classical conventions is a constant element in Kampaṉ's art. Seen in relation to the central story of Rāma and Sītā's common fate, the entire *Irāmāvatāram* might well appear as an extended love poem in the *bhakti* mode.[20] Like earlier Tamil *bhakti* poets, Kampaṉ conflates heroic or panegyric themes (*puṟam*) with *akam* or "interior" elements, largely subordinating the former to the latter in nonexplicit ways. But in Kampaṉ the narrative follows the prescribed structure of the Sanskrit epic, with the result that the classical love situations of Tamil poetry—premarital courtship and stolen union, the several forms of separation and longing, as well as later quarreling and conflict—are now scattered somewhat unpredictably, without orderly sequence, throughout the text. They emerge from time to time, usually with very powerful implications: thus Rāma's crossing of the wilderness as a young man recalls *pālai* themes; premarital passion, *kaḷavu*, is suggested in Mithila; Sītā, pining in Lanka, appears as the impatient heroine of the *neytal* coastal landscape; and here the *pālai* atmosphere is again present at the moment of reunion. In itself, this is instructive, for *pālai*, the landscape of separation at its most severe, embodies that aspect of the love experience felt to inhere in all others, including union.[21] Love, even in union, is largely predicated on the sense of separateness and separation. We can see how appropriate this classical element is to the underlying metaphysics of Sītā's encounter with Rāma—an encounter structured around rejection—and we observe the delicate and calculated artistry of the poet who, following Nammāḻvār and other Vaiṣṇava *bhakti* poets in Tamil, turns the ancient conventions to his devotional purpose.

TIRADE AND TRIAL

Sītā's response is of a different order altogether than in Vālmīki. It resumes and extends themes that have already been broached by the Tamil text, and it does so in the context of a complaint aimed directly at Rāma, both as husband and, implicitly, as god. Irony is the least of Sītā's weapons. More than in any other passage of the *Irāmāvatāram*, she blasts Rāma directly and with literal intent.[22] To those familiar with the Tamil tradition, she calls up the image of the bereaved Kaṇṇaki from the classical *kāvya Cilappatikāram* (especially cantos 18 and 19)—a woman crying out bitterly against an unjust fate. But, closer to home, there are also affinities between her outburst and Kampaṉ's major formulation of the problem of theodicy in the outraged speech by the dying Vālin, shot by Rāma from an ambush.[23] Like Vālin, Sītā is both angry and bewildered; she feels betrayed, and wholly justified in her own prior actions, which have nonetheless led to this unacceptable conclusion; her anger is entirely focused on Rāma, its compelling, proper target.

One feels from the fury and precision of her words that the poet is largely speaking for himself through her mouth.

It is not a long speech. She begins by mentioning Hanumān, who came to Lanka, saw her, and promised her that Rāma would soon arrive. Did he not then inform Rāma of her dreadful suffering? Next she addresses Rāma's preposterous claim that she, Sītā, had ruined the world's finest ideals, especially those relating to womanhood, simply by being born:

> All that I suffered,
> all the care
> with which I kept my chastity,
> my goodness,
> and at what cost,
> and for so long a time—
>
> all this seems crazy now,
> a futile waste,
> since you, O best of beings,
> don't understand it in your heart. (VI.37.74)

Pittu, lunacy, again: her earlier, unwitting prophecy, couched as a rhetorical question, has come true. Tidings of good fortune have led unexpectedly to this taste of madness. She preserved her precious chastity, *kaṟpu*, with such scrupulous, even ferocious, care, but it was all for nothing, a futile waste (*avam*), a kind of mistake (*piḻaittatu*, echoing Rāma's term, *piḻai*, above). As impressive as this conclusion is the logic behind it: the true failure is Rāma's, on the level of feeling and understanding (*uṇarvu*, again echoing Rāma's earlier statement). Lacking *uṇarvu*, he—the god—can make only aberrant and inhuman claims; and the effect is to translate human notions of right or goodness into lunacy.

This question of knowledge or understanding becomes more and more central:

> The whole world knows
> that I'm a faithful wife (*pattiṉi*):
> not even Brahmā on his lotus
> could change my foolish mind.
> But if my lord, who is like the eye
> that sees for everyone,
> should deny this,
> what god could teach him otherwise? (75)

Everyone knows the truth except Rāma, who should be able to see it outright, for he is the universal eye, *kaṇṇavaṉ*—punning, perhaps, on *kaṇavaṉ*, husband, as well as on Kaṇṇaṉ, or Kṛṣṇa. The pun takes up Rāma's simile—the diseased eye squinting in the light of a lamp—in the Sanskrit text. The god sees without really seeing, and surely Sītā is right: there is no god above him to teach him otherwise. Her own stubborn mind, intent on faithfulness as an act of inner autonomy, is thus truly foolish (*pētaiyēṉ*; *pētai* can also mean simply "woman")—the second quality, after lunacy, that Kampaṉ seems to claim for himself in the introductory verse we examined.[24] The coordinates laid out in that verse are uncannily retraced in this one; only devotion, *bhakti*, is still missing.

Having laid the blame where it belongs, Sītā can conclude with an ambiguous eulogy of womanhood (again following Vālmīki's Sītā). The *trimūrti*, Brahmā, Śiva, and Viṣṇu—called, no doubt sardonically, *dharmamūrti*, the incarnation of dharma—might be able to see the whole universe "like a myrobalan in the palm of the hand," but "can they know the state of a woman's heart?"[25] Obviously not, judging by her own husband's conduct—and *he* is that Dharmamūrti himself. All that is left is for her to execute Rāma's command: there is nothing better now, she says, than dying.

She asks Lakṣmaṇa to light the fire; he does so "as if he had lost his own life" (79), after receiving a sign from Rāma's eyes. As Sītā approaches the pyre, the world goes into crisis: not only the gods, all other living beings, and the cosmic elements, but also the four Vedas and Dharma cry out in horror. She worships her husband and demands that Fire burn her if she has erred in thought or word. Then

> as if she were going home
> to her palace on the lotus
> that rises up from the flooding waters,
> she jumped in;
> and as she entered, that fire was scorched
> by her burning faithfulness (*kaṟpu*),
> as milk-white cotton
> goes up in flame. (85)

She is, after all, the goddess Lakṣmī/Padmā, who reigns in state upon the lotus. For her, the experience inside the pyre is drenched in watery associations, as if she had plunged not into fire but into a flood. But for the unfortunate god of fire, Agni, who has to receive her, the moment is one of excruciating, fiery torment. This is yet another innovation in Kampaṉ: Fire is burned by Sītā's fire. *Kaṟpu*—chastity, self-control, faithfulness—is no abstract ethical virtue but a substantial and dynamic reality that suffuses the woman's inner being. The effect of the trial is thus even more dramatic than in Vālmīki. Not only does Sītā emerge unsinged, but she actually scorches the god of fire himself, who screams out in pain and protest (*pūcal iṭṭ' araṟṟum*, 86) to Rāma. Lifting Sītā in his hands, Agni points out that the beads of perspiration, formed on her body by her anger at her husband (*ūṭiya ciṟṟattāl*, 87), were not dried up by his flames, while the flowers she wears in her hair still drip honey and are filled with bees, "as if they had been steeped in water." Sītā's ordeal has been something akin to a refreshing bath, but

Agni's eye detects the still evident traces of the rage that drove her to undergo this test. In terms of Tamil poetics, the confrontation has become an instance of *ūṭal*, the lovers' quarrel, heightened to an almost lethal degree.

Now Agni is angry at Rāma: "You did not think about this divine flame of *kaṟpu*, and so you have destroyed my power; were you furious with me, too?" This prompts another cutting statement from Rāma, for whom the test is still, clearly, not over: "Who are you, appearing in this fire, and what are you saying? Instead of burning this vile woman (*puṉmai cāl orutti*), you praise her!" (90) He insists on Sītā's mean and lowly character, even at this late stage. Agni must therefore spell out the truth for him, first presenting his credentials: "I am Agni; I came here because I could not bear the blazing fire of faithfulness in this woman. People get married before me, resolve their doubts before me." And, at last, a verse no less biting than Rāma's:

Didn't you hear
when the gods and sages
and all that moves and is still
in the three worlds
screamed, as they struck their eyes?
Have you abandoned dharma
and resorted to misery instead? (94)

Rāma accused Sītā of "abandoning us"; Agni throws the expression back at Rāma and, in a manner that goes far beyond anything in Vālmīki, illuminates the real import of Rāma's attitude. This god incarnate has "abandoned dharma" and, in the gloss of one modern commentator, resorted to adharma.[26] The consequences are, according to Agni, potentially disastrous:

Will rain fall,
will the earth still bear its burden
    without splitting in two,
will dharma go the right way,
or can this universe survive

if *she* becomes enraged?
If she utters a curse,
even Brahmā on his lotus
will die. (95)

To the moral issue is now added an overriding argument from identity. Sītā is the great goddess herself—though Rāma hardly seems to know this. He does, however, bow to Agni's verdict and accept Sītā back, welcoming her with a surprisingly laconic, almost grudging acknowledgment:

You [Agni] are the imperishable witness
for this whole world.
You spoke words I can't condemn.

You said she is wholly
without blame.
Blameless, she must not
be sent away. (97)

That is all: Rāma does not address Sītā directly. Still, Kampaṉ gives Rāma an epithet here: he is *karuṇaiy uḷḷattāṉ*, a man whose heart is compassion. Has a transformation taken place? Or has the underlying compassion of the god been released, at last, back into the world? Or is the poet simply enjoying the irony he has built into this context?

Let us briefly take stock before we turn to the final section of the narrative. There is no doubt that this couple's reunion is far more embittered, in the Tamil text, than in its Sanskrit prototype. They speak to one another with shocking verbal abandon. Rāma's doubts and suspicion have turned into a violent denunciation, an a priori pronouncement of guilt that focuses on Sītā's alleged hedonism and lowly birth. Her reply incriminates him: he stands condemned, in her eyes, for a terrible failure of understanding that has led to blatant injustice. The ordeal itself assumes a watery rather than fiery character for Sītā, while Agni, tortured by her superior power, becomes her advocate. As such, he still has to argue with Rāma about Sītā's purity of character; somewhat reluctantly, or at any rate uneffusively, Rāma gives in. There is as yet no hint at all that the entire scene is only a trial to persuade an external audience (the world, or Rāma's subjects) of something Rāma already knows. On the contrary, his lack of *uṇarvu*—the knowledge that is a form of feeling, of empathetic understanding—is a major issue, still unresolved, and one which has implications on the divine level, where Rāma as god is implicitly accused of acting against dharma. Finally, and perhaps most conspicuously, the logical sequence of the Sanskrit narrative has been disturbed. There, Agni appears with Sītā in his hands only *after* the revelation by Brahmā of Rāma's divine identity. It is the revelation, with its dramatic epistemic consequences for the hero, that breaks through the calculations and anxieties that have constrained him and paves the way for Sītā's restoration. Here, however, Sītā is restored, on Agni's pleading, *before* Brahmā speaks. Why this reversal? How does it fit into the overall transformation that Kampaṉ has worked on this passage?

THE SILENCE OF A GOD

In the Tamil text, it is not Rāma who provokes the revelation with agonized questions about his identity, but the gods who decide to do so for their own inscrutable reasons: "The time has come to tell Rāma the truth" (98). Brahmā speaks, addressing Rāma—as have many others, at various points throughout the text—by a clear epithet of Viṣṇu's, *neṭiyōy* ("Long One"

= Trivikrama). He utters fourteen verses of the familiar *stotra* type—a short hymn of praise, again like others scattered through the poem. Perhaps most remarkable, in comparison with the epiphany described in Vālmīki, is the largely impersonal content of these verses: they are an exercise in the application of orthodox cosmological and philosophical categories, drawn especially from Sāṅkhya, to the *bhakti* context of worship. The type is familiar from other South Indian *bhakti* narratives, especially the *Bhāgavata Purāṇa* and its vernacular descendants.[27] Thus the incarnate god, Rāma in this case, is repeatedly identified with the Vedāntic absolute. "Do not think of yourself," Brahmā says, "as a man born into an ancient royal family; you are no other than the truth spoken as the conclusion of the Vedas" (i.e., Vedānta, 99). Similarly, Rāma is told that he is the primeval Puruṣa, the twenty-sixth *tattva*, higher than all the evolutes of matter (*pakuti* = *prakṛti*), the supreme truth (*paramārtha*, 101); he cannot be measured by the usual criteria of knowledge, and sensual perception is no use, but the Upaniṣads proclaim his existence (105–6); those who are sunk in the illusion of having parents, who do not know their own selves, suffer endlessly, but those who know Rāma as father achieve release (103). It is Rāma's illusion, *māyai*, that produces the world, though he himself, like others, does not fully understand this state (99); he also preserves the world with his own form (as Viṣṇu) and destroys it (as Śiva). A single verse introduces the avatar concept: he comes to destroy pride, to rout the demons, and to make the gods take refuge with him. All this leads up to the practical conclusion, which is something of a non sequitur: "This being the case," Brahmā says, "do not hate our mother (Sītā), who gave birth to us and to the triple world and who has demonstrated the glory of married life" (112).

Perhaps the argument is wholly based on this affirmation of identity: as the goddess, Sītā is hardly to be judged by human social standards, and Rāma must in any case take her back. But the hymn does not quite suffice, for now Śiva also puts in an appearance (though there is no precedent for this in Vālmīki) in order to present the message more forcefully and more simply. "It seems," he says, "that you do not know yourself (*uṉṉai nīy oṉṟum uṇarntilai*); you are the primordial deity (*mūrtti*), and this Sītā, mother of the three worlds, resides upon your breast" (113). Śiva's intervention thus confirms the mythic identity of Rāma as Viṣṇu and reiterates the notion of his ignorance. For good measure, Śiva adds that if one errs with respect to the goddess who gave birth to the worlds, many living beings will die; Rāma should thus forget the aversion or scorn (*ikaḻcci*) he has felt for her. On this note of recommended forgetfulness, the divine revelation abruptly ends.

And Rāma is silent. He makes no acknowledgment whatsoever of all that has just been said. Indeed, he will have nothing more to say until, somewhat later, Daśaratha asks him to name his boon. Here, in fact, it is Daśaratha alone who makes the important statement—to Sītā—that the ordeal was meant only to demonstrate publicly her chaste character, "as one passes gold through fire to reveal its purity" (123).[28] Rāma utters nothing to this effect. Silence has engulfed him, despite the tremendous announcement he has just heard. In Vālmīki's version, we may recall, the revelation is followed by Agni's restoration of Sītā and then, immediately, by a voluble, self-justifying outburst by Rāma, who wants to make clear to everyone that he acted only *pratyayārthaṃ tu lokānām*—to establish Sītā's innocence in the eyes of the world. But in the Tamil text, where a dialogic loquaciousness is something of the rule,[29] the hero who has just been told he is God offers no response at all.

It is a pregnant silence, well suited to the subtleties and tensions of the moment, as Kampaṉ sees it. In a reunion that proceeds via rejection and renewed separation, speech easily issues into silence. Clearly, the fundamental theme of loss and recovery has taken a new form in Kampaṉ's poem. Anamnesis—the hero's regaining of memory through perceiving his divine identity—is not, for Kampaṉ, the essential point. In fact, it is in a sense quite beside the point: the embodied god's consciousness of himself *as god* is never what is at stake in the Tamil text. When Śiva tells Rāma that he does not know himself, he is pointing to a very different content of unknowing than that intended by Vālmīki in this same context. On closer inspection, we find this pattern—Rāma recognized as God and praised as such in a *stotra* like that sung by Brahmā, which elicits nothing but silence from its divine object—recurring frequently in the *Irāmāvatāram*.[30] Each time it happens, Rāma ignores the eulogies showered upon him. It is always as if the text shifts levels, for a passing moment, opening up the dimension of discovery and celebration of explicitly recognized divinity before reverting, after the hymn, to the ongoing narration. Or as if, once the intimation of Rāma's divinity is externalized, once it is articulated in language (usually by one of his victims), Rāma's own task is finished. One wonders if he even hears the *stotra* that others offer to him. This aspect of his awareness—the god-hero's own recognition of his "true" identity, apparently veiled by his humanity—is not presented to us by Kampaṉ and seems not to constitute one of this poet's concerns.[31]

We might formulate this observation somewhat differently. What we see in Kampaṉ is a shift away from the psychology of recovery and the play of memory to a different thematic, which seeks to map out in detail the actual human experience of the god in the world. This works both ways: many passages in Kampaṉ explore the god's own experience of human limitations, and above all of human emotions, generally those of loss, shame, helplessness, but also occasionally of wonder and joy. If he forgets, it is not so much his identity that becomes hidden as some much more immediate and interpersonal concern—Sītā's sufferings, for example, although at times the problem is quite the opposite, when Rāma evinces a very human inability to forget some troubling anxiety or hurt. (Thus, as we saw, Śiva begs him to learn forgetfulness, 114.) But in the episode of Sītā's trial, as so often in this poem, the real center lies in *our* response—in the experience that we, as devotees, as listeners, have of Rāma's nearness. The god acts or speaks, and the world around him somehow assimilates his presence. It is, almost by definition, a frustrating and often enigmatic presence, marked by strong tendencies on the part of the god to withdraw into silence, to block connection, to toy capriciously with those around him, to hide.

And the result can be angry protest. In our episode, Sītā speaks like any of Rāma's other victims. She has reason to be angry: his conduct seems perverse to the point of cruelty, even if he is axiomatically a hero of compassion, as the text so often states. She protests a real failing on the level of *uṇarvu*, the god-man's capacity to feel and understand what she, or any other human being, must know or undergo. She says that Rāma does not truly know what she has suffered and is suffering now, and that without this knowledge on his part her endurance becomes an exercise in futility. Since Rāma is no ordinary husband—since Sītā knows, on some level, his cosmic and mythic identity[32]—she is expressing a frustrated demand that the god share fully our essential perceptions and our sorrows. But in contrast to the Vālin episode, where the revelation of Rāma's own broken heart turns the tide of Vālin's bitterness (IV.7.118), here he unfortunately fails to comply with this all-too-human expectation. Again a transformation has taken place, from the notion of a clouded and temporarily forgotten self-knowledge, in Vālmīki, to the god's actual unfeeling ignorance, in Kampaṉ. The content of the missing knowledge is quite different in each case. In Kampaṉ, Sītā speaks of a failure of the divine imagination, a failure that informs, at this moment, her own experience of Rāma. (It is also striking that, from this point onward, Sītā has very little to say in Kampaṉ's text.) On another level, by not expressing Sītā's truth publicly, by allowing the ordeal to proceed out of an apparent lack of feeling, Rāma demonstrates again the inherent asymmetry in the relations between the divine and the human. This imbalance in the intensity and content of *uṇarvu* is surely part of what Śiva is referring to when, in the Tamil text, he tells Rāma that he does not know himself. The process of discovery has also been, in a sense, reversed: whereas Vālmīki's hero is a man who finds himself to be god by hearing and living out his story, and is graced by moments of anamnesis, Kampaṉ's protagonist is a god who discovers repeatedly, often to his own amazement, the painful cognitive and emotional consequences of being human.

Silence, separation, and the failure to feel or to understand: these are the undercurrents surging through the story of Sītā's trial in Kampaṉ's text. Like other points in this great love poem, this episode highlights the conflicts rather than the serenities or certainties of passionate feeling. In this way, the final meeting of Rāma and Sītā follows the more general paradigm of the lovers' thorny career in Tamil poetry and its extensions into the sphere of *bhakti* devotionalism. Lovers, like devotees, are not meant to be at peace.

But this is by no means the only conclusion to be drawn from Kampaṉ's treatment of this passage, for the two versions we have examined reveal outstanding contrasts in theme and structure. In addition to Kampaṉ's careful exploitation of the conventionalized language of Tamil love poetry (especially as reformulated by Nammāḻvār), there are four major points of divergence and transformation:

1. In Vālmīki, the real test is Rāma's, while Sītā's ordeal is proclaimed a show for the benefit of a skeptical world. In Kampaṉ, her trial seems altogether real: her love and commitment to Rāma, despite his verbal hostility, and her readiness to die for her truth, are put to the test—and Sītā wins, like the devotee who so often triumphs over the god.

2. Her rejection is thus equally real in the Tamil text, which offers no space for the notion of a public demonstration or trial until Daśaratha's late commentary on the events. Rāma himself never mentions this possibility. More important still, his repudiation of Sītā has metaphysical implications: union, whether of lovers or of a devotee with god, presupposes separation.

3. Vālmīki's sequence is overturned in Kampaṉ: Agni restores Sītā *before* Rāma hears Brahmā's revelation of his, Rāma's, divinity (which thus serves no pressing function as far as Sītā's status is concerned; she has already been reintegrated into Rāma's life, and no great upheaval in consciousness is required to facilitate the move). The sense of this change in sequence, as of Rāma's subsequent silence in the face of the gods' impressive news, becomes clear from the contrasting axiology and problematics of Kampaṉ's text. The central thematic concern of the episode in Sanskrit—the transition in Rāma's self-awareness in the face of Sītā's suffering and his own responsibility—is almost irrelevant to Kampaṉ's discourse. There is no point at which Rāma has to ask himself, "Who am I?" Instead, the Rāma of the *Irāmāvatāram*, who is clearly god for the Tamil poet, for his audience, and probably for himself, is caught up in the emotional complexities of human experience: this is what he must come thoroughly and intimately to know, as others come to perceive *him* through their responses to his embodied presence and puzzling deeds. Sītā's ordeal is yet another richly articulated opportunity for this course of asymmetrical mutual exploration.

4. Finally, Vālmīki's description of the ordeal returns us, together with the epic hero, to the frame of the work, in which the themes of the hero's self-awareness and self-forgetfulness are so subtly and powerfully embedded. The glimpses he gets of his divine nature develop logically out of the structure of that frame. But this frame is wholly absent from Kampaṉ's work, which opens instead with vivid images of flux—of rushing water, and of lives.

Significantly, the Tamil poet reverts to these images as he begins to narrate the episode of the ordeal, and they spring to mind again with the oxymoronic depiction of Sītā's fire as a cool, liquid bath. Kampaṉ's poem has traced a course from the initial deluge to a culminating fire that is itself another kind of flood. These metaphors are imbued with meaning. If in Vālmīki, Sītā's trial by fire sparks the flash of recovered memory in Rāma, in Kampaṉ it re-presents the experience of the divine river of life flowing mysteriously through and out of bodies, playing with awareness, infusing and transcending these fragile vessels. The god both propels this movement onward—perhaps through the elements of his unknowing (98)—and overflows with it himself into and beyond human form. He also remains paradoxically subject to the concomitant law of continuous separation, with the inevitable ensuing sensation of recurrent, indeed continuous, loss. Perfection is a process, magical, unfinished, flawed.

NOTES

1. *Irāmāvatāram* II.1.83. I cite the edition with commentary by Vai. Mu. Kōpālakiruṣṇamācāriyar, *Kamparāmāyaṇam* (Madras: Vai. Mu. Kōpālakiruṣṇamācāriyar Kampeni, 1971).

2. See David Shulman, "Divine Order and Divine Evil in the Tamil Tale of Rāma," *Journal of Asian Studies* 38, no. 4 (August 1979): 651–69.

3. See, for example, Bhavabhūti, *Uttararāmacarita*, Act I, where Rāma calls himself a "monster" and an Untouchable because of what he must do to Sītā—in order to preserve the good name of his family and his kingship; moreover, "the world itself is upside down" and "Rāma was given life only in order to know pain" (v. 47). In Kālidāsa's *Raghuvaṃśa*, 14.31–68, Rāma says he simply cannot bear the libel spreading among his subjects, "like a drop of oil in water," and the poet adds that those who are rich in fame (*yaśas*) value it more than their own bodies, and a fortiori more than any object of sense perception (35). Although this reduces Sītā's status considerably, Rāma is said to be truly torn as to the proper course; and the poet allows Sītā to express (to Lakṣmaṇa) something of the horror and protest that his decision entails.

4. The argument is developed in part in David Shulman, "Toward a Historical Poetics of the Sanskrit Epic," forthcoming in the *International Folklore Review*.

5. A Tamil *Uttarakāṇḍa*, attributed to Oṭṭakkūttar, Kampaṉ's legendary rival, does exist; the tradition (which is quite prepared to credit Kampaṉ with various inferior works such as *Ēreḻupatu*) insists that this does not belong to Kampaṉ's oeuvre.

6. I cite *Śrīmad Vālmīkirāmāyaṇa*, ed. by K. Chinnaswami Sastrigal and V. H. Subrahmanya Sastri (Madras: N. Ramaratnam, 1958), which generally follows the Southern recension.

7. Note following VI.118.11a: *Śrīmad Vālmīkirāmāyaṇa*, ed. Chinnaswami Sastrigal and Subrahmanya Sastri, 901.

8. See the discussion of this incident in Wendy Doniger O'Flaherty, *Hindu Myths* (Harmondsworth: Penguin Books, 1975), 198.

9. See discussion in my paper, "The Yakṣa's Questions," in a forthcoming volume on enigmatic modes edited by Galit Hasan-Rokem and David Shulman. This verse is omitted by the Critical Edition (it appears as 3247* in the notes).

10. I cannot agree with Robert Goldman, who explains the wide attestation of this section in the manuscript tradition and its consequent incorporation into the Critical Edition as the result of its being a "late and sectarian passage accepted with little change by all scribes": Robert P. Goldman, *The Rāmāyaṇa of Vālmīki*, vol. 1: *Bālakāṇḍa* (Princeton: Princeton University Press, 1984), 44–45, n. 85.

11. This point will be taken up in greater detail in the forthcoming paper cited in note 4.

12. The corresponding (and contrasting) passage in the *Mahābhārata* is the final chapter of the *Svargārohaṇaparvan* (XVIII.5), in which each of the heroes regains his divine self—but only after an apocalyptic war and the violent deaths of most of the dramatis personae. There it is death in battle that closes the cycle and allows a kind of negative reintegration, albeit not in this world but in the divine sphere.

13. *Pittar, pētaiyar, pattar* (= *bhaktas*): *taṟciṟappuppāyiram*, 8.

14. Some scholars read this image in reverse: see the note by Kōpālakiruṣṇamācāriyar on this verse (*Kamparāmāyaṇam*, 666).

15. Translated by A. K. Ramanujan, p. 42 of this volume.

16. *ōtiyav uṭampu tōṟum uyir eṉa*: translated by A. K. Ramanujan, p. 43 of this volume.

17. I cannot explore here the relation between the notion of fluid *uyir* filling endless bodies and the Tamil ideal of "liquefaction," of melting and mingling in love; but see the fine discussion by Margaret Trawick Egnor, *The Sacred Spell and Other Conceptions of Life in Tamil Culture* (Ph.D. diss., University of Chicago, 1978), 13, 20–21, 50, 104–6.

18. See VI.119.15 in the Sanskrit text: "I received my name but not my birth from Janaka; I came from the earth. You devalue my conduct, you who are a judge of good conduct."

19. On *pālai*, see George L. Hart, *The Poems of Ancient Tamil: Their Milieu and Their Sanskrit Counterparts* (Berkeley and Los Angeles: University of California Press, 1975), 221–29; Paula Richman, *Women, Branch Stories, and Religious Rhetoric in a Tamil Buddhist Text*, Foreign and Comparative Studies, South Asia series no. 12 (Syracuse: Maxwell School of Citizenship and Public Affairs, Syracuse University, 1988), 62–68. Cf. David Shulman, "The Crossing of the Wilderness: Landscape and Myth in the Tamil Story of Rāma," *Acta Orientalia* 42 (1981), 21–54.

20. In this respect, it bears a surprising resemblance to another Tamil genre, the *kōvai*, a collection of love verses somewhat artificially arranged in preordained narrative sequence, from the lovers' first sight of one another until their final union. See Norman Cutler, *Songs of Experience: The Poetics of Tamil Devotion* (Bloomington: Indiana University Press, 1987), 82–91. In Kampaṉ, of course, this orderly sequence is ruled out.

21. *Tolkāppiyam, poruḷatikāram* I.11; cf. Rm. Periyakaruppan, *Tradition and Talent in Cankam Poetry* (Madurai: Madurai Publishing House, 1976), 168–73.

22. There are other points in the *Irāmāvatāram* where Sītā complains, ironically, about Rāma. For example, at V.5.7, Sītā cries out from her captivity: "You told me to stay home in the great city, not to come to the forest; you said you would return in a

few days. Where is that vaunted compassion (*aruḷ*) of yours now? I am all alone, and you are consuming my lonely life!" But verses such as these, reminiscent of the laments at unbearable separation in Nammāḻvār (e.g., *Tiruvāymoḻi* 5.4), are not meant to be taken at face value; they are a way of giving voice to the heroine's impatience and despair.

23. For a detailed discussion of this episode, see my "Divine Order and Divine Evil in the Tamil Tale of Rāma."

24. The insistence on autonomy in the form of service or devotion, and in a context of rejection, is a topos known also from Nammāḻvār. Thus *Tiruvāymoḻi* 1.7.8: "Though he looses his hold on me, not even he can make my good heart let go of him."

25. The myrobalan in the hand is a proverbial image signifying intimate closeness.

26. Kōpālakiruṣṇamācāriyar on *vēr' ēvam eṉṟ' oru poruḷ* (VI.37.94; *Kamparāmāyaṇam*, 780).

27. See Friedhelm Hardy, *Viraha-bhakti: The Early History of Kṛṣṇa Devotion in South India* (Delhi: Oxford University Press, 1983), 526–47; David Shulman, "Remaking a Purāṇa: Viṣṇu's Rescue of Gajendra in Potana's Telugu *Mahābhāgavatamu*," forthcoming in a volume of *purāṇa* studies edited by Wendy Doniger (O'Flaherty).

28. Daśaratha speaks to this effect in Vālmīki, too, but only after Rāma himself has announced that the trial was only intended to convince the world.

29. Large parts of the *Irāmāvatāram* read like dramatic dialogues that seem to assume a context of performance; the art of the dialogue in Kampaṉ deserves a separate study. All major events spark extended comments from nearly every potential speaker. In this regard, see the insightful remarks by Stuart Blackburn in this volume.

30. A good example is the demon Virādha's *stotra* to Rāma, who has just dispatched him, at III.1.47–60. Similar passages accompany the deaths of Kabandha, Vālin, and other of the avatar's victims; they occur as well, in shorter forms, when various sages encounter Rāma. We should also recall that the poet consistently keeps Rāma's true identity before our eyes by using divine-mythic epithets for him and his entourage.

31. Cf. the similar conclusion by George Hart and Hank Heifetz in their introduction to *The Forest Book of the Rāmāyaṇa of Kampaṉ* (Berkeley and Los Angeles: University of California Press, 1988), 6: "Again and again, he [Rāma] is recognized as an incarnation of Viṣṇu by those who meet or confront him, but Rāma rarely shows a direct awareness of himself as the supreme god."

32. Thus (at V.5.6, for example) Sītā may even address Rāma, in absentia, as "Nārāyaṇa."

SIX

A *Rāmāyaṇa* of Their Own: Women's Oral Tradition in Telugu

Velcheru Narayana Rao

As a boy growing up in a Brahmin family in the northeastern district of Srikakulam in Andhra Pradesh, I used to hear my mother humming in the mornings:

> *leve sītammā māyammā muddulagumma leve bangaru bomma leve*
> *leci rāmuni lepave vegamu leḍikannuladāna leve*
> *tĕllavāravaccĕnū*

> Wake up Sīta, my mother, my dear, you are my golden doll
> Wake up yourself and wake up Rāma, you have the eyes of a doe
> It is morning!

She had a notebook in which she had written down a number of songs, many of them on the *Rāmāyaṇa* theme, which she would sing on occasions when women gathered at our house. The notebook my mother carried is lost now, but those songs and many others like them are still sung by women in Andhra Pradesh. They tell a *Rāmāyaṇa* story very different from the familiar one attributed to Vālmīki.[1]

The *Rāmāyaṇa* in India is not just a story with a variety of retellings; it is a language with which a host of statements may be made. Women in Andhra Pradesh have long used this language to say what they wish to say, as women.[2] I shall discuss two separate groups of songs, those sung by upper caste Brahmin women and those sung by lower caste women, although my major focus will be on the former. I shall demonstrate that while the two groups of songs represent a distinctly female way of using the *Rāmāyaṇa* to subvert authority, they are still very different from each other, both in the narratives they use and in the specific authority they seek to subvert.

SOME BACKGROUND

While upper caste men in Andhra associate the *Rāmāyaṇa* with the Sanskrit text attributed to the legendary Vālmīki, the Andhra Brahmin women do not view Vālmīki as authoritative. Vālmīki appears in their songs as a person who was involved in the events of Sītā's and Rāma's lives and who composed an account of those events—but not necessarily the correct account. Like most of the participants in the tradition, these women believe the *Rāmāyaṇa* to be fact and not fiction, and its many different versions are precisely in keeping with this belief. Contrary to the usual opinion, it is fiction that has only one version; a factual event will inevitably have various versions, depending on the attitude, point of view, intent, and social position of the teller.

The events of the *Rāmāyaṇa* are contained in separate songs, some long and some short. These are sung at private gatherings, usually in the backyards of Brahmin households or by small groups of older women singing for themselves while doing household chores. Altogether, about twenty-five of them are especially popular, which together constitute a fairly connected story of the epic.[3] Most of these songs, especially the longer ones, are also available in printed "sidewalk" editions, although the oral versions vary in small details from the printed versions.[4]

Since it is difficult for a man to be present at women's events, I could not record all the songs myself. With the help of two female colleagues, however—Kolavennu Malayavasini of Andhra University, Waltair, and Anipindi Jaya Prabha of the University of Wisconsin-Madison, both of whom are Brahmins—I was able to acquire a number of *Rāmāyaṇa* songs on tape. The few songs I was able to record were sung by Malayavasini and Jaya Prabha, who demonstrated singing styles to me while reading the words from a printed book. My information about the context of singing, the singers, and their audience comes partly from my childhood experience and partly from Malayavasini and Jaya Prabha.

Brahmins are perhaps the most widely studied community in India with the result that South Asian anthropological literature offers considerable ethnographic information about Brahmins in general. However, the Brahmins of Andhra Pradesh have not been that well studied, and in particular little is known about Brahmin women of Andhra. Unfortunately, the following brief sketch cannot be intended as a full ethnographic study of Brahmin women, but it will at least provide the background for my conclusions in this paper.

Brahmins (Telugu: *brāhmaṇulu* or, more colloquially, *brāhmalu*) is a cover word indicating a cluster of endogamous groups in Andhra. These groups have independent names,[5] but in terms of the fourfold hierarchical order of Hindu society, they are all placed in the highest category, namely, the *brāhmaṇa*. Vegetarian and considered ritually pure by virtue of their birth,

Brahmins have held the highest level of social respect in Hindu society for centuries. Brahmin families have a very high percentage of literacy, and the men have traditionally been scholars, poets, and preservers of learning both religious and worldly. Brahmins have thus set the standards of Sanskritic culture, and their dialect is considered correct speech. Other castes imitate this dialect in order to be recognized as educated.

In Andhra, women of Brahmin families are segregated from men, though they are not veiled as are women of North India, nor are they kept from appearing before men in public, as are women of the landed castes. But they are encouraged to live a sheltered life. In premodern Andhra, before the social reform movements and legislation of the late nineteenth and early twentieth centuries, Brahmin girls were married before puberty to a bridegroom arranged by their parents. He was often much older than the bride, and the Brahmin wife was not allowed to remarry if her husband died. Even today widows are considered inauspicious and undesirable; they cannot, for instance, bless young brides at weddings. They are also denied access to ornaments, colored clothes, bangles, turmeric, and the red dot on the forehead, which are symbols of auspiciousness. In some families, especially those belonging to the Vaidiki subdivision of the caste, widows have to shave their heads. However, older widows are respected for their age, especially if they have raised a family, and younger women look up to them for guidance and help. They are repositories of caste lore and often good at singing songs. Auspicious women, in contrast to widows, are treated with affection. They are looked upon by their men as sources of family prosperity, and their rituals are considered sacred and valuable. Men are expected to facilitate such rituals by staying away from them but providing all the necessary resources: until recently, a woman was not allowed to own property, except gold given to her as a gift by her parents or husband.

Proper behavior on the part of a wife requires that she obey her husband and parents-in-law, as well as her husband's older brothers and older sisters. Any disobedience is severely punished, and defiant women are disciplined, often by the mother-in-law. In a conflict between the mother and the wife, a son is expected to take his mother's side and punish his wife. In fact, a man is often ridiculed as effeminate if he does not discipline his wife into obedience. Female sexuality is severely repressed; a proper Brahmin woman has sex only to bear children, who should preferably be male. Pursuit of sexual pleasures is offensive to good taste, and a woman is severely punished for any deviance in word or deed. Women should be modest; an interest in personal appearance or a desire to be recognized for physical beauty is discouraged. Women should not even look into a mirror except to make sure that they have put their forehead dot in the right spot. According to a belief popular in Brahmin families, a woman who looks into a mirror after dusk will be reborn as a prostitute. However, women often guide their husbands from behind the scenes in decisions that have a bearing on family wealth and female security, which suggests that this code of obedience, if creatively manipulated, can be a source of power.

Brahmin women who sing the *Rāmāyaṇa* songs discussed in this essay generally come from families relatively less exposed to English education and urbanized styles of life, in which singing such songs is going out of fashion. They are literate in Telugu, but most of them are not formally educated. Their audience consists of women from similar backgrounds, usually relatives and neighbors, and may also include children, unmarried young women, or newly married brides visiting their mother's house for a festival. Often a marriage or similar event provides an occasion for a number of women to gather. The audience does not generally include women of other castes. While adult men are not supposed to be present at such gatherings, young boys stick around. Nonetheless, men do hear these songs, or more precisely overhear them, even though they tend to pay no attention to them, as it is "women's stuff," not worth their time.

Not every singer knows all of the approximately twenty-five popular *Rāmāyaṇa* songs. There is a general recognition, however, that a certain person knows the songs; such a person is often called upon to sing. Some singers have learnt certain songs well, but when a singer does not know a song adequately, she uses a notebook in which she has recorded the text. Singers do not need special training, nor do they consider themselves experts. No musical instruments accompany the singing of these songs, and the tunes are simple, often monotonous. At least one song has refrains, *govindā* at the end of one line and *govindā rāma* at the end of every other line, suggesting that it may be used as a work song.[6] Some of these songs only take about twenty minutes to half an hour to sing, but others are very long, taking several hours to sing.[7]

The precise age of the *Rāmāyaṇa* songs is not easy to determine. While they are accepted as traditional, and therefore must be fairly old, there is no reliable way of dating them since oral tradition has a tendency to renew the diction while keeping the structure intact. It is also difficult to determine to what extent the songs are truly oral compositions. All are orally performed, but at least some of them were written by a single individual. Several songs contain a statement of *phalaśruti* (the merit which accrues from listening to the song), some of which include the author's name, and a few even mention an author in the colophon.[8] That the singers as well as the authors of the songs are acquainted with literary texts is beyond doubt: many songs have references to writing and written texts. However, the singing styles are passed down from person to person, and the performance is often from memory—though, as we noted, a singer does not mind also using a book. In short, we do not know whether these songs were composed orally and then preserved in writing, or were originally written compositions.

Nearly every scholar who has studied these songs has either assumed or concluded that their authors were men. Only Gopalakrishnamurti has suggested that many of these songs were composed by women, and I am convinced he is right.[9] Judging from the feelings, perceptions, cultural information, and the general attitudes revealed in the songs, it seems likely that all of them—except one minor song, a waking-up song for Sītā, which happens to mention a male author—were women's works. Certainly, the songs are intended for women: many of the songs mention the merit women receive from singing or listening to them.

Even a cursory look at the subject matter of the songs indicates that female interests predominate among the themes. Together they comprise a very different *Rāmāyaṇa* than that told by Vālmīki or other poets of literary versions.

1. *Rāmāyaṇa* in summary, narrated with Śāntā (Rāma's elder sister) as the central character
2. Kausalyā's pregnancy, describing her morning sickness
3. Rāma's birth
4. A lullaby to Rāma
5. Bathing the child Rāma
6. Sītā's wedding
7. Entrusting the bride Sītā to the care of her parents-in-law
8. Sītā's journey to her mother-in-law's house
9. Sītā's puberty
10. Several songs describing the games Rāma and Sītā played
11. Sītā locked out
12. Sītā describing her life with Rāma to Hanumān in Lanka
13. Incidents in Lanka
14. Sītā's fire ordeal
15. Rāma's coronation
16. Ūrmilā's sleep
17. Sītā's pregnancy
18. The story of Lava and Kuśa, Sītā's twin sons
19. Lava and Kuśa's battle with Rāma
20. Lakṣmaṇa's laugh
21. Śūrpaṇakhā's revenge

Significantly, these songs do not mention many of the familiar *Rāmāyaṇa* events. Daśaratha's glory, the rituals he performed in order to obtain children, Viśvāmitra's role in training Rāma as a warrior, the Ahalyā story, the events in the forest leading to the killing of demons, Rāma's grief over Sītā's loss, Rāma's friendship with Sugrīva, the killing of Vālin, the search for Sītā, the exploits of Hanumān, and the glories of the battle in Lanka—none of these incidents receive much attention in these songs. On the other hand, events of interest to women are prominently portrayed and receive detailed attention: pregnancy, morning sickness, childbirth, the tender love of a husband, the affections of parents-in-law, games played by brides and grooms in wedding rituals. Moreover, significant attention is given to the last book of the *Rāmāyaṇa*, the *Uttarakāṇḍa*: some of the longer songs in my recorded collection as well as in the printed book relate to the events of the *Uttarakāṇḍa*, especially Sītā's abandonment and Lava and Kuśa's battle with Rāma.

THE SONGS

As the saying goes among men in Andhra, "The news of the birth of a son is pleasant but not the process of the birth." Men are not very interested in the details of pain women undergo in childbirth. Perhaps not surprisingly, then, literary *Rāmāyaṇas* in Telugu describe Rāma's birth in glorious terms. They relate how the king and his kingdom were delighted by the news, and describe in eloquent phrases the festivities celebrated all over the city of Ayodhya and the gifts given to Brahmins. Only in the women's song versions of the *Rāmāyaṇa* do we find a description of Kausalyā in labor, graphically depicting the pain associated with it. The song describes how the child is delivered while the pregnant woman stands upright, holding on to a pair of ropes hung from the ceiling.[10]

> Now call the midwife, go send for her.
> The midwife came in royal dignity.
> She saw the woman in labor, patted her on her back.
> Don't be afraid, Kausalya, don't be afraid, woman!
> In an hour you will give birth to a son.
> The women there took away the gold ornaments,
> They removed the heavy jewels from her body.
> They hung ropes of gold and silk from the ceiling.
> They tied them to the beams, with great joy
> They made Kausalya hold the ropes.
> Mother, mother, I cannot bear this pain,
> A minute feels like a hundred years.

Attention to ritual is common in many *Rāmāyaṇas*, but the rituals are the grand Vedic rituals, in which Brahmin priests play the leading part. Rituals in the women's songs pertain to more domestic matters, in which women are prominent. The only man present is usually the bridegroom Rāma, and as the bridegroom in women-dominated rituals, he is controlled by and subservient to the demands of the women surrounding him. In addition to the rituals, the songs also describe various games Sītā and Rāma play during the wedding and in the course of their married life in the joint family. In all such games Sītā comes out the winner. Rāma even tries to cheat and cleverly escape defeat, making false promises of surrender.

Another point repeatedly stressed in the songs is the auspicious role women have in Brahmin households as the protectors of family prosperity. Women are personifications of the goddess Lakṣmī, the goddess of wealth, and it is a well-known belief that the women of a household bring prosperity to the family by their proper behavior and ruin it by improper behavior. In these songs the bride enters the house of her new husband, always with her auspicious right foot first. It is the women who perform all the appropriate actions to remove the evil eye from the newborn baby. Women, again, serve a delicious feast to the Brahmins and the sages who come to bless the newborn. The ceremonies described in these songs—the naming ceremony and the ceremony of placing the boys in new cribs (especially made for the occasion, their designs and decorations described in detail)—show how important women are on all those occasions. Even the humor is feminine: when Kausalyā gives the women boiled and spiced *senagalu* (split peas) as a part of a ritual gift, they complain among themselves that the *senagalu* were not properly salted.

A song about Sītā's wedding presents a reason—not found in the Sanskrit text of Vālmīki—why Sītā's father Janaka decides on an eligibility test for Sītā's future husband. In her childhood, Sītā casually lifted Śiva's bow, which was lying in her father's house. Janaka was amazed at her strength and decided that only a man who could string that bow would be eligible to marry her. Only a hero can be a match for a hero. Several literary *Rāmāyaṇa* texts, including Tulsīdās's *Rāmcaritmānas*, also give this explanation, which is therefore not unique to women's *Rāmāyaṇa* songs. But this event gains a special significance in the context of women's hopes for a husband who is properly matched to them. In an arranged marriage, where the personal qualities of the future husband are often left to chance, women dream of having a husband who loves them and whom they love. Significantly, therefore, the song describes Sītā's feelings for Rāma, whose charms have been described to her by her friends. Sītā falls in love with him and suffers the pangs of separation (*viraha*) from him. Closely following the conventional modes of love in separation, the song delicately presents Sītā's fears that Rāma might not succeed in stringing the bow. She prays to all the gods to help him to string it.

The song then describes how Rāma falls in love with Sītā. He arrives and sees the bow. He has no doubt that he can easily break it. But he wants to make sure that Sītā is really beautiful. He asks his brother Lakṣmaṇa to go and see Sītā first. In his words:

> If a meal is not agreeable, a day is wasted
> But if the wife is not agreeable, life is wasted.

He asks Lakṣmaṇa to make sure that Sītā has a thin waist, that her skin is not too dark, that her hair is black and her feet small. The breaking of the bow itself, which is prominently and powerfully described in literary *Rāmāyaṇas*, is presented in an almost perfunctory manner in the women's songs: it is the mutual love between Rāma and Sītā that is prominent in the song. All too often, women in this community find that there is little real love between them and the husband who has been chosen for them. An elaborate description of the mutual love and desire of Rāma and Sītā thus serves as a wish fulfillment. The wedding festivities that follow are seen through women's eyes—every detail related to women's roles in the wedding ceremony is carefully described, even the saris the women wear. Toward the end, an incident that portrays Sītā as an innocent girl is narrated. Rāma shows her a mirror. Seeing her image in the mirror, Sītā thinks that it is a different woman, to whom Rāma has already been married. Why did Rāma marry her if he has a wife already? Has he not vowed to live with one wife and no other? Rāma quietly moves closer to the mirror and stands by her side. Sītā, seeing Rāma's reflection also in the mirror, recognizes her innocence and shyly bends her head down.

A song entitled "Sītā Locked Out" describes a delicate event in which Sītā is delayed in coming to bed because she has work to finish in the house. Rāma waits for her, but, growing impatient, closes the bedroom door and locks it from inside. Sītā arrives and pleads with him to open the door. He stubbornly refuses.[11] Sītā quietly informs Kausalyā, who has already left for Daśaratha's bedroom. Kausalyā comes out, knocks on Rāma's door, and admonishes him for locking Sītā out. Rāma has to obey his mother: Sītā knows how to manipulate the situation in her favor by enlisting Kausalyā's help. Kausalyā is represented here as the ideal mother-in-law every daughter-in-law dreams of in a joint family, a mother-in-law who shows warmth and support for her daughter-in-law and who helps to bring her closer to her husband.[12]

Men's *Rāmāyaṇas* have no great use for Śāntā, who is sometimes nominally mentioned as Daśaratha's foster daughter and who is married to Ṛśyaśṛṅga. But for women she is a very important person in the *Rāmāyaṇa* story. In Brahmin families, an elder sister is allowed to command, criticize, and admonish her younger brother. As Rāma's elder sister, Śāntā often intervenes on behalf of Sītā in these songs.

Śāntā's importance in women's *Rāmāyaṇas* is best represented by a long song called "Śāntagovindanāmālu," which describes Śāntā's marriage. A striking feature of this song, which narrates most of the early part of the *Rāmāyaṇa*, is the importance women have in all the events: at every important juncture, women either take the initiative themselves and act, or advise their husbands to take a specific step. Men's position is presented as titular; the real power rests with the women.

The story tells how Lakṣmī, Viṣṇu's consort, decides to be born on the earth to help Viṣṇu, who will be born as Rāma. She descends to the earth and is born as Sītā on a lotus flower in Lanka. Rāvaṇa finds her and gives her to Mandodarī. When Sītā is twelve years old, he wants to marry her as his second wife. The Brahmins, however, advise Rāvaṇa that Sītā will destroy Lanka and that therefore she should be cast into the sea. The song then moves on to narrate other events leading to Rāma's birth.

The two most significant stories in the early books of Vālmīki's *Rāmāyaṇa* are the birth of Daśaratha's sons and Kaikeyī's evil plot to send Rāma away to the forest. In the first story women have no role to play except as passive bearers of children; in the second, the evil nature of women is highlighted in the descriptions of Kaikeyī's adamant demands to have her son Bharata invested as the heir to the kingdom and to banish Rāma to the forest for fourteen years.

The narrative in "Śāntagovindanāmālu" ingeniously transforms both these events so that women acquire the credit for the birth of sons and the evil nature of Kaikeyī's demand is eliminated. First, according to this song, Kausalyā advises Daśaratha that they should adopt Śāntā as their daughter. This daughter will bring good luck to the family and they will have sons. This is a powerful change indeed. The usual Brahmin family belief is that the firstborn should be a son. A firstborn daughter is greeted with disappointment, though it is not always openly expressed. This story suggests that a firstborn daughter is actually preferable because she, as a form of the goddess Lakṣmī, blesses the family with prosperity, which then leads to the birth of sons. Moreover, it is significant that the whole strategy is planned by a woman—whereas in the Vālmīki *Rāmāyaṇa*, for example, the sage Ṛśyaśṛṅga performs a sacrifice for Daśaratha which leads to the birth of sons. What is interesting here is that Daśaratha listens to his senior queen's advice. Kaikeyī, however, initially refuses to go along because she will gain nothing from the plan. But Sumitrā convinces Kaikeyī, who finally accepts the plan on the condition that Bharata, her son, will inherit the kingdom. Śāntā is duly adopted and brought to Ayodhya with great honors, where she is received as the very goddess of wealth. When she grows of age she is married to Ṛśyaśṛṅga, again on the advice of Kausalyā. The song then describes in fine detail the festivities of the wedding and the harmonious atmosphere of the palace, where the women are in control.

The innocence, fun, love, and gentle humor of the songs come to an end and serious problems in Sītā's life begin with the events of the later portion of the *Rāmāyaṇa*—events that take place after Sītā is brought back from her captivity in Lanka. But the women described in these songs are far from meek and helpless: they are portrayed as strong, quite capable of protecting their position against the unfair treatment meted out to them by Rāma.

One song depicts how, after abandoning the pregnant Sītā, Rāma decides to perform a sacrifice. Since ritual prescribes that he have a wife present, he has a golden image of Sītā made, to be placed by his side at the ritual. The image has to be bathed, and the person to do the bathing must be Rāma's sister, Śāntā. However, when Śāntā is called to perform the bathing, she refuses because she was not consulted before Sītā was abandoned.

A more serious situation develops when Rāma's sacrificial horse is captured by his sons, Lava and Kuśa. He does not know that Sītā is still alive and being taken care of by the sage Vālmīki in his forest hermitage, nor does he know that Lava and Kuśa are his sons. Appeals by Lakṣmaṇa and Rāma to the young boys fail to convince them to surrender the horse. In fact, they will not even reveal their identities. In the inevitable battle that ensues, all of Rāma's best fighters, including Hanumān and Lakṣmaṇa, get killed. Finally, Rāma himself goes to battle, and even he is killed. When Sītā comes to know about this, she grieves and chastises her sons for killing their father and their uncle. Vālmīki, of course, comes to the rescue and brings everybody back to life.[13]

Even then, the boys insist that Rāma bow to their feet before he gets his horse back. Is he not the cruel husband who banished his pregnant wife? Rāma, realizing now that Sītā is alive and that these boys are his sons, wants to see her, and so Vālmīki arranges for Sītā to be brought before him. Sītā dresses in her best jewelry to meet Rāma, but Lava and Kuśa run into the hermitage to prevent their mother from meeting him. How can she go to a husband who has treated her so cruelly? To resolve the problem, all the gods appear on the scene, Brahmā, Śiva, and Indra in the company of their wives. The gods take Rāma's side, while their wives support the boys. Śiva's wife, Pārvatī, advises the boys not to surrender, while Brahmā's wife, Sarasvatī, makes the boys insist that Rāma should bow to them first. The gods advise the boys to accept the arbitration af the Sun god, but the boys reject that idea: Rāma belongs to the solar dynasty, so the Sun will not be impartial. How about the Moon god? No, Viṣṇu saved the Moon when Rāhu and Ketu swallowed him. Therefore, the Moon's arbitration cannot be trusted. Nor is Indra an acceptable arbiter because he owes favors to Viṣṇu, who cheated the demons out of their share of ambrosia and gave it all to him. Vālmīki's name is suggested, but even he is not impartial, since he wrote the *Rāmāyaṇa* in praise of Rāma. Brahmā, Śiva, and Ṛśyaśṛṅga—all are rejected one after the other. Rāma has no choice. He decides to fight the boys. Pārvatī opposes this idea, suggesting instead that Rāma bequeath Ayodhya to the boys and go to the forest. Ultimately, a compromise is reached: Rāma should bow to the boys, intending thereby to honor his parents. So Rāma bows to his sons' feet, uttering Kausalyā's name, and thus the dispute is resolved.

Finally the family is reunited, and Rāma embraces Lava and Kuśa. But even then the boys refuse to go to Ayodhya, for they feel that they cannot trust a father who planned to kill his sons while they were in the womb. Only after much pleading do the boys agree to go with their father. Soon after they reach Ayodhya they demand to see the "grandmother" (Kaikeyī) who banished Sītā to the forest! They announce that Sītā is under their protection now and nobody can harm her anymore.

Among the male characters, Lakṣmaṇa receives very affectionate treatment in these songs. He is closer to Sītā, understands her problems, supports her, and even protects her in her time of troubles. In Vālmīki, Rāma banishes Sītā to the forest under the pretext of fulfilling her desire to see the hermitages, instructing Lakṣmaṇa to leave her in the woods and return. According to the women's version, Rāma orders Lakṣmaṇa to kill her. Lakṣmaṇa takes her to the forest but, realizing that she is pregnant, decides not to kill her. He kills a hare instead and shows its blood to Rāma as evidence. Rāma then prepares for her funeral and asks Lakṣmaṇa to go to the hermitages and invite the sages' wives to the ceremonies. When Lakṣmaṇa goes to the forest, Sītā asks him if Rāma is preparing for her funeral. To spare her further pain, Lakṣmaṇa tells the lie that they are performing a special ritual to rid the palace of evil influences. Lakṣmaṇa's wife, Ūrmilā, protests against her husband's cruelty in killing Sītā. She demands that she be killed too, as does Śāntā. Unable to stand their anger and their determination, Lakṣmaṇa tells them the truth: Sītā is alive, pregnant, and will deliver soon. Lakṣmaṇa goes to the forest to visit with her after she has delivered.

Another song in this collection concerns Ūrmilā, whom Vālmīki barely mentions. What happens to Ūrmilā when Lakṣmaṇa leaves for fourteen years to accompany his brother to the forest? According to the women's version, Ūrmilā and Lakṣmaṇa make a pact: they trade their sleeping and waking hours. Ūrmilā will sleep for the entire fourteen years while Lakṣmaṇa will stay awake so that he can serve his brother without interruption. Fourteen years later, when Rāma has been successfully reinstated on the throne and Lakṣmaṇa is serving him at the court, Sītā reminds Rāma that Lakṣmaṇa should be advised to go visit his wife, who is still sleeping. Lakṣmaṇa goes to Ūrmilā's bedroom and gently wakes her up. Ūrmilā does not recognize him, however, and thinks that a stranger has entered her bedchamber. She questions him, warning him about the sin of desiring another man's wife.

> If my father Janaka comes to know about this,
> he will punish you and will not let you get away.
> My elder sister and brother-in-law
> will not let you escape with your life.

As a proper wife she does not even mention the name of her husband. Instead, she refers to him indirectly:

> My elder sister's younger brother-in-law
> will not let you live on the earth.

Then she tells him how, in the past, men who coveted others' wives suffered for their sin.

Did not Indra suffer a disfigured body
because he coveted another man's wife?
Was not Rāvaṇa destroyed along with his city
because he desired another man's wife?

That the sleeping Ūrmilā could not possibly have known about Rāvaṇa kidnapping Sītā and his eventual death at Rāma's hands is immaterial.

Lakṣmaṇa gently identifies himself, whereupon Ūrmilā realizes that he is none other than her husband. The rest of the song relates in loving detail how affectionately they embrace each other. Kausalyā receives them, prepares a bath for them, and feeds them a delicious meal. Lakṣmaṇa and Ūrmilā sit side by side—as husband and wife rarely do in conventional Brahmin families—and the members of the family tease them. When they are sent to the bedroom Lakṣmaṇa combs and skillfully braids Ūrmilā's hair while Ūrmilā asks him about all the events of the past fourteen years. How could Rāvaṇa kidnap Sītā when a man like Lakṣmaṇa, courageous as a lion, was present? Lakṣmaṇa relates the story of the golden deer, telling her how Sītā spoke harsh words to him and forced him to leave her alone and look after Rāma instead. All the major events of the epic have now been narrated briefly, and the song ends wishing all the listeners and singers a place in heaven.

A related song also takes as its starting point Lakṣmaṇa and Ūrmilā's pact. When the goddess of sleep visits Lakṣmaṇa in the forest, he asks her to leave him alone for fourteen years and go to his wife instead. She can come back to him exactly fourteen years later, when he returns to Ayodhya. Sure enough, as Lakṣmaṇa is serving Rāma in the court hall after their return from Lanka, the goddess of sleep visits him. Amused at her punctual return, Lakṣmaṇa laughs. Lakṣmaṇa's sudden laugh amidst the serious atmosphere of the court makes everybody wonder. The song describes how each person in the hall thinks that Lakṣmaṇa laughed at him or her. Thus Śiva, who is present in the court, thinks that Lakṣmaṇa laughed at him because he brought a low caste fisherwoman (Gaṅgā, actually the river Ganges) and put her on his head, while Śeṣa, the ancient snake, thinks that Lakṣmaṇa was ridiculing him because he served Viṣṇu for a long time but is now serving Viṣṇu's enemy, Śiva. Aṅgada assumes that Lakṣmaṇa was laughing at him for joining the service of his own father's killer, Rāma. Sugrīva has his insecurities too: he had his brother killed unfairly and stole his brother's wife. Vibhīṣaṇa revealed the secrets of his brother's kingdom to Rāma and thus caused the ruin of Lanka. Hanumān is bothered by the fact that he, a mighty warrior, was once caught by a young soldier, Indrajit. Bharata and Śatrughna, too, have something to be ashamed of: they were given the empire as a result of their mother Kaikeyī's cunning plot, which deprived Rāma of his position as future king. Even Rāma thinks that Lakṣmaṇa laughed at him because he, Rāma, has taken back a wife who has lived in another man's house—while Sītā thinks that Lakṣmaṇa laughed at her for having lived away from her husband. Furthermore, she was the one who suspected Lakṣmaṇa's intentions when he insisted on staying with her to protect her in the forest. She spoke harshly to him, forcing him to leave her alone and go help Rāma, who appeared to be in danger from the golden deer—thus causing the chain of events that led to the battle of Lanka. Everyone in the court has a secret shame, and Lakṣmaṇa's laugh brings their insecurities to the surface. In this skillful way the song suggests that no character in the *Rāmāyaṇa* is free from blemishes.

Angry at Lakṣmaṇa for his improper act of laughing in court, Rāma draws his sword to cut off his brother's head, at which point Pārvatī and Śiva intervene. They suggest that Lakṣmaṇa should be asked to explain his reasons for such irreverent behavior: he is young and should not be punished harshly. When Lakṣmaṇa explains, Rāma is embarrassed at his rash and uncontrolled anger. He asks Vasiṣṭha how he, as a proper king, should expiate his sin of attempting to kill his innocent brother. Vasiṣṭha advises Rāma to massage Lakṣmaṇa's feet. So a bed is made for Lakṣmaṇa, and, like a dutiful servant, Rāma massages his feet as Lakṣmaṇa sleeps comfortably. When Lakṣmaṇa wakes up and sees what Rāma is doing, he dutifully dissuades his glorious elder brother, the very incarnation of god Viṣṇu, from serving him.[14]

Rāvaṇa's sister Śūrpaṇakhā's role in the women's *Rāmāyaṇa* songs is especially noteworthy. Rāma and his brothers are living happily in Ayodhya when Śūrpaṇakhā happens to see them. She desires to avenge her brother Rāvaṇa's death, but she is a woman. If only she were a man, she could have fought against Rāma and killed him—but as a woman, she can only disrupt his happiness. So she decides to plant suspicions in Rāma's mind about Sītā's fidelity. Taking the form of a female hermit, Śūrpaṇakhā goes to the palace and asks to see Sītā. Although Sītā hesitates, surprised that a forest hermit has come to see her, after some persuasion she consents to see her. The hermit asks Sītā to paint a picture of Rāvaṇa, but she replies that she never set eyes on the demon's face; she looked only at his feet. So the hermit asks Sītā to paint the feet, and Sītā draws a picture of Rāvaṇa's big toe.

Śūrpaṇakhā takes the drawing and completes the rest of the picture herself—strong ankles, thighs, and the rest. She then asks Brahmā, the creator god, to give life to the image so she can see her dead brother again. When Brahmā does so, Śūrpaṇakhā brings the picture back to Sītā, drops it in front of her, and runs away saying, "Do what you want with this picture." When the image of Rāvaṇa starts pulling at Sītā, asking her to go to Lanka with him, Sītā grows perturbed. Ūrmilā, Śāntā, and all the other women in the palace try to get rid of the picture. They make a big fire and throw the picture in, but it does not burn. Then they throw the picture into a deep well, but it comes back up. By no means can they destroy it. Finally Sītā utters Rāma's name, which temporarily subdues the image.

Suddenly Rāma enters the house. Not knowing what to do with the picture, Sītā hides it under her mattress. Rāma approaches Sītā and embraces her, wishing to make love to her. He unties her blouse, but Sītā is distracted. Puzzled, Rāma tries to show his affection by describing in many words how he loves her. When he takes her to bed, however, Rāvaṇa's picture under the mattress throws him off the bed. Thinking that Sītā threw him off, Rāma is angered. He turns around and sees Rāvaṇa's picture. This convinces him that Sītā is really in love with another man and that women are unreliable.

He decides to banish Sītā to the forest along with her picture, but all the women of the palace protest. They explain to Rāma how a certain hermit made Sītā draw Rāvaṇa's picture; they tell him that Sītā is pure, but Rāma does not listen. In his anger, he speaks rudely to his mother, Kausalyā, who pleads in favor of Sītā. When Sumitrā, Lakṣmaṇa's mother, intervenes, he tells her that she could have Sītā as her daughter-in-law, suggesting thereby that Sītā could be Lakṣmaṇa's wife. Ordering that Sītā be killed in the forest, he leaves the house for the royal court. Ūrmilā, Māṇḍavī, and Śrutakīrtī, the wives of Rāma's three brothers, go to Rāma to protest his unfair punishment of Sītā. One after another they assure Rāma that Sītā was not at fault. Finally, Śrutakīrtī tells him:

> We are all born in one family,
> married into one family.
> Our sister is not the only one
> who loves Rāvaṇa now.
> We all love him together
> so kill us together.
> Because we are women
> who stay within the palace,
> your actions pass without check.

This united front only makes Rāma more angry. He commands Lakṣmaṇa to take Sītā away to the forest, cut off her head, and bring the sword back (thus setting the stage for the events described above).

THE STRUCTURE OF THE SONGS

The structure of these songs, which open with praise of Rāma before moving on to the story at hand, might appear somewhat commonplace, but becomes significant in relation to the time and place of their performance. The songs are usually sung in the late afternoon, after the midday meal, when the men of the family have all retired to the front part of the house to take a nap or chat on the porch, the younger among them perhaps playing cards. Having been served a good meal, they now want to be left alone, to relax and rest, until evening. Their daily chores completed, the women are now free from marital and family obligations, at least for the moment. This is their own time, during which they can do what they please—provided, of course, that they don't violate the norms of good behavior. Very much like the place in the house where the songs are sung, then, this time period is largely insulated from the demands of the men, for whom women must otherwise play their dutiful roles.

A Brahmin house is divided into three areas. The front is where the men sit, conduct business, receive guests, or chat among themselves. Except when they are called for meals or when they retire for the evening, men do not usually go into the interior of the house, and when they do, they indicate their arrival by coughing or calling to one of the women from outside, who then comes into the middle part of the house to receive them. The middle part of the house is a relatively neutral area, where men and women meet together. In the back of the house are located a kitchen and a verandah opening into the backyard, often with a well in it. It is here that women gather. Women visitors, servants, and low caste men use the back entrance of the house to converse with the women.

At the front of the house, the conventional male-dominated values reign supreme, but the back part of the house, and to a somewhat lesser extent the interior, are primarily the women's domain. Women are relatively free here from the censuring gaze of their men, and thus enjoy some measure of control over their own lives. Men are even ridiculed for lingering in the back of the house, although male relatives of the wife's family may enter, as can the husband's younger brothers if they are much younger than the wife.

The structure of the songs precisely replicates the structure of the house. Each song begins with a respectful tribute to Rāma, the king. Rāma in these songs is not only God, as in *bhakti Rāmāyaṇas*, but also the *yajamāni*, the master of the house—albeit a master who is not entirely in control. This opening dutifully made, the song moves toward the interior—and the people who inhabit the interior of the songs are mostly women. Much like certain male relatives, however, some men are allowed to enter this area: Lakṣmaṇa, the younger brother-in-law; and Lava and Kuśa, the young twins.

SĪTĀYANA

Women in these songs never openly defy propriety: they behave properly, even giving themselves advice that the male masters of the household would accept and appreciate. The tone of the songs is innocently gentle, homely, and sweet—no harsh or provocative language, no overt or aggressive opposition to male domination. Daughters-in-law thus take great care to observe the conventions in addressing mother-in-law Kausalyā and sister-in-law

Śāntā. Likewise, on several occasions proper behavior is preached to young brides, as when Sītā is told to:

> Be more patient than even the earth goddess.
> Never transgress the words of your father-in-law and mother-in-law.
> Do not ever look at other men.
> Do not ever speak openly.
> Do not reveal the words your husband says in the interior palace,
> even to the best of your friends.
> If your husband is angry, never talk back to him.
> A husband is god to all women: never disobey your husband.

While proper respect is always paid to authority, what follows on the heels of that respect can seem strikingly different. There are polite but quite strongly made statements that question Rāma's wisdom, propriety, honesty, and integrity. However, Sītā herself never opposes Rāma or her other superiors: as a new bride, Sītā is coy, innocent, and very obedient to her husband and the elders of the family. Rather, criticism against Rāma is leveled only by women who have the authority to do so, like Rāma's mother, Kausalyā, or his elder sister, Śāntā, a mother surrogate. Rāma's brothers' wives question Rāma, too, but in order to do so, they need the support of Śāntā. Rāma's young sons, Lava and Kuśa, are also permitted to criticize their father, provided they are acting in their mother's defense.

Both the affections and the tensions of a joint family come out clearly through these songs. Beneath the apparent calm of the house, joint family women often suffer severe internal stress. The songs reveal a similar atmosphere in their use of language. The general style of the language is deceptively gentle. Very few Sanskrit words are used, the choice of relatively more mellifluous Dravidian words lending to the texture of the songs an idyllic atmosphere of calm and contentment. However, the underlying meanings reveal an atmosphere of subdued tensions, hidden sexuality, and frustrated emotions. On occasion, even the gentle words acquire the sharpness of darts, hitting their targets with precise aim. Under the pretext of family members teasing each other, every character is lampooned. No one's character is untainted; no person loves another unconditionally. Even Sītā's chastity is open to doubt: the picture episode suggests that Sītā harbors a hidden desire to sleep with Rāvaṇa, her drawing of Rāvaṇa's big toe making veiled reference to his sex organ. The final picture that emerges is not that of the *bhakti Rāmāyaṇas*, with an ideal husband, an ideal wife, and ideal brothers, but of a complex joint family where life is filled with tension and fear, frustration and suspicion, as well as with love, affection, and tenderness.

The *Rāmāyaṇa* songs also make a statement against the public *Rāmāyaṇas*, the *bhakti Rāmāyaṇas*, which glorify the accepted values of a male-dominated world. In the songs, it is the minor or lowly characters who come out as winners. Ūrmilā, Lakṣmaṇa, Lava and Kuśa, Śāntā, and even Śūrpaṇakhā have a chance to take their revenge. Sītā does not fight her own battle alone: others fight it for her. She even enjoys the freedom she acquires by the (false) report of her death; for once, she can exist without living for Rāma. As Rāma prepares for her death ceremonies, burdened by the guilt of having her killed unjustly, Sītā gives birth to twins and awaits her final victory over Rāma, won through her agents, her sons. In the final analysis, this is her *Rāmāyaṇa*, a *Sītāyana*.

NON-BRAHMIN SONGS

A similar strategy of subverting authority while outwardly respecting it is found in the *Rāmāyaṇa* songs sung by non-Brahmin women. These are not as long as the Brahmin women's songs, nor are they as prominent in the non-Brahmin women's repertoire as they are in Brahmin women's. Although the *Rāmāyaṇa* is often alleged to be universally popular in India, closer examination will, I believe, reveal that the epic's popularity increases with the status of the caste. At any rate the number of *Rāmāyaṇa* songs sung by non-Brahmin women that are available in published collections is relatively small, though the songs are by no means less interesting. My information regarding these songs comes almost entirely from these published collections, and as such my use of the data is rather constrained.

The label "non-Brahmin" masks more than it reveals. Unfortunately, the published information about these songs does not record the precise caste of the singer. As Ganagappa informs us, the songs are sung by women when they are working in the fields, grinding flour, or playing *kolāṭaṁ* (a play of music and dance in which the players move in circles as they hit wooden sticks held in each other's hands). Female agricultural labor in Andhra largely comes from Mālas, a caste of Untouchables, and other castes of very low status. Women of these castes work in the fields with men, make their own money, and thus live relatively less sheltered and controlled lives. Separation of the sexes is not practiced to the same extent as among the upper castes, although women are seen as inferior to men, paid lower wages, and given work which is supposed to require less skill, like weeding and transplanting, as opposed to ploughing, seeding, and harvesting. Women also work in groups, which are often supervised by a man. The household chores that these women perform are also distinct from those of the men, but the separation is not as clear cut as it is among upper castes. Lower caste men, for example, do not consider it demeaning to feed children and take care of them.

Women of these low castes have the same kinds of family responsibilities as Brahmin women do: raising a family, bearing (male) children, being sexually faithful to their husbands, and obeying their husbands and mothers-in-law. But the low-caste women are not as dependent on their husbands as are Brahmin women. Widows are not treated as inauspicious, nor are their heads shaved; and they are not removed from family ritual life. Among some non-Brahmin castes widows even remarry.[15]

The *Rāmāyaṇa* songs sung by non-Brahmin women reflect this difference. These songs also concentrate on women's themes: Sītā's life in the forest, Ūrmilā's sleep, Sītā's request that Rāma capture the golden deer, Rāvaṇa's kidnapping of Sītā, and the battle between Rāma and his sons, Kuśa and Lava. But there is little interest in descriptions of woman's role in ritual, in their wish for importance in family decisions, or in saris and ornaments, nor is there much allusion to the inner conflicts of a joint family. Also significantly absent are hidden sexuality, feminine modesty, and descriptions of games played by husband and wife.

Interestingly, there is a song describing how Rāma grieves when Lakṣmaṇa swoons in battle and how Hanumān brings the mountain with the life-giving herb *saṃjīvini.* Another song describes how Vibhīṣaṇa advises his brother Rāvaṇa in vain to surrender Sītā and how he deserts Rāvaṇa to join Rāma. Their mother advises Vibhīṣaṇa to take half of Lanka and stay. Describing the glory of Lanka she says:

> The god of wind sweeps the floor here in Lanka.
> The rain god sprinkles cow-dung water to keep it clean.
> The fire god himself cooks in our kitchen,
> cooks in our kitchen.
> Three hundred thirty-three million gods take
> shovels and crowbars and work for us as slaves,
> all the time, work for us as slaves.

It is fascinating to see how the song reverses the hierarchy and relishes the description of gods working as slaves, for in truth it is the low-caste women and men who must work as slaves for their masters, the "gods on earth." The chores of sprinkling cow-dung water in the front yards and cooking are women's work, while digging earth for the landed masters is the work of low-caste men. The song thus refers jointly to the tasks of both men and women of the low castes, opposing their situation to that of the upper castes.

Another short song in this collection describes the glory of houses in Lanka where Rāvaṇa and his brothers live.

> Steel beams and steel pillars, whose palace is this?
> Lovely Srīrāma [Sītā], this is Kumbhakarṇa's palace.
> Teak beams and teak pillars, whose palace is this?
> Lovely Srīrāma, this is Indrajit's palace.
>
> . . .
>
> Silver beams and silver pillars, whose palace is this?
> Lovely Srīrāma, this is Rāvaṇa's palace.[16]

Sung during *kolāṭaṁ* play, this group song, its lines repeated again and again, enchants the listeners with its play on words and sound, the increase in value of the house keeping pace with the increase in the tempo of singing. Here, it is Rāvaṇa, not Rāma, who is described in glorious terms befitting a king. We hear of Rāma more as a name in the devotional refrain than as the hero of the epic story.

Among the other male characters Lakṣmaṇa again receives affectionate treatment as Sītā's younger brother-in-law. As surrogate father he takes care of Sītā's sons. He puts oil on their scalps, feeds them milk, and they urinate on his clothes. Lakṣmaṇa loves it; his face glows like the full moon.

The joint family does merit a favorable description in a song depicting Sītā's answer to the demon women guarding her in Lanka.

> Cool lemon trees and fine *pŏnna* trees all around
> have you seen, Sīta, Rāvaṇa's Lanka.
> Time and again you think of Rāma,
> who is this Rāma, Sīta of Rāgavas?
> Rāma is my man, Lakṣmaṇa, my *maridi.*
> Barta and Śatrīka are my younger *maridis.*
> Kausalya is my real mother-in-law,
> Kaika, the elder one and Saumitri, the younger.
> Ūrmiḷa and I are daughters-in-law.
> All the world knows, Janaka is my father.
> All the directions know, Daśaratha is my father-in-law.
> All the earth knows, the earth goddess is my mother.[17]

So Sītā is neither alone nor unprotected. When threatened by an alien power, she can count on all the members of her extended family to come to her support.

An incident that makes Sītā look somewhat childish in the upper-caste *Rāmāyaṇas* is her demand for the golden deer, even though Rāma tells her that the animal is a demon in magical disguise. In the *Rāmāyaṇa* of the low-caste women, though, Sītā does not insist on getting the animal like a spoiled child; she says instead:

> You give me your bows and arrows
> I will go right now and get the animal.

His ego hurt, Rāma rushes forth to capture the golden deer.

These songs are sung in rice fields and play areas—not in the private backyards of houses as the Brahmin songs are. Interestingly, songs collected from the fields where women sing as they work begin with a straightforward narration but end almost abruptly; they seem rather unfinished. One wonders if the open structure of the work songs does not reflect the low-caste women's lack of interest in finishing what really does not belong to them. Rather than indicating an inability to produce a finished song, the songs' structure is thus an expression of rejection: like the open fields where they work, the story of the *Rāmāyaṇa*, with its regal settings and brahminical values, really belongs to others. The same women can, moreover, sing beautifully finished songs when the theme interests them, as, for example, the *kolāṭaṁ* play song describing the glory of the houses Rāvaṇa and his brothers live in. And there is that devotional mention of Rāma's name, perhaps a thin facade covering the actual lack of interest in Rāma's stature as a hero.

CONCLUSIONS

Why do women sing these songs? Edwin Ardener has proposed a theory of muted groups, who are silenced by the dominant structures of expression.[18] India's lower castes and women fall in this category. However, muted groups, according to Ardener, are not silent groups. They do express themselves, but under cover of the dominant ideology.

The contents of the women's *Rāmāyaṇa* songs do not make their singers or listeners feminists. If anything, the Brahmin women to whom I talked consider singing these songs an act of devotion, a proper womanly thing to do in the house. Nor have men who have listened to these songs or read them in print objected to their use by the women of their households. None of the scholars (of both sexes) who have written on the Brahmin *Rāmāyaṇa* songs perceive in them a tone of opposition to the public *Rāmāyaṇas*, the "male" versions.[19]

Do the women consciously follow the meaning of the songs when they sing them for themselves? They have so routinized their singing that they seem to receive the meaning subliminally, rather than self-consciously. Furthermore, the very same women who sing these songs also participate in the public, male *Rāmāyaṇa* with all the devotion appropriate to the occasion. Does the contrast between what they sing at home and what they hear outside the home receive their attention? Do they discuss these issues among themselves? The texts women sing are not esoteric. Their language is simple, their message clear; they protest against male domination. I believe it is the controlled context of their performance that makes their use properly "feminine." Perhaps the value of the songs consists precisely in the absence of conscious protest. The women who sing these songs have not sought to overthrow the male-dominated family structure; they would rather work within it. They have no interest in direct confrontation with authority; their interest, rather, is in making room for themselves to move. It is this internal freedom that these songs seem to cherish. Only when such freedom is threatened by an overbearing power exercised by the head of the household do the women speak up against him, even then subverting his authority rather than fighting openly against him. These songs are a part of the education Brahmin women receive, a part of brahminic ideology, which constructs women's consciousness in a way suitable to life in a world ultimately controlled by men.

In sharp contrast to the Brahmin women's songs, the songs sung by the low-caste women seem to reflect their disaffection with the dominant upper-caste masters for whom they work rather than with the men of their own families. As low-caste women, these singers are doubly oppressed. As women, they share some of the feelings of the upper-caste women, and to that extent they understand Sītā's troubles. Perhaps more intriguing, however, is the lack of interest in Rāma and the attention shown instead to Rāvaṇa and Lanka, in an apparent rejection of Rāma. But again, as in the Brahmin women's songs, the rejection is not open and confrontational, but subtle and subversive.

NOTES

Sanskrit loan words in Telugu shorten the long vowel at the end of feminine nouns: Sīta, Ūrmiḷa. In the passages quoted from the songs these names appear without the final long vowel and with Telugu diacritics.

I am grateful to Kolavennu Malayavasini for collecting these *Rāmāyaṇa* songs for me. Her cultural insights and her knowledge of the *Rāmāyaṇa* song tradition have been very useful to me. Thanks are also due to Jaya Prabha, who collected several songs from her mother. Peter Claus and Robert Goldman read and commented on an earlier version of this paper when it was presented at the 40th annual meeting of the Association for Asian Studies in San Francisco, March 1988. Joyce Flueckiger, A. K. Ramanujan, Joe Elder, Kirin Narayan, and Paula Richman read a later draft and made a number of suggestions for improvement. I am grateful to all of them. Responsibility for the interpretation (and misinterpretation) is entirely mine.

1. The songs women sing on the *Rāmāyaṇa* theme have received extensive attention from Telugu scholars for some time. The earliest collections of these songs were made by Nandiraju Chelapati Rao, *Strīla Pāṭalu* (Eluru: Manjuvani Press, 1899), and Mangu Ranganatha Rao, *Nūru Hindū Strīla Pāṭalu* (c. 1905). The existence of these early collections is reported in Sripada Gopalakrishnamurti's introduction to another collection, *Strīla Rāmāyaṇapu Pāṭalu*, ed. "Krishnasri" (Hyderabad: Andhrasarasvataparishattu, 1955), but they were unavailable to me. A more recent collection of folksongs, which includes several shorter women's *Rāmāyaṇa* songs, is that of Nedunuri Gangadharam, *Minneru* (Rajahmundry: Sarasvathi Power Press, 1968). A small but extremely interesting collection, which includes *Rāmāyaṇa* songs collected from low-caste women, is found in Sriramappagari Gangappa, ed., *Jānapadageyarāmāyaṇamu* (Gunturu: By the author, 1983). Another collection, also by Gangappa, is *Jānapadageyālu* (Vijayawada: Jayanti Publications, 1985), which includes a number of the *Rāmāyaṇa* songs already published in his 1983 collection.

Earlier studies of these songs include: Hari Adiseshuvu, *Jānapadageyavāñmayaparicayamu* (Gunturu: Navyavijnanpracuranalu, 1954; repr. 1967), 245–50; Birudaraju Ramaraju, *Telugujānapadageyasāhityamu* (Hyderabad: Janapadavijnanapracuranalu, 1958; 2d ed. 1978), 78–126; Tumati Donappa, *Jānapadakaḷāsampada* (Hyderabad: Abhinandanasamiti, Acarya Tumati Donappa Mudu Arvaila Pandaga, 1972; repr. 1987); Panda Samantakamani, *Telugusāhityamulo Rāmakatha* (Hyderabad: Andhrasarasvataparishattu, 1972), 248–69; T. Gopalakrishna Rao, *Folk Ramayanas in Telugu and Kannada* (Nellore: Saroja Publications, 1984); and Kolavennu Malayavasini, *Āndhra Jānapada Sāhityamu: Rāmāyaṇamu* (Visakhapatnam: By the author, 1986). Donappa includes several *Rāmāyaṇa* songs from the Rayalasima region of Andhra Pradesh, unavailable in any other published collections. In addition, Gopalakrishna Rao mentions K. Srilakshmi's "Female Characters in Folk Songs Based on Ramayana" (M. Phil. thesis, Osmania University, Hyderabad, 1980), but unfortunately I was not able to consult it.

2. To continue the language metaphor, it may be said that there are *Rāmāyaṇas* whose grammar is less conventional, such as the DK (Dravida Khazagam) version popular in Tamilnadu: see Richman's essay in this volume. There are also several such *Rāmāyaṇas* in Telugu, most notably a recent feminist, Marxist version by Ranganayakamma entitled *Rāmāyaṇa Viṣavṛkṣam* (The Rāmāyaṇa: A poison tree), 3 vols. (Hyderabad: Sweet Home Publications, 1974–76).

3. It should be noted that the popularity of these songs is waning: most young Brahmin women who attend college or university no longer sing these songs.

4. In 1955 Andhrasarasvataparishattu, a literary service organization in Hyderabad, assembled forty-two of these songs in one volume entitled *Strīla Rāmāyaṇapu Pāṭalu,* with a critical introduction by Sripada Gopalakrishnamurti, but no information is given about the methods of collection, the singers, or the context of singing. Absent also is information regarding the tunes to which these songs were sung. It is possible that the book drew chiefly or entirely on earlier printed sources. Gopalakrishnamurti's otherwise valuable introduction is silent about these matters. Even though the title page of the book says that it is edited by "Krishnasri"—presumably a pseudonym—the introduction indicates that Gopalakrishnamurti was not directly involved in the collection of these songs.

5. For example, Vaidikis, Niyogis, Golkōṇḍavyapāris, Madhvas Drāviḍas, etc., each group boasting numerous subdivisions.

6. In a work song, the lead singer sings the main text, while the refrain is repeated by the group of women working along with her. On my tape, however, one singer sings both the text and the refrain.

7. I was not able to acquire sung versions of several of the long songs, but they are available in print.

8. The author of "Kuśalavula Yuddhamu" says that the song was composed "on behalf of" (*tarapuna*) the *Rāmāyaṇa* of Vālmīki, referring to himself/herself in the third person but without giving a name: *varusaga idi vālmīki rāmāyaṇamu tarapuna vrāsenu ī kavitānu.* Because of the use of the masculine *kavi,* "poet," in this line, scholars have concluded that the author is a man. It is not improbable that *kavi* would be used to indicate a woman poet: the feminine term *kavayitri* is more pedantic. In another song, "Kuśalavakuccalakatha," the author refers to herself as *sati,* "auspicious woman," again without mentioning her name. Quite possibly women poets preferred not to give their names because to do so would be immodest. Only one song, "*Sīta Mēlukolupu,*" mentions its author's name: Kurumaddali Venkatadasu, a man. Gopalakrishnamurti thinks that two other songs, "Laṅkāyāgamu" and "Laṅkāsārathi," were also composed by men, because men as well as women sing them.

9. See Gopalakrishnamurti's introduction to *Strīla Rāmāyaṇapu Pāṭalu,* ix–x.

10. Apparently this was the practice in premodern Andhra; it is attested in carv-

ings on temple carts and *kalamkāri* cloth paintings.

11. In another song, also with a "locked out" theme, it is Rāma's turn to be locked out and Sītā refuses to open the door for him. See M. N. Srinivas, "Some Telugu Folk Songs," *Journal of the University of Bombay* 13, no. 1 (July 1944): 65–86, and no. 4 (January 1945): 15–29. See David Shulman, "Battle as Metaphor in Tamil Folk and Classical Traditions," in *Another Harmony: New Essays on the Folklore of India*, ed. Stuart H. Blackburn and A. K. Ramanujan (Berkeley and Los Angeles: University of California Press, 1986), 105–30, for a study of this song in a different perspective.

12. In reality, the mother-in-law is often a hindrance to the union of wife and husband. Women's folksongs make many references to quarrels between mother-in-law and daughter-in-law.

13. Again, this motif is not unknown in literary *Rāmāyaṇas:* for example, the Bengali *Rāmāyaṇa* of Kṛttivāsa tells a similar story. Interestingly, many of the themes in the women's *Rāmāyaṇas* are similar to ones found in Jain versions. It is possible that the Jain versions were popular with Telugu Brahmin women, or, alternatively, that the Jain *Rāmāyaṇa* authors borrowed from the women's versions—or both. At this stage of our research, it is difficult to tell for sure.

14. In another version, Rāma suggests that he will serve Lakṣmaṇa in another birth; for now, it would be improper for an older brother to serve a younger one. Thus, in the next avatar, Rāma (i.e., Viṣṇu) is born as Kṛṣṇa and Lakṣmaṇa as Balarāma, Kṛṣṇa's older brother—so Lakṣmaṇa now receives Rāma's services. (I am grateful to Jaya Prabha for this information.)

15. For information on castes among whom widow remarriage is permitted, see V. Narayana Rao, "Epics and Ideologies: Six Telugu Folk Epics," in *Another Harmony*, ed. Blackburn and Ramanujan, 131–64.

16. The reason why Srīrāma here stands for Sītā is unknown to me.

17. In Sanskrit the name is Rāghava; Bharta and Śatrīka are Bharata and Śatrughna; Kaika is Kaikeyī; and Saumitri is Sumitrā. (Such adaptations of Sanskrit names are common in the dialects of the castes described here.) *Maridi* is a Telugu kinship term for a husband's younger brother.

18. Edwin Ardener, "Belief and the Problem of Women" and "The Problem Revisited," both in *Perceiving Women*, ed. Shirley Ardener (London: Dent, 1975), 1–17 and 19–27, respectively.

19. Ramaraju, however, comments that the events in the later part of the song "Kuśalvula Yuddhamu" are "blemished by impropriety" (*anaucitīdoṣaduṣitamulu*), apparently referring to the harsh words Lava and Kuśa speak against their father, Rāma: *Telugujānapadageyasāhityamu*, 117.

SEVEN

The Raja's New Clothes: Redressing Rāvaṇa in *Meghanādavadha Kāvya*

Clinton Seely

Michael Madhusudan Dutt (1824–1873) stated quite candidly:

> People here grumble that the sympathy of the Poet in Meghanad is with the Raksasas. And that is the real truth. I despise Ram and his rabble, but the idea of Ravan elevates and kindles my imagination; he was a grand fellow.[1]

This confession—really more a proud declaration—appears in a letter to Raj Narain Bose during the period when Dutt was writing his magnum opus, *Meghanādavadha Kāvya* (The slaying of Meghanāda), a poem retelling in nine cantos an episode from the *Rāmāyaṇa*, composed in Bengali and published in 1861. Unlike more traditional Rāma tales, the poem begins in medias res and focuses on Rāvaṇa's son Meghanāda, telling of his third and final fight in defense of the *rākṣasa* clan, his demise, and his obsequies. If one analyzes Dutt's characters closely, one finds that the main protagonists—Rāma, Lakṣmaṇa, and Rāvaṇa—are consonant with those characters as found in the most widely known Bengali *Rāmāyaṇa*, composed in the fifteenth century by Kṛttivāsa. Likewise, the events are fundamentally those narrated in one portion of Kṛttivāsa's *Rāmāyaṇa*: Rāvaṇa's two sons, Vīrabāhu and Meghanāda, are slain, the latter by Lakṣmaṇa; Rāvaṇa slays Lakṣmaṇa; Lakṣmaṇa, with help of a special herb procured by Hanumān, is revived. Nothing in *Meghanādavadha Kāvya* leads the reader to assume any other conclusion than that Rāvaṇa will eventually die at the hands of Rāma, as happens in the *Rāmāyaṇa*. But despite Dutt's rather remarkable adherence to traditional characterizations and events (remarkable, given his declared contempt for Rāma and his rabble), his poem engenders in the reader a response vastly different from that produced by the more traditional Rāma story. Nirad C. Chaudhuri may have put it most succinctly:

> We regarded the war between Rama and Ravana, described in the *Ramayana*, as another round in the eternal struggle between right and wrong, good and evil. We took Rama as the champion of good and the Demon King Ravana as the champion of evil, and delighted in the episode of Hanumana the Monkey burning Lanka, the golden city of Ravana. But Dutt would be shocking and perplexing us by his all too manifest sympathy for the Demon King, by his glorification of the whole tribe of demons, and his sly attempts to show Rama and his monkey followers in a poor light. . . . He had read Homer and was very fond of him, and it was the Homeric association which was making him represent a war which to us was as much a struggle between opposites and irreconcilables as a war between rivals and equals. When we were thinking of demons and of gods (for Rama was a god, and incarnation of Vishnu himself), Dutt was thinking of the Trojans and the Achaeans. Ravana was to him another Priam, Ravana's son Meghanad a second Hector, and Ravana's city, which to us was the Citadel of Evil, was to Dutt a second Holy Troy.[2]

If both the characterizations and the events in Dutt's poem correspond, by and large, to the *Rāmāyaṇa*'s core story, how did Dutt manage to "shock" and "perplex" people such as Chaudhuri? Other readers, moreover, take an even more extreme position and conclude that Dutt did not render Rāma and Rāvaṇa as equals (as is the case with the *Iliad*'s arch foes, Achilles and Hector) but reversed their conventional roles altogether, fashioning Rāvaṇa as the hero—the epitome of the sympathetic and respected raja, beloved by his subjects, as well as a devoted brother, husband, and father.[3] How can a work that purports to have as its template a rather predictable story skew the reader's perception of its protagonists so effectively? The answer is complex, for the talented and skillful Dutt employed various literary strategies to accomplish his ends. Elsewhere I have discussed how Dutt used similes to subvert the reader's preconceptions about the traditional epic tale by consistently aligning the *rākṣasas* with various heroes of Hindu Indian literature. By the process of elimination Rāma and Lakṣmaṇa, the nominal heroes of the *Rāmāyaṇa*, become associated with the opposers of these heroic exemplars. In what follows, I extend my earlier argument, moving from the level of simile to that of storytelling, and argue that Dutt's epic poem tells not one tale but four tales simultaneously, with the three subordinate stories—three of the most prominent tales in Bengali Hinduism—running counter to and subtly undermining the dominant Rāma story.[4] As this essay's title suggests, at one level *Meghanādavadha Kāvya* is a tale about the invisible, almost subliminal, cloaking of Rāvaṇa in the finery of heroism, while "Ram and his rabble" go about stripped of their traditional garb of glory. But first a bit of background for those unfamiliar with Michael Madhusudan Dutt and Bengal of the nineteenth century. And like Dutt's opus, we begin at a beginning, but not necessarily the beginning.

BACKGROUND: MULTIPLE TRADITIONS

In 1816 a group of the leading Indian residents of Calcutta established Hindoo College, which opened its doors to Hindu students the following year, expressly "to instruct the sons of the Hindoos in the European and Asiatic languages and sciences."[5] Hindoo College proved to be the intellectual incubator for an amorphous group known as Young Bengal—youths eager to assimilate new and progressive ideas as well as to denounce what they viewed as superstitious, obscurant practices among their fellow Hindus. Starting in 1833, when he was nine years old, Dutt attended the junior department of this college.[6] He had been born in a village in Jessore district (now in Bangladesh) into a fairly well-to-do Hindu family. Dutt's father commanded Persian, still the official language of British India's judicial system, and was employed in Calcutta's law courts. It was to Calcutta that the senior Dutt brought young Madhusudan for his education.

Even outside institutions of formal education, there was at this time considerable enthusiasm for English and for knowledge of all kinds. Various periodicals helped satisfy this need, as did a number of societies. One of these, the Society for the Acquisition of General Knowledge, came into being in 1838 with a membership of around 150 of Calcutta's educated elite, including one "Modoosooden" [Madhusudan] Dutt.[7] With such a supportive environment at Hindoo College and within the upper echelons of society (epitomized by the Society), it is not surprising that Madhusudan Dutt began his literary career writing in the English language. English, after all, was the language of the literature he had been taught to respect, the literature for which he had cultivated a taste. As his letters to a classmate make clear, he dearly loved English literature and wanted fiercely to become a writer in English. Boldly he sent off some of his poetry to a couple of British journals, identifying himself to the editor of *Bentley's Miscellany*, London, in this way:

> I am a Hindu—a native of Bengal—and study English at the Hindu College in Calcutta. I am now in my eighteenth year,—"a child"—to use the language of a poet of your land, Cowley, "in learning but not in age."[8]

Of his fantasies there can be no doubt, as a letter to his friend Gour Dass Bysack reveals:

> I am reading Tom Moore's Life of my favourite Byron—a splendid book upon my word! Oh! how should I like to see you write my "Life" if I happen to be a great poet—which I am almost sure I shall be, if I can go to England.[9]

In 1843, the year after he wrote the above letters, Dutt went even further in his acceptance of things Occidental: he embraced Christianity, in the face of very strong opposition from his father. As a Christian, Dutt could no longer attend Hindoo College and so transferred to Bishop's College, where his curriculum included Greek, Latin, and Hebrew.[10] At the start of 1848, he left Bengal suddenly, going south to Madras, where he secured employment as a schoolteacher and married, within his profession, the daughter of a Scottish indigo planter. Early on during his sojourn in Madras, the first signs appear of a shift in aspirations from that of becoming a noted poet in English to that of devoting his creative energies to writing in his mother tongue, Bengali.

A year after he arrived in Madras, Dutt published "The Captive Ladie," a very Byronic tale (the epigram for the first canto came from "The Giaour") in two cantos of well-modulated octosyllabic verse. One reviewer—J. E. D. Bethune, then president of the Council of Education, whose opinion Dutt personally sought—advised Dutt to give up writing in English and put his talents to work on Bengali literature. Wrote Bethune to Dutt's friend Bysack, who concurred and passed the advice on to Dutt:

> He might employ his time to better advantage than in writing English poetry. As an occasional exercise and proof of his proficiency in the language, such specimens may be allowed. But he could render far greater service to his country and have a better chance of achieving a lasting reputation for himself, if he will employ the taste and talents, which he has cultivated by the study of English, in improving the standard and adding to the stock of the poems of his own language, if poetry, at all events, he must write.[11]

Bethune went on to say that from what he could gather, the best examples of Bengali verse were "defiled by grossness and indecency." He suggested that a gifted poet would do well to elevate the tastes of his countrymen by writing original literature of quality in Bengali, or by translating. Dutt's biographer points out that such counsel was not reserved for Dutt alone but offered by Bethune to the assembled students of Krishnagar College.[12] Given Bethune's stance, it seems safe to assume that he was not simply judging literary merit in the case of "The Captive Ladie." (The piece is actually quite effective poetry.) Rather, he wanted to encourage the writing of Bengali literature, not just good literature per se. It should be noted, moreover, that the following year Bethune was among the founders of the Vernacular Literature Society.[13]

Bysack rephrased parts of that letter and then encouraged Dutt to heed Bethune's words:

> His advice is the best you can adopt. It is an advice that I have always given you and will din into your ears all my life. . . . We do not want another Byron or another Shelley in English; what we lack is a Byron or a Shelley in Bengali literature.[14]

The precise impact of Bethune's and Bysack's advice cannot be known with certainty. In an oft-cited letter to Bysack a month later, Dutt boasted of a nearly impossible daily regimen of language study: "Here is my routine; 6

to 8 Hebrew, 8 to 12 school, 12–2 Greek, 2–5 Telegu and Sanskrit, 5–7 Latin, 7–10 English." He added that "I devote several hours daily in Tamil" and concluded, with rhetorical panache: "Am I not preparing for the great object of embellishing the tongue of my fathers?"[15]

Earlier that year, though, even before Bethune's unexpected, unenthusiastic reception of "The Captive Ladie," the first signs of Dutt's impending conversion to his mother tongue for creative writing had already shown themselves, well before "The Captive Ladie" had even been published. He wrote Bysack, asking him to send from Calcutta two books. The books requested were the Bengali re-creations (not really translations) of India's Sanskrit epics and were among the first books printed in Bengali, published from the Baptist missionaries' press at Serampore. The stories and characters from these two epics, known to Dutt from childhood, provided about half the raw material for what he would write in Bengali, including *Meghanāda-vadha Kāvya.*

In 1856, at the age of thirty-two, Dutt returned to Calcutta. Between 1858 and 1862, when he finally got an opportunity to go to England (to study law), Dutt wrote and published in Bengali five plays, three narrative poems, and a substantial collection of lyrics organized around the Rādhā-Kṛṣṇa theme. Along with all this, he found time to translate three plays from Bengali into English.

By the latter half of the nineteenth century, the original ideals of the Young Bengal group—an earnest, enlightened quest for knowledge coupled with a rejection of what they viewed as demeaning superstition—had been misinterpreted by some to mean aping the British and flouting social norms. In particular, patronizing dancing girls, meat-eating, and the drinking of alcohol (taboo among devout Hindus), along with speaking a modicum of English, came to symbolize for some their "enlightenment." Quite otherwise was Dutt's embrace of things Occidental. He had a good liberal education, was a practiced writer (although much of that practice had been in English), and had drunk deeply from European and Indian literature. Of a fellow writer Dutt wrote in 1860:

> Byron, Moore and Scott form the highest Heaven of poetry in his estimation. I wish he would travel further. He would then find what "hills peep o'er hills"—what "Alps on Alps arise!" As for me, I never read any poetry except that of Valmiki, Homer, Vyasa, Virgil, Kalidas, Dante (in translation), Tasso (Do) and Milton. These *kavikulaguru* [master poets] ought to make a fellow a first rate poet—if Nature has been gracious to him.[16]

There was little or no doubt in his mind that in his case Nature had indeed been kind. And by the end of the 1850s he felt himself prepared "for the great object of embellishing the tongue of my fathers." The pattern—of beginning one's literary life writing in English and then switching to one's mother tongue—was not an uncommon one. R. Parthasarathy, himself an Indian poet who also writes in English (not his mother tongue), refers to Dutt as "the paradigm of the Indian poet writing in English . . . torn by the tensions of this 'double tradition.'"[17] But it was in Bengali that Dutt made his lasting literary contributions, foremost among them *Meghanādavadha Kāvya*.

THE TEXT: EPIC DEPARTURES

To reiterate, *Meghanādavadha Kāvya* tells of the third and decisive encounter between Rāvaṇa's son and Rāma's forces, wherein Meghanāda is slain by Rāma's brother Lakṣmaṇa. In the first of his nine cantos, Dutt introduces us to Rāvaṇa and Meghanāda on the day prior to the slaying; at the epic's conclusion, Rāvaṇa performs Meghanāda's obsequies, a scene that dramatically unifies Dutt's narrative while also foreshadowing the closure of the *Rāmāyaṇa*'s larger conflict, Rāma and Rāvaṇa's battle over Sītā. The reader can assume that events following Meghanāda's demise will largely correspond to those found in the traditional *Rāmāyaṇa*, since Dutt's narrative throughout has conformed in essence to that epic. But Rāma's story is merely the warp, if you will, of Dutt's poem; three other tales form the woof of this *Rāmāyaṇa* fabric, interweaving with Rāma's tale to create texture and, most importantly, to subvert the main narrative's purport—the aggrandizement of Rāma.

Complex narrative structuring was by no means introduced into Indian literature by Dutt. Sanskrit boasts a type of multisemic narrative which, if read one way, tells a certain tale (of Kṛṣṇa, for instance) and, read another way, tells a different story (of Rāma, for example). The two—or more—tales are simultaneously present in the same text, but, depending on choices the reader makes, one or the other story becomes manifest. Sanskrit, by its very nature, allows for ambiguous reading, and certain poets exploited that ambiguity for artistic effect. Owing to euphonic assimilation (*sandhi*), word boundaries can become difficult to discern. A string of phonemes can be variously divided to produce diverse words; different parsings of a sentence can thus produce diverse readings. On the simplest level, to take an example from the *Rāmāyaṇa* itself, we have the mantra-like utterance by Ratnākara, a thief who, thanks to the purifying nature of a spell, becomes Vālmīki, devotee of Rāma and author of the *Rāmāyaṇa*. A penitent Ratnākara is directed to chant the name of Rāma, but he demurs, claiming he is too vile a sinner. So Ratnākara is instructed to speak the word *marā*, meaning dead. By chanting *marā marā* continuously—*marāmarāmarā*—Ratnākara does in fact say Rāma's name, by virtue of the contiguity of the two phonemes *rā* and *ma*. Divide the phonemes one way and one gets "dead"; divide them another way and Rāma springs to life.

In his survey of Sanskrit literature, A. B. Keith mentions somewhat more sophisticated examples. In a poem entitled the *Rāghavapāṇḍavīya* "we are told simultaneously the stories of the *Rāmāyaṇa* and the *Mahābhārata*," while another work, the *Rasikarañjana*, "read one way, gives an erotic poem, in another, a eulogy of asceticism." And yet a third narrative, the *Rāghavapāṇḍavīyayādavīya*, narrates the tales of Rāma, of Nala, and of the *Bhāgavata Purāṇa* simultaneously, using the same phonemes in the same order.[18]

Written Bengali, in which word boundaries are more recognizable and permanent, does not lend itself as readily as Sanskrit to such linguistic virtuosity. Though individual words may, apropos of *kāvya* or poetic literature, have more than one meaning, whole sentences or paragraphs cannot be construed to contain certain words in one reading and different words in another. Nevertheless, in the tradition of his Sanskrit poetic forefathers, Dutt creates in *Meghanādavadha Kāvya* a multistory narrative. On the denotative level, it is simply an episode out of the *Rāmāyaṇa*, but read another way, primarily through its similes, *Meghanādavadha Kāvya* dons the clothing of Kṛṣṇa to tell Kṛṣṇa's tale. Read even differently, Dutt's poem alludes to the *Mahābhārata* and its internecine struggle between Kurus and Pāṇḍavas. And read from yet one more perspective, the fabric of *Meghanādavadha Kāvya* glitters with the myth of Durgā and her annual autumnal visit to Bengal, when Bengali Hindus celebrate Durgā Pūjā [worship], the grandest public festival of the Hindu year.

All the subsidiary interwoven stories are present in one and the same reading of *Meghanādavadha Kāvya*, albeit in far less narrative detail than Rāma's story, just as the threads in fine cloth can be discerned but tend to blend into the total design. Because all are manifest and thus not only can but must be read and apprehended simultaneously, each tale affects the reader's understanding of all the other tales. As one reads of Meghanāda's demise and Rāma's impending victory—a joyous event for any Hindu—one also reads the more dolorous tale of Kṛṣṇa, who grew up in bucolic Vraja, delighting the cowherd maidens, but who then had to leave, never to return. The conflation of characters, in this case Kṛṣṇa and Meghanāda, serves to confuse the reader's response: is the reader made uncomfortable by the departure of Kṛṣṇa or by the death of Meghanāda? The resulting subversion of the main story by a secondary tale leads at least some readers, as Chaudhuri attests, to react with shock and perplexity. Have the *rākṣasas* been glorified beyond what they are in more traditional *Rāmāyaṇas*? Well, no, not directly. Has Rāma been shown in a poor light? Not exactly. These characters are precisely what they have always been. But Dutt's submerged tale of Kṛṣṇa has complicated matters for the reader. In similar fashion, as one reads the episode drawn from the *Rāmāyaṇa*, one is also presented with a vignette from the *Mahābhārata* as well as the mythic tale of Durgā, each bittersweet stories, each in its own way countering the emotional impact of *Meghanādavadha Kāvya*'s main story line.

Let us examine the three substrata stories more closely. The tale of Kṛṣṇa is told entirely through similes, all of which compare him with Meghanāda. These similes are drawn from two periods in his life. According to his hagiography, Kṛṣṇa was born in Mathura (also called Madhupura) but taken immediately after his birth to Vraja (Gokula) to escape the wrath of King Kaṃsa, his uncle. In Vraja, by the banks of the Yamunā, Kṛṣṇa grows up to become the lover of the *gopīs*, the local cowherds' wives, Rādhā chief among them. There comes a time, however, when the idyll must end. Kṛṣṇa leaves Vraja and returns to Mathura, there to slay his wicked uncle. That done, he moves on to the city of Dvaraka. But for Bengali Vaiṣṇavas, it is the time Kṛṣṇa spent in Vraja with his *gopī* lovers that is most cherished.

Dutt's Kṛṣṇa similes are by no means randomly scattered throughout his poem. In the first half of *Meghanādavadha Kāvya*, while Meghanāda is still living with his fellow *rākṣasas*, the Kṛṣṇa similes refer to Vraja in the happy days when the deity resided there. Early in the first canto, for example, a passage describing Rāvaṇa's sumptuous court runs: "Constant spring breezes delicately wafted scents, gaily/transporting waves of chirping, ah yes! enchanting as the/flute's melodic undulations in the pleasure groves of/ Gokula."[19] Toward the end of the same canto, we find Meghanāda, first compared to the moon (lord of night) and then to Kṛṣṇa (the herdsman), at ease. He has defeated Rāma in open warfare not once but twice and assumes, reasonably enough, that the *rākṣasas* have won the war.

> That best of champions dallied with
> the maids of shapely bodies, just as the lord of night sports
> with Dakṣa's daughters, or, O Yamunā, daughter of the
> sun, as the herdsman danced beneath *kadamba* trees, flute to
> lips, sporting with the cowherds' wives upon your splendid banks!
> (1.648–53)

Alerted to the danger facing his father (for Rāma is not dead as the *rākṣasas* suppose), Meghanāda leaves his wife behind in that country retreat and returns to the walled city and his father's court. We see in the opening lines of canto 3 that young Pramīlā—who is likened to Rādhā, the maid of Vraja—does not react to the separation from her beloved husband with equanimity.

> In Pramoda Park wept Pramīlā, youthful Dānava
> daughter, pining for her absent husband. That tearful moon-
> faced one paced incessantly about the flower garden
> like the maid of Vraja, ah, when she, in Vraja's flower
> groves, failed to find her yellow-clad Kṛṣṇa standing beneath
> *kadamba* trees with flute to lips. That lovelorn lady would
> from time to time go inside her home, then out, just like a
> pigeon, inconsolable in her empty pigeon house. (3.1–9)

Donning warrior's garb, Pramīlā marches with her legion of women (a borrowing by Dutt from the *Aśvamedhaparva* of the Bengali *Mahābhārata*) through Rāma's ranks—Rāma grants her passage—and rejoins her husband in the walled city. Then in canto 5, Meghanāda is awakened by doves on the morning of the day he is to do battle once again. He wakes Pramīlā, kissing her closed eyelids: "Startled, that woman rose in haste—as do the cowherds' wives/at the flute's mellifluous sounds" (5.387–88). Later that same morning he leaves Pramīlā, who watches him walk away from her for, unbeknownst to her, the last time.

> Wiping her eyes, that chaste wife departed—as cowherds' wives,
> about to lose their lover, bid farewell to Mādhava
> on Yamunā's shores, then empty-hearted return to their
> own empty homes—so, weeping still, she entered her abode. (5.604–7)

Just as Kṛṣṇa (Mādhava) left pleasant Vraja to slay the evil Kaṃsa, so Meghanāda leaves, intending to slay Rāma. Neither one will return. Kṛṣṇa goes to Dvaraka; Meghanāda dies. The remaining two Kṛṣṇa similes are set during the time after Kṛṣṇa has gone away.

Meghanāda is slain in canto 6. Though at that moment his death is known only to Lakṣmaṇa and Vibhīṣaṇa, it affects the three individuals emotionally closest to him: his father's crown falls to the ground; his wife's right eye flutters, an inauspicious sign; and his mother faints. "And," adds Dutt, "asleep in mothers' laps, babies cried/a sorrowful wail as Vraja children cried when precious/Śyāma [Kṛṣṇa] darkened Vraja, leaving there for Madhupura"(6.638–41). It is not until the ninth and final canto that another Kṛṣṇa simile occurs, once more depicting Vraja after Kṛṣṇa's departure. As the funeral cortege for Meghanāda files out of the walled city of Lanka toward the sea, "that city, now emptied, grew dark like Gokula devoid of Śyāma" (9.308–9). Again, the Kṛṣṇa woof, created here with similes, is woven into the *Rāmāyaṇa* story. If the two tales typically evoked the same audience response, then the anticipated reaction would simply be intensified. But in this case, the traditional audience responses are discordant: sadness at the loss of Kṛṣṇa; glee over Rāma's triumph.

Similar subversion of the expected reader response to Rāma's victory is fostered by the *Mahābhārata* woof. The *Mahābhārata* is a compendium of stories, a far more eclectic text than the *Rāmāyaṇa*; the many *Mahābhārata* similes in *Meghanādavadha Kāvya* are drawn from diverse episodes. One set of these similes, however, focuses on the specific tale of the ignominious slaughter of the Pāṇḍavas' sons by Aśvatthāman. This particular episode takes place at the end of the war, after the outcome is clear. Although both sides have sustained heavy losses, the five Pāṇḍavas have won. The Kaurava Duryodhana, the great enemy of the Pāṇḍavas, lies dying, his hip broken. At this point Aśvatthāman, a cohort of Duryodhana's, decides to slip into the Pāṇḍava camp and slay the five Pāṇḍava warriors out of spite. Under cover of darkness, Aśvatthāman and his accomplices proceed to the victors' bivouac, at the gate of which stands the god Śiva, as Sthāṇu (a veritable pillar). Aśvatthāman manages to get by Śiva and penetrate the enemies' camp. Once inside, he kills those he takes to be the senior Pāṇḍavas but who are in fact their five young sons. Pleased with himself, Aśvatthāman hastens to tell the senior Kaurava, Duryodhana, what he has done.

The first canto of *Meghanādavadha Kāvya* contains a reference to the encampment of the Pāṇḍavas, couched in a series of similes describing Rāvaṇa's grand court. "Before its doors/paced the guard, a redoubtable figure, like god Rudra [Śiva]/trident clutched, before the Pāṇḍavas' encampment's gateway" (1.53–55). This same *Mahābhārata* episode is alluded to again in canto 5 when Lakṣmaṇa, preparing to slay Meghanāda, must first proceed to the Caṇḍī temple situated in a nearby forest. As he approaches, his way is blocked by a huge Śiva, whom he must pass in order to enter the woods. Lakṣmaṇa circumvents Śiva and overcomes several other obstacles in his path before successfully reaching the temple. It is there that Lakṣmaṇa is granted the boon of invisibility for the following day so that he may enter the *rākṣasas*' walled city undetected. Just as Aśvatthāman had first to bypass Śiva before entering the Pāṇḍavas' camp under cover of darkness in order to slay what turned out to be their sons, so Lakṣmaṇa must get past Śiva, then penetrate under the cloak of invisibility the *rākṣasas*' stronghold to slay Rāvaṇa's son Meghanāda.

In the very next canto, Lakṣmaṇa does slip into the *rākṣasas*' city and kill Meghanāda. As Lakṣmaṇa and his accomplice flee the walled city, Dutt describes their action with a combination of two similes, one natural, the other based on the same episode from the *Mahābhārata:*

> The two left hurriedly, just as a hunter, when he slays
> the young of a tigress in her absence, flees for his life
> with wind's speed, panting breathlessly, lest that ferocious beast
> should suddenly attack, wild with grief at finding her cubs
> lifeless! or, as champion Aśvatthāman, son of Droṇa,
> having killed five sleeping boys inside the Pāṇḍava camp
> in dead of night, departed going with the quickness of
> a heart's desire, giddy from the thrill and fear, to where lay
> Kuru monarch Duryodhana, his thigh broken in the
> Kurukṣetra War. (6.704–13)

And like Aśvatthāman, who ran to tell Duryodhana what he had done, Lakṣmaṇa runs to Rāma to bring him news of the slaying. Here again, two tales simultaneously told, one from the *Mahābhārata* and the other from the *Rāmāyaṇa*, produce contrary effects: delight when Lakṣmaṇa slays Meghanāda; disgust at Aśvatthāman's heinous act. Small wonder the reader is perplexed.

Yet a third tale is woven into *Meghanādavadha Kāvya*, that concerning goddess Durgā's annual *pūjā*. According to myth, on the sixth day of the waxing moon of the autumn month of Āśvin, Durgā arrives at her natal home, there to stay until the tenth day, when she must return to her husband Śiva's home on Mount Kailasa. Her short visit is the occasion for Bengal's greatest public Hindu festival, the Durgā Pūjā, during which she is worshiped in the form of the ten-armed goddess who slays Mahiṣāsura, the buffalo demon. On that tenth day, called the *vijayā* (victorious) tenth, she as the victorious one is bid farewell for another year as she leaves to rejoin her spouse. Durgā's departure is, as departures tend to be, a somewhat bittersweet affair, for although she wants to return to her husband's side, she is sad to leave her parents and friends. Her mythic parents, Menakā and Himālaya, are loath to let their daughter go. The eighteenth-century Bengali poet Ram Prasad Sen, a devotee of the mother goddess in all her sundry manifestations, sang eloquently and passionately of the plight of Menakā (or any mother), who had to say goodbye to her daughter for yet another year. Those songs, called *vijayā* songs, were no doubt sung in Dutt's time and can still be heard today. Dutt captures this bittersweetness, setting an unexpected tone for his poem in the very first canto when he describes Lakṣmī—she who must leave Lanka—with a simile drawn from the Durgā Pūjā. Lakṣmī is the goddess of good fortune; as Rājalakṣmī, she is the raja's luck or fortune. Lanka's grandeur (a feature common to all *Rāmāyaṇas*, not just Dutt's) attests to the presence of good fortune in Rāvaṇa's realm, but with the advent of Rāma, Lakṣmī must soon leave Lanka.

> With face averted, moon-faced Indirā [Lakṣmī] sat
> glumly—as sat Umā [Durgā] of the moonlike countenance, cheeks
> cradled in her palms, when the tenth day of the waxing moon
> of Durgā Pūjā dawned, with pangs of separation at
> her home in Gaur [Bengal]. (1.502–5)

In one way or another both the warp and woof of *Meghanādavadha Kāvya* narrate departures and death. Kṛṣṇa left Vraja. The Pāṇḍavas won the war but lost their sons and kinsmen. Every year, on the tenth day of the waxing moon of Āśvin, Durgā must depart. And Meghanāda is slain. The first three are attended by sorrow; the fourth should be a cause for joy, were it not for the subversion wrought by the other three.

In the concluding canto, Dutt again accentuates the Durgā Pūjā theme. As the cortege exits the city gates, Pramīlā's horse is led riderless while Meghanāda's war chariot goes empty:

> Out came the chariots moving slowly, among them that
> best of chariots, rich-hued, lightning's sparkle on its wheels,
> flags, the colors found in Indra's bow, on its pinnacles—
> but this day it was devoid of splendor, like the empty
> splendor of an idol's frame without its lifelike painted
> image, at the end of an immersion ceremony. (9.251–56)

On the tenth lunar day of the Durgā Pūjā the iconic representation of the goddess, in all her ten-armed splendor, slaying the buffalo demon is immersed in the Ganges. It is then that the life-force of the deity, which entered the idol several days before and has been present throughout the celebrations, leaves and travels back to Mount Kailasa. The images are made from straw tied around bamboo frames; the straw is covered with clay, which when dry is painted, and the image meticulously clothed to represent the supreme goddess. When such an icon is immersed in the river, the clay eventually washes away, leaving a stick and straw figure exposed. Just so appears Meghanāda's chariot without its vital warrior.

When the funeral procession reaches the seashore, a pyre is built of fragrant sandalwood, onto which is placed Meghanāda's corpse. Pramīlā mounts the pyre and sits at her dead husband's feet—the decorated pyre being likened to the goddess's altar during Durgā Pūjā (9.375–76). From Mount Kailasa Śiva now commands Agni, god of fire, to transport the couple to him: like Durgā after the immersion of her icon, Meghanāda and Pramīlā will travel directly to Śiva. Dutt invites—nay, forces—his reader to feel toward Meghanāda and Pramīlā what they feel toward Durgā on the day of her departure. The loss of a traditional enemy becomes, by the subversive power of Durgā's tale, a cause for lamentation.

When the funeral fire is finally out, the *rākṣasas* purify the site with Ganges water and erect there a temple. To wash away some of the pollution which attends death, they then bathe in the sea. Dutt concludes his epic poem as follows:

> After bathing in waters of the sea, those *rākṣasas*
> now headed back toward Lanka, wet still with water of their
> grief—it was as if they had immersed the image of the
> goddess on the lunar tenth day of the Durgā Pūjā;
> then Lanka wept in sorrow seven days and seven nights. (9.440–43)

The Durgā Pūjā similes in the first and final cantos not only lend symmetry to *Meghanādavadha Kāvya* but also, more than any of the other tales, presage Rāvaṇa's death. In Bengal, it is the Durgā Pūjā that Hindus celebrate during the waxing Āśvin moon, coming to an end on the tenth of that month, the victorious tenth. In some parts of India, however, the Rām Līlā, a reenacting of Rāma's divine play is performed in that season, culminating on the very same tenth of Āśvin with the slaying of Rāvaṇa by Rāma.[20] Thus, the Durgā Pūjā similes in Dutt's text not only relate in part the tale of Durgā's annual leaving but also imply the story of Rāma's victory over Rāvaṇa, for Durgā's and Rāma's tale occur simultaneously in mythic time. If the substratum story, Durgā's tale and her departure, effect a bittersweet response, then the elation at Rāma's triumph—when the two tales are perforce read together—cannot but be vitiated. That was unquestionably Dutt's intent, for, as we recall, he had declared his dislike for Rāma and his admiration for Rāma's foe. But dislike Rāma or not, Dutt kept his Rāma character true to the *Rāmāyaṇa* tradition, preferring to let his similes and simultaneously told secondary tales complicate his reader's response.

THE RECEPTION: MIXED BLESSINGS

Different audiences received *Meghanādavadha Kāvya* differently, though in general it met with approbation and congratulations. Dutt himself, no disinterested judge, tells us through his letters that his poem was gaining acceptance almost daily.

> The poem is rising into splendid popularity. Some say it is better than Milton—but that is all bosh—nothing can be better than Milton; many say it licks Kalidasa; I have no objection to that. I don't think it impossible to equal Virgil, Kalidasa and Tasso. Though glorious, still they are mortal poets; Milton is divine.
>
> Many Hindu Ladies, I understand, are reading the book and crying over it. You ought to put your wife in the way of reading the verse.[21]

Even before the entire work had been published (cantos 1 through 5 appeared first), a man of letters of the day and patron of the arts, Kali Prosanna Singh, understood the importance of Dutt's accomplishment and felt it essential that Dutt should be honored. This was done under the aegis of the Vidyotsahinī Sabhā (Society for Those Eager for Knowledge), one of various private organizations formed during the nineteenth century by educated Bengalis in Calcutta. Singh's letter of invitation to a small circle of guests read in part:

> Intending to present Mr. Michael M. S. Dutt with a silver trifle as a mite of encouragement for having introduced with success the Blank verse into our language, I have been advised to call a meeting of those who might take a lively interest in the matter.[22]

Following the ceremony, Dutt wrote to Raj Narain Bose:

> You will be pleased to hear that not very long ago the Vidyotsahini Sabha—and the President Kali Prosanna Singh of Jorasanko, presented me with a splendid silver claret jug. There was a great meeting and an address in Bengali. Probably you have read both address and reply in the vernacular papers.
>
> On the whole the book is doing well. It has roused curiosity. Your friend Babu Debendra Nath Tagore [Rabindranath's father], I hear, is quite taken up with it. S— told me the other day that he (Babu D.) is of opinion that few Hindu authors can "stand near this man," meaning your fat friend of No. 6 Lower Chitpur Road [where Dutt resided], and "that his imagination goes as far as imagination can go."[23]

And still later, writing to the same friend:

> Talking about Blank-Verse, you must allow me to give you a jolly little anecdote. Some days ago I had occasion to go to the Chinabazar. I saw a man seated in a shop and deeply poring over Meghanad. I stepped in and asked him what he was reading. He said in very good English—
>
> "I am reading a new poem, Sir!" "A poem!" I said, "I thought that there was no poetry in your language." He replied—"Why, Sir, here is poetry that would make any nation proud."[24]

And again:

> I have not yet heard a single line in Meghanad's disfavour. The great Jotindra has only said that he is sorry poor Lakshman is represented as killing Indrojit in cold blood and when unarmed. But I am sure the poem has many faults. What human production has not?[25]

Jotindra Mohan Tagore's reservation aside, few if any readers (and it should be noted that "readers" implies the educated elite who could in fact read this erudite work) took umbrage at Dutt's iconoclasm. As Pramathanath Bisi, a contemporary literary scholar, tells us:

> Disgust toward "Ram and his rabble," the sparking of one's imagination at the idea of Rāvaṇa and Meghanāda—these attitudes were not peculiar to Dutt. Many of his contemporaries had the very same feelings. What was native seemed despicable; what was English, grand and glorious. Such was the general temperament. . . . Dutt cast Rāvaṇa's character as representative of the English-educated segment of society.[26]

We may not choose to accept all of Bisi's statement at face value, but history forces us to conclude that Dutt's attitudes were indeed not peculiar to him alone. *Meghanādavadha Kāvya* did not go unappreciated: by the time Dutt died in 1873, his epic poem had gone through six editions.

Four years after Dutt's death, Romesh Chunder Dutt (not a relative), one of the most respected intellectuals of the day, wrote in his *The Literature of Bengal*:

> Nothing in the entire range of the Bengali literature can approach the sublimity of the Meghanad Badh Kabya which is a masterpiece of epic poetry. The reader who can feel, and appreciate the sublime, will rise from a study of this great work with mixed sensations of veneration and awe with which few poets can inspire him, and will candidly pronounce the bold author to be indeed a genius of a very high order, second only to the highest and greatest that have ever lived, like Vyasa, Valmiki or Kalidasa, Homer, Dante or Shakespear.[27]

As might be expected, however, over the years not everyone has been enamored with *Meghanādavadha Kāvya*. Rabindranath Tagore, born the year it came out, was one of Dutt's harshest critics. Dutt's "epic" was an epic (*mahākāvya*) in name only, he declared. Tagore found nothing elevating or elevated about Dutt's characters or in his depiction of the events. There was no immortality, as he put it, in any of the protagonists, not even in Meghanāda himself; none of these characters, he contended, would live with us forever.[28] Tagore published those opinions when he was twenty-one. Later, in his reminiscences, he recanted:

> Earlier, with the audacity that accompanies youth, I had penned a scathing critique of *Meghanādavadha Kāvya*. Just as the juice of green mangos is sour—green criticism is acerbic. When other abilities are wanting, the ability to poke and scratch becomes accentuated. I too had scratched at this immortal poem in an effort to find some easy way to achieve my own immortality.[29]

But despite the retraction, Tagore never accepted Dutt fully. Edward Thompson, Tagore's English biographer, quotes Tagore as follows:

> "He was nothing of a Bengali scholar," said Rabindranath once, when we were discussing the Meghanadbadh; "he just got a dictionary and looked out all the sounding words. He had great power over words. But his style has not been repeated. It isn't Bengali."[30]

Whether something is or is not the genuine article, whether it is "really Bengali," has been for some time a criterion by which Bengali critics judge the artistic accomplishments of their fellow artists. Pramatha Chaudhuri, colleague of Tagore and editor of one of the most prestigious and avant-garde journals from the early decades of this century, *Sabuja Patra* (Green leaves), wrote in the initial issue of that magazine:

> Since the seeds of thought borne by winds from the Occident cannot take root firmly in our local soil, they either wither away or turn parasitic. It follows, then, that *Meghanādavadha Kāvya* is the bloom of a parasite. And though, like the orchid, its design is exquisite and its hue glorious, it is utterly devoid of any fragrance.[31]

But what Pramatha Chaudhuri looked upon as suspect has since come to be recognized as the normal state of affairs. As our colleague A. K. Ramanujan, a man of many literatures, has commented:

> After the nineteenth century, no significant Indian writer lacks any of the three traditions: the regional mother tongue, the pan-Indian (Sanskritic, and in the case of Urdu and Kashmiri, the Perso-Arabic as well), and the Western (mostly English). Poetic, not necessarily scholarly, assimilation of all these three resources in various individual ways seems indispensable.[32]

Perhaps Dutt was just a bit ahead of his time.

Attacked by Tagore and Pramatha Chaudhuri as un-Bengali, Dutt's poem has also been praised for—of all things—being in line with international communism. Since in *Meghanādavadha Kāvya* Rāma is more man than incarnation of Viṣṇu, Bengali Marxists lauded Dutt, in their underground publication *Mārksavādī* (The Marxist), for debunking religion and the gods.[33]

Though now, like Milton's *Paradise Lost*, read more as part of a university curriculum, as the first great modern work of Bengali literature, than as a best-seller, there was a day when *Meghanādavadha Kāvya* qualified as required reading for the educated Bengali-speaking public at large, the sine qua non of the cultured Bengali. Of Dutt's standing in Bengali literature, an assessment by Nirad C. Chaudhuri, though made some four decades ago, still applies today. "In addition to his historical importance," wrote Chaudhuri, "the absolute value of his poetry is also generally undisputed; only his reputation, like that of every great writer, has had its ebbs as well as tides, its ups and downs; and his most modern Bengali critics have tried to be as clever at his expense as the modern detractors of Milton."[34] Also generally undisputed has been the conclusion that Dutt's *rākṣasa* raja is decked out in some very regal new clothes. That this conclusion has been so widely accepted proves how deceiving appearances can be, for Rāvaṇa, in truth, wears no new attire. Instead, the master poet has slyly—to borrow Chaudhuri's term—woven his central *Rāmāyaṇa* episode so as to suggest heroic raiment for Rāvaṇa rather than for Rāma. Clothed in cunning finery, *Meghanādavadha Kāvya* presents a deceptive exterior. The raja—redressed though he may be—wears no new clothes, even though the reader sees what in fact is not there.

NOTES

1. Yogindranath Bose, *Māikela Madhusūdana Dattera jīvana-carita* (The life of Michael Madhusudan Dutt) (5th ed.; Calcutta: Chakravarti, Chatterjee, & Co., 1925), 489. We are most fortunate to have a sizable collection of Dutt's letters preserved for us by his friends and published in the above biography and, in expanded form, in Ksetra Gupta, ed., *Kavi Madhusūdana o tāṁra patrāvalī* (Poet Madhusudan and his letters) (Calcutta: Grantha Nilaya, 1963). Nearly all of these were written in English, as is the case with the one cited here; a rare few are in Bengali. We also know he wrote in Italian, to Satyendranath Tagore, because Dutt himself tells us so, and in French, while he lived at Versailles—one of these letters being to the king of Italy, on the occasion of Dante's sixth birth centenary.

2. Nirad C. Chaudhuri, *The Autobiography of an Unknown Indian* (New York: Macmillan, 1951), 188.

3. See, for instance, Mohitlal Majumdar, *Kavi Śrīmadhusūdana* (Poet Madhusudan) (3d ed.; Calcutta: Vidyodaya Library, 1975), 44–45; Nilima Ibrahim, *Bāṁlāra kavi Madhusūdana* (Bengal's poet Madhusudan) (3d ed.; Dhaka: Nawroz Kitabistana, 1978), 56; Suresh Candra Maitra, *Māikela Madhusūdana Datta: jīvana o sāhitya* (Michael Madhusudan Dutt: His life and literature) (Calcutta: Puthipatra, 1975), 192; and Mobasher Ali, *Madhusūdana o navajāgṛti* (Madhusudan and the Renaissance) (3d ed.; Dhaka: Muktadhara, 1981), 91.

4. Those interested in subversive similes and how Dutt used them might like to

read my "Homeric Similes, Occidental and Oriental: Tasso, Milton, and Bengal's Michael Madhusudan Dutt," *Comparative Literature Studies* 25, no. 1 (March 1988): 35–56.

5. Sushil Kumar De, *Bengali Literature in the Nineteenth Century, 1757–1857* (2d ed.; Calcutta: Firma K. L. Mukhopadhyay, 1962), 480.

6. The earliest biography of Dutt gives his age as "about thirteen" at the time he entered Hindoo College—in 1837, according to that source: Bose, *Jīvana-carita*, 25 and 48. An editor of Dutt's collected works cites a subsequent scholar's opinion—that the year was in fact 1833—and then notes that the college magazine dated 7 March 1834 mentions Dutt reading aloud at the college's awards ceremony: Ksetra Gupta, ed., *Madhusūdana racanāvalī* (The collected works of Madhusudan) (Calcutta: Sahitya Samsad, 1965), xi. Hindoo College was at that time divided into a junior and a senior school, the former admitting boys between the ages of eight and twelve. See *Asiatic Journal* (September–December 1832), 114–15; cited in Brajendranath Bandyopadhyay, ed., *Saṁvādapatre sekālera kathā* (From the periodicals of bygone days) (Calcutta: Bangiya-Sahitya-Parisad-Mandir, 1923), 2:15.

7. Goutam Chattopadhyay, ed., *Awakening in Bengal in Early Nineteenth Century (Selected Documents)* (Calcutta: Progressive Publishers, 1965), 1:lxi–lxvii.

8. Bose, *Jīvana-carita*, 114; letter dated October 1842.

9. Bose, *Jīvana-carita*, 60; letter to Gour Dass Bysack dated 25 November 1842.

10. Gupta, *Madhusūdana racanāvalī*, xiv.

11. Bose, *Jīvana-carita*, 159–60; letter of J. E. D. Bethune to Gour Dass Bysack dated 20 July 1849.

12. According to Bethune:

> If you do your duty, the English language will become to Bengal what, long ago, Greek and Latin were to England; and the ideas which you gain through English learning will, by your help, gradually be diffused by a vernacular literature through the masses of your countrymen . . . . [I have told] those young men in Calcutta, who have brought for my opinion, with intelligible pride, their English compositions in prose and verse . . . . [that they] would attain a more lasting reputation, either by original compositions in their own language, or by transfusing into it the master-pieces of English literature.

Quoted in Bose, *Jīvana-carita*, 160–61.

13. Nilmani Mukherjee, *A Bengali Zamindar: Jaykrishna Mukherjee of Uttarpara and His Times, 1808–1888* (Calcutta: Firma K. L. Mukhopadhyay, 1975), 169–70. The founders met in 1850; the Society came into being in 1851.

14. Bose, *Jīvana-carita*, 161–62; letter of Bysack to Dutt, undated.

15. Bose, *Jīvana-carita*, 182; letter to Bysack dated 18 August 1849.

16. Bose, *Jīvana-carita*, 322; letter to Raj Narain Bose dated 1 July 1860.

17. Quoted in Homi Bhabha, "Indo-Anglian Attitudes," *Times Literary Supplement*, 3 February 1978, 136.

18. A. Berriedale Keith, *A History of Sanskrit Literature* (London: Oxford University Press, 1920), 137–39.

19. Canto 1, lines 55–58; subsequent citations appear in the text. All translations of *Meghanādavadha Kāvya* are mine.

20. Although the length of the entire Rām Līlā performance varies in different

towns and villages, the crucial event, the slaying of Rāvaṇa, happens on the same day everywhere. See Norvin Hein, *The Miracle Plays of Mathura* (New Haven and London: Yale University Press, 1972), 76–77 and appendix.

21. Bose, *Jīvana-carita*, 480; letter to Raj Narain Bose, undated [1861].

22. Bandyopadhyay, ed., *Saṁvādapatre sekālera kathā*, 2:16.

23. Bose, *Jīvana-carita*, 480–81; letter to Raj Narain Bose, undated [1861].

24. Bose, *Jīvana-carita*, 487; letter undated [1861]. Dutt's metre in *Meghanādavadha Kāvya* and in his earlier, shorter work (which he referred to as an "epicling"), *Tilottamā sambhava* (The birth of Tilottama), is a blend of Milton and medieval Bengali's most common narrative verse structure, called *payāra*, a rhymed couplet of fourteen-foot lines, with partial caesura after the eighth foot in each line. In Dutt's supple hands, Milton's iambic pentameter gives way to *payāra*'s fourteen syllables, while *payāra*'s rhyming and eight-six scansion are sacrificed to the demands of Miltonic blank verse, replete with enjambment. To a friend, he wrote: "You want me to explain my system of versification for the conversion of your skeptical friend. I am sure there is very little in the system to explain; our language, as regards the doctrine of accent and quantity, is an 'apostate', that is to say, it cares as much for them as I do for the blessing of our Family-Priest! If your friends know English let them read the Paradise-Lost, and they will find how the verse, in which the Bengali poetaster writes, is constructed." Bose, *Jīvana-carita*, 320–21; letter to Raj Narain Bose dated 1 July 1860.

25. Bose, *Jīvana-carita*, 494; letter dated 29 August 1861. Jotindra Mohan Tagore may have been the first to take exception to the way Dutt has Lakṣmaṇa slay Meghanāda. Rather than engaging his adversary in open combat, Lakṣmaṇa enters by stealth the *rākṣasa*'s place of worship and fells an unarmed Meghanāda, who is doing *pūjā* to Agni at the time and would have become invincible had he been allowed to complete the ritual. Many critics have subsequently concurred with Jotindra Mohan Tagore that Dutt might have gone a bit too far by casting Lakṣmaṇa in this rather cowardly role. Dutt was, however, drawing on an aspect of the *Rāmāyaṇa* tradition here. Although Lakṣmaṇa does not slay Meghanāda by stealth in the *Rāmāyaṇa*, in Kṛttivāsa's telling of the tale, Hanumān travels to the netherworld and there is instructed by Māyā how, by stealth, to slay Mahirāvaṇa. Dutt has Māyā (also referred to as Mahāmāyā) instruct Lakṣmaṇa precisely how to vanquish his formidable opponent. Dutt thus borrowed a stratagem from Kṛttivāsa but had a different character (albeit still on Rāma's side) make use of it.

26. Pramathanath Bisi, *Bāṁlā sāhityera naranāri* (Men and women in Bengali literature) (Calcutta: Maitri, 1953; repr. 1966), 25.

27. AR CY DAE (Romesh Chunder Dutt), *The Literature of Bengal; Being an Attempt to Trace the Progress of the National Mind in Its Various Aspects, as Reflected in the Nation's Literature; from the Earliest Times to the Present Day; with Copious Extracts from the Best Writers* (Calcutta: I. C. Bose & Co., 1877), 176.

28. Rabindranath Tagore, "*Meghanādavadha kāvya*," in *Ravīndra-racanāvalī* (The collected works of Rabindranath Tagore) (Calcutta: Visvabharati, 1962), Addenda 2:78–79.

29. Tagore, *Jīvanasmṛti* (Reminiscences), in *Ravīndra-racanāvalī* (Calcutta: Visvabharati, 1944), 17:354.

30. Quoted in Buddhadeva Bose, "*Māikela*" (Michael), in his *Sāhityacarcā* (Literary studies) (Calcutta: Signet Press, 1954), 35.

31. Pramatha Chaudhuri, "*Sabuja patrera mukhapatra*" (Sabuj Patra's manifesto), in *Nānā-kathā* (Miscellany) (Calcutta: By the author, 3 Hastings Street, [1919]), 109–10.

32. A. K. Ramanujan, "On Bharati and His Prose Poems" (paper presented at the 16th annual conference on South Asia, Madison, Wisconsin, November 1987), 3.

33. *Mārksavādī* no. 5 (September[?] 1949): 132.

34. Chaudhuri, *The Autobiography of an Unknown Indian*, 183.

EIGHT

Creating Conversations: The Rāma Story as Puppet Play in Kerala

Stuart H. Blackburn

The Rāma story in India is an oral tradition. Although texts do stabilize certain variants, and may engender other variants, the diversity of the tradition—the many *Rāmāyaṇas*—is a function of the many genres, the many languages, and the many occasions on which the Rāma story is orally performed. By tale-tellers and epic-singers, temple pundits and schoolteachers, and any number of unknown tellers and tellings, the story is spoken, chanted, sung, mimed, retold, and explained. Several contributions to this volume draw attention to this variety of tellers and tellings, and implicitly to their audiences. Here, too, is diversity. The audience may be the immediate listeners, whose role in performance varies from that of active participant (as respondent to a spoken line) to silent spectator. Some audiences are physically absent, such as patrons, who are meant only to overhear the performance or learn of it later. The audience may also be a god or goddess, as when a text is ritually performed with no human onlookers. And combinations of these audiences often coexist in a single performance event.[1]

Audiences seem especially important in the Rāma story tradition. Several major texts, including the *Rāmcaritmānas* and the *Adhyātma Rāmāyaṇa*, are cast in dialogue form, Śiva narrating the story to Pārvatī. Even in Vālmīki's variant, Nārada summarizes the first chapter to the poet. Whether or not this focus on narration offers further evidence for the essentially oral nature of the *Rāmāyaṇa*, these texts include another type of audience: an internal audience, created by tellers within their text. This internal audience is what I found in studying performances of the shadow puppet play in Kerala. The puppeteers did not perform for a conventional audience, since few people, often absolutely no one, remained throughout the night to hear their chanting and exegesis of the Rāma story; instead, they created conversations among themselves.

The Kerala shadow puppet play itself illustrates the diversity of the

Rāmāyaṇa tradition in that it performs a classical Tamil text in a Malayalam folk context.[2] The plays are presented in a long series of overnight performances, often running twenty or more nights, as part of the annual festival in central Kerala to the goddess Bhagavati. Although the puppet stage, called a "drama house," is built outside the temple proper, the performances are explicitly linked to the temple: its lamp is used to light the little lamps inside the drama house that cast the puppet shadows on the screen; the screen is handed to the puppeteers by the temple oracle-priest on the first night of performance; each night the performance is blessed by the oracle-priest; and each night hundreds, sometimes thousands, of individuals make donations to the puppeteers (in advance of the performance), who in return will ask the goddess to bless them, cure their leg sores, return runaway cousins, or restore a brother's lost livestock. From this public perspective, the puppet plays are recitations, an extended verbal ritual (*pūjā*) intended to win benefits for its patrons.

Textually, the puppet plays are based largely on Kampaṉ's epic poem, the *Irāmāvatāram*, composed in the Chola court during the twelfth century. Of Kampaṉ's more than 12,000 verses, the puppeteers sing between 750 and 1,150, depending on whether the story is begun in the Forest Book or the War Book and on how many nights the puppeteers perform. Approximately one-fifth of the verses, however, are drawn from unidentified sources and introduce episodes and motifs not found in Kampaṉ.[3] All the verses are carefully memorized, syllable by syllable, and recalled in performance by the initial word of the first line. Following each chanted verse, the puppeteers launch into their own commentary, sometimes glossing the verse line by line but more often digressing into mythological stories, grammatical explication, or improvised dialogue between the epic characters. All this is carried out by a small group of three to five men, who sit on wooden benches or woven mats and manipulate the puppets behind a white cloth screen.

Outside there is an open space, where a few people lie asleep on mats, sometimes waking to watch for a moment before dozing off again. Puppeteers speak of a "golden age," before movies, videos, and television, when large crowds watched their performances. This claim is not entirely fabrication. Even today, when the puppet play coincides with a popular entertainment event such as a folk drama or a fair, the open space in front of the drama house is crowded; perhaps a hundred people will watch the puppets for an hour before drifting off. It is also true that at particular sites certain episodes regularly muster crowds of fifty or more, most of whom remain mostly awake for most of the night. However, these are the exceptions: usually the Kerala puppeteers chant their verses and expound their interpretations to no one beyond the cloth screen.

Several aspects of the puppet play work to discourage a conventional audience. The language of the verses is an allusive medieval Tamil, read by scholars only with the aid of written commentaries and scarcely understood by the local Malayalam-speakers;[4] nor is the commentary (delivered in a dialect of Tamil heavily influenced by Malayalam, the local language) a conversational idiom. Second, the puppet play is primarily a commentarial rather than narrative tradition: the burden of performance is the convoluted interpretation of the verses, which tire even the epic character forced to listen to them, as we shall learn below. Third, the dominant role of commentary produces performances that are static, more like a frieze than a film. The slow pace of these performances was critically noted in 1935 by the first recorded Western observer of the tradition and again in the late 1940s by a Kerala scholar, who made this recommendation:

> If the olapavakuthu [puppet play] is to survive (and it would be a great pity if it did not), it will apparently have to undergo considerable renovation in the reduction of exposition, a change that would have the desirable effect of quickening the movements of the figures on the screen and bringing the *kūthu* [play] nearer the natural desire of people for rhythmic representation.[5]

That this appraisal fails to appreciate the less obvious dimensions of the puppeteers' art is what I hope to demonstrate in this essay.

Any potential audience is also distanced by the medium of shadow puppetry, which drops a screen between the performers and listeners. This is not true of shadow puppetry in Java and Bali, for example, where the screen is free standing and the performers are open to public view; indeed, patrons and favored members of the community are invited to sit behind the screen to fully appreciate the puppeteers' art.[6] In Kerala, however, the stage is a permanent building and the screen seals the puppeteers within, cut off from the public in a private space of their own.

This divide, I believe, deeply affects the Kerala puppeteers' telling of the Rāma story. Specifically, because these puppet plays have virtually no external listeners or viewers (audience in the ordinary sense), they have generated internal audiences. On the outside the performances are a ritual act; but on the inside they are an uninterrupted conversation, both within the text and among the puppeteers themselves. In their telling of the Rāma story, talking is no less important than the events of the tale.[7] Even in the eventful War Book, which dominates the puppet play, the martial action is defused through dialogue. Puppets do fight battles, weapons are hurled, even stuck into puppets' chests, but the art of the Kerala puppeteers is the art of conversation.

In adapting a medieval epic poem to shadow puppet play, the Kerala tradition has created several levels of conversation. On the textual level, the leather puppets speak in three separate dialogues: as Brahmins, at the opening of every performance; as epic characters speaking through verse and commentary; and, intermittently, as gods commenting on the epic action.

The second of these conversations, that between epic characters, is the most important, but all three contribute to the total dialogic effect of the puppet performance.

The very first words of every performance are spoken by two Brahmin puppets who dance around the Gaṇeśa puppet pinned to the center of the screen, a feature not found in Kampaṉ's text. Their presence in Kerala is an instructive innovation because the puppet play might have been framed differently—narrated by the single voice of one of the famous puppeteer-poets saluted in the introductory devotional songs, for instance. Instead the performance is framed by a dialogue between the two Brahmin puppets, named Muttuppaṭṭār and Gaṅgaiyāṭi. Once the initial songs to Gaṇeśa and Sarasvatī have faded away, Muttuppaṭṭār speaks to his companion and welcomes other Brahmins (not represented by puppets):

"Welcome, Gaṅgaiyāṭi, welcome."
"I am here, Muttuppaṭṭār."
"Is Kuñcappappaṭṭār here?"
"I am here also, Muttuppaṭṭār."
"Has Comācippaṭṭār arrived?"
"I have come, Muttuppaṭṭār."
"We have all come chanting the name 'Gōvinda-Rāma,' the most powerful name in the world."
"How is that?"

Muttuppaṭṭār's answer to this question leads to a description of Hindu cosmology and local sacred geography, ending with an enumeration of the fruits of devotion. After forty-five minutes of invocations and preliminaries, the Brahmin puppets are removed. Then the first narrative verse—spoken by one epic character to another—is sung and the commentary is added, as part of that dialogue. This is followed by more verses and more commentary, over and over again, until the early morning. In this way the Brahmin puppets set in motion a conversation that continues throughout the telling of the Rāma story, ending only when the performance itself comes to a close.

The peculiar nature of that conversation is illustrated by the opening scene of the Kumbhakarṇa episode, translated below. Kumbhakarṇa, Rāvaṇa's brother, has taken the field after Rāvaṇa's humiliating defeat by Rāma the previous day. As the demon warrior and his elephant army enter the screen from the left, Rāma and his army of monkeys stand on the right. The lead puppeteer introduces the scene, chants a verse from Kampaṉ, in which Rāma addresses Vibhīṣaṇa (Rāvaṇa's other brother, who defected to Rāma's side) and then begins his commentary:

"With thirteen thousand soldiers, Kumbhakarṇa entered the field, and from a distance Rāma saw his figure emerge. He turned to Vibhīṣaṇa."

"Who stands there, shoulders so wide
that many days would pass for the eyes
to scan from right to left? Is he
a battle-hungry warrior? Or Mount Meru on legs?"[8]

"Vibhīṣaṇa, yesterday we defeated Rāvaṇa and his two hundred thousand demon soldiers; I felled him, knocking off his crown. Now he knows that he cannot win, and I am wondering, 'Will he release Sītā and end this war? Or will he send more demons to be killed?' But look, over there! Some huge warrior has taken the field—god, he is enormous! Even to run your eyes from his right shoulder to his left would take days! He cannot be human-born. Looks more like a mountain risen from the earth, like Mount Meru, flanked by the cosmic elephants, with the nine planets circling his head. Who is this mountain-man?"

"Rāma, look closely—what do you see?"

"I don't know. Could it be Rāvaṇa in disguise—changing his twenty arms and ten heads for these two arms and single head? Is this his *māyā* frightening us again? Tell me, tell me quickly."

"Listen, noble one (*āriya*), he is
the younger brother of the raja of
this earth's (*aṭi talam*) beautiful Lanka,
and he is my older brother;
Wearing anklets of black death
and wielding a cruel trident,
he's called Kumbhakarṇa,
oh, lord of victory."[9]

"Rāma, notice that the poet calls you *āriya* or 'noble one.' We also call you *pūjyaṉ*, which means not only 'worthy' but something else as well. It means 'nothingness,' a cipher. True, we add, say, ten to twenty to find out a total. But more useful is a symbol of nothingness, and everything at the same time. That's you, Rāma. Nameless, formless, you are the unknowable *brahman*, the hidden essence. You are *svayambhū*, self-generating reality.

"Of course, some will ask, 'Why worship this nothingness?' Our answer is that the nothing takes form to protect us. You, too, assume the eight dispositions (*guṇa*): love, compassion, and so on, like the rest of us. So what separates you from us? Well, the Śaiva texts describe three layers of body: visible, subtle, and inner. The visible body is that known to the naked eye. Inside is another, the subtle body, which can be known by yoga and meditation; and inside it is a still more subtle body, which is known only by wisdom. Humans and gods alike have these three layers, but there is a difference. All the outer bodies of all the beings in the world equal the outer body of god; all the inner bodies of all the beings form the inner body of god; all the innermost bodies are subsumed in god's innermost body. In short, god's body is this world.

"People debate the nature of god. Some say he has name and form, some deny it. But, Rāma, the simple truth is this: god takes bodily form to protect this world in times of crisis. Because you are an example of that compassion, we call you *pūjyaṉ*."

"Yes, but who is that giant warrior bearing down on us?"

"Right, now look at the rest of the first line. *Aṭi talam* refers to the earth, because one walks on it. This is an example of a 'derived noun.' The other class of nouns is derived from conventional usage. Then each of these two categories can be either 'general name' or 'special name.' Hence, there are four classes of nouns. For instance, we use the word *paṅkam* to mean 'mud' (*cēṟu*). Other things that come from mud, like the word *paṅkayam* for 'lotus,' are derived nouns—even though many would consider 'lotus' a noun by convention. Still, few people use the word *paṅkayam* and use instead *centāmarai*, which is a 'special-derived noun.' Similarly, *mūkkaṇṇaṉ* means 'three-eyed' and is a derived noun when we use it to mean 'coconut'; but when we use it to mean Śiva, it is a 'special-derived-noun.' This phrase *aṭi talam* is also a 'special-derived-noun' because it was coined by a single person but for a special reason. And that person was Vāmana, the dwarf-avatar of Viṣṇu."

"Vibhīṣaṇa, I appreciate your learned explanations, but first tell me, Who is this gigantic warrior almost upon us?"

"That's what I am telling you, Rāma, by explaining this phrase *aṭi talam*. Long ago a raja and his son Mahābali built the magnificent city of Asurapati, from where the demons ruled the three worlds. Soon the gods and sages petitioned Brahmā for relief from the demons' violence; Brahmā sent them to Nārāyaṇa, who assured them that he would end their troubles once and for all.

"'First,' he said, 'we must churn the milk ocean to acquire ambrosia. Bring that huge Mandara mountain, the long snake named Vāsuki, the sixteen-phased moon Candra, and that other snake, Kārkōṭṭaṉ. But for this you gods need the help of the asuras, especially their king, Mahābali.'

"With the demons' help, the gods set up Mount Mandara as the churning stick, using the moon as a latch and a horse as a pin to fasten the stick to the tortoise as the resting place. Vāsuki was wrapped around the stick, and, with the gods holding his tail and the demons his head, they began to churn. They churned and churned . . ."

For two hours Vibhīṣaṇa speaks to Rāma, and while he speaks, he raises his right hand two or three times to make a point. No other movement is visible on the screen. In the epic action, however, Kumbhakarṇa and his huge armies, the earth quaking beneath them, rapidly advance on Rāma. Any reader may share Rāma's growing anxiety about "that giant warrior bearing down upon us," as Vibhīṣaṇa expatiates on the epithet "noble one," tells the story of Mahābali, explains the classifications of nouns, all the time ignoring Rāma's pleas, and finally finishes with a long account of the Mārkaṇḍeya story. By exaggerating and playing on the difference in pace between the rambling commentary and the imminent battle of the text, and not, as one might expect, hiding this discrepancy to maintain the illusion of narrative reality, the puppeteers establish the primacy of speech over action, of their interpretation over Kampaṉ's text. And even their exegesis is cast in dialogue, spoken by one epic character to another.

We might note also that this particular scene has been staged, in a pattern repeated throughout the puppet performance, as a conversation: a warrior appears on the battlefield; Rāma (or Lakṣmaṇa) asks who he is, and Vibhīṣaṇa then describes his birth, weapons, and boons. Vibhīṣaṇa speaks similar words in Kampaṉ, but there his words occupy a mere thirteen verses—about 3 percent of the episode—whereas the puppeteers stretch them to cover two hours, or one-third of the night's performance. The folk tradition also entirely omits the string of verses in which Kampaṉ describes Kumbhakarṇa's appearance, his chariot, his armor, and his armies (or else slips these verses into Vibhīṣaṇa's speech). The same principle of omitting descriptive verses in favor of conversation has determined the folk tradition's adaptation of every episode from Kampaṉ's text. Nowhere is there description of landscape or person, except as addressed to a listener.

The tropism toward dialogue is clearest in the consistent alteration of reported speech in Kampaṉ to direct speech in performance. This alteration at times requires a new line, or even two, but the most common technique is very simple: the final word of a Kampaṉ verse is changed from "he said" (*eṉṟār*) to "I say" (*eṉkiṟēṉ*) or to an expletive, a vocative, or an imperative. An example of the last case is the famous first verse of the Śūrpaṇakhā episode, which likens the beauty of the Godāvari river to poetry. When the puppeteers chant this verse, they make one minor change: the finite verb "saw" (*kaṇṭār*) becomes "look, brother" (*tampi kāṇāy*), so that the entire verse is addressed by Rāma to Lakṣmaṇa. Thus, instead of "The warriors saw the Godāvari," we hear:

> Look, Lakṣmaṇa, here is the Godāvari,
> lying as a necklace on the world
> nourishing the rich soil
> rushing over waterfalls
> flowing through the five regions
> in clear, cool streams
> like a good poet's verse.[10]

The shift to dialogue also allows the puppeteers to express emotions that remain mute in Kampaṉ. Voicing hidden or forbidden feelings is a characteristic of folk tradition everywhere, and the Rāma literature is no exception—as when Sītā draws a picture of Rāvaṇa, which then assumes physical form beneath her bed; or when, as a ferocious goddess, she kills him; or when Lakṣmaṇa marries Śūrpaṇakhā.[11] Perhaps the epic's pretense of virtue prompted the Telugu proverb: "The *Rāmāyaṇa* is about illicit sex, the *Mahābhārata* about lies."[12] In the Kerala puppet play, these suspect feelings are often kept private yet given greater immediacy when a character addresses himself, replacing the last phrase of Kampaṉ's verse ("he thought," "she feared") with "O, Heart!" (*maṉacē*). Rāma or Vibhīṣaṇa, then, is not simply described as thinking the words to himself; he says them to himself. Inner thoughts, too, have a listener in the puppet play.

Misgivings about war, which are faint, almost whispered, in Kampaṉ, are loudly and continually voiced in the puppet play. This difference may be illustrated by comparing Kampaṉ's treatment with the puppeteers' treatment of the same scene. When Rāma sees Lakṣmaṇa and the monkeys lying dead, felled by Indrajit's snake-weapon (*nāga-astra*), he falls down in grief over his brother's body, and cries out:

PUPPET PLAY

"No more war!
  and no more fame!
No victory bow!
  no wife! no kingdom!
Even Śiva who gave me life,
  I renounce them all,
If you, Lakṣmaṇa,
  do not live."

"We left our father and mother
  and we left Ayodhya
But like the Vedas,
  we have never been apart;
Now you've left me, Lakṣmaṇa,
  and this earth is not my home;
Let my soul leave me,
  if Yama is ready to take it."

KAMPAṈ

Strong-shouldered Rāma looked at
  his bow, at the knots of the
  snake-weapon,
Looked at the still, dark night,
  at the gods in heaven
    and screamed,
  "I'll rip up this earth!"
Then, biting his coral lips, he
  pondered what wise men said.

He rubbed Lakṣmaṇa's feet
  with his soft hands;
Opened Lakṣmaṇa's lotus-
  eyes and peered inside.
His heart beat quickly as
  he looked at the sky and
  lifted him to his chest.
Laying him on the earth,
  he wondered, "Is that
  devious Indrajit near?"[13]

In both versions Rāma is bitterly angry at his brother's (apparent) death, but they differ in their expression of that anger. In the first of Kampaṉ's verses, Rāma screams in frustration but then recedes into defeated silence; in the first folk verse, by contrast, he explicitly condemns war and its instruments. The power of this folk verse grows with the repetition of the pained cry *veṇṭē* ("No more!"). A repetition (*kaṇṭār*, "he saw") also organizes the Kampaṉ verse: Rāma's pain is suggested by his looking, first at his useless bow, then at the merciless gods—by what he sees more than what he says. Rāma remains similarly mute in the second Kampan̲ verse, his feelings kept within his eyes, heart, and mind. In the second folk verse, however, he again speaks without reserve. Verbal denunciation rings through the folk verses, whereas revenge is visually projected in the Kampan̲ verses.

The puppet play also voices furtive emotions through dialogue between characters. More misgivings about war, and about Rāma himself, are expressed by Rāma's general, the good Jambuvan̲. When Rāvaṇa sends in his reserve army, Jambuvan̲ flees the field and explains to Aṅgada:

"What can our seventy divisions do against their thousand? We'd only make a meal for them! I'm not ready to die yet."

"Jambuvan̲, don't say that! Once, at my father's death, you spoke to me with brave words and now you talk of retreat!"

"You're young, Aṅgada, and cannot understand what these demons can do in battle. Rāvaṇa has sent them, and this time Rāma will not defeat him."

"But, there's Lakṣmaṇa, and Hanumān . . . surely . . ."

"Don't be naive. Do you think we are anything more than bodyguards to them? Did anyone protect [my son] Vasantan̲ when Kumbhakarṇa mauled him? And no one will stop the pain when you die, either. Better to escape into the forest, drink pure water, and eat fresh fruits. Let Rāma win or lose—what's it to us anyway? Why should we die for them?"[14]

In a later episode, "The Revival of Vasantan̲" (considered a late interpolation in Kampan̲), the horror of death again prompts Jambuvan̲ to accuse Rāma of disloyalty. After Rāvaṇa's death and Vibhīṣaṇa's coronation as raja of Lanka, Rāma, Sītā, Lakṣmaṇa, and the monkeys prepare to return to Ayodhya in Rāvaṇa's old chariot. At this happy moment, Jambuvan̲ speaks angrily, refusing to enter the chariot because, he says, "I am old and have seen many amazing events, but never have I seen someone take back so quickly what they have given." His charge, that Rāma is reclaiming the chariot that only minutes ago he gave to Vibhīṣaṇa when crowning him, seems somewhat contrived, but we soon learn its underlying motivation: Jambuvan̲ is angry at Rāma for his indifference to Jambuvan̲'s son, Vasantan̲, killed while fighting for Rāma's cause. Rāma may well celebrate—his wife and brother are still alive—but what of the thousands of monkeys who died in their defense? Are they to be forgotten in the triumphant return to Ayodhya?

Jambuvan̲'s refusal to ignore the reality of death in the celebration of victory characterizes the emotions given new voice in the puppet play. The folk tradition will not accept platitudes or categories uncritically; in the key Śūrpaṇakhā and Vālin episodes, it shows that the Rāma-avatar is flawed and that the claims of the *bhakti* epic are easily deflated. My favorite example of this check on the epic's excessive posturing is the puppeteers' treatment of

Hanumān's mission to bring back medicinal herbs needed to revive Lakṣmaṇa and the monkeys. Jambuvan̲ speaks excitedly:

"Listen, Hanumān, we have only three-quarters of an hour to revive Lakṣmaṇa and the others. Then the sun rises and Indrajit will behead them all!"

"Yes."

"Before that, you must travel seventy-three thousand yoganas to the Medicine Mountain, find a special healing herb, and return."

"Are you joking?"

"Joking?"

"Seventy-three thousand yoganas in three-quarters of an hour? And return? It's . . . impossible."

"But, Hanumān, if you don't . . ."

"That far, that quickly, to locate a rare herb for an incurable disease? Ridiculous, that's all."

In the puppet play, even Hanumān, the ideal Rāma devotee, cannot resist poking fun at epic hyperbole.

The puppet play's countervailing comic voice, however, belongs more often to characters either insignificant or absent in Kampan̲'s text. The most important of these figures are the Standard Bearer, nowhere found in Kampan̲ but always stationed next to Rāvaṇa on the cloth screen, and Rāvaṇa's messengers, present but nondescript in Kampan̲.[15] The Standard Bearer stirs from his silent pose when he and Indrajit, Rāvaṇa's son, inspect the bodies of Lakṣmaṇa and the monkeys felled by Indrajit's snake-weapon. His comic dialogue with the great demon warrior (considered more dangerous than Rāvaṇa) serves to undermine Indrajit's pretensions to power. They meet unexpectedly on the battlefield and the Standard Bearer speaks first, parodying the sounds of war:

"Bing-bang, bing-bang! Who are you?"

"Me? I just shot the snake-weapon, the whole point of this night's performance."

"Oh, and you came here in this chariot, I suppose."

"Right. How'd you come?"

"I'm the Standard Bearer; I just grabbed onto the chariot and came along for the ride."

"What do you want?"

"Problem is your snake-weapon did not kill them; it only knocked them out. I'll finish them off by stabbing them with the tip of my staff. Anyway, let's walk along this battlefield and inspect each body. If my staff doesn't finish them off, you can always shoot another snake-weapon."

"All right."

"Who's this, lying here?"

"It's Nalaṉ, the one who built the causeway to Lanka by carrying all those stones on his head."

"A contractor, huh?"

"Yes. Give the 'boss' a good stab."

"And this one?"

"That's Blue-Man (*nīlaṉ*)."

"Oh, I need some of that."

"Of what?"

"You see, my wife hasn't washed her sari for a week and . . ."

"Not blue-soap (*nīlam*), stupid! Blue-Man. Besides, do you wash your wife's saris?"

"If you saw them, you'd understand why no one else would touch them. Anyway, who is low enough to be my washerman?"

Apparently a servant's staff is more potent than the epic's most fearsome weapon. The same point is made later when the epic battle grinds to a standstill because the Standard Bearer refuses to hold the standard without receiving his pay. This servant-figure, anonymous but indispensable, appears fully assimilated into the epic when he requests and receives *mokṣa* (religious liberation) from Rāma. But this supreme act of *bhakti* is compromised when he flinches in fear of death. As with Jambuvaṉ's anger and grief at the moment of the return to Ayodhya, the puppet play speaks of mortality precisely when the epic wishes to celebrate victory or religious devotion.

At other times, the Standard Bearer and messengers laugh when epic characters mourn. If the Rāma story in the puppet play is pervaded by a single emotion, it is grief, especially over loss in death. But the most powerful scenes of grief—when Rāma cries (twice) for his dead brother and allies, and when Rāvaṇa cries over his dead son, Indrajit—are hedged around with a comic element supplied by these folk figures. Rāma's mourning is immediately preceded by the slapstick, puns, and dirty laundry of the scene translated above in which the Standard Bearer and Indrajit inspect bodies on the field; the same scene is repeated later (before Rāma mourns those felled by the Brahmā-astra) with the same jokes, to the same effect. An even more obvious undermining of grief occurs just before Rāvaṇa learns of Indrajit's death. Returning from the battlefield with this information, the messengers sing a mock dirge to Indrajit. Then, when Rāvaṇa asks them for the "news" (of his son), they trifle with him, informing him of the latest gossip in the vegetable market. Finally, anticipating Rāvaṇa's tears just before they tell him about Indrajit, the messengers comment sarcastically, "It's monsoon time again!"

This dialogue between epic characters, which we have been listening to in both verse and commentary, comprises most of the long hours of performance. The introductory dialogue between Brahmins is brief by comparison, while the third dialogue, that between Indra and the gods, is intermittent. Unlike the epic characters, but like the Brahmin puppets, Indra and the gods do not participate in the epic action; they comment on it as omniscient narrators. Indra and the gods occasionally appear in Kampaṉ's text, too, commenting on and influencing the epic action, especially when Indra sends Rāma his chariot and charioteer in the final battle against Rāvaṇa. But in the shadow puppet play, Indra appears frequently and always with another puppet, who represents the other gods collectively; and, whereas in Kampaṉ Indra speaks directly to the epic characters, in the puppet play he speaks only to his companion puppet.

A good example of this third-level dialogue occurs when Rāvaṇa enters his palace humiliated, having lost the first battle with Rāma:

"Tell us, Indra, how did Rāvaṇa feel when he entered the palace?"

"He was disgraced. Having lost his chariot, he walked on foot, dragging his long arms along the ground, just as the sun set in the west."

"He entered just as the sun set—is there any special meaning to that?"

"I'll come back to that. First it is important to say that this twenty-armed Rāvaṇa was defeated by the two arms of Rāma."

"Śrī Rāma's right and left arms, right?"

[At this point, a man who I had thought was fast asleep in the corner of the drama house jumped up and spoke, displacing one of the puppeteers:]

"What was your question? Something about the setting sun?"

"Nothing really, Indra. Some say that the setting sun symbolized Rāvaṇa's life, its decline, I mean."

"No! No! Nothing of the sort. Demons fight at night because you can't defeat them in the darkness. The point of this line is that the first battle took place during the day and thus Rāma was able to defeat Rāvaṇa. To say that Rāvaṇa's entering the palace at sunset symbolizes the end of his life is sheer nonsense! It simply indicates the fact the battle took place in daylight and nothing more. Now if you want to talk about Rāma's two hands . . . [that's another story]."

Pinned high on the cloth screen, above the epic characters, Indra and the gods are spectators as well as narrators. From the very first episode in the puppeteers' text, when they petition Viṣṇu to defeat their enemies, the gods have kept a close watch on Rāma. Viṣṇu's eagle, Garuḍa, for instance, spies Rāma grieving on the battlefield and flies down from Mount Meru to tear free the knots of the snake-weapon that bind his brother. Rāma and Rāvaṇa, for their part, are not unaware of their distant audience. Nowhere is this more evident than in the last scene of the great battle: Rāvaṇa tells Rāma to spare no effort in offering the gods a good spectacle, and, before he kills the demon raja, Rāma addresses the gods: "Gods, I, Rāma, now kill Rāvaṇa."

To summarize the discussion thus far: The puppet play is performed as dialogue on three levels, each of which has its listeners, an audience internal to the performance. The interaction among the Kerala puppeteers, however, is more complex than these puppet voices. When the puppets converse as Brahmins at the opening of the performance, or as epic characters in verse or commentary during the narrative, or as gods above the action, only their shadows are projected on the public side of the cloth screen. Inside the drama house, however, another kind of exchange, a private "conversation," is carried on among the puppeteers themselves.

The puppeteers always perform in a pair, a lead man and a respondent, and in shifts: two men will begin and, after a few hours, one or both of the performers will be relieved by others who have been resting. The long hours of narration and interpretation, then, amount to a tête-à-tête between the lead puppeteer and his respondent. At times, when a puppeteer launches into a diatribe on his favorite point of Hindu philosophy, the performance may resemble a monologue. Nonetheless, however far a speech may wander, it eventually reverts to dialogue by concluding with a question to the respondent, or when the respondent himself puts a question to the first puppeteer. The dialogic nature of the commentary is also continuously, if a little monotonously, maintained by the partner, who responds with a drone-sound ("ahhhhh") whenever the lead man pauses for thought or breath. In addition, every speech, again regardless of its length, begins and ends with standardized vocatives. Thus Rāma is always addressed as "Rāma-god," Lakṣmaṇa as "Young-god," Vibhīṣaṇa as "Raja of Lanka," and so on. While these labels are addressed to the epic character, they also function as signposts to a puppeteer lost within a detailed commentary. When one man plunges into the story of the "Churning of the Ocean" and resurfaces to the epic story forty minutes later with the question, "So what do you think?" his partner is likely to have forgotten who is speaking to whom and is rescued only when the man mercifully adds, "Raja of Lanka?"

Dialogue between puppeteers during the commentary is more obvious when, as is usual, they trade speeches of two or three minutes' length. And when they speak in a rapid-fire exchange, improvising freely, anyone sitting behind the cloth screen realizes that the puppets on the screen are less interesting than the puppeteers. On one occasion, during the confrontation between Indrajit and Hanumān on the battlefield ("Hey, runt, where's your weapons? Come and fight like a man!"), the puppeteer speaking for Indrajit challenged his partner, jabbing his finger and shouting at him; the puppeteer playing Hanumān merely raised his eyebrows and responded with cool disdain. In their long and complicated telling of the Rāma story, a puppeteer will react to his partner with every kind of emotion—frustration with his wordiness, respect for his wit and knowledge, gentle humor at his sleepiness.

Familiar tactics of talk are employed by puppeteers to control the flow of conversation among themselves. "Let that be," one man interrupts the other's account of Rāvaṇa's palace, "and explain how you got here, Vibhīṣaṇa." Certain senior puppeteers are notorious for their long-winded discourses and apparent disregard for time; others in the drama house, fearful that the sun will in fact rise before Hanumān returns with the medicinal herbs, wrestle with them to hasten the pace of the commentary. As the senior puppeteer glides effortlessly through Jambuvaṉ's account of the origin of the worlds, for example, he is cut short: "I see, Jambuvaṉ, so that's how you were born; but what can we do about Lakṣmaṇa's death?" No one likes to be cut off, and some puppeteers will fight to maintain control of the commentary, raising their voice or speaking faster. The most effective way to silence your opponent and regain control, however, is suddenly to recite a line from the verse you are explaining (which everyone else has in all likelihood forgotten). By an instinct born of long training, your partner will almost certainly drop whatever he was trying to say and chant the rest of the line, leaving you free to continue on.

Inside the drama house, cut off from their conventional audience, the puppeteers perform for themselves. The learned quotations, the rapid replies, the skill at parody, the displays of logic—all are calculated to win respect from the little band of fellow puppeteers and drummers, and the occasional stray connoisseur.[16] Even when only two puppeteers are awake, they take pride in setting right the meaning of the setting sun, explaining how Rāvaṇa got his name, or laughing at the foolish messengers. Likewise, there is a measure of shared shame when someone fails, forgets the next verse, or begins with the wrong line. That is why some puppeteers, even those with ten years' experience, take a notebook of verses, and sometimes quotations, into the drama house; one may refer to this book, but not read directly from it. Only once, in three research trips, did I see a puppeteer completely at a loss. The young man suddenly went blank in mid-verse: "I don't know the verses in this part," he murmured to his partner and then hung his head, while the other man glared at him but carried on.

The quality of a performance matters on the other side of the cloth screen, too. If not the reception by the half-awake "audience" on the ground, the opinions of the patrons and temple officials determine which puppeteer group will be hired next year; and the loss of patronage at even one temple delivers a hard financial blow. I have no precise data on how these influential men form judgments about performances, but from my conversations with them it is clear that they hold definite views. Although patrons and officials rarely stay through the night, they do listen to the long introduction by the Brahmin puppets and hear informal reports from many people during the course of the festival. Almost as important to the puppeteers are the hundreds, sometimes thousands, of individual patrons who give a single rupee in the hope of securing blessings from Bhagavati. They will not be present in the middle of the night when the puppeteers sing their names to the goddess, but the general reputation of the puppeteers will determine how many villagers offer them money.[17]

Another external audience for the puppet play is the goddess Bhagavati, as the origin legend of the tradition explains:

> The goddess who guarded the gates to Brahmā's treasury grew proud and was cursed to serve as guard to Rāvaṇa's treasury in the city of Lanka. For thousands of years she protected Rāvaṇa's wealth, until Rāma and his monkey armies attacked the city. When Hanumān attempted to enter and she blocked his path, the monkey slapped her with his tail and sent her to Śiva's heaven. Once there, she complained: "For years and years I have suffered under Rāvaṇa and now, just as he is to be killed by Rāma, I am here and cannot see this special event." Śiva then gave her a boon: "You shall be born on earth as Bhagavati and I will be born as the poet Kampaṉ. I will write the story of Rāvaṇa's death and you may watch it every year in your temple."[18]

In the origin legend, as in the patronage system, Bhagavati is the public audience. The puppeteers play to please her.

However, even Bhagavati hears words and see shadows on one side of the cloth screen only. Neither she nor the patrons nor the sleeping listeners play any role in the performance; they overhear it. Such extreme distance between performers and external audience distinguishes the shadow puppet play from most other kinds of oral folk performance. Tales, proverbs, folk theater and so on are partially, sometimes largely, shaped by audience reaction; this is why donations to performers in most Indian folk traditions are offered during the performance and not beforehand, as in the Kerala puppet play. Although every performance involves a degree of separation between performer and audience, the distance shrinks when a teller draws on the local setting for details of his story. And the gap all but disappears when listeners play a role in the performance, as a spirit-possessed dancer in a ritual or as a respondent in a joke.

Interaction between performers and audience gives a performance vitality and popularity, but communication is difficult through a screen of shadows. In Kerala, the distance inevitable in shadow puppetry is increased, rather than decreased, because the puppeteers are completely enclosed inside a drama house and use a medieval Tamil text, making little concession to spectator taste for music or movement. Observers and scholars, as noted earlier, have faulted the Kerala tradition for its apparent unresponsiveness, which has tended to alienate its audience. But the absent audience may have contributed to the complexity of the puppeteers' art. Converting Kampaṉ's text to dialogue, the puppeteers created internal audiences: every word spoken by a Brahmin, an epic character, or a god is addressed to another puppet; every speaker is paired with a listener with whom he interacts. And the most important audience for the Kerala puppet plays are the puppeteers themselves. In commentary, in chanting verses, and in manipulating puppets, these men constantly interact with each other, responding to jokes, jibes, and personalities. This is true of actors on any stage, but the Kerala puppeteers' full performance is visible only to the audience inside the drama house.

NOTES

This essay is based on fieldwork carried out in Kerala in 1984, 1985, and 1989 with support from the Fulbright Program (CIES), and on research supported by the National Endowment for the Humanities.

1. The pioneering study of audiences in folk performances is Roger Abrahams, "The Complex Relations of Simple Forms," in *Folklore Genres*, ed. Dan Ben-Amos (Austin: University of Texas Press, 1976), 193–214. On audiences in puppet performances, see Frank Proschan, "Cocreation of the Comic in Puppetry," in *Humor and Comedy in Puppetry: A Celebration of Popular Culture*, ed. Dina Sherzer and Joel Sherzer (Bowling Green, Ohio: Bowling Green University Press, 1987), 30–46.

2. For a more complete description of the Kerala shadow puppet tradition, see Friedrich Seltmann, *Schattenspiel in Kerala* (Stuttgart: F. Steiner, 1986); and Stuart H. Blackburn, "Hanging in the Balance: Rāma in the Shadow Puppet Theater of Kerala," in *Gender, Genre, and Power in South Asian Expressive Traditions*, ed. Arjun Appadurai et al. (Philadelphia: University of Pennsylvania Press, 1991).

3. These episodes and motifs—for example, the killing of Sambukumāraṉ, the son of Śūrpaṇakhā, or Rāma's admission of guilt in the Vālin episode—are, however, known in the wider *Rāmāyaṇa* literature.

4. On Kampaṉ's language, see George L. Hart and Hank Heifetz, *The Forest Book of the Rāmāyaṇa of Kampaṉ* (Berkeley and Los Angeles: University of California Press, 1988), 7–19.

5. Stan Harding, "Ramayana Shadow-Play in India," *Asia* (April 1935): 234. J. H. Cousins, "Dance-Drama and the Shadow Play," in *The Arts and Crafts of Kerala*, ed. Stella Kramrisch, J. H. Cousins, and R. Vasudevan Poduval (1948; repr., Cochin: Paico Publishing House, 1970), 212.

6. For a discussion of the interaction between puppeteers and their patrons and audiences in Java, see Ward Keeler, *Javanese Shadow Plays, Javanese Selves* (Princeton: Princeton University Press, 1987). Shadow puppet performances in India (except Kerala) use a temporary enclosed stage.

7. Philip Lutgendorf makes a similar point concerning interpretation of Tulsīdās's Rāma story: "The View from the Ghats: Traditional Exegesis of a Hindu Epic," *Journal of Asian Studies* 48, no. 2 (May 1989): 272–88.

8. The Kampaṉ verse is VI.15.111 (*tōḻotu tōḷ*) in the death of Kumbhakarṇa episode (Vai. Mu. Kōpālakiruṣṇamācāriyar edition, Madras, 1976); all further reference to Kampaṉ verses are to this edition. One Kampaṉ verse recited during this excerpt has been eliminated from the translation because the commentary simply restates it.

9. VI.15.114 (*āriyaṉ aṉiya*). The folk alteration of this Kampaṉ verse exemplifies the general principle of converting indirect to direct speech: its first line revised, the entire verse is now spoken by Vibhīṣaṇa.

10. III.5.1 (*puviyiṉukku*) in the Śūrpaṇakhā episode of the Forest Book.

11. See the essays by Ramanujan and Narayana Rao in this volume. For Śūrpaṇakhā's marriage to Lakṣmaṇa, see Komal Kothari, "Performers, Gods, and Heroes in the Oral Epics of Rajasthan," in *Oral Epics in India*, ed. Stuart H. Blackburn et al. (Berkeley and Los Angeles: University of California Press, 1989), 116.

12. "*Rāmāyaṇam raṅku, Bhāratam boṅku*"; collected from Sampath Kumar, Hyderabad, July 1988.

13. VI.18.224 and 223 (*villiṉai* and *tāmarai*) in the Nākapācam episode of the War Book.

14. A Kampaṉ verse, VI.30.43 (*aṉumaṉ*, of the Mūlapala Vatai episode in the War Book), not sung by the puppeteers in this scene, contains a proverb found in some form in all South Indian languages: "If Rāma rules or Rāvaṇa rules, what's the difference?"

15. The other major figure given a voice in the puppet plays is the oracle-priest of Bhagavati temples.

16. These learned quotations (*piramāṇam*) in Tamil, and occasionally in Sanskrit, are aphorisms cited by the puppeteers to illustrate a point.

17. The singing of these blessings is called a *nāṭakam* (here, "dance"). Rāvaṇa summons celestial dancing women, and the puppets representing these dancers are placed on the screen while the puppeteers (as singers in Rāvaṇa's court) sing devotional songs.

18. The legend is not known to all puppeteers, nor does it appear to have a textual source, although it is invariably mentioned in articles on the Kerala tradition. I collected this version from a puppeteer in a village near Palghat in 1985.

PART THREE

Tellings as Commentary and Programs for Action

NINE

E. V. Ramasami's Reading of the *Rāmāyaṇa*

Paula Richman

On the first day of August in 1956, E. V. Ramasami (henceforth E.V.R.) set out for the Madras marina to lead his followers in burning pictures of Lord Rāma, hero of the *Rāmāyaṇa*. This symbolic action would represent a reversal of the culmination of North Indian performances of the *Rāmāyaṇa*, in which images of the epic's villain, Rāvaṇa, are put to the flames as spectators watch in delight.[1] Rejecting Rāma as hypocritical and weak, worthy only of scorn, E.V.R. saw Rāvaṇa as the true hero of the tale. E.V.R.'s iconoclastic reading comprised more than just another exegesis of a religious text, however. It was the centerpiece of his campaign against brahmanical Hinduism, conducted in the context of his assertion of Dravidian, that is, South Indian, identity.[2]

The day before the proposed burning of Lord Rāma's picture, important political leaders implored E.V.R. to cancel the event, so as not to offend orthodox Hindu Tamilians. P. Kakkan, president of the Tamilnadu Congress Committee, argued that the desecration of Rāma images would constitute an "anti-social" act that would betray the strong faith in God by which Gandhi won independence for India. E.V.R. remained unmoved by such arguments, noting that "there was bound to be a difference of views regarding any measure aimed at bringing social reform."[3]

On the following day, the Deputy Commissioner of Police promptly arrested E.V.R. when he stepped out of his house to head toward the marina. E.V.R. seemed prepared for this eventuality: in addition to his picture of Rāma and his box of matches, he carried a bedroll to spread on the hard prison floor. Soon afterward, his wife went down to the beach to tell the assembled crowd of the arrest. Some of the protestors, who had brought pictures of Rāma and little wooden matchboxes, began to burn pictures on their own. As *The Hindu* reported:

> Then for another half-an-hour, a number of persons . . . played hide and seek on the road and on the sands with the police and from time to time one would come forward and be arrested. One of these managed to slip onto the sands and burn a picture of Sri Rama, but he was arrested.[4]

Police reinforcements arrived at the beach, several people began to throw stones, the police made a few half-hearted charges brandishing their *lathis* (weighted staffs), and then most people went home. Approximately 890 people were arrested either before or during the event. E.V.R. was released after two and a half hours but declined to continue the protest, saying that the event had more than fulfilled its purpose.[5]

E.V.R.'s Rāma-burning campaign was neither an isolated incident nor the stunt of some prankster. From the late 1920s through to the end of his life, he developed a serious and thorough critique of the characters and values of the *Rāmāyaṇa*, of which the 1956 agitation was simply one manifestation. E.V.R. reads the *Rāmāyaṇa* as a text of political domination: his interpretation of the text is intended to awaken South Indians to their oppression by North Indians and to their true identity as Dravidians. Through his exegesis of the *Rāmāyaṇa*, E.V.R. exposes what he sees as the shoddy values of brahminism, reveals what he understands as Rāma's greed for power and desire to dominate, and sets out what he takes to be Rāvaṇa's true greatness. By the end of his endeavor, conventional readings of the text lie in shreds.

In this article, I focus upon the logic of E.V.R.'s reading of the *Rāmāyaṇa*, particularly the manner in which he politicizes the text. First, I provide a brief biographical and historical overview of his life and milieu, concluding with a discussion of how he used print to disseminate his ideas. Second, I analyze one popular pamphlet which contains a comprehensive formulation of his ideas. Third, I consider some of the precedents for E.V.R.'s reading and then his innovations. The essay concludes with an evaluation of E.V.R.'s exegesis of the *Rāmāyaṇa* as a contribution to public discourse in South India. Throughout, my goal is to demonstrate the pivotal role that E.V.R.'s attack on the *Rāmāyaṇa* played in fusing religious texts and political issues in Madras during the middle third of this century.

ROOTS AND METHODS OF E.V.R.'S ATTACK ON THE RĀMĀYAṆA

Running through E.V.R.'s life is his growing disillusionment with Hinduism, accompanied by an ever-increasing distrust of and activism against brahmanical privilege.[6] Accounts suggest that even as a youth E. V. Ramasami Naicker (he later dropped the caste name) rebelled against brahmanical prescriptions for proper social behavior. Born in 1879 into a family of Baliga Naidus, a Telugu *jāti* of traders and cultivators, he grew up in Erode, a fairly important mercantile town in the Coimbatore district of Madras.

Because E.V.R. insisted upon associating with boys of lower castes, his father removed him from school at age ten.[7] His marriage was arranged when he was thirteen, and he entered the family business, becoming prosperous thanks to his shrewd business sense.

At the age of twenty-five, however, E.V.R. grew dissatisfied with mercantile life and became a *sādhu* (wandering holy man). During his journeys across India, visiting cities such as Banaras and Calcutta, he gained a broader perspective on the nature of his country and its religion. But hand in hand with his widening experience came a disgust with a Hindu priesthood that he saw as exploiting the masses under the guise of "spiritual advancement." After a short time he became disillusioned, returned home, rejoined society, and entered regional politics.[8]

E.V.R.'s early political activities already indicate his concern with the rights of non-Brahmins. In 1920 he joined the Non-cooperation Movement and became active in the Indian National Congress party, following its Gandhian principles devoutly. His most famous exploit was his participation in a satyagraha campaign in Vikom, Kerala, undertaken to give Untouchables access to certain roads hitherto forbidden to them, his deeds earning him the title "Hero of Vikom."[9] All these activities were well within the reform program of Gandhi and the Congress party.

Although the Tamilnadu Congress Committee elected E.V.R. its secretary, his sensitivity to the problems of non-Brahmins (especially Untouchables) began to make him unpopular among the Brahmin elite. He antagonized them further by protesting when a Congress-run school instituted segregated eating facilities for Brahmins and non-Brahmins. Later he demanded that positions on municipal councils be reserved for non-Brahmins. In 1925 he withdrew from the Congress party, henceforth attacking it as a vehicle for Brahmin domination.

Even while still involved with Congress, E.V.R. had increasingly turned his attention to the denunciation of brahmanical Hinduism. In 1922 he advocated the burning of both the *Rāmāyaṇa* and *The Laws of Manu*, a famous *dharmaśāstra* text that sets out the proper conduct for different castes and, in so doing, glorifies Brahmins. By 1924 he had founded a publication called *Kuṭi Aracu* (People's government) to advocate social reform, aimed at destroying religious privilege and constraint.[10] After abandoning the Congress in 1925, he organized the "Self-Respect Movement" for "Dravidian Uplift."

During this period E.V.R. came to view Hinduism as a web of deceit designed to maintain the supremacy of the Brahmin—whom he linked with North Indian Sanskritic (non-Tamilian) culture—and to oppress non-Brahmins.[11] He therefore set out to reveal the insidious nature of orthodox religion. First in the line of attack were Hindu myths, which he read in a strictly literal fashion, delighting in finding seeming contradictions. Treating the myths as if they were historical accounts, he denounced the actions of the gods as obscene, stupid, and immoral, and advocated atheism instead.[12] Next E.V.R. excoriated Hindu rituals—which were, after all, the domain of Brahmin priests. In place of traditional Hindu rituals he substituted community-based "Self-Respect" ceremonies, the most famous of which was the "Self-Respect Marriage," at which Vedic rites were omitted and an elder of the community or one of the leaders of the Self-Respect Movement (rather than a priest) presided.[13] Finally, he ridiculed the entire notion of caste, rejecting social separation and purity/pollution observances as entirely unnecessary. Traditional Hindu concepts of endogamous communities were to be systematically broken down through the encouragement of intercaste marriages, widow remarriage, and other acts designed to undermine the exclusiveness of *jāti*. He also advocated a separatist Dravida Nadu (Dravidian country) in place of a community based on the *varṇadharma* (caste duties) of pan-Indian tradition.[14]

Political activism and opposition to brahmanical Hinduism led E.V.R. to espouse an increasingly separatist direction for Tamils. When in 1937 the Congress ministry proposed introducing Hindi—a language derived from Sanskrit and spoken chiefly in the north—as a compulsory subject in schools, E.V.R. interpreted it as an offensive attempt to impose North Indian culture upon South India. The anti-Hindi protests he organized brought him both notoriety and a jail sentence. Several years later E.V.R. aligned himself with the Justice Party, a group devoted to attacking Brahmin domination and pressuring the British for provincial autonomy. By 1944 he had taken control of the Justice Party, shaping it to his own concerns. He reorganized it and renamed it the Dravida Kazagham (Dravidian Federation), commonly known as the DK. Following Indian independence in 1947 and the ensuing social and political realignments, E.V.R.'s activities not only continued but his anti-Northern and antibrahmanical rhetoric became more strident.

In particular, E.V.R. singled out the *Rāmāyaṇa* to censure. For E.V.R., the *Rāmāyaṇa* story was a thinly disguised historical account of how North Indians, led by Rāma, subjugated South Indians, ruled by Rāvaṇa. Although his ideas were comparatively radical—and potentially disorienting—to a population of devout Hindus, many people responded enthusiastically. Why? His "North vs. South" interpretation of the *Rāmāyaṇa* was successful with a Tamil audience partly because of the political context in which E.V.R. was operating. To succeed, a leader must have more than personal "charisma"; that leader must articulate and legitimate a message that followers see as addressing their own situation.[15] In order to understand the enthusiastic reception Tamilians gave to E.V.R.'s ideas we must therefore examine certain features of his time and region: the rise and fervor of Dravidian sentiment in South India, the uneasy power relationships that existed between Brahmins and elite non-Brahmins, and the role of print in the intellectual life of Madras.[16] Let us explore each of these in turn.

E.V.R.'s championing of fervent Dravidian separatism must be understood in its pan-Indian context. During this period various groups—both regional and religious—were choosing to define themselves as separate and demanding some sort of official, usually political, recognition of their uniqueness.[17] E.V.R.'s assertion of Dravidian identity, which postulated a golden age of Dravidian society in the distant past (before the coming of Rāma) that could be reestablished if South Indians would only throw off the yoke of North Indian domination, to some extent conformed to this trend. In much the same way that other South Asians sought, for example, the creation of a separate Islamic state (Pakistan), E.V.R. desired a separate Tamil state and identity for South Indians, linking the articulation of that identity with a critique of the *Rāmāyaṇa*.

Moving from a pan-Indian to a regional context, one finds that Brahmins—the target of E.V.R.'s most vitriolic criticism—had become exceptionally successful in Madras toward the end of the nineteenth century. Subramaniam argues that Brahmins were in an excellent position to enter the middle class as mediators between the British and those they ruled in Madras, because, owing in part to British respect for high-status groups, they had not fared as badly under British rule as other more dominant land-owning groups ("clean" Śūdras, such as Vellalas). In addition, their tradition of learning enabled them to take advantage of educational opportunities and thus to enter the British-run civil service.[18]

In contrast, members of dominant non-Brahmin *jātis* who moved from their villages to urban areas experienced considerable social disorientation. In pre-British society, many land-holding non-Brahmins enjoyed a relatively high and clearly defined status, articulated in their ritual interaction with those around them in the local community. But as large numbers moved to the comparative anonymity of urban areas, where land-holding dominance was not a decisive factor, they had to negotiate their place in a new urban hierarchy that tended to favor the educated Brahmins.[19] In E.V.R.'s view, these non-Brahmins were the indigenous, authentic Dravidians, now oppressed by the foreign rule of the "Aryan" Brahmins, whose conquest of the South was described mythically—and more important, legitimated—by the *Rāmāyaṇa*.

In this situation, non-Brahmins sought not only to secure access to government positions previously dominated by Brahmins but to reform society. As Irschick argues, "Though the Government of Madras instituted quotas in job recruitment, education and other areas for those it considered backward, these quotas could have no real effect unless both egalitarian strands within Indian tradition and Western ideas could be used to claim parity for all groups in society and politics."[20] The rejection of caste hierarchy (as defined by brahmanical Hinduism and epitomized, in E.V.R.'s eyes, by Rāma's rule) was one way of claiming such parity. According to E.V.R., South Indian life before arrival of the Aryans (his term for North Indians) had been free of such societal divisions, and he demanded a return to such a society.

The fact that E.V.R. could disseminate his demands so widely reflects in part the unprecedented growth and power of print at this time.[21] Although full-length books were too expensive for most people to purchase and too time-consuming for most members of the professional class to read, inexpensive pamphlets reached a wide audience. E.V.R.'s brief articles on topics such as the *Rāmāyaṇa*, with their simple prose style and bombastic but witty rhetoric, made his message readily accessible to anyone interested in hearing it.[22] He was in fact a prolific writer of short, aggressive journalistic pieces, designed to arouse popular passions and amplify social, political, and religious grievances. His writings on the *Rāmāyaṇa* were just such pieces.

For E.V.R., who possessed a canny ability to make the most of the resources available to him, this mobilization of the power of print was characteristic. He founded a series of journals and fortnightly magazines, established a press in order to issue his many publications, and knew how to attract extensive newspaper coverage for his public campaigns and protests. His 1956 Rāma-burning agitation, whose rationale had previously been explained in writings published by his press, brought him front-page headlines.[23]

E.V.R.'s reading of the *Rāmāyaṇa* is most fully developed in two works: *Irāmāyaṇappātiraṅkaḷ* (Characters in the *Rāmāyaṇa*) and *Irāmāyaṇakkuṟippukaḷ* (Points about the *Rāmāyaṇa*).[24] Although the latter is a sophisticated and thorough textual study of the *Rāmāyaṇa*, the less scholarly *Irāmāyaṇappātiraṅkaḷ* has done the most to shape E.V.R.'s followers' perceptions of the *Rāmāyaṇa*. Since this text is one of his earliest, most comprehensive, most popular, and most frequently reprinted works on the *Rāmāyaṇa*, it will be the focus of the discussion below.

The extensive publication and translation history of *Characters in the Rāmāyaṇa* indicates both its centrality in E.V.R.'s writings on the *Rāmāyaṇa* and the enthusiastic reception it has continued to receive from readers. First published in 1930, the work was in its tenth printing in 1972. The first English translation appeared in 1959, a second edition came out in 1972, and a third in 1980.[25] With the appearance of this translation, as well as a Hindi translation, the text's audience was no longer limited to Tamil readers. While the work's Tamil title suggests that E.V.R. will consider the actions of each character, the English version's title, *The Ramayana (A True Reading)*—though not an exact translation of the original title—is in some ways more illuminating, for it indicates E.V.R.'s goal of revealing to the reader the "correct" interpretation of the *Rāmāyaṇa*.

The format and price of the book ensured its availability to readers. Less a book than a long pamphlet, *Characters in the Rāmāyaṇa* measures approximately 8½ by 5½ inches, contains a little under one hundred and twenty pages of large type, and—thanks to its flimsy binding—falls apart after a few readings. Fortunately, it also sells for a price that most people can easily afford: the 1972 edition, for example, cost only a single rupee (at that time, about fifteen cents).

An entire business developed out of the publication of such works, a business which gave high priority to polemical texts. *Characters in the Rāmāyaṇa* was published by the Periyār Cuyamariyātai Piracāra Niṟuvaṉa Veḷiyīṭu or (as it calls itself in its English publications) Periyar Self-Respect Propaganda Institution Publications. This institution, whose headquarters are in Trichy, the city whence issued the 1956 announcement that images of Rāma should be burned on the first of August, conceives of its mission in a disarmingly straightforward way: to produce propaganda, namely, material self-consciously designed to change people's opinions. The printers, Tirāviṭaṉ Accakam (Dravidian Printers), are also committed to the proliferation of works extolling Dravidian culture.

E. V. RAMASAMI'S INTERPRETATION OF THE RĀMĀYAṆA

The motivating force behind E.V.R.'s exegesis of the *Rāmāyaṇa* remains the desire to see in it a struggle between North and South India. For E.V.R. "northern" means brahmanical, caste-ridden, and Sanskritic, while "southern" means nonbrahmanical, egalitarian, and Tamil—value judgements that are embedded in his interpretation. In *Characters in the Rāmāyaṇa* E.V.R. vehemently attacks the respect with which Tamilians have traditionally viewed the *Rāmāyaṇa*, arguing that the story is both an account of and a continuing vehicle for northern cultural domination. Reversing the conventional understandings of villain and hero, he also calls upon readers to abandon their "superstitious" beliefs and embrace a desacralized view of the world.

The structure of *Characters in the Rāmāyaṇa* is tripartite. E.V.R. begins with a brief rationale for writing the text, pointing to the pamphlet's crucial role in enlightening Tamils about the "real" message of the *Rāmāyaṇa* (11–16). The heart of the pamphlet is its long middle section, which enumerates and critically evaluates the deeds performed by most of the major characters in the epic (17–88). The text culminates with a short collection of quotes from *aṟiñar*, "learned men," whom E.V.R. feels confirm and thus legitimate his understanding of the *Rāmāyaṇa* (91–104).

In the opening section, E.V.R. justifies his enterprise, claiming that his study of the *Rāmāyaṇa* should reveal to Tamilians that they have been deluded by northern propaganda into believing that Rāma was exemplary as well as divine, when in fact, E.V.R. argues, he was neither. First and foremost, then, we see that E.V.R. wants to "demythologize" (my term, not his) Rāma for Tamilians. But he wants to go even further, to establish that, in addition to being an ordinary mortal, Rāma was not a particularly admirable one.

E.V.R. acknowledges that Tamilians will not find it easy to accept this view of Rāma, attributing this reluctance to their illiteracy and the power of "superstition" among them. He notes with disappointment how most Tamilians (aside from Muslims and Christians) have long venerated the *Rāmāyaṇa*. But for E.V.R., insofar as the commonly held understanding of the *Rāmāyaṇa* is essentially North Indian, it is a key part of the ideology which keeps South Indians in an inferior position, and so must be discredited. He thus argues that the *Rāmāyaṇa* lures Dravidians into the Aryan net, destroys their self-respect, and stymies their development (11). For E.V.R., this examination of the *Rāmāyaṇa* is no mere intellectual exercise; on the contrary, he has taken on the absolutely crucial task of liberating Tamilians from their feelings of cultural and racial inferiority.

E.V.R.'s specific textual analysis follows in the very long middle section of the pamphlet, which might be characterized as an extensive annotated list of charges. Rather than constructing an argument in a discursive manner, he piles example upon example, doubtless intending to overwhelm the reader into accepting his thesis by the sheer number of instances in which the poem's putative heroes commit acts of wrongdoing. He picks his way through the *Rāmāyaṇa*, character by character, vilifying those who join forces with Rāma and praising those who oppose him. In Table 1, I summarize the major charges that E.V.R. levels against thirteen characters, to each of whom he devotes a separate chapter.

E.V.R. uses these charges to accuse those who venerate the *Rāmāyaṇa* of ignoring or condoning myriad acts of improper behavior. As the table shows, a number of the epic's characters are censured because they depart from the norms established for marital or kinship relations. Thus E.V.R. condemns Sītā for criticizing her husband and Kausalyā for not respecting her spouse; he intimates that Sītā was unchaste in Rāvaṇa's house; Lakṣmaṇa and Śatrughna earn abuse for making unfilial statements about their father and disregarding their father, respectively; Bharata insults both parents, thereby drawing E.V.R.'s scorn; both Sugrīva and Vibhīṣaṇa are reviled for betraying their brother. It is ironic that E.V.R. condemns these characters on the basis of prescriptions for behavior which find elaborate expression in the very *dharmaśāstra* text he considers so obnoxious: *The Laws of Manu*. This text, which E.V.R. deeply hates and elsewhere attacks for its praise of Brahmins, contains passages detailing the proper relationships for husband and wife, father and son, and brothers.[26] These passages have traditionally set the standards for proper Hindu behavior—the same behavior that E.V.R. demands (and finds lacking) in the deeds of *Rāmāyaṇa* characters.

E.V.R. also censures a number of characters because they cannot bring their sensual passions and desires under control. He reads the *Rāmāyaṇa* as

TABLE 1. E. V. Ramasami's Charges Against *Rāmāyaṇa* Characters

Character	*Role*	*Charges against the character*
Daśaratha	Rāma's father, ruler of Ayodhya	Was enslaved by passion; broke promises; acted stupidly
Sītā	Wife of Rāma	Criticized her husband; felt attraction to Rāvaṇa; was unchaste; cared too much for jewelry
Bharata	Daśaratha's second son (by Kaikeyī)	Heaped abuse on his mother; insulted his father; had many wives
Lakṣmaṇa	Third son of Daśaratha (by Sumitrā), loyal companion to Rāma	Was attracted to Sītā; tortured (demon) females; made unfilial statements about his father; was hot-headed
Śatrughna	Fourth son of Daśaratha (by Sumitrā), companion to Bharata	Insulted Kaikeyī; abused and disregarded his father
Kausalyā	Senior wife of Daśaratha, mother of Rāma	Possessed excessive concern for the success of her son; was jealous of Kaikeyī and hostile to her; did not respect her
Sumitrā	Youngest wife of Daśaratha, mother of Lakṣmaṇa and Śatrughna	Was eager for Rāma to become king; was prejudiced against Bharata
Sumantra	Charioteer and advisor to Daśaratha	Counseled the king to do improper deeds; spoke derisively of Kaikeyī; lied
Vasiṣṭha	Daśaratha's family guru	Participated in the plot to crown Rāma; hurriedly fixed a day for the coronation so that Bharata would not find out
Hanumān	Rāma's monkey companion, who set fire to Lanka	Is said to have performed miraculous deeds which scientific reason indicates are impossible; unjustly set fire to Lanka and thus killed many innocent people; used obscene language when conversing with Sītā
Sugrīva	King of monkeys, ally of Rāma	Betrayed his brother; joined Rāma only to get rid of his brother
Aṅgada	Son of Vālin, general in Sugrīva's army	Befriended those who killed his father; did not really love Sugrīva
Vibhīṣaṇa	Brother of Rāvaṇa	Betrayed his brother and caused his death in order to gain the kingship of Lanka; did not feel anger when his sister was dishonored by Lakṣmaṇa

portraying Daśaratha enslaved by passion, Sītā overly fond of jeweled ornaments, Lakṣmaṇa desirous of Sītā, Kausalyā as excessively ambitious for the success of her son, and Lakṣmaṇa too hot-headed to control his flaring temper. Again, E.V.R. condemns these people in a way that echoes a central ideal of brahmanical Hinduism—that one must cultivate detachment toward passions and desires. The virtue of detachment is a constant theme in the *Upaniṣads* and in Vedāntic works, to say nothing of the *Bhagavad Gītā* and yogic texts; even the *dharmaśāstras* uphold the benefits of self-restraint.

Although E.V.R. vigorously criticizes all of the above-mentioned characters, his greatest contempt is directed at Rāma himself, whose actions are seen as the epitome of North Indian domination. In accordance with his enumerative style of discourse, E.V.R. cites fifty incidents of seemingly improper behavior on Rāma's part. Rather than explain each one, I will summarize his major criticisms and the patterns of reasoning which stand behind these accusations.

One of E.V.R.'s most elaborately mounted attacks concerns Rāma's supposed coveting of the throne of Ayodhya, which E.V.R. interprets as a sign of Rāma's desire for domination. Ignoring the common understanding—that Rāma merely responded to Daśaratha's request that he be crowned and had all the qualities of a responsible king—E.V.R. portrays Rāma as scheming to grab the throne. He alleges that Rāma craved royal power and acted in a virtuous and affectionate way towards his father, Kaikeyī, and Ayodhya's citizens only to gain such power. Then, says E.V.R., Rāma improperly conspired with his father to have himself installed on the throne before his brother Bharata returned from his stay with his uncle (33–35).

Rāma's alliance with Sugrīva and the ensuing killing of his brother, Vālin, come in for special denunciation, as one might expect, because Rāma apparently unfairly murders the monarch of a southern kingdom. In focusing upon this always problematic incident, E.V.R. expresses an ambivalence found in many diverse tellings of the *Rāmāyaṇa* about whether Rāma erred in killing Vālin as he did—from the back and without having announced his presence. With equal vehemence, however, E.V.R. emphasizes not only the stealthy killing but the fact that Brahmins praise such a man. That they do so is evidence of their attempt to foist an unheroic Rāma upon South India as an exemplar of proper behavior (11–13).

Rāma's treatment of his wife, Sītā, draws particular criticism from E.V.R. because he takes it as emblematic of Rāma's oppression of those less powerful than himself. After her grueling and terrifying captivity in Lanka, Rāma subjects Sītā to a despicable ordeal and then still refuses to accept her back. As E.V.R. comments, "Even though Vālmīki proclaimed the chastity of Sītā, Rāma did not believe it, so she had to die" (38). For E.V.R., this hostile attitude toward women is part and parcel of the North Indian worldview.

The manner, glorified in North Indian texts, in which Rāma drove his wife to submit to such ordeals helps to keep Indian women in a state of subjugation.

E.V.R. reserves his greatest outrage, however, for Rāma's treatment of Śūdras, the lowest group in the four-part brahmanical caste ranking and one of the major audiences of his pamphlet. He notes that Rāma killed a Śūdra named Śambūka because he was performing asceticism, which Vedic tradition prohibits to those not twice-born (that is, Śūdras and Untouchables). Rāma murdered this Śūdra in order to revive a Brahmin boy who had died—that such an untimely death could strike a Brahmin family signaled that somewhere someone (in this case Śambūka) was committing an offense against dharma. After summarizing this incident, E.V.R. extrapolates from it to present-day South India. "If there were kings like Rāma now, what would be the fate of those people called Śūdras?" he asks, implying that Śūdras would never be safe from murder if such a king still ruled (41). Since over 60 percent of South Indians are regarded as Śūdras, at least by Brahmins, E.V.R. stirs the rage of a good number of his readers by emphasizing this event.

Although E.V.R. surveys many other incidents in the epic, castigating Rāma for everything from meat-eating to killing females (39), the trend of his critique is already clear. For E.V.R., Rāma personifies "North Indian values" and is accordingly identified with North Indian dominance of lower castes and women. Equally pernicious, according to E.V.R., is the attempt by Brahmins to put forth this vicious and immoral person as virtuous—and even divine.

Just as E.V.R. regards the traditional heroes as villains, he proposes more positive evaluations of characters who have long been condemned, such as Kaikeyī, the mother of Bharata. Those seeking to portray King Daśaratha in a sympathetic light have conventionally held his youngest wife, Kaikeyī, to be the real villain of the epic, holding her responsible for the king's decision to deprive Rāma of the throne and exile him. In contrast, E.V.R. points out that Kaikeyī was fully within her rights when she asked the king to fulfill the two boons he had granted her when she once saved his life (61).[27]

In his analysis of the Vālin episode, E.V.R. makes another revisionist interpretation, an interpretation all the more significant because of the ambivalence with which tradition has viewed Rāma's killing of Vālin. The words of the modern writer R. K. Narayan, who has produced his own telling of the Rāma story, are instructive here:

> Rama was an ideal man, all his faculties in control in any circumstances, one possessed of an unwavering sense of justice and fair play. Yet he once acted, as it seemed, out of partiality, half-knowledge, and haste, and shot and destroyed, from hiding, a creature who had done him no harm, not even seen him. This is one of the most controversial chapters in the Ramayana.[28]

E.V.R. points out that Vālin could not be defeated in an open fight (implying that a desire to win lay behind Rāma's devious action) and that he assumed Rāma to be an honest and fair person and died as a result—although E.V.R. overstates the matter when he claims that "Vālin was blameless in every way" (63).[29]

Vālin figures only briefly in the analysis, however. Not surprisingly, Rāvaṇa receives more attention because for E.V.R.—who identifies Rāvaṇa as a monarch of the ancient Dravidians—he exemplifies the South Indians, whose culture was unfairly suppressed by North Indians. Although E.V.R. neglects to provide specific textual references, he begins his praise of Rāvaṇa by listing the virtues that Vālmīki attributes to Rāvaṇa: Rāvaṇa has mastered the Vedas and *śāstras*, he protects his family and kin, he acts courageously, he practices *bhakti*, he is the beloved son of a god, and he has received several boons (67). One wonders why E.V.R. would consider knowledge of "Aryan" texts like Vedas a recommendation, but what follows is even more revealing. Focusing on the influence of other characters on Rāvaṇa's actions, E.V.R. gives us a new construct of Rāvaṇa.

Rather than seeing Rāma as effectively vanquishing Rāvaṇa, E.V.R. interprets Rāvaṇa's death as the result of his brother's betrayal. When Vibhīṣaṇa, Rāvaṇa's brother, approaches Rāma and asks to join him, E.V.R. harshly condemns his abandonment of his brother, viewing this action as motivated by Vibhīṣaṇa's desire to possess and rule Lanka (67). The great Rāvaṇa was thus undone by his brother's villainy; his death, argues E.V.R., should not be seen as evincing any lack of courage.

Nor should Rāvaṇa's abduction of Sītā be interpreted as the result of lust, according to E.V.R. He argues that Rāvaṇa takes Sītā to Lanka as an honorable act of retaliation against Rāma's insult and Lakṣmaṇa's disfigurement of Rāvaṇa's sister, Śūrpaṇakhā. Śūrpaṇakhā had fallen in love with Rāma, openly offering herself to him in marriage; by way of punishment, Lakṣmaṇa cut off her nose and ears. As a dutiful brother, Rāvaṇa had no choice but to avenge his sister's cruel disfigurement—but, as E.V.R. points out, Rāvaṇa would never stoop to something as low as mutilating Sītā in the same horrible way. In fact, notes E.V.R., Rāvaṇa never forced himself upon the captive Sītā. In such matters, he practiced proper self-restraint, never touching a woman without her consent (68). At the level of metadiscourse, E.V.R. goes so far as to argue that one must not condemn Rāvaṇa for abducting Sītā because she was left alone in the forest specifically so she could be abducted (69). In other words, by abducting Sītā, Rāvaṇa is simply performing an action which he is destined to perform—an interpretation which assumes an inexorability about the events in the *Rāmāyaṇa*.

Rāvaṇa's sense of propriety also manifests itself in his unwillingness to kill animals, which E.V.R. takes as evidence of his compassionate Dravidian nature. He notes that Rāvaṇa hated *devas* (gods), *ṛṣis* (sages), and Brahmin priests because they performed sacrificial rituals and drank intoxicating liquor (*soma*). Rāvaṇa refused to participate in such rituals because they involved the torture of poor helpless animals (68). By portraying Rāvaṇa as rejecting the killing of animals, E.V.R. plays on the vegetarian inclinations of many of his followers, arousing their sympathy for Rāvaṇa.

In a cryptic but intriguing comment near the end of his characterization of Rāvaṇa (69), E.V.R. even claims that Rāvaṇa was a responsible and responsive political leader, a benign ruler. Because the *Rāmāyaṇa* records instances where Rāvaṇa consults with his ministers and debates ensue, E.V.R. claims to see traces of an inclusive political process, which belie the conventional brahmanical claims that Rāvaṇa was a cruel despot.

Especially given that Rāvaṇa represents Dravidians, it is somewhat noteworthy that E.V.R. does not devote much attention to any of the other characters in Rāvaṇa's family, even though he dealt at length with Rāma's father, mothers, brothers, and wife. Although E.V.R. says that so-called demons like Rāvaṇa are in fact admirable Dravidians, Śūrpaṇakhā's actions—her open expression of sexual desire, for example—are not praised, nor even mentioned, except as they relate to Rāvaṇa's duty to revenge her honor. E.V.R. is similarly silent about Mandodarī, and about Khara, Mārīca, Dūsaṇa, and other of Rāvaṇa's supporters. The fact that E.V.R. spends so much time castigating Rāma and his family and so little time praising the actions of Rāvaṇa and his family indicates that E.V.R. aroused more ire by lambasting North Indians than by defining and defending precisely what constitutes South Indian culture and identity.

The final brief section of *Characters in the Rāmāyaṇa* consists of an appeal to authority. Scholarly discourse in Tamil has traditionally taken note of the opinions of learned men. One main area of analytic discourse consisted of commenting on texts: those trained in grammar construed complex verses, gave parallel passages, and provided exegesis, an enterprise which generally included quotations from scholars of the past.[30] In fact, a good commentary would record what a large number of learned men had said on the subject. E.V.R.'s thirteen-page section entitled "Opinions of Learned Men [*aṟiñar*] about the Rāmāyaṇa" serves the same function.

Rather than citing the opinion of traditional religious and literary scholars, however, E.V.R. quotes distinguished authorities of other types—historians, politicians, other public figures, members of the Indian Civil Service. Also cited in his "Opinions of Learned Men" section are many handbooks or histories of India with titles such as *Ancient Indian History and Civilization*, *Dravidians and Aryans*, and *Civilization in Ancient India*. The historians cited include both North Indians (Muslim and Bengali) and Europeans.[31] E.V.R. also quotes from the works of the North Indian Swami Vivekananda, as he does from the pan-Indian classic *The Discovery of India*, by the North Indian "Pandit" Jawaharlal Nehru, nationalist leader and prime minister of India from 1947 to 1964.[32] When E.V.R. quotes members of the prestigious Indian Civil Service, he includes "I.C.S." after their names in order to indicate their status. Similarly, he includes after the names of historians all their degrees (B.S., M.A., Ph.D., L.L.D.) *and* precedes their names with "Ṭākṭar" (Dr.) whenever possible. Both Henry Johnson's and William Wilson Hunter's names are preceded by "Sir." Clearly, E.V.R. wants to impress upon his readers the illustriousness of those scholars and national figures who appear to confirm his interpretation.

In addition, E.V.R. cites various prominent Tamilian scholars. He quotes J. M. Nallaswami Pillai, an important figure in the Saiva Siddhanta movement and editor of its journal, *Siddhanta Deepika*, as well as Maraimalai Atigal, an eminent Tamil literary savant whose ideas form the ideological foundation of the Pure Tamil movement.[33] Along with such non-Brahmin literary and religious figures, E.V.R. also quotes respected Brahmin scholars such as S. Krishnaswami Aiyangar, a historian of religious and philosophical texts, and K. A. Nilakanta Sastri, a prominent historian of South India. E.V.R. thus willingly cites the opinions of Brahmins, non-Brahmins, and Western "foreigners" to prove his thesis that Brahmins were aliens in South India who oppressed non-Brahmins.

E.V.R.'s citation method also deserves notice. The section of quotes comes at the end of his argument, rather than in the course of it, and thus serves not as documentation but as affirmation. His quotes from Nehru's *Discovery of India* are representative of his citation style throughout this section of *Characters in the Rāmāyaṇa*. He notes several of Nehru's comments about the *Rāmāyaṇa* in relation to Aryan expansion in South India and gives a page number for each quote—but he cites no edition, no facts of publication. Like other authors of the popular pamphlet literature of his time, E.V.R. cites not so his reader can go to the original text but simply to take advantage of the cited author's status. Nor does he give any context for the quotes cited: each is simply listed, along with all the others, as validation for his interpretation of the *Rāmāyaṇa*. By stringing together forty-seven quotes from historians and politicians about the ancient move of northerners to South India, E.V.R. seeks to demonstrate that learned men support his claims—although those learned men might not agree with the use to which their words have been put.

PRECEDENT AND INNOVATION IN E.V.R.'S INTERPRETATION

Little in E.V.R.'s interpretation of the *Rāmāyaṇa* is absolutely new. Rather, it is the manner in which E.V.R. assembles, packages, argues, and dramatizes his interpretation that is innovative. A truly modern social critic, he publishes with a careful eye to public reception and dramatizes his interpretations through public performances. Although his forms may be innovative, one can find precedents for the various components of his message in many places.

In attacking the hypocrisy of Brahmins, E.V.R. places himself in a long line of Tamil writers who have bitterly criticized brahmanical tradition. Among the many examples that demonstrate E.V.R.'s continuity with this strand of Tamil polemicism, one is particularly ancient and notable. In Cīttalai Cāttaṉār's *Maṇimēkalai*, a Buddhist text that most scholars believe dates from the sixth century A.D., one finds the story of Āputtiraṉ, a character with an E. V. Ramasami–like view of Hinduism.[34] The illegitimate son of a renowned Varanasi Brahmin's wife, Āputtiraṉ gets into a debate with the leaders of his Brahmin community. Because he has thoroughly studied the Vedas, he is able relentlessly to cite embarrassing facts about the ancient brahmanical sages in order to discredit his opponents' lineages. Like E.V.R., Āputtiraṉ cites all kinds of improprieties about their births: some, for example, were conceived when their fathers ejaculated while watching dancing girls, others are the sons of animals, and so on.[35] Next, Āputtiraṉ confronts Indra, king of the gods, informing the deity that he is indifferent to Indra's heaven because it is full of beings who care only for their own pleasure, rather than for doing good. As we have seen, E.V.R., too, ridicules stories about Brahmins and brahmanical deities, portraying them as self-serving and unworthy of admiration.

Anti-Brahmin sentiment continues to surface periodically in South Indian literature. Surveying anti-Brahmin and egalitarian movements in South India, Irschick reminds us that this strand of rhetoric played an important role in the writings of some of the Siddhars, a group of Tamil ascetics, the majority of whom lived between the fifth and tenth centuries.[36] Ramanujan's translations of Vīraśaiva poems dating from the tenth to twelfth centuries reveal Lingayat contempt for traditional Hindu institutions, including the role of Brahmins.[37] Closer to E.V.R.'s own time are the writings of the religious poet Ramalingaswami (1823–1874), a saint extremely critical of caste distinctions. Irschick points out that in 1929 E.V.R.'s own press published an anthology of Ramalingaswami's songs with an introduction by A. Citamparanar, who also wrote an influential biography of E.V.R.'s early life.[38] E.V.R. considered Ramalingaswami important enough to the Self-Respect Movement to revive his writings and publish them in a form available and understandable to a general audience. Maraimalai Atigal, called by one scholar "the most articulate pioneer" of ideological resistance to Brahmin domination, slightly preceded E.V.R. and shared with him a sharply critical attitude toward Brahmins and brahmanical Hinduism.[39]

If E.V.R.'s antibrahminism connects him to a continuous strand of South Indian culture, his positive assessment of Rāvaṇa has precedents in the *Rāmāyaṇa* tradition itself. Several Jain writers contest the prevailing characterization of Rāvaṇa in their *pratipurāṇas* ("counter-*purāṇas*"), of which

Vimalasūri's *Paumacariyam* (c. 473 A.D.) is an excellent example. In a notable reversal, this text begins its narrative with an account of Rāvaṇa's lineage, rather than that of Rāma.[40] Vimalasūri portrays Rāvaṇa as noble, admirable, and knowledgeable about religious texts, and as one who has learned a great deal through ascetic practices. As Ramanujan's essay in this volume demonstrates, this *pratipurāṇa* gives us a totally different perspective on Rāvaṇa from that found in most Hindu versions. Dineshchandra Sen calls our attention to another Jain *Rāmāyaṇa*, by Hemacandra (1089–1172), in which Rāvaṇa again acts in spiritually admirable ways. In one key scene Rāvaṇa sits in the forest meditating, remaining serene and single-minded despite all the attempts of *yakṣas* (forest spirits) to distract him from his endeavor by transforming themselves first into seductive damsels and then into terrifying jackals and snakes. Dineshchandra Sen comments that Rāvaṇa's acts of meditative discipline "show his high character and a majestic command over passions, worthy of a sage, which unmistakably prove him to be the real hero of the Dravidian legend."[41] In a similar vein, Rāvaṇa figures as a sage and a responsible ruler in the Buddhist *Laṅkāvatāra Sūtra*, where he invites the Buddha to his kingdom of Lanka and then listens intently to his religious discourse.[42]

As Seely's analysis reveals, the Bengali author Michael Madhusudan Dutt (1824–1873) also wrote a "reverse *Rāmāyaṇa*," which some scholars feel may have been shaped in part by the Jain *Rāmāyaṇa* tradition.[43] Of at least equal importance, however, is the role of the colonial context in which Dutt was writing. Nandy sees Dutt's epic as enabling him to accept certain martial values in Indian culture and reject brahmanical ascetic ones.

> Madhusudan's criteria for reversing the roles of Rāma and Rāvaṇa, as expressed in their characters, was a direct response to the colonial situation. He admired Rāvaṇa for his masculine vigour, accomplished warriorhood, and his sense of *realpolitik* and history; he accepted Rāvaṇa's "adult" and "normal" commitments to secular, possessive this-worldliness and his consumer's lust for life. On the other hand, he despised "Rāma and his rabble"—the expression was his—because they were effeminate, ineffectual pseudo-ascetics, who were austere not by choice but because they were weak.[44]

Both Dutt and E.V.R. wrote in a colonial context. For different reasons, each came to see Rāvaṇa as the real hero of the Rāma story, a choice that had deep political resonances.

E.V.R.'s attempt to discredit the assumptions of orthodox Hinduism through an exaggeratedly literal reading of its texts is consonant with a form of discourse popular in the second half of the nineteenth century. In religious debates, Hindus, Muslims, Sikhs, and Christians routinely disparaged the religious beliefs of their opponents, as Barbara Metcalf has shown.[45] In so doing, they often relied on a hyperliteral reading of mythic texts. To see just how literal such a reading can be, consider this quote from Dayananda Sarasvati, the leader of the Arya Samaj, who responded to the description of a heavenly army of horsemen found in Revelations 9:16 in this way:

> Where would so many horses stay in heaven? Where would they graze? Where would they dwell and where would they throw out the dung? How awful would be the bad smell of the dung! We Aryas have washed our hands of such a heaven, such a God and such a religion.

Quoting this passage, Kenneth Jones comments: "Since the goals of these writers were to discredit Christianity and make it difficult for missionaries to defend it in public debates and in print, absolute literalism proved a useful and welcome tool."[46] E.V.R. used the same technique of hyperliteral readings in his attempt to discredit and desacralize the *Rāmāyaṇa*.

Even E.V.R.'s view of the *Rāmāyaṇa* as an account of Aryan domination of Dravidian culture has roots in earlier discourse. Irschick has carefully traced how the ideas of P. Sundaram Pillai, a Tamil Vellala (1855–1897), began to focus attention on the meaning of the *Rāmāyaṇa* in the context of discussions about Dravidian and Aryan culture.[47] Sundaram Pillai published some of his views on the self-sufficiency and grandeur of Dravidian civilization during his lifetime, but his theories about the *Rāmāyaṇa* were disseminated after his death by his friends. T. Ponemballem Pillai wrote an article for the *Malabar Review* in which he summarized Sundaram Pillai's view of the *Rāmāyaṇa* as written to "proclaim the prowess of the Aryans and to represent their rivals and enemies the Dravidians, who had attained a high degree of civilization in that period, in the worst possible colour."[48] A somewhat later writer, M. S. Purnalingam Pillai, ended his *Ravana the Great: King of Lanka* by describing Rāvaṇa as "a mighty hero and monarch, a conqueror of worlds, and a fearless resister of the Aryan aggressions in South India."[49] With these writers began a controversy about the political meaning of the *Rāmāyaṇa*, to which E.V.R. soon added his own strident reading of the text.

Thus each of the major characteristics of E.V.R.'s interpretation of the *Rāmāyaṇa*—his attack on brahmanical tradition, his positive assessment of Rāvaṇa, his hyperliteral reading of Hindu texts, and his North/South reading—finds a precedent in some genre of South Asian writing. E.V.R. has synthesized these different themes, transforming the disparate pieces into something new and coherent. The manner in which he brings these elements together is both innovative and powerful: his reading of the *Rāmāyaṇa* is hostile and comprehensive, seductive and witty, rhetorically adroit and politically astute.

The single-minded and relentless virulence of E.V.R.'s interpretation is striking. Insofar as he seeks to contest the central values of Vālmīki's telling of the story, his overall aim is similar to that of the Jain *Rāmāyaṇas*—but E.V.R. goes beyond mere contesting. In accord with his North/South principle of interpretation, he atomizes the text and reassembles its events for his own purpose. He could have presented the story chronologically, interpreting events in the order they occur. Instead, like a lawyer putting together a set of accusations, E.V.R. assembles his case by selecting and forming into a daunting list particular events or bits of dialogue that become the basis of his harsh indictment of most of the Ayodhyan characters. Both the hostility and the comprehensiveness of his attack mark E.V.R.'s interpretation of the *Rāmāyaṇa* as singular.

Not only is his analysis thorough but his styles of argumentation are many. Certain strategies of exegesis appear again and again. He anachronizes the text, condemning customs from centuries earlier on the basis of modern norms. He literalizes the text, subjecting mythic material to scientific analysis in order to "prove" that such events could not have occurred. He conflates the dual nature of Rāma, ignoring that, according to myth, Rāma is both human *and* divine (he is the god Viṣṇu as well as a human avatar), which allows him to criticize Rāma for things he must do as part of his avatar mission while also making fun of him for showing human emotions. E.V.R. even goes so far as to condemn a character on the strength of minor character flaws, ignoring the majority of (positive) actions performed by that character. When necessary he has it both ways, in one context portraying a character as a victim and in another as an oppressor, depending on his polemical needs.

E.V.R.'s use of evidence is typical of the pamphlet style of his time, and, while seductive, the evidence itself is sparsely documented. The reader is told that E.V.R.'s analysis grew out of an exhaustive study of the Vālmīki *Rāmāyaṇa* and Tamil translations of it done by Brahmins. E.V.R. almost never, however, cites a specific edition of the text or the interpretation of one or another commentator on a particular passage or even specific verse numbers, though he sometimes cites *sargas* (chapters) in *kāṇḍas* (books). For example, in his eight-point analysis of Rāvaṇa, he provides only two citations, neither one referring to specific verses—even though one of the eight points contains a direct quote. Likewise, discussing his fourth point, E.V.R. says "Vālmīki himself said" but fails to tell us where Vālmīki said so (*Characters in the Rāmāyaṇa*, 68). Such a documentation style indicates neither deliberate sloppiness nor a desire to distort evidence. Rather, it is governed by audience: E.V.R. intended his exegesis as a way of expounding Dravidian ideology to the popular reader, not to scholars.

In part, E.V.R.'s style of argumentation derives from oral presentation. His speeches were unforgettable events. Respectable women (who would not think of mingling directly with those they perceived as the "common riffraff" who frequented such events) would crowd onto nearby verandas and listen to his speeches over loudspeakers. Even Brahmins—often the subject of his attack—attended his speeches to hear his cutting yet humorous satire. Those who attended his public lectures continue to comment even today on how wickedly funny they found them. Hence it comes as no surprise to find that his writing is also designed both to delight and to stir up his audience. His written language has much of the power of his oral art. His simple sentences, numbered points, and loosely connected structure comprise a kind of "jab rhetoric" with which he can attack the *Rāmāyaṇa*. E.V.R. is also deliberately crude or coarse in places, incorporating into his argument innuendoes about Rāma's vileness or Sītā's lack of faithfulness.[50] As an orator and a writer addressing a mass audience, he uses wit and titillation to play upon the half-guilty pleasure of seeing a familiar object of piety in a totally new, somewhat ridiculous, light.

E.V.R.'s self-presentation also plays a large role in the delivery of his message. His publications characteristically bear his picture: long white beard, glasses, white hair. Inside *Characters in the Rāmāyaṇa*, the reader really encounters more of E.V.R. than Rāma. The inside back covers of most editions contain, in addition to the titles and prices of his other publications, lists of celebratory accounts of his accomplishments, such as *Periyar E. V. Ramasami* (*A Pen Portrait*)—a phenomenon that has persisted beyond his death (in 1973). Consider the following announcement inside the front cover of the 1980 English edition of *The Ramayana* (*A True Reading*):

> The importance of this book
>
> The English and Hindi Editions of this book were banned by the Uttar Pradesh Government. The High Court of the U. P. lifted the ban and the U. P. Government appealed to the Supreme Court against the judgment of the High Court. In the Supreme Court, the appeal preferred by the U. P. State was dismissed in 1976 as the Supreme Court did not see any reason to interfere with the judgment of the U. P. High Court.[51]

As this statement indicates, the significance of the work now extends beyond the boundaries of Tamilnadu: through its translation into both English and Hindi, it has attracted attention in North India. The pamphlet was considered so threatening that the government of Uttar Pradesh (where Rāma's royal city of Ayodhya is located and where Hindu-Muslim riots continue over a mosque at the alleged site of Rāma's birth) felt compelled to ban its publication—although, as the publishers note with satisfaction, the government's attempt to suppress the text has been unsuccessful.[52] The announcement of course gives the reader the impression that the pamphlet contains forbidden, and hence desirable, reading matter, thus adding to E.V.R.'s notoriety.

Not a man to stop at mere words, E.V.R. encouraged the enactment of his interpretation of the *Rāmāyaṇa* in dramatic performance as well. The DK drama inspired by E.V.R.'s exegesis and known by the mocking name of

"*Keemayana*" (*keema* is a nonsense sound) toured throughout Tamilnadu. The play's portrayal of Rāma as a drunkard and Sītā as a wanton woman earned it the comment "hoodlums stage filth in Trichy" in one review.[53] The high (or low, depending on the viewer's perspective) point in the performance occurred when participants beat images of Rāma with their (polluting) leather sandals. Similarly, E.V.R.'s scheduled burning of images of Rāma in 1956 testifies to his desire to dramatize his exegetical attack. By reversing the North Indian ritual of Rāvaṇa-burning, he not only enacts his verbal attack on Rāma but reminds Tamilians of the urgent need for them to embrace his political interpretation of the *Rāmāyaṇa*.

CONCLUSIONS

This account of E. V. Ramasami's interpretation of the *Rāmāyaṇa* confirms that even in the modern period the *Rāmāyaṇa* continues to be reread in ways that reflect and shape the concerns of both exegete and audience. As we have seen, the skeletal Rāma story affords a structure around which poets build new tellings. For E.V.R., the story provides the framework for a deeply political telling. He reinterprets and re-presents the *Rāmāyaṇa*, a sacred and traditional text, so as to undermine radically both its sacrality and the traditional understanding of its incidents.

E.V.R.'s telling of the *Rāmāyaṇa* is consonant with many of the biographical and political features of his own life. Thus his denial of the epic's sacrality echoes his own youthful disillusionment with Hinduism, while his condemnation of Rāma as an agent of North Indian oppression parallels his attack on Brahmins as dominating both the Congress Party and local positions of power. What makes his reading of the text more than an idiosyncratic response to the *Rāmāyaṇa*, however, is the extent to which E.V.R. imbued this response with political purpose and self-consciously presented his reading for public consumption. The impressive reprint history of *Characters in the Rāmāyaṇa* attests to the success of his interpretation in the realm of public discourse. In vilifying Rāma and elevating Rāvaṇa, E.V.R. does far more than simply present a new assessment of familiar characters. By demythologizing Rāma, he translates what had generally been thought of as sacred mythic truth into the political sphere, using his exegesis of the text to articulate the need to resist what he saw as oppressive North Indian cultural and political domination of South India.

E.V.R.'s exegesis of the *Rāmāyaṇa* is accordingly presented so as to have the maximum public impact. It uses dramatic rhetoric, it attacks, it pokes fun, it shocks, and it insists. Although one might be tempted to dismiss E. V. Ramasami as an isolated eccentric, this would be unwise, for his exegesis of the *Rāmāyaṇa* was pivotal. As the 1956 Rāma-burning agitation indicates, E.V.R. not only sought but gained front page media coverage for his opinions. Reassessing the traditional characters and incidents of the epic with polemical flamboyance, he created a rhetoric of political opposition that shaped public discourse for a group much larger than his relatively small band of followers.

Part of E.V.R.'s legacy rests with the DMK (Dravida Munnetra Kazagham, or Progressive Dravidian Federation), a group composed of some of his most brilliant followers, who split off from the DK to form their own organization. Men such as C. N. Annadurai, Mu. Karunanidhi, and Shivaji Ganesan, who worked in filmmaking as screen writers, producers, and actors, continued E.V.R.'s dramatic style of public rhetoric to decry brahmanical suppression of Dravidian identity. At first a mere splinter group, the DMK eventually came to equal and then vastly surpass the DK in importance. Because a number of prominent DMK members were active in the film industry, moreover, they had access to another powerful medium for publicizing their message to huge numbers of people. By 1967 DMK political power was established, the DMK continuing to dominate the political arena in Tamilnadu until the group splintered.[54] Members of the DMK learned a great deal from E.V.R., particularly in relation to public discourse and political performance. They moved readily and smoothly from the realm of myth (Rāvaṇa, Rāma) to film, from public agitation to mass meetings, from political criticism to political power.

In fact, one could argue that what the DMK came to offer Tamilians outdistanced E. V. Ramasami. If E.V.R. was the great assembler of rhetoric, of interpretations, and of public performances, DMK filmmakers created even more extravagant celluloid products with clearly identified villains and heroes, moral messages, and colorful drama. If E.V.R. was the great polemicist in the public arena, the DMK went further, transforming grass-roots Dravidian sentiment into institutionalized political power. If E.V.R. was the great self-promoter, the DMK became increasingly sophisticated and daring in its strategies to gain media coverage and a popular following. If E.V.R. was the stage director of histrionic public acts, the DMK film personalities and politicians were his true successors. Far from dying out, his style was incorporated, updated, and intensified. To understand some of the roots of the highly charged conflicts in Tamilnadu public discourse during recent decades, one must take into account a largely ignored phenomenon, E.V.R.'s critique of the *Rāmāyaṇa*.

NOTES

I am grateful to Marguerite Barnett, Sara Dickey, Michael Fisher, Sandria Freitag, Charles Hallisey, Eugene Irschick, Pat Mathews, Susan Munkres, Sumathi Ramaswamy, James Ryan, Sandra Zagarell, Eleanor Zelliot, Abbie Ziffren, and the members of the faculty seminar on religious innovation at the University of Washington, as well as students in my 1989 and 1990 seminars, for their comments on earlier drafts of this article. I also appreciate the financial support of Oberlin College, from whom I received a faculty research grant for this project.

For convenience's sake I have referred to E. V. Ramasami [Naicker] throughout the article as E.V.R. The common Tamil abbreviation is Ī. Ve. Rā., but that becomes a bit cumbersome in English prose, and most English writers refer to him as E.V.R. When writing his name out in full, I have omitted diacritics because "E. V. Ramasami" was the standard English form of his name in his publications. The same is true for other important Tamil figures of his period who used English spellings of their names.

1. E.V.R. decided to burn images of Rāma in order to protest the fact that All-India Radio had refused to transmit a speech he made on the occasion of celebrating the birthday of the Buddha. See the front page of the *Indian Express*, 2 August 1956. For a description of the burning of Rāvaṇa in the Rāmlīlā, see Linda Hess and Richard Schechner, "The Ramlila of Ramnagar," *The Drama Review* 21, no. 3 (September 1977), 63.

2. Technically, the term *Dravidian* refers to the family of languages spoken throughout South India. But the leaders of the Tamil separatist movement have expanded the term to encompass everything that they identify as South Indian culture.

3. *The Hindu*, 1 August 1956; *Indian Express*, 1 August 1956; *Tiṉamaṇi*, 1 August 1956. The Tamilnadu Congress was dominated by Brahmins, so Kakkan's appeal did not have much effect on E.V.R.

4. *The Hindu*, 1 August 1956.

5. *Tiṉamaṇi*, 2 August 1956, provides a breakdown of the number of people arrested throughout Tamilnadu. In Madras more than 90 people were arrested, while 120 were jailed in Tiruchirappalli (Trichy). For E.V.R.'s comment after his release, see the *Indian Express*, 2 August 1956.

6. In this very brief overview of E.V.R.'s life, I highlight only the events relevant to the development of his interpretation of the *Rāmāyaṇa*. For the details of his life, see the widely consulted biography of his early years by A. Citamparaṉār, *Tamiḻar Talaivar* (Erode: Kuṭi Aracu Press, 1960; repr. Trichy: Periyar Self-Respect Propaganda Institution, 1979); also, Ē. Es. Vēṇu, *Periyār Oru Carittiram* (Madras: Pūmpukār Piracuram, 1980). In addition, a number of other works give some biographical information: K. M. Balasubramaniam, *Periyar E. V. Ramasami* (Trichy: Periyar Self-Respect Propaganda Institution, 1973); D.G.S., *Periyar E. V. Ramaswamy: A Proper Perspective* (Madras: Vairam Pathippagam, 1975); Ki. Vīramaṇi, *Periyār Kaḷañciyam* (Madras: Periyar Self-Respect Propaganda Institution, 1977); Anita Diehl, *E. V. Ramaswami Naicker-Periyar: A Study of the Influence of a Personality in Contemporary South India* (Lund: Scandinavian University Books, 1977).

7. For an analysis of the significance of E.V.R.'s youthful rebellions against caste, see Marguerite Ross Barnett, *The Politics of Cultural Nationalism in South India* (Princeton: Princeton University Press, 1976), 34–36.

8. Citamparaṉār, *Tamiḻar Talaivar*, 41–51. For a discussion of E.V.R.'s involvement in regional politics, see Christopher J. Baker and David A. Washbrook, *South India: Political Institutions and Political Change, 1880–1940* (Delhi: Macmillan, 1975), 27; Christopher Baker, "Leading up to Periyar: The Early Career of E. V. Ramaswami Naicker," in *Leadership in South Asia*, ed. B. Pandey (Bombay: Vikas, 1978), 503–34;

and Christopher Baker, *The Politics of South India, 1920–1937* (Cambridge: Cambridge University Press, 1976), 192–94.

9. This place is also spelled Vaikom, Vykom, and Vaikkom in English. For a discussion of this event, see E. Sa. Visswanathan, *The Political Career of E. V. Ramasami Naicker* (Madras: Ravi and Vasanth Publishers, 1983), 42–46.

10. Over the years E.V.R. launched a number of serials including *Puraṭci* (Revolt), *Pakuttaṟivu* (Discernment), and *Viṭutalai* (Liberty).

11. Although E.V.R. is famous for the statement, "If you see a Brahmin and a snake on the road, kill the Brahmin first," he seems to have said such things largely to shock. In several places, he claimed he hated not individual Brahmins but brahminism as an institution. In a somewhat similar spirit, in an article for *The Hindu*, while maintaining that "Aryan" and "Dravidian" are two distinct groups, he commented: "My desire is not to perpetuate this difference but to unify the two opposing elements in society." See Barnett's analysis of his statement in *Politics of Cultural Nationalism in South India*, 71.

12. Much of E. V. Ramasami's exegesis of myths was intended for shock value and involved a deliberate overly literal reading of texts. For other texts which use the same kind of rhetoric, see *Visittira Tēvarkaḷ Kōrṭṭu* (Wonderful court of deities) (Madras: Artisan and Co., 1929), in which various Hindu gods are tried in court for their improper deeds. (I am indebted to Eugene Irschick for this reference.) The *purāṇas* also came in for criticism. The procession which culminated E.V.R.'s 1971 Superstition Eradication Conference contained painted tableaux of many scenes from the *purāṇas* in which gods are engaged in what E.V.R. perceived to be obscene behavior. I discuss this and similar events in "Smashing, Burning, and Parading: E. V. Ramasami's Anti-Religion Agitations, 1953–1971" (paper presented at the Conference on Religion in South India, Brunswick, Maine, June 1989). For an analysis of E.V.R.'s contribution to atheism, see V. Anaimuthu, *Contribution of Periyar E.V.R. to the Progress of Atheism* (Tiruchirappalli: Periyar Nul Veliyittakam, 1980).

13. See Periyar E. V. Ramasami, *Self-Respect Marriages* (Madras: Periyar Self-Respect Propaganda Institution, 1983), which, according to the preface of this edition, is a translation of his *Vāḻkkai Tuṇai Nalam*, first published in 1958. For more information about the self-respect marriage, see Nambi Arooran, *Tamil Renaissance and Dravidian Nationalism* (Madurai: Koodal, 1980), pp. 162–63; Lloyd Rudolph, "Urban Life and Populist Radicalism: Dravidian Politics in Madras," *Journal of Asian Studies* 20, no. 3 (May 1961), 289.

14. See Eugene F. Irschick, *Politics and Social Conflict in South India: The Non-Brahman Movement and Tamil Separatism, 1916–1929* (Berkeley and Los Angeles: University of California Press, 1969), 34. In 1939 E.V.R. organized a conference during which he called for a separate and independent Dravida Nadu, a concept that paralleled the idea of Pakistan, at that time gaining support among the Muslim community. Robert L. Hardgrave, *The Dravidian Movement* (Bombay: Popular Prakashan, 1956), comments: "Naicker gave full support to the scheme for Pakistan and tried to enlist League support for the creation of Dravidasthan. . . . At the time of partition, Naicker tried to secure the help of Jinnah, so that Dravidasthan might be formed simultaneously with Pakistan. Jinnah refused assistance, and the British ignored the Dravidian agitations" (27, 32).

15. See Peter Worsley, *The Trumpet Shall Sound: A Study of "Cargo" Cults in Melanesia*, 3d ed. (New York: Schocken Books, 1968), ix–xxi.

16. This brief overview of E. V. Ramasami's milieu cannot possibly do justice to the complexity of the changes occurring in South India at the time. The reader interested in discussions of other historical and political factors during this period should consult the studies of Barnett, Irschick, Visswanathan, Hardgrave, Arooran, Diehl, and Baker cited above, as well as Robert L. Hardgrave, "The Justice Party and the Tamil Renaissance," in *The Justice Party Golden Jubilee Souvenir* (Madras: Shanmugam Press, 1968), 73–75; P. D. Devanandan, *The Dravida Kazhagam* (Bangalore: Christian Institute for the Study of Religion and Society, 1960); Dagmar Hellmann-Rajanayagam, *Tamilsprache als Politisches Symbol: Politische Literatur in der Tamilsprache in den Jahren 1945 bis 1967*, Beiträge zur Südasienforschung Südasien-Institut Universität Heidelberg, vol. 74 (Wiesbaden: Franz Steiner, 1984).

17. Scholars have paid a great deal of attention to this process of asserting some kind of nonnational identity, variously labeling it *primordialism*, *nativism*, or *revivalism*. See Hardgrave, *Political Sociology*, 6, for a discussion of primordialism in relation to the assertion of Dravidian identity. For a discussion of the concept of primordialism as an analytic category in anthropology, see Clifford Geertz, "The Integrative Revolution: Primordial Sentiments and Civil Politics in the New States" in *Old Societies and New States*, ed. Clifford Geertz (New York: Free Press, 1963); Charles F. Keyes, "Towards a New Formulation of the Concept of Ethnic Group," *Ethnicity* 3, no. 3 (September 1976), 202–13. For an analysis of the Dravidian material in relation to the concept of revivalism, see Eugene F. Irschick, *Tamil Revivalism in the 1930s* (Madras: Cre-A, 1986), 3–37.

18. V. Subramaniam, "Emergence and Eclipse of Tamil Brahmins," *Economic and Political Weekly*, Special Number (July 1969), 1133–34. Irschick provides statistical evidence of "the consistently strong domination of the Brahmans in many upper levels of government service." See his *Politics and Social Conflict in South India*, 13, as well as Hardgrave's discussion of Brahmin/non-Brahmin relationships (*Essays in the Political Sociology of South India*, 11).

19. Barnett, *Politics of Cultural Nationalism in South India*, 25.

20. Irschick, *Tamil Revivalism*, 31.

21. Srinivasan's study of the development of periodicals in Madras shows the effectiveness of journals, pamphlets, and newssheets in shaping public opinion and bringing grievances to the attention of the government. See R. Srinivasan, "Madras Periodicals and Modernization of Values," *Journal of the University of Bombay* 40, no. 76 (Arts Number, October 1971), 150.

22. In addition to pamphlets, E.V.R. used another popular medium, theater, as well (see pages 193–94). The DK sponsored performances of the *Rāmāyaṇa* based on E.V.R.'s interpretation of the text. Baskaran has shown the tremendous political power of theatrical performances in South India for the nationalist movement, a power that E.V.R. appropriated. See Theodore Baskaran, *The Message Bearers: Nationalist Politics and the Entertainment Media in South India, 1880–1945* (Madras: Cre-A, 1981), 21–42.

23. For the rationale behind actions such as the Rāma burning, see, for example, articles in *Kuṭi Aracu* on 3 March 1929, 18 December 1943, 8 January and 15 January 1944, 12 February 1944, 20 September 1947, and 13 January 1951. See also *Viṭutalai*

on 5 November 1948, 27 May 1956, 29 July 1956, 9 August, 15 August, and 17 August 1956, and 13 September 1956. These articles have been reprinted in a collection of E.V.R.'s writings titled *Periyār Ī. Ve. Rā. Cintaṉaikaḷ*, ed. Vē. Āṉaimuttu, 3 vols. (Tiruchirappalli: Thinkers' Forum, 1974), 3:1430–64.

24. Periyār Ī. Ve. Rāmacāmi, *Irāmāyaṇappāttiraṅkaḷ* (1930; repr. Tirucci: Periyār Cuyamariyātai Piracāra Niṟuvaṉa Veḷiyīṭu, 1972); *Irāmāyaṇakkuṟippukaḷ* (1964; repr. Tirucci: Periyār Cuyamariyātai Piracāra Niṟuvaṉa Veḷiyīṭu, 1972). Whenever I refer to the former text, I will do so by the title *Characters in the Rāmāyaṇa* rather than by the Tamil title. *Characters in the Rāmāyaṇa* thus refers to the original Tamil text with which I am working, as opposed to the later English translation entitled *The Ramayana (A True Reading)*. From now on, page numbers from the Tamil text will be cited in the body of this paper. I have limited my analysis to pp. 1–104: E.V.R.'s discussion of the relationship between the *Rāmāyaṇa* and the *Skanda Purāṇa* (pp. 105–16) lies beyond the scope of my inquiry here.

25. The pamphlet's publication history has been pieced together from the fragmentary information given in the front of various editions and from the bibliography of E. V. Ramasami's writings provided in *Cintaṉaikaḷ*, 1:xcv–xcvi.

26. See Georg Bühler, trans., *The Laws of Manu* (1886; repr. New York: Dover Publications, 1969), 195–96 (V.147–158), 85 (III.55–59), 71–72 (II.225–237). For E.V.R.'s critique of *The Laws of Manu*, see his *Manu: Code of Injustice to Non-Brahmins* (1961; repr. Madras: Periyar Self-Respect Propaganda Institution, 1981).

27. Some of E.V.R.'s conclusions about Kaikeyī are consonant with those presented by Sanskritist Sally Sutherland in her paper titled "Seduction, Counter-Seduction, and Sexual Role Models: Bedroom Politics in Indian Epics" (forthcoming in the *Journal of Indian Philosophy*).

28. R. K. Narayan, *The Ramayana: A Shortened Modern Prose Version of the Indian Epic* (Harmondsworth: Penguin Books, 1977), 97.

29. For an analysis of the ambivalent presentation of this episode in the twelfth-century rendition of the *Rāmāyaṇa* by Kampaṉ, see David Shulman, "Divine Order and Divine Evil in the Tamil Tale of Rāma," *Journal of Asian Studies* 38, no. 4 (August 1979), 651–69.

30. Kamil Zvelebil, *The Smile of Murugan: On Tamil Literature of South India* (Leiden: E. J. Brill, 1973), 247–60.

31. Notable among the authors cited are R. C. Dutt, R. Mukherjee, S. C. Dass, Nagendra Ghosh, Feroz Khan, James Murray, H. G. Wells, Vincent Smith, Sir William Wilson Hunter, and Sir Henry Johnson.

32. Swami Vivekananda, *Speeches and Writings of Swami Vivekananda* (Madras: G. A. Natesan, 1922). The passage that E.V.R. quotes is located on p. 530, but since E.V.R. himself gives no page reference or bibliographical information, I cannot tell whether he consulted this edition. Jawaharlal Nehru, *The Discovery of India* (New York: J. Day, 1946). This is the first edition; again E.V.R. gives no indication which edition he used.

33. Maṟaimalaiyaṭikaḷ, *Aṟivuraikkottu* (1921; repr. Madras: Pari Nilayam, 1967). The passage E.V.R. quotes is located on pp. 150–51 in this edition.

34. For a translation and analysis of the story of Āputtiraṉ, see Paula Richman, *Women, Branch Stories, and Religious Rhetoric in a Tamil Buddhist Text*, Foreign and Comparative Studies, South Asia series no. 12 (Syracuse: Maxwell School of Citizenship

and Public Affairs, Syracuse University, 1988), 123–42. Although there is no solid evidence that E.V.R. drew on the *Maṇimēkalai*—which is the only extant Tamil Buddhist text—he greatly admired Buddhists, considering them his intellectual precursors.

35. Compare E.V.R.'s chapter entitled "The Hoax about Gods" in *Periyarana*, ed. and trans. M. Dharmalingam (Trichy: Periyar Self-Respect Propaganda Institution, 1975), 81–109.

36. Irschick, *Tamil Revivalism*, 83. On the Siddhars, see also Kamil Zvelebil, *The Poets of the Powers* (London: Rider and Co., 1973).

37. A. K. Ramanujan, *Speaking of Śiva* (Harmondsworth: Penguin Books, 1973).

38. Irschick, *Tamil Revivalism*, 85–89; see note 6, above, for the biography.

39. G. Devika, "The Emergence of Cultural Consciousness in Tamilnadu between 1890 and 1915: A Study of the Ideas of Maraimalai Atikal" (Master of Philosophy thesis, Jawaharlal Nehru University, 1986), 1.

40. K. R. Chandra, *A Critical Study of Paumacariyaṁ* (Muzaffarpur: Research Institute of Prakrit, Jainology and Ahimsa, 1970), 120–38.

41. Dineshchandra Sen, *The Bengali Ramayanas* (Calcutta: University of Calcutta, 1920), 28.

42. D. T. Suzuki, trans., *The Laṅkāvatāra Sūtra* (Boulder, Colo.: Prajna Press, 1978), 4–6.

43. See Clinton Seely, "The Raja's New Clothes," in this volume. Irschick notes that Madhusudan Dutt wrote his work after he returned from a trip to Madras (*Politics and Social Conflict in South India*, 284, n. 23). Nandy mentions that Asit Bandopadhyay, a Bengali literary critic, traced Dutt's interpretation of the *Rāmāyaṇa* to a Jain *Rāmāyaṇa*: Ashis Nandy, *The Intimate Enemy: Loss and Recovery of Self under Colonialism* (Delhi: Oxford University Press, 1983), 19, n. 29.

44. Nandy, *The Intimate Enemy*, 20.

45. See Barbara Metcalf, *Islamic Revival in British India: Deoband, 1860–1900* (Princeton: Princeton University Press, 1982), for an analysis of this form of debate.

46. Kenneth Jones, "Hindu-Christian Polemics in Nineteenth-Century Punjab" (paper presented for the panel "Vernacular Religious Polemics and Social Change in Nineteenth-Century India," 37th annual meeting of the Association for Asian Studies, Philadelphia, 1985), ms. p. 16; Dayananda Sarasvati is quoted on ms. p. 12. The passage from Revelations reads, in the King James version: "And the number of the army of the horsemen were two hundred thousand thousand; and I heard the number of them."

47. Irschick, *Politics and Social Conflict in South India*, 283–84.

48. T. Ponemballem Pillai, "The Morality of the Ramayana," *Malabar Quarterly Review* 8, no. 2 (June 1909), 83. V. P. Subramania Mudaliar also summarizes Sundaram Pillai's ideas concerning the *Rāmāyaṇa* and caste: see "A Critical Review of the Story of Ramayana and An Account of South Indian Castes Based on the Views of the Late Prof. P. Sundaram Pillai, M.A.," *Tamil Antiquary* 1, no. 2 (1908): 1–48.

49. M. S. Purnalingam Pillai, *Ravana the Great: King of Lanka* (Munnirpallam: The Bibliotheca, 1928), 78. Such works were only the beginning of a set of explorations into the *Rāmāyaṇa* from a Dravidian perspective. See, for example, Cantiracēkara Pālavar, *Irāmāyaṇa Ārāycci*, 5 vols. (Madras: Kuṭi Aracu Patippakam, 1929–49); Aṟiñar Anna, *Kamparācam* (Madras: Bharati Patippakam, 1986).

50. At times E.V.R. criticizes Rāma for being cruel to Sītā after she returns from Lanka, but in other places he implies that she was a wanton woman who became pregnant by Rāvaṇa (*Characters in the Rāmāyaṇa*, 27 and 48–49). Cf. Rudolph, who describes the way "Dravidian" interpretations of the *Rāmāyaṇa* have focused on Sītā in this way: "Sita is no longer the devoted Hindu wife, the model for Brahmanical culture; rather she is Ravana's paramour who did not resist but 'clung like a vine' when she was abducted. Whether Sita struggled or clung has become, like many other points in this epic, a matter for bitter, even violent dispute" ("Urban Life and Populist Radicalism," 288).

51. Periyar E. V. Ramasami, *The Ramayana* (*A True Reading*), 3d ed. (Madras: Periyar Self-Respect Propaganda Institution, 1980). *E. V. Ramasami* (*A Pen Portrait*) was written in 1962 by "an admirer" (repr. Madras: Dravidian Kazhagam, 1984).

52. For an account of these riots, see Michael H. Fisher, *A Clash of Cultures: Awadh, the British, and the Mughals* (Riverdale: Riverdale Company, 1987), 227–34.

53. *Organiser*, 1 May 1971. For a discussion of the origin of the drama, see Vēṇu, *Periyār Oru Carittiram*, 19–20.

54. For the DMK's use of film, see Robert Hardgrave, "When Stars Displace the Gods: The Folk Culture of Cinema in Tamil Nadu," in his *Essays in the Political Sociology of South India*, 92–100. For accounts of the relationship between the DK and the DMK, see ibid., 39–80; Barnett, *Politics of Cultural Nationalism in South India*, 69–158; P. Spratt, *D.M.K. in Power* (Bombay: Nachiketa Publications, 1970), chap. 2.

TEN

Rāmāyaṇa Exegesis in Tenkalai Śrīvaiṣṇavism

Patricia Y. Mumme

In Indian religious traditions and philosophical schools (*darśanas*), the fund of scriptural texts is ever expanding. There is hardly any genre of literature that has not been used as scripture by some group of religious scholars somewhere in India. Folklore, epic, drama, aesthetic theory, treatises on grammar, love poetry—all have joined ranks with the more obviously "sacred" genres of myth, hagiography, and liturgy to become the scripture of religious communities and grist for their theological mills. This phenomenon extends to both classical and popular variations of the Rāma story, which continue to be plumbed by widely diverse religious communities in India for messages they can relate to their own systems of meaning, often in very creative ways.

The Śrīvaiṣṇava tradition in Tamilnadu, especially the Tenkalai subsect, has made ample use of epic and *purāṇic* scripture in general, and the *Rāmāyaṇa* in particular, in their theological discourse. A brief outline of the development of Śrīvaiṣṇava theology will show how the authors of the Tenkalai school came to use passages from the *Rāmāyaṇa* to explicate some of their distinctive theological claims.

THE ŚRĪVAIṢṆAVA TRADITION IN SOUTH INDIA

Yāmuna (fl. 11th C.) and Rāmānuja (fl. 12th C.), the founders of the Viśiṣṭādvaita school of Vedāntic philosophy and the Śrīvaiṣṇava religious tradition, make no appeal to the *Rāmāyaṇa* in their written works, and little to other epic or *purāṇic* literature. But they were faced with the task of trying to legitimate their school's qualified nondualistic interpretation of Hindu scripture for a potentially hostile audience. Thus they not only wrote in Sanskrit but appealed mostly to the more authoritative Upaniṣads, the *Bhagavad Gītā*, and the *śāstras*. As the Śrīvaiṣṇava tradition became more popular over the next few generations, however, many of Rāmānuja's successors started writing works intended to make Śrīvaiṣṇava teaching accessible to a wider audience than intellectual philosophers.

During the twelfth and thirteenth centuries some of Rāmānuja's successors—especially those in Kanchipuram—continued the exposition of Viśiṣṭādvaita Vedānta in Sanskrit. At the same time, others—notably a circle in Srirangam—developed a large body of commentatorial literature in Tamil Maṇipravāḷa, a form of Sanskritized Tamil understandable to the larger Śrīvaiṣṇava community, even women and non-Brahmins. In this literature, well-known stories from the epics and *purāṇas*, as well as passages from the beloved hymns of the Āḻvārs, are frequently cited to support and illustrate Śrīvaiṣṇava teaching. By the thirteenth century the different specializations of the Kanchi and Srirangam schools were evident in the kinds of literature they were producing. It is not surprising, given the different audiences and intentions of these two schools, that doctrinal differences between them also began to develop.[1]

The doctrinal rift first surfaced when Vedānta Deśika (1269–1370) criticized many of the claims of the Srirangam school. About a century later, Maṇavāḷamāmuni (d. 1443) reaffirmed the teachings of his Srirangam predecessors, especially Piḷḷai Lokācārya (d. 1310?), by writing commentaries on their most important works. Thus Vedānta Deśika and Maṇavāḷamāmuni came to be revered as the founders and foremost teachers (*ācāryas*) of the two main Śrīvaiṣṇava subsects: the Vaṭakalai (literally "northern school," referring to Kanchi) and the Teṉkalai (literally "southern school," referring to Srirangam). The central issue in the Teṉkalai-Vaṭakalai dispute is soteriological, focusing on how best to understand the path of simple surrender to the Lord (*prapatti*) and its relation to the path of devotion, or *bhaktiyoga*, which—as expounded by Yāmuna and Rāmānuja—must be accompanied by Vedic ritual practice. To understand the thrust of the Teṉkalai use of *Rāmāyaṇa* incidents, one must first contrast their view of surrender to the Lord with that of their Vaṭakalai counterparts.

The more conservative Vaṭakalai school, in its understanding of surrender, is driven by its concern to preserve the validity of *bhaktiyoga*, Vedic ritual, and the Sanskrit scriptures which teach them. At the same time, they do not want to compromise two important principles of Viśiṣṭādvaita philosophy: that the Lord is egalitarian as well as merciful, and that the soul—although dependent on the Lord—has the God-given ability to act (*jīvakartṛtva*). Vedānta Deśika's writings repeatedly affirm that the paths of surrender and devotion are enjoined in scripture as two equally effective means (*upāya*) to mokṣa (spiritual liberation). However, these alternatives are not a matter of choice, for an individual will be qualified for only one of them. The path of devotion (*bhaktiyoga*) is an arduous means to salvation that demands performance of Vedic rituals (*karmayoga*) as an ancillary duty; thus it is restricted to twice-born males (who alone are qualified to perform Vedic rites) endowed with a good education, patience, and physical stamina. Only those who lack one of the qualifications for the path of devotion are allowed to follow the easier and quicker path of surrender (*prapatti*), which does not involve any Vedic rituals. Vedānta Deśika emphasizes that the Lord is ever willing to save all souls but, out of respect for the soul's desire, he will not do so until he receives a sign that indicates one's acceptance of the salvation the Lord offers. The adoption of either of these two means constitutes such a sign. But salvation is not something one earns, for neither surrender to the Lord nor devotion would be effective without the Lord's grace. Nonetheless, the Vaṭakalai see no harm in calling them means (*upāya*) to mokṣa and subsidiary causes of salvation: both surrender and devotion are performed with the soul's God-given ability to act, and one or the other is absolutely necessary before salvation by the Lord's grace can be effected.

The Teṉkalai authors have a much more radical understanding of surrender to the Lord. To them, surrender is a passive, loving response to the Lord's active, saving grace. It is merely a mental phenomenon—a particular change of attitude in which one recognizes one's utter dependence on the Lord—rather than an act performed by the individual soul. Though the Teṉkalai teachers do not deny that the Lord has given the soul the ability to act, they claim it is contrary to the soul's nature of subservience (*śeṣatva*) to the Lord and dependence (*pāratantrya*) on him for one to use that ability to try to save oneself. Any active attempt to save oneself by any means (*upāya*)—including engaging in the devotional or ritual means taught in scripture—will thus violate the soul's inherent dependence on the Lord and obstruct the Lord's saving grace. The Teṉkalai go so far as to claim that, despite what the *śāstras* may teach, neither the path of devotion nor the path of surrender are really means to mokṣa. The only true means, according to the Teṉkalai, is the Lord himself—the soul's rightful master and protector. True, surrender normally involves mutual acceptance: the Lord accepts the soul as an object of his grace (*paragatasvīkāra*) and the soul accepts the Lord as savior (*svagatasvīkāra*). However, the Lord's acceptance of the soul is the sole cause of salvation and hence the true means; the individual's acceptance of the Lord is neither sufficient nor necessary for salvation. The Teṉkalai school affirms the Lord's sovereign freedom to choose whom he wants to save—or to refuse salvation to someone for no reason. (This the Vaṭakalai consider an affront to the Lord's egalitarian mercy.) Because of the Lord's autonomous will, the Teṉkalai argue, all who seek salvation must approach the Lord through the Goddess Śrī, his beloved and merciful consort, who will see to it that the Lord's compassionate desire to save is aroused.

With this overview of the central doctrinal differences between the two schools, we can proceed first to show how the Teṉkalai theologians have used incidents from the *Rāmāyaṇa* as scriptural support for their distinctive claims regarding the nature of surrender to the Lord and then to analyze their method of selecting and interpreting these incidents.

TEṈKALAI EXEGESIS OF RĀMĀYAṆA INCIDENTS

The Teṉkalai teachers, by their own claim, see the *Rāmāyaṇa* as a work of utmost authority and doctrinal importance. Piḷḷai Lokācārya begins his major theological treatise, the *Śrīvacana Bhūṣaṇa*, by explaining the relationship between the Veda and the *dharmaśāstras*, *itihāsas*, and *purāṇas*. Whereas the earlier, ritual portions of the Veda are explained by the *dharmaśāstras*, the more important Vedānta or Upaniṣads, which comprise the latter portion of the Veda, are explicated primarily by the *itihāsas* and secondarily by the *purāṇas*. Of the two principal *itihāsas*, the *Mahābhārata* explains the greatness of the Lord Kṛṣṇa, while "the more excellent *itihāsa*, the *Rāmāyaṇa*, proclaims the greatness of the one who was imprisoned [Sītā]" (*ŚVB* 1–5).[2] Sītā, who is the incarnation of the Goddess Śrī, has a dual importance for the Teṉkalai school. First, as the Lord's beloved wife and the mother of all souls, she is the merciful mediator (*puruṣakāra*) between the soul in need of salvation and the omnipotent Lord. As we will see, the Teṉkalai theologians interpret numerous *Rāmāyaṇa* incidents as revealing the power and salvific importance of her mediation. But according to the Teṉkalai school, Sītā is also a separate soul (*cetana* or *jīva*) like us, dependent and perfectly submissive to the Lord, who is her master and protector. As such, Sītā in the *Rāmāyaṇa* exemplifies the ideal relationship between the soul and the Lord, and Rāmā's rescue of Sītā from Lanka can be seen as an allegory for the process of salvation. Just as Rāma rescued Sītā from Lanka and brought her back to Ayodhya to attend him, the Lord rescues the soul from the throes of *saṃsāra* and takes it after death to Vaikuṇṭha, Viṣṇu's heavenly abode, where the soul can fully realize its subservient nature by serving the Lord directly.[3]

The Teṉkalai authors appeal to several *Rāmāyaṇa* passages in which Sītā's behavior can be held up as a model for the soul's passive dependence on the Lord for its salvation. "With regard to the *upāya*" or means of salvation, says Piḷḷai Lokācārya, "one must be like Pirāṭṭi [Sītā]" (*ŚVB* 80), meaning that to be saved one must entirely relinquish one's own power and effort (*ŚVB* 85). Maṇavāḷamāmuni explains that Sītā "had the power to reduce the host of enemies to ashes and save herself" by the power of her chaste virtue; but she refused to do so, saying, "Since Rāma has not so commanded, and because I must guard my ascetic restraint (*tapas*), I will not reduce you to ashes by the fiery power of my chastity, O ten-necked one."[4] Rather, she said, "If Rāmā were to assault Lanka with his arrows, defeat it, and take me away, that would be fitting of him" (*Rām.* V.39.29). Why, if Sītā was fully capable of saving herself at any point during her captivity, did she not do so? "Pirāṭṭi refused to do anything by her own power, thinking that to save herself by her own efforts—rather than letting Rāma, her hero, protect her—would destroy her dependence (*pāratantrya*)" (*ŚVB* 82). Maṇavāḷamāmuni explains that, like Sītā, we should not try to save ourselves by pursuing some particular means to salvation but should preserve our dependent nature and wait in faith for the Lord to save us.

Piḷḷai Lokācārya and Maṇavāḷamāmuni also cite other *Rāmāyaṇa* incidents, though not involving Sītā, to prove that resorting to means other than the Lord himself can actually hinder salvation. Once, in the midst of battle, Rāvaṇa was shaken by a thunderous blow from Rāma's lance. Despite this, he continued to cling to his bow. But when struck by Rāma's arrow, Rāvaṇa dropped his bow; only then did Rāma allow him to withdraw from the battlefield (*Rām.* VI.59.135). Maṇavāḷamāmuni explains how this incident relates to the process of salvation:

> Rāvaṇa, overwhelmed by Rāma's archery, became agitated and tried to escape. But as long as he held the bow, Rāma did not allow him to leave. The bow, which he eventually dropped, was not an effective means (*sādhana*) for conquering his enemy while he was holding it. Not only that, but the permission Rāma later gave him, saying "I will let you go," was not given during the time he was holding the bow. Thus [the bow] can be said to be an impediment that kept him from leaving. In the same way, if there remains even the slightest involvement in these other means, they will not only fail to be effective means (*upāya*) to the goal [of salvation], but will actually turn out to be obstructions to the ultimate attainment. (*Mumu* 203)

Rāvaṇa expected the bow to help him have his way with his enemy, but the bow only prevented him from saving himself by escaping. Like Rāvaṇa's bow, the apparent means to salvation, including the path of devotion and ritual works, will not help us and must actually be dropped in order for salvation to occur. Piḷḷai Lokācārya underscores this point by citing the example of Daśaratha, Rāma's father, who had to banish Rāma in order to remain true to a promise he had made to one of his wives (*Mumu* 204). Maṇavāḷamāmuni explains:

> The great king [Daśaratha] lost the fortune he had—namely, living with Rāma, who is said to be the dharma incarnate—by clinging to the dharma of truthfulness, which was merely a semblance [of dharma], thinking that he could not refuse to honor a boon he had previously granted. In the same way, remaining engaged in the other illusory means [such as *bhaktiyoga*] will certainly make for loss of the great fortune of living with the divine being himself, [the Lord who is] the eternal dharma. (*Mumu* 204)

Thus, according to the Teṉkalai authors, even the means to salvation enjoined as dharma in authoritative scripture (*śāstra*) can obstruct salvation if one clings to them rather than to the Lord himself as one's savior.

Both Teṉkalai and Vaṭakalai authors also frequently refer to the Brahmāstra incident in the Rāma story to illustrate an important point on which both schools agree: surrender to the Lord himself must be carried out in complete faith that he alone will be one's means to salvation. In other words, surrender cannot be combined with any other means for salvation, or it will not be effective. The significance of the Brahmāstra incident is fully explained in Aruḷāḷa Perumāl Emperumāṉār's *Jñānasāra*, an early Tamil text on which Maṇavāḷamāmuni commented. However, to my knowledge, no such incident appears in Vālmīki's *Rāmāyaṇa*.[5] The story has it that Rāvaṇa's demon army of *rākṣasas* used the Brahmāstra, a divine weapon which binds its enemies and thus renders them helpless, against the monkey Hanumān, who was acting as Rāma's emissary. But the Brahmāstra only works if the user has complete faith in it. When the *rākṣasas* decided to bring in a jute cord to further secure the bound Hanumān, just to be on the safe side, the Brahmāstra slipped off. Maṇavāḷamāmuni explains: "The Brahmāstra that had tied him slipped off by itself at the moment another cord was tied on. In the same way, if one who has resorted to this *upāya* [the Lord himself] engages in another *upāya*, [the first] will leave him" (*JS* 28). For the Teṉkalai *ācāryas*, the analogy between the Brahmāstra and *prapatti* (surrender) is instructive: one might think that means such as devotion and ritual action will enhance the efficacy of one's surrender to the Lord, but in fact these will cause one to lose the Lord. The path of surrender demands complete cessation of one's own efforts and faith in the capacity of the Lord alone to bring about salvation.

If the Teṉkalai and the Vaṭakalai concur in their interpretation of the Brahmāstra incident, the Teṉkalai teachers also use examples from the *Rāmāyaṇa* to support one of their more controversial claims: that the Lord can save whomever he chooses, without waiting for that soul to surrender to him and thus request acceptance. Nor is the Lord obligated to save one who surrenders to him, even if such surrender is performed perfectly. The Teṉkalai hold that, because of the Lord's unconstrained sovereignty (*niraṅkuśa-svātantrya*), he need pay attention neither to the individual's desire or lack thereof nor to the soul's merits or sins when deciding whether or not to grant salvation. As Piḷḷai Lokācārya says: "When the soul thinks to obtain the Lord, this surrender is not a means. When the Lord decides to obtain the soul, not even sins can stand in the way. Both are seen in the case of Bharata and Guha" (*ŚVB* 142–144). Maṇavāḷamāmuni begins by explaining how it is the Lord's initiative which has the salvific power, not our surrender to him:

> It is the owner who comes and takes possession of his property. In the same way, it is the Lord alone—the soul's master and owner—who approaches, while the dependent soul must wait to be accepted. If one thinks to attain the autonomous (*svatantra*) Lord by one's own act of acceptance, this intention will fail. Any surrender so conceived will not be a means to attain the Lord. . . . But when the sovereign Lord and master himself decides by his own will to obtain

> the soul who is his dependent property, even the worst sins will not be obstacles. These [first] two [sentences] show that the acceptance on the part of the soul (*svagatasvīkāra*) is not realy the means (*upāya*) for salvation; rather, the acceptance on the part of the Lord (*paragatasvīkāra*) is the means. (*ŚVB 142–143*)

Maṇavāḷamāmuni then explains how the differing fates of Bharata, Rāma's devoted brother, and Guha, a lowly hunter who accompanied Rāma to the forest, affirm this crucial theological point:

> These [truths] are illustrated by [the examples of] Bharata and Guha. Bharata wanted to bring Rāma back [to Ayodhya], crown him, and live by serving him, in accord with [Bharata's] true nature [as a soul subservient to the Lord]. With this in mind, Bharata—in the company of his ministers—approached Rāma and sought refuge, surrendering at his holy feet. But for Bharata, the good deed of surrender performed in this manner—since it was not what the Lord and savior had in mind—became an evil. But for Guha, Rāma himself came forward and accepted him. Indeed, Guha's very faults were accepted as an offering; thus the evilness of his offenses became merits. For isn't the very definition of merit and sin said to be "merit is whatever pleases him; sin is the opposite"? (*ŚVB* 145)

The Teṉkalai authors further point out that neither Guha nor even Hanumān had any desire to be accepted as Rāma's companions. "But even without any desire on their part, acceptance by the Lord (*paragatasvīkāra*) occurred to Hanumān on the banks of the Pambā and to Guha on the banks of the Gaṅgā"; they were accepted when the Lord himself took the initiative and approached them (Maṇavāḷamāmuni on *ŚVB* 150). If surrender, signifying one's acceptance of the Lord, were a prerequisite for that acceptance, then the sincere surrender of the virtuous Bharata would have been effective and his request fulfilled. Conversely, the sinful hunter Guha and the lowly monkey Hanumān—neither of whom expressed a desire for the Lord's acceptance—would not have become Rāma's close companions. But such was not the case. These examples, the Teṉkalai argue, demonstrate that the soul's surrender to the Lord cannot be considered an effective means to salvation, and that the Lord's freedom to accept whomever he wants is completely unconstrained.

The Teṉkalai authors go on to cite two *Rāmāyaṇa* incidents featuring Sītā as evidence for their radical claim that efforts to accumulate merit or remove sin, aimed at earning the Lord's favor, instead insult the Lord's sovereign power and run contrary to the soul's dependent nature. When Rāma and Sītā were dwelling in the forest, Rāma declared that he would not allow Sītā to be adorned with even a necklace during their lovemaking, for fear that it would interfere with their intimate union (*ŚVB* 162).[6] Maṇavāḷamāmuni explains that even though one may expect merits to enhance the Lord's pleasure when he communes with the soul, they end up obstructing his pleasure, just like clothes and jewelry interfere with the intimacy desired by a lover.

In fact, says Piḷḷai Lokācārya, "while ornaments are not desired, dirt is desired" (*ŚVB* 165), alluding to an incident after the victory over Lanka. Rāvaṇa vanquished, Rāma ordered Vibhīṣaṇa to fetch Sītā. "Have Sītā, the divine-limbed Vaidehī, brought here before me quickly, adorned with sacred ornaments, her hair washed," he instructed (*Rām.* VI.117.6–7). When Vibhīṣaṇa reported this to Sītā, she at first protested, claiming that she wanted to see her husband at once, before bathing. But Vibhīṣaṇa insisted, so she did as she was told. When she appeared before Rāma freshly bathed and adorned, however, Rāma became angry and greeted her with harsh words: "Like a lamp to one with a diseased eye, you are not a welcome sight for me" (*Rām.* VI.118.17–18). Why was he angry? Hadn't Sītā done as she was told? Maṇavāḷamāmuni claims that Rāma really desired to see her body with all its dirt, "unadorned, like a lotus plant without the lotus" (*Rām.* V.15.21). He didn't mean what he told Vibhīṣaṇa, and he expected Sītā to know his mind. Maṇavāḷamāmuni explains that "Vibhīṣaṇa did not know Rāma's true intention but only relayed the words he spoke. But even so, Sītā should have refused to bathe and just gone to see him in the state she was in while imprisoned in Rāvaṇa's house. But she didn't do this. She quickly bathed and came, which made him angry, for he wanted to see her in her [dirty] state" (*ŚVB* 166). The interpretation of this incident hinges on an implied analogy between scriptural commandments and Rāma's command to Vibhīṣaṇa. Even though the *śāstras* declare that the Lord hates sins and even prescribe methods to expiate them, these statements do not reflect the Lord's true intention. He wants to commune with the soul in its sinful state and will be angered if one tries to win his favor by purifying oneself. His desire for the soul cannot be obstructed by sins, but it can be thwarted by attempts to remove them.

However, the Teṉkalai authors do not simply leave the individual who desires salvation with no recourse but to wait patiently for the Lord to approach. This is where the Teṉkalai doctrine of the necessity of Śrī as mediator assumes importance. Śrī, the Lord's beloved wife and consort, is ever willing to act as *puruṣakāra* or mediator, to intercede with the Lord on behalf of the soul who seeks salvation. Thus one should approach her first and request her intercession, rather than risk rejection by going directly to the Lord and requesting salvation. Piḷḷai Lokācārya views the entire *Rāmāyaṇa* as testimony to the power and necessity of the mediation of the merciful Goddess, incarnate as Sītā (*ŚVB* 5–6). He claims the Rāma story shows that the Lord never saved or accepted anyone without some form of intercession on the part of Sītā. On every such occasion, the Teṉkalai authors find some symbolic evidence of the Goddess's mediation. When Rāma accepted Hanumān and Sugrīva, it was because they carried the jewels Sītā dropped as she was abducted by Rāvaṇa. Vibhīṣaṇa approached Rāma and surrendered to him directly, but this surrender was effective only because he had been instructed by Sītā before he left Lanka. When Guha was accepted, Rāma made reference to Sītā (*ŚVB* 151). Thus, Piḷḷai Lokācārya claims, salvation is gained only through the Goddess (*Mumu* 118–19).

According to the Teṉkalai school, the efficacy of the Goddess's mediation is based on her merciful nature and her special relationship with the Lord, both of which are demonstrated in the *Rāmāyaṇa*. She is the very embodiment of the Lord's mercy, and yet she is without his sovereign power to punish; therefore she will always be tenderhearted toward sinful souls, whom she sees as her children. Because the Lord loves her dearly and always does what she says, he will never reject one who approaches him with the recommendation of the Goddess. Doesn't the *Rāmāyaṇa* show that the Lord always follows his wife's command, even when it brings peril? At Sītā's urging, Rāma left the hermitage to pursue the magic deer, which brought about Sītā's capture. Surely the omniscient Lord knew what would happen, but he went after the deer anyway, out of his love and desire to please her. So, Maṇavāḷamāmuni asks, is there any doubt that she can make the Lord overlook the soul's faults and accept it when she so requests? (*Mumu* 129). Piḷḷai Lokācārya says, "Need we point out that the one who made Hanumān forgive can also make the one who follows her words forgive?" (*Mumu* 129). Maṇavāḷamāmuni then explains this allusion to an incident that emphasizes the tenderhearted mercy of Sītā, who could not be angry even at the demonesses (*rākṣasīs*) who had tormented her while she was imprisoned in Lanka:

> Hanumān had taken full account of the sins of the *rākṣasīs* who had threatened and chided Sītā for ten months; he was eager to inflict severe punishment. But it was she who made the strong-willed Hanumān relent and forgive them by means of her instruction, saying such things as "Who has committed any sin?" [*Rām.* VI.116.38] and "No one has done anything wrong at all" [*Rām.* VI.116.43]. (*Mumu* 129)

Because Sītā was there to plead with Hanumān not to destroy the demonesses, they were spared. Similarly, when the crow Kākāsura attacked her breast, Rāma was eager to punish it. But when the crow fell at Rāma's feet, begging for mercy, Sītā was moved, so for her sake Rāma spared it (*Rām.* V.38.34–35). Piḷḷai Lokācārya says, "Because of her presence, the crow was saved. Because of her absence, Rāvaṇa was destroyed" (*Mumu* 135–36). Maṇavāḷamāmuni clarifies:

> It was because of the presence of the lady who subdues the autonomy of the sovereign Lord and arouses his compassion that the crow who had committed a heinous crime was mercifully spared. . . . Rāvaṇa was helplessly trapped in a similar way, even though he had not committed the extreme offense of the crow [for he had not physically attacked Sītā]. But she was not present, and as a result Rāvaṇa perished, the target of Rāma's arrows. (*Mumu* 135–36)

Thus, according to the Teṉkalai *ācāryas*, the *Rāmāyaṇa* proves that when one invokes the merciful Goddess as mediator before approaching the Lord for salvation, one need not fear rejection by the Lord on account of his unbridled autonomy or one's own sins.

RĀMĀYAṆA INCIDENTS AS PARABLES

The Teṉkalai school's reading of *Rāmāyaṇa* incidents is unique, yet their methods of structuring and interpreting these incidents have parallels in other scriptural traditions. What is immediately striking is that the Teṉkalai school is not very interested in the main plot, the didactic portions of the epic, or even the literal meaning of statements made by Rāma or Sītā. Rather, they focus on a few relatively obscure events in the Rāma story, which, when interpreted allegorically, lend support to their soteriological doctrines. It is not that the *Rāmāyaṇa* as a whole is an allegory to the Teṉkalai, at least not in the manner of a work like *Pilgrim's Progress*. In Bunyan's book each character is univalent, representing a single concept. But in the Teṉkalai reading of the *Rāmāyaṇa*, different characters symbolize different theological realities at different moments. For example, Sītā can represent the soul waiting to be saved or Śrī, the mediator. Thus the soul and the goal of salvation can be represented by almost any character and the goal he or she is seeking. Sītā seeking to escape from Lanka, the *rākṣasas* seeking to bind Hanumān, Rāvaṇa seeking to vanquish Rāma—all become allegories for the soul seeking salvation. The Teṉkalai teachers seem to select these isolated incidents on the basis of a perceived parallel between the relation of the actors in the narrative and the relation of the theological concepts they wish to illustrate.[7] The allegorical identification is sometimes fully spelled out, and sometimes merely hinted at, so that listeners are encouraged to extend the metaphor, to fill in the blanks and draw the theological conclusion themselves.

All this brings the Śrīvaiṣṇava reading of *Rāmāyaṇa* incidents very close to the genre of parable. Parables are also brief narratives or stories that are akin to metaphors and are often interpreted analogically or allegorically. The allegorical meaning of parables, especially those in religious scriptures, is sometimes fully explained, and sometimes only hinted at. However, the relation between parable and allegory is a bone of scholarly contention in the field of religious studies. Traditionally, the parable has been seen as closely akin to metaphor, analogy, example-story, and allegory. In this view, a parable is defined as an extended metaphor built around a narrative structure; though often interpreted analogically, parables are generally too brief and unsystematic to be considered full-fledged allegories. However, some recent scholars, such as John Dominic Crossan, have tended to emphasize the distinction in both form and function between parables and allegories. Crossan and others would argue that parables are not intended to be interpreted allegorically, even though theologians have often co-opted (and perhaps misused) scriptural parables by reading them allegorically in order to support their own metaphysical or ethical viewpoints. Though we cannot go into the details of this argument here, some ideas gleaned from this scholarly dispute on the structure, interpretation, and theological significance of parables can both illuminate and be illuminated by the Śrīvaiṣṇava use of *Rāmāyaṇa* incidents.

In Crossan's view, a parable is defined by certain structural characteristics:

> There is in every parabolic situation a battle of basic structures. There is the structure of expectation on the part of the hearer and there is the structure of expression on the part of the speaker. These structures are in diametrical opposition, and this opposition is the heart of the parabolic event. . . . What actually happens in the parable is the reverse of what the hearer expects.[8]

Crossan uses this structural model to analyze biblical parables in both the Old and New Testaments. For example, he points out that in Jesus' parable of the good Samaritan (Luke 10:30–35) the hearer expects the priest and Levite to help the victim and the Samaritan to refuse assistance, but the story shows exactly the opposite (107). In the parable of the Pharisee and the publican (Luke 18:10–13) one expects God to hear and accept the prayer of the righteous Pharisee and reject the prayer of the sinful publican, but just the opposite happens (102).

This conflict between the reader's expectations and the narrative outcome seems to be the central dynamic of the Teṉkalai telling of *Rāmāyaṇa* incidents no less than of biblical parables. Indeed, in recounting the *Rāmāyaṇa* incidents they select, the Teṉkalai *ācāryas* deliberately highlight the paradoxical nature of the outcomes. One would expect Sītā, as an incarnation of the Goddess Śrī, to use her power to save herself and escape Lanka. Why did she not do so? One would expect Rāvaṇa's bow to help him achieve his aim. Why did Rāma let him escape only after he dropped it? One would expect the addition of a jute cord to reinforce the efficacy of the Brahmāstra. Why did it fail? One would expect the merciful Rāma to honor the request of his own virtuous brother, Bharata, who humbly surrendered to him with the request that he return to Ayodhya and allow Bharata to serve him. Why did Rāma refuse him and yet actively seek the companionship of the lowly Guha and Hanumān, who had not even expressed a desire for this companionship, much less surrendered to him? One would expect Rāma to be pleased when Sītā appeared before him bathed and adorned as he had requested. Why did he get angry?

The Teṉkalai versions of *Rāmāyaṇa* incidents thus seem to have the paradoxical structure of parables. They do not, however, fully confirm Crossan's theory about the function and meaning of parables. He claims that the intent of parable, as a genre, is diametrically opposed to that of allegory and example-story. The parable's central paradox is designed to attack the hearer's culturally conditioned standards of expectation, to subvert all theology (or "myth," as he calls it)—meaning all received views of reality and ethical standards. Allegories and example-stories, on the other hand, serve to explain and support a given worldview. He claims that the New Testament redactors turned Jesus' parables—which were genuine parables intended to confront the hearer with an authentic religious experience transcending all conceptualization—into allegories and example-stories that supported the eschatology and moral teachings of the early church. Thus in the context of the Gospel of Luke, the parable of the good Samaritan becomes an example-story teaching love for one's neighbor, while the parable of the Pharisee and publican teaches that the honest humility of a sinner is better in God's eyes than the self-righteousness of the holy. Crossan suggests that the central dynamic of reversed expectations in the parable runs counter to the theological aims of example-stories and allegories; therefore, he claims, Jesus' parables often end up as rather poor examples of the latter (120). Crossan thus questions whether one "could ever succeed in making a smooth change from parable to example and allegory" (123).

Crossan has been criticized for drawing too sharp a distinction between theology ("mythical religion," as he calls it) and the parabolic religion of transcendence, which is anti-theology.[9] Isn't it possible that parables—even with their characteristic paradoxical structure—not only seek to subvert a prevailing worldview but also to establish a new one? Can the paradoxicality at the heart of the parable actually serve the allegorical meaning and theological aims of their interpreters, rather than acting as obstacle to them?

The Teṉkalai school's "parabolized" readings of *Rāmāyaṇa* incidents suggest that the answer to both questions is yes, and that Crossan's critics are right. The Teṉkalai theologians seem to use their interpretations of *Rāmāyaṇa* incidents both to criticize the prevailing worldview and to assert their own theological claims. Furthermore, the paradoxical structure of these incidents and their allegorical interpretation do not seem to be at odds (as Crossan's analysis of New Testament parables would suggest); rather, they work together to accomplish both aims. In the Teṉkalai *ācāryas'* telling of *Rāmāyaṇa* incidents, the paradox at the surface or narrative level of each incident serves as a hook to draw the listener toward the allegorically derived theological level of meaning. So why did Rāma get angry at Sītā? Why didn't Rāvaṇa's bow help him? Why did the Brahmāstra slip off? Why did Rāma reject Bharata? The reader or listener, disturbed by the paradox, must "stay tuned" for its resolution. The allegorical interpretation, when disclosed as the hidden meaning of the incident, resolves the surface paradox and thereby affirms the particular doctrinal viewpoint the author wishes to promote.[10] But this doctrinal viewpoint nevertheless subverts some of the most cherished assumptions of the Hindu worldview (many of which are staunchly defended by the Vaṭakalai school): that the Lord hates sins and loves virtue, and that salvation and the favor of the Lord can be achieved by means of devotion and ritual action, as taught in scripture. Against this backdrop of expectation, the Teṉkalai reading of these paradoxical *Rāmāyaṇa* incidents boldly demonstrates why these incidents do not turn out as expected: the assumptions of the underlying worldview are wrong. The Lord does not hate sin but in fact longs to commune with the soul with all its sin; scripturally enjoined means performed by one's own efforts don't help one achieve salvation but interfere with it; even surrender itself is not a fail-safe means to win the Lord's favor, and he is not bound to honor it.

In one sense, the theological function of the Teṉkalai interpretation of *Rāmāyaṇa* incidents is not so different from the aim of the New Testament interpretation of Jesus' parables. In the gospels, Jesus' parables are used to ridicule the legalism of the Pharisees and to teach a radical morality of love which cannot be reduced to a structured code of ethical principles that state precisely what God demands of human beings. Similarly, the Śrīvaiṣṇava *Rāmāyaṇa* incidents subvert and ridicule the *śāstric* legalism that the Vaṭakalai defend and yet simultaneously teach a radical soteriology that cannot be reduced to a scripturally prescribed system of devotional and ritual actions; there is no surefire recipe for salvation.

The effectiveness of metaphor, parable, and allegory in oral and written discourse has been noted at least since the time of Aristotle. Religious teachers in particular have appreciated how powerfully one can bring home a theological point to an audience through the use of these techniques. One wonders whether the average Christian would truly understand (or even remember) Jesus' commandment to love one's neighbor as oneself without the parable of the good Samaritan. Similarly, although Pāñcarātra texts clearly teach that when one surrenders to God, one must abandon all other *upāyas*, most Śrīvaiṣṇava devotees understand this principle through the analogy their founding teachers have made with the Brahmāstra incident in the Rāma story. Even though the Śrīvaiṣṇava use of *Rāmāyaṇa* incidents does not support Crossan's radical distinction between the intentions of parable and theology, the value of his analysis, as I see it, is to suggest that the paradoxes at the heart of parables may be the secret to their theological vigor as well as their rhetorical impact. In Crossan's words, they "shatter the structural security of the hearer's world and render possible the kingdom of God" (123); or, as the Teṉkalai theologians might prefer to say it, they shatter the structural security of the *śāstric* worldview and render possible the soul's true subservience to the Lord.

ABBREVIATIONS

JS — *Jñānasāra* of Aruḷāḷa Perumāl Emperumāṉār with Maṇavāḷamāmuni's commentary. In *Jñānasāram Prameyasāram*, ed. Vidvan Venkatacharya and Tiruvenkatacharya. Kanchi: Śrīvaiṣṇava Mudrāpaka Sabhā, 1916.

Mumu — *Mumukṣuppaṭi* of Piḷḷai Lokācārya with Maṇavāḷamāmuni's commentary. Edited and published by S. Krishnaswami Iyengar. Trichy: n.d.

Rām. — *Śrīmad Vālmīki Rāmāyaṇa*, according to the Southern Readings, ed. T. Krishnacharya. 2 vols. Madras: T. K. Venkobacharya, 1930.

ŚVB — *Śrīvacana Bhūṣaṇa* of Piḷḷai Lokācārya with Maṇavāḷamāmuni's commentary. Ed. P. Raghava Ramanuja Swami. Madras: R. Rajagopala Naidu, 1936.

NOTES

1. For more information on the divergence between the schools, see my *Śrīvaiṣṇava Theological Dispute: Maṇavāḷamāmuni and Vedānta Deśika* (Madras: New Era Publications, 1988).

2. See the list of abbreviations, above.

3. Another doctrinal difference between the two schools hinges on the issue of whether Śrī is a *jīva* or individual soul (the Teṉkalai view), or an aspect of the Lord himself (the Vaṭakalai view). Although this issue might seem unrelated to the basic soteriological dispute, I submit that the Teṉkalai insist on Śrī's status as *jīva* in part so that they may continue to use the example of Sītā in the *Rāmāyaṇa* to support their soteriological doctrines. If Sītā were not a dependent soul like us, then her attitude and behavior in the context of her rescue by Rāma would not be a model for salvation that we could emulate.

4. *Rām.* V.22.20, quoted by Maṇavāḷamāmuni in *ŚVB* 82.

5. Maṇavāḷamāmuni's commentary on *JS* 28 quotes a Sanskrit passage he attributes to the *Sanatkumāra Saṃhitā* in which the analogy between *prapatti* and the Brahmāstra is made, but I have not been able to locate this passage in available editions.

6. *hāro'pi nārpitaḥ kaṇṭhe sparśasaṃrodhabhīruṇā* |
āvayor antare jātāḥ parvatās sarito drumāḥ ||

This śloka, quoted in full by Maṇavāḷamāmuni in *ŚVB* 162, is not found in current editions of Vālmīki's *Rāmāyaṇa*.

7. It is important to note that although the Teṉkalai *ācāryas* prefer to cite the Vālmīki *Rāmāyaṇa* when possible, they are not limited to its version of events in applying their allegorical method. References to incidents from the Rāma story contained in the hymns of the Āḻvārs and Pāñcarātra texts, for example, are also cited. It is the Rāma legend as a whole that has scriptural authority, not just Vālmīki's version.

8. John Dominic Crossan, *The Dark Interval: Towards a Theology of Story* (Niles, Ill.: Argus Communications, 1975), 66. Subsequent references to this work are given in the text.

9. Frank Burch Brown and Elizabeth Struthers Malbon, "Parabling as a *Via Negativa*: A Critical Review of the Work of John Dominic Crossan," *Journal of Religion* 64, no. 4 (October 1984), 537.

10. I am indebted for this idea to Gunther Cologne, "The Parable as a Literary Genre" (M. A. thesis, Arizona State University, 1984). Cologne points out that "it is exactly the paradox of the parable, the unquieting and disturbing effect created through the reversal of the hearer's expectations, that causes him or her to search for an explanation" (22). Cologne's insight, based on his analysis of literary parables and Rabbinic *mashals*, certainly seems to apply to the Śrīvaiṣṇava telling of *Rāmāyaṇa* incidents. Furthermore, it can help reinstate the structural and functional connection between parable and allegory which Crossan et al. have artificially severed.

ELEVEN

The Secret Life of Rāmcandra of Ayodhya

Philip Lutgendorf

Both teller and hearer should be
treasuries of wisdom,
for Rām's tale is mysterious.[1]

RĀMCARITMĀNAS

The hero of the *Rāmāyaṇa*—the Sanskrit epic attributed to the sage Vālmīki, but better known to Indians through later vernacular retellings such as the immensely popular Hindi *Rāmcaritmānas* of the sixteenth-century poet Tulsīdās—is often regarded as a paragon of the sort of virtues catalogued in a credo I was made to memorize as a boy: "trustworthy, loyal, helpful, friendly, courteous, kind, obedient, cheerful, thrifty, brave, clean, and reverent"; in short, as the Eagle Scout of Hindu mythology. Such a view was furthered by Victorian scholars of the Hindu tradition, who viewed Rām as the most palatable alternative to that young reprobate, Kṛṣṇa, and praised the *Rāmāyaṇa* for, as F. S. Growse noted approvingly, its "absolute avoidance of the slightest approach to any pruriency of idea"—which was the Victorian way of saying that it didn't contain any sex.[2] The legacy of this mindset is still with us, both in the West and perhaps even more in India, where it has been promoted by English-medium education and the puritanical revisionism of the "Hindu Renaissance," which largely internalized the colonial critique of the "sensuality" and "effeminacy" of devotional Hinduism. The contrast between Rām as "exemplar of social propriety" (*maryādā puruṣottam*) and Kṛṣṇa as "exemplar of playfulness" (*līlā puruṣottam*) has long been recognized by Hindus, of course, but the notion of *maryādā*—a term suggesting dignity, restraint, limits—seems in modern times to have taken on a particularly prudish if not reactionary connotation. But if our Victorian forebearers gratefully hailed Rām as the one ray of light in a "degenerate" late-*bhakti* Hinduism, the wheel of time and fashion has now revolved to the point that some of us may dismiss him, as one of my teachers once did, as a tiresome prig—"so good you can't bear him!" Significantly, a major portion of the research that in recent decades has sought to situate devotional texts within the context of historical and contemporary religious practice has been concerned with Kṛṣṇa and his devotees, and there has been a relative neglect—only now beginning to be corrected—of the parallel and no less influential traditions of *Rām-bhakti*.[3]

The revolving fashions of academic scholarship have little immediate impact, of course, on grass-roots devotees, and in the roughly eight centuries since Rām's cult became visible and prominent in Northern India, its mythology and theology have acquired a breadth and depth that belies any simplistic dichotomy between a Dionysian Kṛṣṇa and an Apollonian Rām. If we leave the milieu of urban middle-class apologetics and the medium of English—a language in which few Indians give vent to any aspect of their inner lives—we find the boundary between *maryādā* and *līlā* and their respective divine representatives considerably more permeable. Apart from certain sharply drawn sectarian divisions—and to some extent even within them—the choice of Rām or Kṛṣṇa as personal deity (*iṣṭadev*) seems to depend as much on such factors as regional identity, family custom, and choice of guru as on a sharp distinction between the personalities of the two heroes. At the folk level, their characters, deeds, and even names bleed into one another. Watching Rām Līlā plays and listening to *Rāmcaritmānas* expounders in Uttar Pradesh, I was struck by the earthiness and humor with which Rām, Sītā, and their companions—no less than Kṛṣṇa, Rādhā, and their circle—were depicted, and also by the importance given the romantic episodes in the story: the beloved "flower garden" scene in Tulsīdās's version (*phulvārī*), in which Rām and Sītā meet for the first time, and the tumultuous and extended celebration of the couple's wedding, complete with scurrilous women's folksongs (*gāliyāṃ*). Rām may be an exemplar of decorum, but he is also a prince and later a king—an enjoyer of the earth's delights. If he is self-controlled and devoted to one wife (*ek patnī vrat*), he is certainly not, in the popular view, celibate; he is, for most of his saga, a happily married householder in that stage of life in which one is supposed to savor the joys of *kāma*—the pleasure principle in classical Indian thought.

My purpose in this essay is to briefly introduce the theology and religious practices of a group of devotees who chose to focus on this very aspect of the Rām story, and who, perhaps for this reason, have been almost entirely ignored by scholars of Hindu devotional traditions. Adherents of the "connoisseur tradition" or *rasik sampradāy* viewed Rām not only as the supreme manifestation of divinity but also as the ultimate embodiment of erotic sentiment, and focused on his passionate union with his eternal feminine energy (*śakti*) in the form of Sītā. Such devotees represented an important current within the Rāmaite devotional tradition from at least the latter half of the sixteenth century onward, represented by scores of influential teachers and by a copious literature in the Avadhī dialect of Eastern Hindi; their influence remains significant even today. Thus the majority of important temples in Ayodhya, the pilgrimage city most closely associated with the *Rāmāyaṇa*, are controlled by *rasik* sects, and their iconography and liturgy encodes the esoteric theology developed by sectarian teachers. Similarly, the guided meditations and visualizations favored by the *rasiks* remain a vital part of the spiritual practice of many contemporary Vaiṣṇava initiates. I will return later to the subject of the origins and history of the movement but will first focus on its metaphysics and praxis as presented in the writings of influential preceptors. A primary source for this description is the signal work in Hindi that traces the development and teachings of the tradition, Bhagavati Prasad Singh's 1957 monograph, *Rām bhakti meṃ rasik sampradāy* (The *rasik* tradition of Rām *bhakti*). This has been supplemented by recent research in Ayodhya by Hans Bakker and Peter van der Veer, and by my own study of *Rāmcaritmānas* performers and devotees.

THE NATURE OF RASIK SĀDHANĀ

The term *rasik*—by which the adherents of this tradition have commonly referred to themselves—means one who savors *ras* ("juice, essence, aesthetic sentiment") and in mundane contexts can connote a connoisseur of the arts or of any kind of refined pleasure—a bon vivant or even a playboy. Its use among Vaiṣṇava devotees reflects the sixteenth-century Gauṛīya Vaiṣṇava theologians' reinterpretation of classical Sanskrit aesthetic theory in the service of the ecstatic devotionalism promulgated by Kṛṣṇa Caitanya, the renowned mystic of Bengal. In the writings of Rūpa Gosvāmī and his successors, the classical notion of the transformation of individualized, transient emotion (*bhāva*) into universalized aesthetic experience (*rasa*) was reformulated to express the devotee's attainment of spiritual bliss through contemplation of the deeds of Kṛṣṇa. The central importance of drama for the classical aestheticians was not lessened by the new interpretation, for Vaiṣṇavas saw their Lord as the archetypal actor, repeatedly assuming roles in his universal "play" or *līlā*.[4] The writings of the Gosvāmīs and their successors, such as Rūpa's own influential compendium *Bhaktirasāmṛtasindhu* (Ocean of nectar of the essence of devotion), explicitly link this theology of play to the daily practice of initiated devotees, both through a liturgical script for use in rituals and through internal role-playing and visualization. The initiated devotee, like the theatrical connoisseur of classical times, aspired to become a cultivated spectator of the cosmic drama—one equipped with the intellectual, emotional, and indeed physical training necessary to inwardly savor its *ras*, an experience which would culminate not merely in aesthetic rapture but in "bodily liberation" (*sadeh mukti*) into the highest state of bliss. But since this drama was considered ultimately to encompass or underlie all phenomenal life, the only way to be its spectator was to become its participant. In the "theater" of the Vaiṣṇava *rasiks*, to enter the audience necessarily meant to enter the play.

The play itself was in each case a selectively edited version of a well-known and much longer scenario. Just as *rasik* devotees of Kṛṣṇa excerpted, from the god's total legend, a certain phase of his adolescence and attributed to it not only a special charm but the most profound theological significance, so Rām *rasiks* focused on a single phase of their Lord's story—the idyllic period when the newly married Rām and Sītā, having returned from Sītā's home city of Mithila, enjoyed each other's company amidst the palatial comforts of Ayodhya. Although this period is generally held to have lasted some dozen years, it receives no elaborate treatment in most of the standard versions of the *Rāmāyaṇa* (Tulsīdās, for example, discreetly shifts from the couple's joyful return to Ayodhya after the wedding, in 1.361, to the anticipation, only a single stanza later, of Rām's elevation to the status of heir apparent). This neglect did not, however, daunt Rām's *rasik* devotees, who in their songs and meditations delighted in endlessly elaborating on the pleasures of this idyllic interlude, which precedes the beginning of what is usually regarded as the "real" story of the *Rāmāyaṇa*. It would be as pointless for the noninitiate to inquire, in connection with this scenario, where the Rām of that latter story had gone—the long-suffering prince who relinquished his kingdom to preserve his father's honor, lost his wife to a lustful demon king, and led an army of monkeys to eventual victory over his foe—as it would be to ask a Gauṛīya Vaiṣṇava why the princely Kṛṣṇa of the *Mahābhārata* does not figure in their enchanted pastoral realm of Golok. Devotees of both sects were of course aware of the wider cycle of their Lord's adventures, and both groups devised similar explanations to account for their exclusive focus on one facet of it. The Lord, they said, has two *līlās*—one earthly and manifest (*laukik*, *prakaṭā*) and the other transcendent and hidden (*alaukik*, *aprakaṭā*). According to the Rāmaite view, in the former the quality of "majesty" (*aiśvarya*) predominates, and Rām establishes dharma in the world as the *maryādā puruṣottam*. This is also termed his "*līlā* to be known or understood" (*jñey līlā*), and it encompasses the conventional events of the *Rāmāyaṇa* story. But beyond this, they say, there is a secret *līlā* known only to certain fortunate adepts, in which the quality of erotic attractiveness or *mādhurya* predominates and in which Rām expresses his ultimate reality. This is his "*līlā* to be contemplated" (*dhyey līlā*), and it is deliberately omitted from most versions of the *Rāmāyaṇa*, although it may be glimpsed through those portions of the story dealing with Rām's exploits at the youthful age at which the quality of eroticism is most perfectly manifested.

And just as, in Kṛṣṇa *bhakti*, the earthly locale of Vrindavan was transformed into the transcendent sphere of *Golok* (literally, "the world of cattle") wherein Kṛṣṇa's romantic *līlā* eternally unfolded, so the mundane city of Ayodhya (which likewise was growing in importance as a pilgrimage center during the formative period of Rām-*rasik* theology, the late sixteenth to mid seventeenth centuries[5]) was re-visioned as the eternal realm of *Sāket lok*—

"the world of Saket." There the supreme godhead, known to other traditions as Parabrahma, Īśvar, or Śrī Kṛṣṇa, resided eternally in his ultimate form or *svarūp* as sixteen-year-old Rāmcandra and his *parāśakti* or feminine energy, Sītā. Saket was conceived as a vast and beautiful city, foursquare in plan, surrounded by magnificent pleasure parks to which the divine retinue often repaired for excursions. Every part of the city was filled with pleasure: its streets were flecked with gold dust and its balconies encrusted with luminous gems, perfumed fountains played in its squares, and it was dotted with magnificent gardens in which spring always held sway. But the greatest splendor radiated from the city's center, at which lay the immense House of Gold (Kanak Bhavan)—the palace presented to Sītā on her marriage to Rām. Like the city, the palace too was foursquare and many-gated, containing a labyrinth of chambers and passages oriented around a central courtyard which contained the most beautiful of all gardens. At the center of this garden stood a dais in the shape of a thousand-petaled lotus, and at the heart of the lotus a gem-studded throne-couch. Upon this couch was enacted the supreme mystery: the eternal union of the two divine principles in human form, worshiped and served by their intimate attendants who alone could gain entry to this inner sanctum. The tantric influence on this conception is apparent; iconographically it is especially evident in the intricate charts (*yantra, maṇḍala*) created as aids in *rasik* visualization, showing the plan of the House of Gold with its four gates and maze of allegorically labeled chambers.[6]

In calling the divine city of Saket a "visualization" I invoke a term increasingly used by Western psychotherapists and healers to describe imagined settings or scenarios intended to promote mental or physical well-being.[7] Yet in the context of *rasik* meditation this term may be somewhat misleading, since the process by which Saket is evoked by the devotee (usually termed *dhyān*—"meditation"—or *smaraṇ*—"remembrance"[8]) might better be called a "realization." Fundamental to *rasik* theology is the belief that the magic city is *real*—more real, in fact, than our conventional world.[9] And its reality is not simply to be "visualized" with an inner eye but is to be experienced with all the senses—that is, through the medium of a body appropriate to this ultimate world. Since Saket is (in current American real-estate parlance) a "limited-access community," only certain categories of bodies need apply: those which stand in one of four primary relationships—of servant, elder, companion, or lover—to the Lord around whom the life of the magic city revolves. Or to put it another way, the devotee cannot simply write himself into the divine drama; in order to get on this stage, he must fill one of the existing parts, and, as with all acting, this involves long and exacting training.

He must, first of all, be an initiated Vaiṣṇava—either a *sādhu* or a householder—in one of the *rasik* branches of the Rāmānandī *sampradāy*. The preliminary stages of initiation involve the five *saṃskārs* common to many Vaiṣṇava sects—the bestowal of a mantra or sacred formula, of the sectarian *tilak* and other bodily marks (*mudrā*), of a rosary (*mālā*), and of a new name, usually ending in the suffix *-śaraṇ*—"one who takes refuge,"[10] a feature which distinguishes *rasik* devotees from other Rāmānandīs, who generally favor the suffix *-dās*, "slave." Together with these outer signs, which effect the purification of the physical body, there begins a program of inner training designed to familiarize the aspirant with the iconography of the divine city and its inhabitants. This often utilizes manuals prepared by the tradition's preceptors (*ācārya*), such as the *Dhyān mañjarī* of Agradās, who resided at Galta, near modern-day Jaipur, during the second half of the sixteenth century and who was regarded by later *rasiks* as the modern founder of their tradition. This "Handmaiden of Meditation" consists of seventy-nine couplets devoted to an evocation of Saket and its inhabitants, culminating in a vision of the luxuriant pleasure park and of the divine dyad (*yugal svarūp*) of Rām and Sītā enthroned within it.[11] More than half of the text is devoted to detailed verbal portraits of the divine pair, belonging to the type known as *nakh-śikh*—"from the toenails to the crown of the head"—a descriptive genre so common in Indian poetry that we may risk dismissing it as a mere convention and forget that in serving to create (in Kenneth Bryant's memorable phrase) a "verbal icon" of the most literal sort, it represents, in fact, a recipe for visualization.[12] Later *rasik* manuals offer similarly detailed instructions for envisioning other key players in the Saket *līlā*, particularly the principal young female companions of Sītā (*sakhī*) and their respective maidservants (*mañjarī*), as well as the comparable young male companions of Rām (*sakhā*).

The most important *rasik* initiation—in theory given only when the guru perceives that the aspirant is inwardly prepared for it through preliminary training and purification—is the "initiation of relationship" (*sambandh dīkṣā*), which establishes the vital personal connection to the supreme *līlā*. Its purpose is the fabrication of a new body, termed the body of "consciousness" or "discipline," or the "divine body" (*cit deh, sādhanā śarīr, divya śarīr*). This is held to be altogether distinct from the three bodies (gross, subtle, and mental) of Advaita metaphysics and is often said to be one's innate or ultimate form, recognized within one by the spiritual guide. Yet although this new body represents one's true identity, the awareness of it depends on emotional experience or *bhāv*, which in the early stages of spiritual discipline must be carefully cultivated.

The training of the *rasik* adept involves total identification with his assigned body—a role-playing more intense than even the most dedicated method actor would undertake.[13] To assist in identification with the new body and cultivation of its *bhāv*, the initiate is provided with a wealth of contextual information. There exist, for example, treatises that catalogue the seven kinds of female friends of Sītā, ranging in age from less than six to more than sixteen years, and provide each with a list of parents, other relatives, and teachers, along with details as to place of birth, favorite activities, and so forth. Similar catalogues exist for the youthful male comrades of Rām.[14] Each initiate is also assigned a special "inner-palace name" (*mahalī nām*) identifying him as one of those privileged to enter the private apartments of Kanak Bhavan. This name, which for members of the *sakhī* branch of the tradition usually ends in a feminine suffix such as *-alī*, *-latā*, *-sakhī*, or *-kalī*, is normally kept secret, although it might be known to other adepts. It is also common to use it as a poetic signature (*chāp* or *bhaṇitā*), especially at the end of compositions purporting to describe mysteries seen in the course of inner service. Thus there exist numerous emotional and erotic lyrics which bear such signatures as "Agra-alī" and "Yugal-priyā" and which are held to be the inspired compositions of the preceptors otherwise known as Agradās and Jīvarām.[15] Indeed, the *rasiks'* propensity for living two lives simultaneously has sometimes resulted in confusion—as in the instances in which manuscript searchers of the Nāgarī Pracāriṇī Sabhā (a Hindi literary society) failed to recognize an initiatory name, resulting in texts by the same person being wrongly assigned to two different authors.[16]

Once established in the emotional mood of the visualized body, the aspirant is ready to begin the most characteristic aspect of *rasik* devotional practice or *sādhanā*: the "mental service" (*mānasī pūjā*) of Sītā-Rām according to the sequence of "eight periods of the day" (*aṣṭayām*)—a cycle mirroring the pattern of daily worship in Vaiṣṇava temples and, ultimately, the protocol of royal courts. Most of the prominent preceptors of the tradition, beginning with Agradās, are held to have composed manuals detailing their own interpretations of the eight periods and of the type of service to be offered during each. Thus, for example, the *Aṣṭayām pūjā vidhi* (Schedule of the eight periods of worship), a Hindi work by the early nineteenth-century preceptor Rāmcaraṇdās, divides the day into five principal segments during which the scene of divine activity shifts among eight "bowers" (*kuñj*) within Saket. In this scenario, a *sakhī*'s day begins with her own elaborate toilette, followed by the singing of gentle songs to awaken the divine couple, who are imagined to be languorously sleeping in an opulent "rest bower." Once awake, they are seated on low stools and ministered to in various ways: their feet are washed, their teeth cleaned, their ornaments and garlands are changed, and they are worshiped with incense and lights, before being led to the "refreshment bower" for the first of many light snacks that will be served to them during the day. This is followed by a lengthy trip to the "bathing bower" for a dip in the holy Sarayu, and then by the donning of fresh clothes, ornaments, unguents, and makeup in the "adornment bower"—all supervised by the ever-hovering *sakhīs*. Once dressed, the divine pair are offered a proper morning meal in the "breakfast bower," where they are served, serenaded, and fanned by female attendants.

After breakfast, the couple again proceed to the Sarayu, where Rām joins his *sakhās* and Sītā her *sakhīs* for boating excursions or "water play" (*jal krīṛā*). This mild exertion is followed by a midday meal in the "refreshment bower" and then by a period of rest, during which the most intimate *sakhīs* remain in attendance on the divine couple, pressing their feet, offering betel preparations, or singing songs to enhance their erotic mood. After a brief nap, the pair is again awakened, worshiped, and escorted to the pleasure parks on the banks of the Sarayu where, suitably dressed and adorned and to the accompaniment of the singing and dancing of *sakhīs*, Rām engages in Kṛṣṇa-style *rās līlā* (dancing and lovemaking) and enjoys a late supper with Sītā, before finally returning to the "sleeping bower" for the night.[17]

The climax of this meditative foreplay is said to be the experience of *tatsukh* (literally, "that delight")—a vicarious tasting of the pleasure shared by the divine couple in their union, as witnessed by attendant *sakhīs* and *mañjarīs*. This dimension of the *sādhanā* has always been controversial, however—for Rāmānandīs no less than for Gauṛīya Vaiṣṇavas—since some adepts of the *sakhī* tradition have maintained the possibility of *svasukh* ("one's own delight"), or a personal experience of mystico-erotic union with Rām. In theory, this was viewed as impossible; however, in the internal world of *dhyān*, some adepts apparently found themselves, like their counterparts in the Christian and Islamic mystical traditions, experiencing things that, according to the book, weren't supposed to happen.[18]

The brief summary of an *aṣṭayām* schedule given above cannot do justice to the painstaking detail in which each period and activity is to be evoked: every article of clothing and jewelry, every morsel of sweetmeats and golden bowl of water, adds iconographic richness and is to be rehearsed over and over again. Moreover, as I have already noted, the adept aims for more than mere visioning: the fragrances of the unguents and incense, the taste of the betel packets (which are daintily pre-chewed for the divine pair by their solicitous attendants), the cool splash of Sarayu water—all are to be imaginatively experienced in the most vivid fashion through the appropriate internal senses.

One may also observe that, in Rāmcaraṇdās's scheme, Rām's faithful male comrades don't get to spend very much time with their Lord, who passes his days largely surrounded by females; but of course, in the *aṣṭayām* schedules prepared by preceptors of the *sakhā* branch of the tradition the division of activities between male and female attendants is more equitable, and the timetable includes such wholesome masculine diversions as elephant processions down the gilded avenues of Saket, solemn durbars, and hunting excursions to nearby forests, in the course of which Rām's comrades of various ages can delight in the intimacy of teasing jokes, songs, and general locker-room camaraderie. B. P. Singh's study of a large number of *aṣṭayām* manuals led him to observe, however, that there appeared to be an increasing emphasis, over the course of time, on erotic sports to the exclusion of all other kingly activities.[19]

To be sure, *aṣṭayām* manuals are poetic compositions—anthologies of verses describing each period of the day, rather like the "twelve months" (*bārah mās*) texts which reckon the months of the year from the perspective of a lovesick woman awaiting her lover's return—and they often contain ingenious conceits which are thought to evoke the author's meditative experiences. But they are also and primarily textbooks for a concrete mystical practice, and indeed one which involves rigorous discipline. The *sādhak* or practitioner of this meditation program must rise by 3:00 A.M., bathe, and purify himself through repetition of the Rām mantra, mentally reassume the *sādhanā* body and persona by systematically reviewing its attributes, and begin offering service to the divine pair when they are awakened at about 4:30—a service which will continue at prescribed intervals throughout the day and night. The aim of this discipline, which may occupy one's whole life, is clearly expressed in the writings of the *rasikācāryas*: what begins as an "imaginative conception" (*bhāvnā*) ends as a reality so compelling that the conventional world fades into shadowy insignificance. Through long practice in visualization, it is said, the adept begins to catch "glimpses" (*jhalak*) of the actual *līlā*; these gradually intensify and lengthen, until he gains the ability to enter Saket at any moment. He becomes a real and constant participant in this transcendent world, a condition regarded, within this tradition, as "liberation in the body" (*sadeh mukti*).[20] Of course, this ultimate state is not attained by all devotees, but it is an ideal to which all may aspire. The intensity with which exemplary initiates have pursued these practices and the extraordinary experiences vouchsafed them are celebrated in sectarian hagiography (some examples of which are given below), while the notion of the heavenly Ayodhya as the soul's ultimate abode is constantly reaffirmed in the Rām devotees' preferred idiom for death: to "set forth for Saket" (*Sāket prasthān*).

Despite the emphasis, especially in the *sakhī* branch of the tradition, on erotic themes, the personal meditations of many *rasik* devotees centered on other personal relationships to Rām. Some chose to visualize the Lord as a young child and to cultivate tender parental emotions toward him (*vātsalya bhāv*).[21] In this they had as a model the character of the legendary crow Kāk Bhuśuṇḍī in *Uttar kāṇḍ*, the seventh book of the Tulsīdās epic, who asserted,

> My chosen Lord is the child Rām,
> who possesses the beauty of a billion Love gods.[22]

Kāk Bhuśuṇḍī was said to return to Ayodhya in every cosmic cycle to re-experience the childhood sports of his Lord, thus paralleling the aspirant's own daily inner journeys to Saket and re-creations of its *līlā*. What was common to all *rasik* practice was an emphasis on the techniques of role-playing and visualization as well as an aesthetic delight in sensorally rich settings, rather than on any specific content.

As in the Kṛṣṇa tradition, so in the *rasik* literature of Rām we find warnings against the externalization of the meditative practices, for the content of the visualizations could easily provoke the misunderstanding and scorn of the uninitiated. Yet paradoxically, since an underlying assumption is that the events seen in meditation are real, the most exemplary devotees are often those whose lives reveal a blurring of the boundary that separates this world from Saket and a spilling over of its *līlā* into the mundane sphere. Such legends confirm the power of the technique and suggest that the devotee's "acting" is less a mental exercise than a way of life.

For example, the early saint Sūrkiśor (fl. c. 1600?), who like Agradās came from the Jaipur region, is said to have visualized himself as a brother of King Janak; hence he regarded Sītā as his daughter and Rām as his son-in-law. So strictly did he observe traditional rules of kinship that, on pilgrimages to Ayodhya, he refrained from taking food or water within the city limits, since a girl's blood relations should not accept hospitality from her husband's family. He had an image of Sītā which he carried with him everywhere and treated exactly as one would a real daughter, even buying toys and sweets for her in the bazaar. It is said that other devotees, shocked by his "disrespectful" attitude toward the Mother of the Universe, stole this image. Heartbroken, he went to Mithila to find his lost daughter, and Sītā, pleased by his steadfastness, caused the image to reappear.[23]

In oral *Rāmāyaṇa* exposition sessions (*Rāmāyaṇ-kathā*), I twice heard the story of the child-saint Prayāgdās. Taunted by other children because he had no elder sister to feed him sweets during the festive month of Śrāvaṇ, he went tearfully to his widowed mother, who appeased him by telling him that he indeed had a sister who had been married before he was born; "Her name is Jānakī, and her husband is Rāmcandra, a powerful man in Ayodhya. She never comes to visit us." The guileless child, determined to see his sister, set out on foot for Ayodhya and after many trials reached the holy city. His requests to be directed to the residence of "that big man, Rāmcandra" met with laughter; everyone assumed the ragged urchin to be insane. Exhausted from his journey, Prayāgdās fell asleep under a tree. But in the dead of night, in the inner sanctuary of Kanak Bhavan temple (a modern re-creation of the legendary House of Gold and one of Ayodhya's principal shrines), the images came alive. Rām turned to Sītā and said, "Dearest, today the most extraordinary saint has come to town! We must go meet him." The divine entourage proceeded in state to Prayāgdās's lonely tree, where the ringing of the great bells around the necks of the elephants awakened the boy. Undaunted by the magnificent vision, he repeated his question to the splendidly dressed man in the howdah and received the reply, "I am Rāmcandra, and here beside me is your sister, Jānakī." But the boy, unimpressed, told the Lord, "You are surely deceiving me, because where I come from we have the custom that when a sister meets her brother again after a long separation, she falls at his feet and washes them with her tears." Devotees delight in describing how the Mother of the Universe, unable to disappoint him, got down from her jeweled palanquin and threw herself in the dust of the road.[24]

The romantic predilections of *rasik* devotees led many of them to focus on the first book of the *Mānas*, the *Bāl kāṇḍ*, which recounts Rām's youthful adventures culminating in his marriage to Sītā. Maharaja Raghurāj Siṃha of Rewa wrote in his epic *Rāmsvayaṃvar* that his guru had instructed him to read *Bāl kāṇḍ* exclusively. A great devotee of the Ramnagar Rām Līlā, he is said to have attended only the early portions of the cycle each year. The *sādhu* Rāmpriyā Śaraṇ, who regarded himself as Sītā's sister, composed a *Sītāyan* in seven books (c. 1703), similarly confining its narrative to Sītā's childhood and marriage. A few preceptors even took the extreme position that the distressing events of Rām's exile, the abduction of Sītā, the war with Rāvaṇ, and so on, were not true *līlā* at all (in which the Lord reveals his ultimate nature), but only divine "drama" (*nāṭak*) staged for the benefit of the world.[25] Another story told of Prayāgdās has the guileless saint happen on an oral retelling (*kathā*) of the *Rāmāyaṇa*'s second book, *Ayodhyā kāṇḍ*, the events of which are altogether unknown to him. He listens with growing alarm as the expounder tells of the exile of Rām, Sītā, and Lakṣmaṇ and their wanderings in the forest, but when he hears that the princes and his "sister" are compelled to go barefoot and to sleep on the ground, he becomes distracted with grief. Rushing to the bazaar, he has a cobbler fashion three pairs of sandals and an artisan make three little rope-beds, and, placing these things on his head, sets out for Chitrakut, enquiring of everyone concerning the wanderers. He eventually makes his way to the forest of Panchvati where, it is said, he is rewarded with a vision of the trio and the opportunity to bestow his gifts.[26]

The influence of the *rasik* tradition appears to have peaked in the eighteenth and nineteenth centuries. B. P. Singh's biographical listing of prominent *rasik* devotees includes many Rāmāyaṇīs (*Rāmāyaṇa* specialists) who were active in the royal court at Banaras, especially under Mahraja Udit Nārāyaṇ Siṃha and his son Īśvarīprasād, both of whom were connoisseurs and munificent patrons of the Rām tradition. Some of these men—such as Rāmgulām Dvivedī, Ragurāj Siṃha, Śivlāl Pāṭhak, and Kāṣṭhajihvā Svāmī—were also involved in the development of the royal Rām Līlā pageant, which became an influential model for Rām Līlā troupes throughout northern India.[27] These connections serve to remind us that the theology and mystical practice of the *rasik* preceptors was not without political implications. In a period of economic and social transformation and ebbing princely authority, they offered devotees and patrons an interiorization of the old Vaiṣṇava royal cult, based on a "new kingdom"

> limitless in extent, and millions of times greater in splendor than any earthly kingdom. Its king is so great that the five elements and time itself stand reverently before him . . . while he himself, in the company of countless maidservants and his own beloved, remains in the Golden House immersed in dalliance. . . . This imaginary kingdom of the *rasiks* is the world of Saket, its sovereign is the divine couple Śrī Sītā-Rām, and the easy path to reach it is through the technique of visualization.[28]

But just as in the theory of *rasik* practice, what begins as imagination ends as a reality so concrete that the real world seems in comparison no more than a dream, so in the case of the Ramnagar Rām Līlā, what began as a play was transformed, under the guidance of the Banaras rulers and their *rasik* advisors, into a city and kingdom not only reimagined but physically reconstructed into an enduring ideological statement.

INTERPRETING THE RASIK TRADITION

Among the few scholars who have examined Rāmaite *rasik* texts and practices, the most common approach has been to stress the highly derivative nature of the tradition. Thus R. S. McGregor, in a short essay on the *Dhyān mañjarī*, attempts to demonstrate that Agradās composed his text under the influence of a Kṛṣṇaite source, the *Rās pañcādhyāyī* of Nanddās.[29] The Sanskrit *Bhuśuṇḍī Rāmāyaṇa*, an esoteric rewrite of the *Rāmāyaṇa* in the light of *rasik* practices, has been termed by B. P. Singh "only a transformation of the *Bhāgavata* [*purāṇa*] text," while Hans Bakker, in his recent study of Ayodhya, labels this *Rāmāyaṇa*'s conceptualization of the holy city "no more than a trivial replica of the sacred topography developed for Braj in the *Vrajabhaktivilāsa* of Nārāyaṇa Bhaṭṭa written in A.D. 1552."[30] The writer who has offered the only ethnographic data on Rāmānandī *rasiks*, Dutch anthropologist Peter van der Veer, characterizes their entire tradition as "the 'Kṛṣṇaization' of Rām *bhakti*."[31] Such evaluations reflect modern scholarship's preference for a historical approach—which seeks to understand religious movements by tracing them back to their presumed origins—and they indeed shed much light on the process of sectarian evolution. Thus it has been shown that from Agradās's time onward Rāmānandī centers in Rajasthan were in close contact with developments in the Braj region, and that many *rasik* adepts received training from Kṛṣṇaite preceptors in Vrindavan.[32] An historical perspective can also offer an antidote to sectarian fallacies—such as the Ayodhya *rasiks*' claim that their tradition is in fact *older* than that of Vrindavan, since, as every pious Hindu knows, Rām carried on his erotic pastimes in the Tretā Yug, the second of the four cosmic epochs, long before Kṛṣṇa was even a gleam in his father Vasudev's eye.

The perspective of social history may also shed light on the underlying causes of the rise of the *rasik* tradition from the sixteenth century onward, though here the interpretation of historical data is more problematic. Joseph O'Connell suggests that the theology and mystical practice of the Vrindavan Gosvāmīs reflected a Hindu retreat from the Muslim-dominated sociopolitical sphere.[33] This view has been echoed by David Haberman, who sees the enchanted and extrasocial realm of Vrindavan as a response to a "serious need for an expression of Hindu *dharma* that placed the world of significant meaning far beyond that sphere controlled by the Muslims."[34] Similarly, Singh has suggested that the practices of the Rāmānandī *rasiks* represented a response to an age dominated by "foreign" political powers.[35] Such theories cannot be overlooked in any comprehensive study of these traditions in their cultural context, particularly in view of the long-standing cultic emphasis on the king's identification with Viṣṇu. Yet at the same time, scholars must be wary of judgments colored by the hindsight of twentieth-century communalism, and especially by the idealization, so often encountered in the writings of modern Hindu scholars, of an imagined pre-Muslim past—a view which often tends to compromise the complexity of Indian society at the grass-roots level, with its intricate web of interacting forces and interests. In this context, it is worth reminding ourselves that the practice of visualization and of the fabrication of inner bodies has a very old pedigree in the subcontinent, extending back long before the establishment of the Delhi Sultanate, and also that the "other worlds" of the *rasiks* came to prominence precisely during a period of generally amicable relations between Hindus and Muslims—most notably during the age of Akbar and his immediate successors—when Hindu nobles occupied powerful positions in the imperial administration and large temples were again being constructed in North India under princely patronage. Similarly, although the rise of the great *rasik* establishments in Ayodhya occurred only after the breakup of central Mughal authority, it was fueled by the patronage of the newly enfranchised maharajas of the eastern Ganges Valley—such as the rulers of Banaras, Rewa, Tikamgarh, and Dumrao—as well as, significantly, by that of the heterodox and religiously eclectic Shi'ite Nawabs of Oudh, who had their capital at Ayodhya until 1765.[36]

Returning to the question of the genesis of Rāmaite *rasik* practices, we may also observe that there is a stigma attached to the label "derivative," which reflects our own culture's valuation of certain kinds of novelty and originality—concepts often viewed very differently in India—and which may lead us to a cursory dismissal of what we judge to be "unoriginal" material. Useful as it is, a historical understanding offers only one perspective on the Rām *rasik* tradition; it tells us nothing of the special attraction of its impressive corpus of literature or of the inventive adaptations that it made within the *Rāmāyaṇa* framework. Singh's study of this neglected tradition documents some nine hundred texts: *aṣṭayām* manuals, hagiographies like the *Rasik prakāś bhaktamāl*, descriptions of the divine city of Saket, and anthologies of songs stamped with the initiatory names of prominent *ācāryas*, as well as such intriguingly titled works as Rāmpriyā Śaraṇ's seven-canto epic, *Sītāyan* (c. 1703), and the earlier *Rāmaliṅgāmṛta* of one Advait of Banaras (1608).[37] If nothing else, the realization that thousands of pious devotees saw nothing wrong in visualizing Rām and Sītā's erotic sports should chasten us in our attempts to apply simplistic categories to Vaiṣṇava traditions: the puritanical Rāmaites here, the sensual Kṛṣṇaites there.

Moreover, the charge of derivativeness can be much more broadly applied, since it is clear that the whole *rasik* orientation in Vaiṣṇava *bhakti* was heavily indebted to the Buddhist and Śaiva traditions of an earlier period and indeed seems to have represented the culmination of a long historical process of the "tantricization" of Vaiṣṇavism. This process was already reflected in the Pāñcarātra literature and in the *Bhāgavata Purāṇa*, and a circa twelfth-century Rāmaite text, the *Agastya Saṃhitā*, includes instructions for an elaborate visualization of Rām and Sītā, enthroned on the pericarp of an immense lotus incorporating all the powers of the cosmos.[38] Agradās's floruit is assumed to have been the second half of the sixteenth century, which would make him a contemporary of the later Vrindavan Gosvāmīs. His rapid adaptation of their teachings bears witness to the fact that *rasik* practice was, by his day, an idea whose time had come—a pan-Vaiṣṇava phenomenon which cut across sectarian lines.

The influence of the Rām *rasik* tradition grew steadily during the seventeenth and eighteenth centuries, and the movement acquired a more public profile through an influential commentary on the *Rāmcaritmānas* composed by Mahant Rāmcaraṇdās of Ayodhya in about 1805, which was said to have openly revealed the secrets of erotic devotionalism (*śṛṅgārī bhakti*) which Tulsīdās had deliberately concealed in his Manas Lake.[39] Van der Veer documents the steadily growing power of *rasik* institutions in Ayodhya from the early eighteenth century onward—in part a reflection of the patronage of wealthy rajas, zamindars, and merchants who were attracted to the movement. Some of these patrons became initiated *sādhaks*, like Maharaja Raghurāj Siṃha of Rewa, himself the author of thirty-two works.[40] Like the tantric tradition before it, the *rasik* movement underwent a popularization, acquiring a vogue among the elite which was reflected in the predominance of *rasik* themes in the poetry and painting of the period. And despite the attacks of the Victorians and the puritanical apologetics of the "Hindu Renaissance," the *rasik* point of view remains much in evidence, especially in Ayodhya, where the majority of important temples are controlled by *rasik* sects and where the most famous shrine—Kanak Bhavan temple—represents a full-scale realization of the mythical House of Gold, complete with Rām and Sītā's opulent bedchamber. It is, of course, difficult to say to what extent the full and arduous *rasik* meditational regimen is currently put into practice.

It may appear to us ironic that celibate Hindu ascetics like Agradās, who typically led lives of great austerity, should have indulged in internal fantasies in which they roamed jewel-studded pleasure houses and witnessed (or, in some cases, participated in) the untiring loveplay of a divine libertine—doubly ironic in that these scenarios were, as Singh has pointed out, dependent for their tangible details of architecture, dress, and courtly protocol on the recent imperial model of the Mughals.[41] We might recall a parallel in the Western Christian tradition, where the favorite text of the monastics of the Middle Ages was the most erotic book in the Bible, the "Song of Songs."[42] But I would like to end with the suggestion that visualization and projection are not unique to religious practitioners, but are inherent also in what scholars of religion do—the imaginative reconstruction of other people's beliefs and practices. In visualizing another world, it is impossible to avoid seeing through the lens of one's own, and we find this reflected as much in Rām's Mughal-style durbar hall as in our own readings of the *rasik* tradition—condemned as "licentious," because the Victorian observer is prudish, or written off as "derivative," because the late twentieth-century observer cherishes novelty. Talking about other people's myths is often only a rather arch way of talking about our own, and this being so, we might remind ourselves that the reigning fantasy world of our commercial culture—reconfirmed daily by countless visual cues in television commercials, billboards, and newspaper and magazine advertisements—bears many superficial resemblances to that of the *rasiks*: a fictive realm in which everyone is young, attractive, and nearly always engaged in erotic play. Yet in two significant respects this untiringly reimaged world of our culture differs strikingly from the realm of Saket: for its characters are not divine (and so not connected to the deeper values supposedly cherished by our society) and its scenarios are not chosen and generated by ourselves, but rather are created for us by the *ācāryas* of a secular and materialist religion, who know wherein the ultimate return lies.

NOTES

Research for this paper was carried out in India between 1982 and 1987, initially under a Fulbright-Hays fellowship and later under a faculty development grant from the University of Iowa. The author wishes to acknowledge the kind assistance of Dr. Bhagavati Prasad Singh of Gorakhpur, and of Pandit Rāmkumār Dās of Maṇi Parvat, Ayodhya, and the helpful suggestions of Paul Greenough, Sheldon Pollock, and Paula Richman.

1. 1.30b. Hanuman Prasad Poddar, ed., *Rāmcaritmānas* (Gorakhpur: Gita Press, 1938; reprinted in numerous editions). Numbers refer to book or *kāṇḍ*, stanza (a series of verses ending in a *dohā* or couplet; when more than one couplet completes a stanza, a roman letter is added to the couplet number), and individual line within a stanza.

2. Frederick Salmon Growse, trans., *The Rāmāyaṇa of Tulasī Dāsa* (Cawnpore: E. Samuel, 1891; repr. New Delhi: Motilal Banarsidass, 1978), lv.

3. Examples of significant work on contemporary expressions of Kṛṣṇa devotionalism include Milton Singer, ed., *Krishna: Myths, Rites, and Attitudes* (Honolulu:

East-West Center Press, 1966); Norvin Hein, *The Miracle Plays of Mathurā* (New Haven: Yale University Press, 1972); and John Stratton Hawley, *At Play With Krishna* (Princeton: Princeton University Press, 1981). The emerging literature on Rām includes Frank Whaling, *The Rise of the Religious Significance of Rāma* (Delhi: Motilal Banarsidass, 1980); Hans Bakker, *Ayodhyā* (Groningen: Egbert Forsten, 1986); and Peter van der Veer, *Gods on Earth* (London: Athlone Press, 1988). On *Rāmcaritmānas* performance, see Philip Lutgendorf, *The Life of a Text: Performing the Rāmcaritmānas of Tulsidas* (Berkeley and Los Angeles: University of California Press, 1991).

4. On the theology and dramatic theory of the Gosvāmīs and its influence on sectarian practice, see David Haberman, *Acting as a Way of Salvation* (New York: Oxford University Press, 1988); and Donna M. Wulff, *Drama as a Mode of Religious Realization* (Chico, Calif.: Scholar's Press, 1984), especially pp. 7–44.

5. On the historical developments which permitted the "reclamation" of Ayodhya by Vaiṣṇavas, see Bakker, *Ayodhyā*, 135–53, and van der Veer, *Gods on Earth*, 38–40.

6. An example appears in Bhagavati Prasad Singh, *Rāmbhakti meṃ rasik sampradāy* (Balrampur, Uttar Pradesh: Avadh Sahitya Mandir, 1957), facing p. 274.

7. There is a growing literature on the therapeutic use of visualization techniques; for an extensive discussion and bibliography, see Jeanne Achterberg, *Imagery in Healing* (Boston: New Science Library, 1985). (I am grateful to Susan Lutgendorf for this reference.)

8. On the meanings of *smaraṇ*, see Haberman, *Acting as a Way of Salvation*, 63–64, 124–26.

9. The ontological status of places and things seen in visualization has begun to concern Western health researchers as well. Therapist Gerald Epstein, for example, has suggested that since visualizations can produce tangible effects on the physical body, they must be regarded as possessing some kind of reality; see "The Image in Medicine: Notes of a Clinician," in *Advances* 3, no. 1 (Winter 1986): 22–31; especially p. 23.

10. Thus the name Rāmpriyā Śaraṇ means "one who takes refuge in Rām's beloved"—i.e., in Sītā.

11. Ronald Stuart McGregor, "The *Dhyān mañjarī of Agradās*," in *Bhakti in Current Research: 1979–1982*, ed. Monika Thiel-Horstmann (Berlin: Dietrich Reimer, 1983), 237–44.

12. Kenneth Bryant, *Poems to the Child-God* (Berkeley: University of California Press, 1978), 72–75. Bryant borrows the phrase "verbal icon" from the title of a book by literary critics W. K. Wimsatt and Monroe C. Beardsley, but significantly reinterprets it for the Indian context.

13. Cf. Haberman's interesting comparison of Vaiṣṇava role-playing with the acting method developed by Constantin Stanislavski: *Acting as a Way of Salvation*, 67–70.

14. See Singh, *Rāmbhakti meṃ rasik sampradāy*, for examples of the catalogues developed for *sakhīs* (pp. 238–40) and for *sakhās* (pp. 245–47).

15. Some non-*rasiks* dispute the attribution of some of the "Agra-alī" songs to Agradās, claiming that they are forgeries perpetrated by latter-day sectarians with a view to proving the antiquity of their tradition (Pandit Rāmkumār Dās; private conversation, July 1987). Such "forgeries" may, however, equally well reflect the widespread practice of assuming the voice and persona of a revered poet-saint in order to

express conventional sentiments associated with his teachings; see John Stratton Hawley, "Author and Authority in the *Bhakti* Poetry of North India," *Journal of Asian Studies* 47, no. 2 (May 1988): 269–90.

16. Singh, *Rāmbhakti meṃ rasik sampradāy*, 9–10.

17. Ibid., 241–42.

18. Ibid., 307–9. On the Kṛṣṇaite side of the debate, see Haberman, *Acting as a Way of Salvation*, 94–114.

19. Singh, *Rāmbhakti meṃ rasik sampradāy*, 240–41.

20. Ibid., 253.

21. See, for example, the three-volume *Mānas* commentary entitled *Bāl vinodinī* (For the amusement of children) by Mahant Gaṅgādās of Ayodhya (Ayodhya: Maṇirāmdās kī Chāvnī, 1969), in which the author regards himself and fellow devotees as child-playmates of Rām. Note also the spiritual practice of the famous nineteenth-century scholar Umāpati Tripāṭhī of Ayodhya, who scandalized his contemporaries by visualizing himself as the teacher of the youthful Rām; van der Veer, *Gods on Earth*, 13–14.

22. Poddar, ed., *Rāmcaritmānas*, 7.75.5.

23. Singh, *Rāmbhakti meṃ rasik sampradāy*, 399.

24. Based on oral versions by Śrīnāth Miśra (13 February 1983) and Rāmnārāyaṇ Śukla (3 August 1983). Singh gives a different version, in which Prayāgdās is sent to Ayodhya by his guru: *Rāmbhakti meṃ rasik sampradāy*, 402.

25. Singh, *Rāmbhakti meṃ rasik sampradāy*, 281; concerning the *Sītāyan*, see p. 394.

26. Ibid., 403.

27. On the history of the Banaras Rām Līlā, see Lutgendorf, *The Life of a Text*, chapter 5.

28. Singh, *Rāmbhakti meṃ rasik sampradāy*, 365. While Singh implies that this invisible kingdom was meant to serve as an alternative to the cultural model presented by the Mughals, he points to the ironic fact that the physical details in which it was imagined were inevitably based on the most recent model of imperial grandeur—the Mughals themselves.

29. McGregor, "The *Dhyān mañjarī* of Agradās," 241–43.

30. Bhagavati Prasad Singh, "*Bhuśuṇḍī Rāmāyaṇa* and Its Influence on the Medieval *Rāmāyaṇa* Literature," in *The Ramayana Tradition in Asia*, ed. V. Raghavan (New Delhi: Sahitya Akademi, 1980), 475–504, at p. 479; Bakker, *Ayodhyā*, 142.

31. van der Veer, *Gods on Earth*, 165–72.

32. Singh, *Rām bhakti meṃ rasik sampradāy*, 171.

33. Joseph T. O'Connell, "Social Implications of the Gauḍīya Vaiṣṇava Movement" (Ph.D. diss., Harvard University, 1970), 171–206; cited in Haberman, *Acting as a Way of Salvation*, 43–44.

34. Haberman, *Acting as a Way of Salvation*, 43.

35. Singh, *Rām bhakti meṃ rasik sampradāy*, 365–66.

36. van der Veer, *Gods on Earth*, 37–40.

37. The title of the latter work poses difficulties for the translator, who may shy away from the (literal but perhaps misleading) "Nectar of the Phallus of Rām." According to B. P. Singh, a major portion of this text is indeed devoted to descriptions of Rām and Sītā's dalliance, but bearing in mind the wider range of meanings of *liṅga* in Indian culture (as "symbol," "signifier," or "emblem of power") one might do

better to render it "Nectar of the Essence of Rām"—it being understood that, for the *rasik* tradition, erotic energy is one of the Lord's essential attributes.

38. Bakker, *Ayodhyā*, 110–17.

39. Singh, *Rām bhakti meṃ rasik sampradāy*, 159; Lutgendorf, *The Life of a Text*, chapter 3.

40. Singh, *Rām bhakti meṃ rasik sampradāy*, 472.

41. Ibid., 365–66.

42. Jean Leclercq, *The Love of Learning and the Desire for God* (New York: Fordham University Press, 1961), 84–86.

TWELVE

Personalizing the *Rāmāyaṇ*: Rāmnāmīs and Their Use of the *Rāmcaritmānas*

Ramdas Lamb

In the religious life of the Rāmnāmīs of Chhattisgarh, the *Rāmcaritmānas* of Tulsīdās plays a fundamental role. There has been an ongoing development in the relationship between the sect and the text since the inception of the Rāmnāmī movement in the late nineteenth century. An understanding of the changing role of the *Mānas*[1] in the Rāmnāmī community, however, requires a certain reevaluation of the concept of "scripture" in Hindu tradition and in particular the two traditional categories of Hindu sacred texts: *śruti*, "that which was heard," and *smṛti*, "that which was remembered."

Śruti generally designates the corpus of Vedic texts—Saṃhitās, Brāhmaṇas, Āraṇyakas, and Upaniṣads—which are said to be eternal reverberations emanating forth from the Transcendent and directly cognized by seers at the beginning of each cycle of creation. Three characteristics are generally held to distinguish this class of texts. (1) *Śruti* constitutes a circumscribed, bounded category of texts—that is, the Vedic texts.[2] (2) These texts, although transmitted by sages who "saw" and "heard" them, are held to be eternal and uncreated, not composed by any human or divine agent.[3] (3) Given that study of the Vedic Saṃhitās has focused on meticulous preservation of the purity of the Vedic sounds, or mantras, which are held to be intrinsically powerful and efficacious, precedence has usually been given to memorization and recitation of *śruti* texts rather than to understanding and interpretation of their meaning.[4]

Smṛti texts can be defined in direct opposition to *śruti*. (1) *Smṛti* is a fluid, dynamic, open-ended category, which includes the *dharmaśāstras*, epics, and *purāṇas* as well as an array of other texts that different groups at different times have regarded as belonging to the class. (2) In contrast to *śruti*, these texts are believed to have been composed by personal authors, either human or divine, and hence are "that which was remembered" rather than "that which was heard." (3) Study of *smṛti* texts involves not only rote recitation of verses but also an understanding and interpretation of their content.

Indologists have traditionally concentrated on brahmanical Sanskritic texts when considering the concept of scripture in India. Perhaps as a result, the orthodox view of *śruti* and *smṛti*, as defined by the above characteristics, has tended to neglect the modifications of these categories that have taken place over the last thousand years. Devotional movements have been largely responsible for the increasing permeability and reinterpretation of these categories. They have precipitated the greatest number of additions to the class of *smṛti* and at the same time have inspired the elevation of multiple sectarian works to the status of *śruti*. Recognizing this, in recent years several scholars have suggested the need for an expanded understanding of *śruti* and *smṛti* that would encompass more fully the dynamic role the sacred word has played in Hindu tradition, particularly in post-Vedic times. For example, Thomas Coburn has suggested that instead of constituting fixed categories of texts, *śruti* and *smṛti* may refer rather to "two different kinds of relationship that can be had with verbal material in the Hindu tradition."[5]

As Coburn's observation implies, despite the apparently secure status of the Vedas themselves as *śruti*, the distinctions between the categories of *śruti* and *smṛti*, as delineated above, do not represent an absolute classification of particular texts. Rather, they form part of a theoretical framework by means of which a variety of texts may be classified according to their status and function within a particular community. A text ultimately attains its sacred status as scripture—and more specifically as *śruti* or *smṛti*—only in relationship to a particular religious community, for it is the community that determines whether a text is "sacred or holy, powerful or portentous, possessed of an exalted authority, and in some fashion transcendent of, and hence distinct from, all other speech and writing."[6]

Historically, several strategies have been adopted to effect a change in the position of sectarian texts with respect to the categories of *śruti* and *smṛti*. Those processes which have played an important role in the evolution of the Rām story in India, from earliest times to the present, will be discussed below.

THE MĀNAS AS ŚRUTI AND SMṚTI

Over the past four hundred years no Hindu text has generated as large and as active a following as Tulsīdās's *Mānas*. Even as a non-Sanskritic text, it has been elevated to the status of *śruti* in the eyes of the populace of North India. More than any other text it has been reinterpreted, recreated, and imitated in a large variety of literary, ritual, and performative genres such as commentaries, oral recitations (*kathās*), dramas (*līlās*), and devotional chanting (*bhajans*). As such the *Mānas* is an especially suitable vehicle for examining the permeability and relativity of the categories of *śruti* and *smṛti*.

It is impossible to say with certainty how early the Rām story achieved scriptural status in India. J. L. Brockington maintains that at least five stages are perceptible in the development of Vālmīki's *Rāmāyaṇa* from its original to its final form. Each stage incorporated additional brahmanical elements into the text, which served to make the story more consistent with orthodox beliefs and practices, with developing brahmanical doctrines, and with the establishment of the Brahmin priest as the mediator of devotion to Rām. Brockington refers to this process of altering the text in the direction of brahmanical values as *brahmanization*.[7]

By the time the *Rāmcaritmānas* was written the Rām story had been sufficiently appropriated and given status by the brahmanical orthodoxy in North India that a large section of the priestly community of Banaras, where the *Mānas* was completed, became outraged by Tulsīdās's rendition of the story in Hindi, rather than in the orthodox Sanskrit. According to popular tradition, this situation led to an event—said to have occurred just after the completion of the *Mānas* and originally recorded by Benīmādhavdās, a disciple of Tulsīdās, in his *Mul Gosāīñ Caritra*—that was extremely significant both for Tulsīdās and for his poem.

According to the legend the Brahmin priests of Banaras were furious that the story of Rām had been written in a vernacular language instead of in Sanskrit, and they denounced the *Mānas* as a debasement of the holy scriptures. Subsequently, Tulsīdās took his work to the main Śiva temple in the city where a test of its validity was devised by a respected Sanskrit scholar. That night the book was placed before the main image in the temple, and on top of it were placed the *śāstras*, the eighteen *purāṇas*, the Upaniṣads, and, finally, the four Vedic Saṃhitās. The temple was then locked for the night. When it was reopened in the morning the *Mānas* was found on top of the pile. Immediately the text and its author were hailed by all present.

This story is often heard in North India when the position of the *Mānas* in relation to the Sanskrit scriptures is discussed. A common interpretation is that the *Mānas* was divinely recognized as equal to the Vedas in sanctity. Many Rām *bhaktas* (devotees), however, say the story shows that the *Mānas* actually supersedes the Vedas in both sanctity and authority. For them, the *Mānas* is not equal to *śruti*: it is itself *śruti*. It is the preeminent text of the present age, the new standard by which to define *śruti*.[8]

The process through which a text is elevated to the status of *śruti* has been termed *vedacization*.[9] Unlike brahmanization this process does not involve a modification of textual content but rather of attributed status. The dual process of brahmanization and vedacization of a number of sectarian works has complicated the traditional division between *śruti* and *smṛti*. Most such works enter the scriptural hierarchy at the level of *smṛti*, as the preferred text of a particular sect. As a given text gains adherents and ritual status, additional sanctity is ascribed to it. Eventually, the text bridges the gap between *śruti* and *smṛti* attribution, taking on dimensions of both. Philip Lutgendorf refers to a text that goes through this process as an "upwardly-mobile scripture."[10]

The *Mānas* in North India provides an excellent example of a sacred text that has assumed characteristics of both *śruti* and *smṛti*. On the one hand, the *Mānas* has the attributes of a *smṛti* text: it was composed by a human author, Tulsīdās, and is written in Avadhi, a regional dialect related to modern Hindi, rather than in Sanskrit, the language of the Vedas. Moreover, as the source of the Rām story, the content of the text is considered as important as its sound value. In the context of the *Mānas* as *śruti*, modification of the text, in its written form as well as in oral presentation, forms a part of the process of continual reinterpretation and recreation of the story.[11] At the same time the *Mānas* clearly has attained quasi-*śruti* status. Its verses are viewed by its adherents as efficacious mantras, the chanting of which can bring about blessings, cure illness, remove obstacles, and even grant power. Like the Vedas the *Mānas* has generated a sizable body of literature that imitates, interprets, and expands on the text. In addition, many Brahmin priests today, albeit some begrudgingly, grant a *śruti*-like position to the *Mānas* and use it ritually as such. Lutgendorf has described the process of vedacization in Banaras and other urban centers of North India through which the *Mānas* has come to be regarded as the "Hindi Veda" and *Mānas* recitation rituals have been transformed into Vedic *yagyas* ("sacrifices") performed by Brahmin priests.[12]

RĀMNĀMĪS AND THE MĀNAS

The Rāmnāmī Samāj is a sect of *harijan* (Untouchable) Rām *bhaktas* from the Chhattisgarh region of Madhya Pradesh. Formed in the 1890s, the sect has become a dominant force in the religious life of the *harijans* of the area. While the "official" text of the sect is Tulsīdās's *Rāmcaritmānas*, an examination of the movement's history and practices reveals the presence and growing importance of oral variants of the *Mānas*, based on Tulsīdās's telling of the Rām story yet distinct from it. In actuality it is these oral variants that circumscribe the Rām story for the Rāmnāmīs.

The founder of the Rāmnāmī sect was an illiterate Chhattisgarhi Camār (member of an Untouchable leather-worker caste) named Parasurām. His father, like many North Indian Rām devotees, had been an avid *Mānas* devotee who would listen to recitations of the text whenever possible and commit verses to memory. Parasurām followed his father's example and from early childhood began memorizing verses from the text. According to the sect's oral hagiography, when Parasurām was in his mid twenties he contracted leprosy but was miraculously cured by a Rāmānandī ascetic.[13] The ascetic then exhorted Parasurām to devote himself entirely to the *Mānas*, viewing the text as his chosen deity, and to ceaselessly practice *rāmnām*, repetition of the name of Rām. As word of the miracle spread, countless villagers came to see Parasurām, who would tell them of the ascetic's teachings, recite stories from the *Mānas*, and speak of the greatness of *rāmnām*. Parasurām's popularity grew, and in less than a year the Rāmnāmī Samāj was born. Those most attracted to Parasurām and his teachings were illiterate *harijan* villagers like himself.

The *Mānas* became the central symbol of the sect on three different levels. On the material level, the physical text was revered as the sect's chosen deity, as is evident in the Rāmnāmī practice of positioning a copy of the text in the center of the group during *bhajan*, treating it as an image of a deity to which they are offering hymns. On the level of sound, the *Mānas* was celebrated as a repository of *rāmnām*, and its verses viewed as mantras possessing transformative power. On the level of meaning, the *Mānas* was cherished by the Rāmnāmīs as their primary source of the Rām story—though actual recitation of the narrative has never been stressed—and a repository of great spiritual wisdom.

In the early years of the movement the Rāmnāmīs focused primarily on the first two levels, paying relatively less attention to the text's meaning, possibly because nearly all of the members of the sect were illiterate.[14] Parasurām could not actually read the *Mānas* well but had memorized large portions of the text, which he would recite in the presence of the other sect members. At this stage in the sect's development the *Mānas* enjoyed a quasi-*śruti* status in that it was revered primarily as a recited text containing potent mantras that did not need to be understood in order to be spiritually efficacious. The text had already attained this status among many North Indian Rām devotees, so the Rāmnāmīs were not assigning a new distinction to it. They merely adopted a prevalent sentiment.

Since most of the group could neither recite from memory nor understand the text of the *Mānas*, group *bhajans* originally centered almost exclusively on the chanting of *rāmnām* rather than on recitation of the *Mānas* itself.[15] As a result, the Name gradually came to supersede the *Mānas* as the central symbol of the sect. Not only did *rāmnām* become the quintessential mantra on which Rāmnāmī devotional chanting focused but its written form was used as a ritual diagram, or *yantra*, and inscribed on their homes, their clothing, and their bodies.[16]

In time, however, members of the sect other than Parasurām began to memorize verses from the *Mānas* and integrate them into their *rāmnām* chanting. Group members would occasionally learn the meaning of the verses they had memorized, although in the early days of the sect the verses were still viewed above all as mantras, the power of which was automatically activated through recitation.

The desire to memorize verses nonetheless led eventually to an increase both in literacy and in understanding of the chanted portions of the text. Because the Rāmnāmīs initially were unfamiliar with the full contents of the *Mānas*, they believed that its teachings were based solely on *gyān* ("religious knowledge"), *bhakti* ("devotion"), and *rāmnām*. However, as understanding of the memorized verses increased, sect members began to realize that the text also contained many verses that support orthodox Hindu beliefs regarding Brahmin social and religious superiority and the inferior status of low castes and women. The Rāmnāmīs were thus confronted with a difficult situation. The text they had been taught to revere as scripture turned out to contain certain teachings that were diametrically opposed to their own beliefs and apparently supportive of the existing social and religious hierarchy that had placed them at its bottom, declaring them unworthy to possess a developed religious life.

This situation inspired a move by many of the younger Rāmnāmīs to learn to read so that they could understand the meaning of the growing number of verses that had been integrated into group *bhajans*. The purpose of this effort was twofold. First, it would allow them to sift through the existing collection of verses and eliminate those that were contrary to the sect's developing belief system. Second, it would aid in the establishment of selection criteria to be employed in the building of a corpus of verses to be chanted, which would in turn help give definition to the sect's philosophy and values. In this way the corpus of memorized verses and the sect's beliefs came to exist in a dynamic interchange, each affecting the development of the other.

As the focus shifted from rote recitation of *Mānas* verses to an understanding of the recited text, from an emphasis on sound to an emphasis on meaning, the status of the *Mānas* began to shift from *śruti* to *smṛti*. No longer viewed as a bounded, inviolable scripture, the text came to be seen as open-ended, capable of being interpreted, elaborated, and when necessary modified. The Rāmnāmīs began both to reinterpret and to expand on the text, emphasizing verses that were in accordance with their values while ignoring others that violated their belief system. The *Mānas* thus became the basis for the sect's own tellings of the *Rāmāyaṇ*, which draw not only on the *Mānas* but on a variety of additional texts.

BEYOND THE MĀNAS: RETELLING THE RĀM STORY

In the early days of the Rāmnāmī movement, the *Mānas* clearly enjoyed a sacrosanct and authoritative status in the sect's devotional practices, and until the 1920s the Tūlsī *Rāmāyaṇ* was the only text from which verses were extracted for use in Rāmnāmī *bhajans*. With the realization that the *Mānas* also contained teachings antithetical to their philosophy, however, the Rāmnāmīs were forced to reevaluate the role of the text in their religious life.

Their increased awareness of the contents of the *Mānas* subsequently opened the door for the inclusion in their chanting sessions of verses from other texts and alternate tellings of the Rām story.

Another pivotal factor influencing the inclusion of supplemental textual material seems to have been the presence in Chhattisgarh of Kabīrpanthīs, followers of Kabīr. The sect had been in the area for over two hundred years, spreading Kabīr's teachings. Praise of *rāmnām* is a recurring theme in much of Kabīr's poetry, and so the Rāmnāmīs, as devotees of the Name, eventually incorporated several of Kabīr's couplets into their *bhajans*. Once verses from Kabīr became a part of the sect's chanting, it was not long before the Rāmnāmīs began to incorporate verses from a variety of other texts as well.

Thus the *Mānas* gradually lost its position as the sole repository of verses used in *bhajan*, although it is still the major source for most Rāmnāmīs. A corpus of approximately five to six hundred *Mānas* verses makes up the bulk of the sect's chanted *Rāmāyaṇ*, to which more than one hundred verses from other texts have been added, becoming an integral part of the group *bhajan*.[17] Author and antiquity play little if any role in the selection of alternative texts or verses, and many of the Rāmnāmīs are entirely unaware of the origin of numerous verses they commonly use in chanting.[18]

There are, however, two major criteria for determining whether a verse may be included in a Rāmnāmī *bhajan*. Its metrical form must be either *dohā* or *caupāī*, the meters in which the majority of the *Mānas* is written,[19] and its content must pertain to Rām, wisdom, devotion, or *rāmnām*, although in certain situations this rule can be dispensed with. (See the section below on *ṭakkar*.) Among the secondary texts that meet these criteria and are consequently drawn on for use in chanting are well-known writings like Tulsīdās's *Dohāvalī* and Kabīr's *Bījak*, as well as lesser-known texts like the *Viśrām Sāgar*, *Sukh Sāgar*, *Vraj Vilās*, *Brahmānand Bhakta*, and Sabal Singh Chauhan's Hindi version of the *Mahābhārata*.[20] The most popular of these auxiliary texts is the *Viśrām Sāgar*, written in the nineteenth century by Raghunāthdās, a member of the Rāmsnehī sect found primarily in Madhya Pradesh and in some areas of Uttar Pradesh. Rāmsnehīs adhere to a *nirguṇ* ("formless") Rām *bhakti* philosophy similar to that of Kabīr.[21] Over the years the *Viśrām Sāgar* has earned such a position of respect among Rāmnāmīs that it is second only to the *Mānas* in terms of the number of its verses that are included in *Rāmnāmī bhajan*.

The Rāmnāmīs' compilation of *dohās* and *caupāīs* from the *Mānas* and other texts represents the sect's own, ever evolving and maturing telling of the Rām story, one which emphasizes those aspects of the story that harmonize with their beliefs and values while ignoring aspects that run counter to them. Those sections of the *Mānas* most consonant with the Rāmnāmīs' philosophy accordingly receive the greatest attention. Conspicuous by their almost complete absence are verses containing references to Brahmins, adherence to caste distinctions, ritual observances, image worship, and devotion to deities other than Rām, as well as those that criticize low castes and women. Most sect members simply ignore such verses, although some have gone to the point of actually deleting offensive couplets from their personal copies of the text. The Rāmnāmīs' telling of the Rām story is instead crafted around teachings concerning *gyān*, various dimensions of *bhakti*, and *rāmnām*. Not very surprisingly, then, the only narrative material from the life of Rām that figures in the sect's chanting centers on events that emphasize his impartial love, compassion, and forgiveness.

Other than Rām the characters that appear most frequently in the Rāmnāmīs' *Rāmāyaṇ* are Sītā (Rām's wife), Bharat and Lakṣmaṇ (his brothers), Hanumān (the monkey god), Niṣādrāj (a chieftain of the Untouchable boatman caste), and Vibhīṣaṇ (a demon devotee of Rām). All of these characters have close devotional relationships with Rām and thus assume important roles in the sect's rendering of the Rām story. Many of the verses used in *bhajan* consist either of words spoken by these characters or words addressed by Rām to one of them. The Rāmnāmīs view the ways in which these figures relate to Rām as ideal manifestations of devotion to him. The last three, Hanumān, Niṣādrāj, and Vibhīṣaṇ, are of special significance to the sect because in their respective roles as monkey, *harijan*, and demon they testify to the fact that any being can take refuge in, have an intimate relationship with, and ultimately attain union with Rām.[22]

In summary, among the early Rāmnāmīs the *Mānas* enjoyed a status approaching that of *śruti*, but as its meaning gradually came to be understood the status of the text itself began to shift. Although the sect still tends to assign the *Mānas* scriptural status, make it the centerpiece of their group *bhajans*, and use its verses as mantras, at the same time they add to and subtract from it as they please, praising some sections while denouncing others. The implications of this change in attitude toward the text will be explored more fully below.

RĀMNĀM BHAJAN

Members of the Rāmnāmī Samāj are spread throughout the eastern districts of Chhattisgarh. This is one of the least developed areas of the North Indian plains: poverty is the norm and travel is arduous. Because group *bhajans* afford the only opportunities many of the sect's members have to get together, such *bhajans* have become the most important unifying activity for the Rāmnāmīs. The style of group *bhajan* has gone through a variety of modifications, however, since the formation of the group nearly one hundred years ago.

The introduction of random verses into their chanting of *rāmnām* has resulted in the sect's unique style of *bhajan*: a chorus of *rāmnām* interspersed with verses in the *dohā* and *caupāī* meters taken primarily from the *Mānas*. Although this is the dominant form of *bhajan*, several variant styles have also evolved that have inspired the development of individualized *Rāmāyaṇs* and reveal the direction in which the sect and its philosophy have matured. These will be discussed below.

The Rāmnāmīs' ritual dress for *bhajan* includes a cotton shawl covered with "Rām" written in *devanāgarī* script, a peacock-feather hat worn primarily by male members of the sect, and a set of bells worn on the ankles by sect members who dance and tapped on the ground by seated *bhajan* participants. The Rāmnāmīs' attire not only identifies them as members of a sect but also serves to attract spectators. This is important to the Rāmnāmīs because they believe that anyone who participates in or even hears *rāmnām* benefits by it. Thus, the larger the crowd that is lured, the greater the advantage of the *bhajan*.

Whenever they sit to chant, the Rāmnāmīs place a copy of the *Mānas* before them, usually elevated on a small wooden bookstand. If no bookstand is available, the text will be placed instead on a piece of cloth or, in some cases, directly on the ground in front of the area where the Rāmnāmīs have gathered. As long as the chanting continues the text will remain open in its place, although it may never be actually read from or even looked at. Rather, the physical text exists in their midst as a symbol, venerated as the source of *rāmnām* and as a repository of teachings concerning *gyān*, *bhakti*, and the glories of the Name. Once the chanting ends, however, so does any reverence shown the physical text. The book is then handled and stored by the Rāmnāmīs as any other book would be.

The refrain of *rāmnām* is approximately forty-eight beats in length and contains twenty-eight repetitions of the name of Rām. A chanter wishing to contribute a *dohā* or *caupāī* from the *Mānas* or another text will notify the other chanters of his intention by vocalizing an extra "RāmRām" more loudly at a fixed point in the latter part of the refrain. The person introducing the couplet recites all but the last line solo, at which time all those familiar with the verse join in its conclusion. The inserted couplet is then followed by the *rāmnām* refrain. During the last few decades the number of inserted verses has increased to the point that nearly every refrain is followed by one. Moreover, the Rāmnāmī repertoire of verses has grown so large that during any particular *bhajan* sitting—unless it is an all-night event—very few are ever chanted twice.

In addition to selecting only verses they deem ideologically and metrically appropriate for their chanting, Rāmnāmīs further individualize their oral *Rāmāyaṇ* by modifying *Mānas* verses themselves. The most common form of modification is the insertion of "RāmRām" or "Rāmnām" into verses, either on their own or as substitutes for alternate names of Rām. Thus "Rāmcandra" becomes "RāmRām" or "RāmRāmnām," "Raghuvīr" becomes "Rām-

Rāmvīr," "Rāmu" and "Rāmahi" become "RāmRām" or "Rāmnām," and so on. "Sītā Rām" is often replaced with "RāmRāmnām," and, where the meter allows, even "Rām" may be replaced by "RāmRām." Such substitutions are the Rāmnāmīs' way of demonstrating where their devotion actually lies: not with the person of Rām, a human incarnation of the divine, but with *rāmnām*, their link to the formless Rām, the Absolute.

Another form of verse modification of *Mānas* couplets involves replacing the words "*brāhmaṇ*" or "*vipra*" with "*rāmnām*" in verses that originally contained praise of Brahmins, redirecting that praise to the practice instead. Consider the following verse from the *Mānas*, commonly recited by North Indian Rām devotees:

> The Lord took human form to help Brahmins, cows, gods, and holy men.

A small change by the Rāmnāmīs gives the verse a meaning much more consistent with their particular beliefs.

> The Lord took human form to help gods and holy men by giving them [the practice of] *rāmnām*.[23]

VARIANTS, VIDVĀNS, AND INDIVIDUAL VERSIONS

Within the framework of group *bhajan*, several variant formats have evolved that have added new dimensions to the sect's oral performance of the Rām story. Of these, two have been especially influential in increasing both the Rāmnāmīs' understanding of and their repertoire of verses from the *Mānas* and other texts. The first of these involves the insertion of a conversation in verse form into the *bhajan* itself. This is a common practice among members of the sect. The second format is a special type of philosophical dialogue or interchange, engaged in by a small but growing number of Rāmnāmīs. This stylized interchange is called *ṭakkar* (literally, "collision" or "quarrel").

Conversation

To the Rāmnāmīs *rāmnām bhajan* is both a religious practice and a form of entertainment. Insofar as it is the focus of their individual spiritual lives as well as of their shared life of devotion as a community, it is a religious practice to be taken quite seriously. At the same time, however, *rāmnām bhajan* gatherings, especially the periodic large ones, are the only opportunity many Rāmnāmīs have to see each other and to escape temporarily from the troubles and concerns of daily life. Thus group chanting sessions are also a time of joy and celebration. In this context *bhajan* is viewed as a source of entertainment, involving at times lighthearted conversation, jesting, and joking.

Besides the corpus of verses from the *Mānas* and other texts that have been incorporated in *rāmnām bhajan*, there is a vast array of other *Mānas* verses covering a broad range of subjects. Although these verses do not directly apply to *bhajan* topics, they are often quite useful for the purpose of conversation. Sect members will occasionally interject such verses into the chanting as a means of greeting one another, joking, complaining about the difficulties of family life, speaking irreverently about priests, politicians, or wealthy landowners, and so on.

For example, seeing a friend after a long time apart, a Rāmnāmī may nod an acknowledgment of the other's presence while reciting the following *Mānas* verse. The words are those of a sage greeting Rām upon his arrival at the former's hermitage.

> I have watched the road day and night with deep concentration. Upon seeing [you] my Lord, my heart has been soothed.[24]

A fitting reply to this welcoming couplet might be:

> Now I have faith, O Hanumān, in the Lord's blessings upon me, for without it the company of saints cannot be gained.[25]

If an unknown member of the sect arrives to take part in a *bhajan* gathering, a Rāmnāmī may want to show hospitality and inquire about the stranger's identity. At the same time he may want to ascertain whether the stranger is aware of the conversation format and gauge his cleverness.

> Are you one of the Lord's servants? My heart is filled with feelings of love.
> Or maybe you are Rām, friend of the poor, who has come to grant me blessings.[26]

With the following brief reply the newcomer could show his humility, his awareness of the conversation, and his knowledge of how to respond:

> Lord, I am [Vibhīṣaṇ] the brother of the ten-headed Rāvaṇ. O Protector of the gods, I was born in the family of demons.[27]

This in turn might prompt the reply:

> Vibhīṣaṇ, you are triply blessed. You have become the jewel of the demon family.[28]

In this manner the Rāmnāmīs combine *bhajan* and conversation, although the process often seems more like a competition to see who can be cleverer in finding verses that apply to a variety of situations. When a verse used in conversation is replied to, a dialogue may begin, which may lead into another stylistic variant of *bhajan* called *ṭakkar*.

Ṭakkar

Nearly all of the Rāmnāmīs know something about the use of *Mānas* verses in conversation, and many of them practice it. Barely half, on the other hand, are even aware of the process of *ṭakkar*, and not more than a tenth actually take an active part in it. Nevertheless, *ṭakkar* and its practitioners, known in the sect as *vidvāns* ("exponents of knowledge"), have provided perhaps the greatest formative influence in contemporary times on the beliefs and practices of the Rāmnāmī Samāj.

As we have seen, the Rāmnāmīs' gradual growth in literacy and ability to understand *Mānas* verses made them aware of the need to sift through and evaluate the text, in order to avoid verses and sections that were discordant with their own beliefs. The designation *vidvān*, traditionally used to refer to a Sanskrit scholar, was given to those Rāmnāmīs who dedicated themselves to deepening their comprehension of the *Mānas* and to gaining the knowledge required to judge which verses from the *Mānas* (and other texts) accorded with the Rāmnāmīs' philosophy and thus might fruitfully be incorporated into the *bhajans*.[29] Although the *vidvāns* constitute only about 10 percent of the sect, they have had tremendous influence as the architects of the sect's philosophy, giving shape and direction to the Rāmnāmīs' beliefs and practices. The vehicle the *vidvāns* employ for the expression and dissemination of their particular philosophical perspectives is *ṭakkar*.

As understood by the Rāmnāmīs, *ṭakkar* is a form of dialogue or interchange between *vidvāns* that takes place during chanting, the language of these interchanges consisting entirely of verses from the corpus of texts collected by the *vidvāns*. The *ṭakkar* process evolved as a direct result of both the conversation style of *bhajan* and the freedom allowed each individual Rāmnāmī in the selection of verses to be memorized for use in *bhajan*. The more literate sect members tended to seek out primarily those verses consistent with their personal philosophical viewpoint.[30] In time, differences as well as similarities in the perspectives of the various sect members became apparent on the basis of the verses favored by each member in the *bhajan* sessions. For example, a Rāmnāmī, finding himself in particular agreement with a verse chanted by another sect member, might choose to display his consensus by offering a verse consonant with the previous one in spirit. Conversely, a sect member could counter an objectionable verse by reciting an opposing couplet. This back-and-forth process of responding to recited verses gradually became formalized in *ṭakkar*.

The term *ṭakkar* literally means "quarrel" or "collision," and the process indeed resembles a school debate or competition more than a discussion of fundamental philosophical differences. As one *vidvān* put it, *vidvāns* use *ṭakkars* for the purpose of plumbing "the depths of each other's knowledge and devotion." In a gaming spirit, Rāmnāmī *vidvāns* like to set parameters or rules for each *ṭakkar*. For example, restrictions may be placed on the subject matter of the *ṭakkar*, the preferred topics being *gyān*, *bhakti*, and *rāmnām*. Alternatively, the verses used in *ṭakkar* may be limited to those drawn from a particular chapter of the *Mānas* or to those taken from texts other than the *Mānas*.[31]

Ṭakkars can take place at any time during *rāmnām bhajan* and may last from several minutes to several hours. When a group chant involves mostly non-*vidvāns*, which is quite common, then short *ṭakkars*, generally lasting only a few minutes, will occasionally take place between the *vidvāns* present, such dialogues often passing almost unnoticed by the rest of the group. When, on the other hand, a large number of *vidvāns* gather together, a much greater percentage of the *bhajan* will take the form of *ṭakkar* of one type or another. An amazingly high percentage of Rāmnāmīs—perhaps as many as 40 percent—are oblivious to the existence of the *ṭakkar* process itself, and an even greater number are generally unaware when such interchanges are actually taking place during the *bhajan*. Those Rāmnāmīs who are least aware of the *ṭakkar* process tend to be the women and older men, the two groups in which illiteracy is the highest. The primary reason for this is that many of the illiterate Rāmnāmīs have simply memorized the verses they chant through listening to their frequent repetition during *bhajans*, without any real attempt to understand what is being chanted. Consequently, their actual comprehension of most verses is minimal and is generally limited to the more commonly repeated ones from the *Mānas*. As was the case in the early days of the movement, such sect members simply have faith that the verses they are listening to or repeating are about *gyān*, *bhakti*, or *rāmnām*, and that is sufficient for them.

On the other hand, many of the younger males have had at least a few years of schooling and have attained a certain degree of literacy. They tend to have a greater curiosity with respect to what is being repeated and thus have a greater capability and likelihood of gaining an understanding of recited verses. In addition, they also have a greater ability to read the *Mānas* and other texts to search out new *bhajan* verses on their own. It is therefore this group of Rāmnāmīs that yields the greatest number of *vidvāns*.

The *ṭakkars* have stimulated the *vidvāns* to undertake an in-depth study not only of the *Mānas* but of various other texts—including Hindi translations of some Sanskrit scriptures—in order to improve their understanding of classical and contemporary Hindu thought as well as to find verses with which to fuel and energize their debates. This study is not necessarily confined to those texts used in *bhajan*, but can extend to Hindi translations of such works as the Upaniṣads, the *Bhagavad Gītā*, *purāṇas*, various *stotras*, and even portions of the Vedic Saṃhitās. If a text is found that is in *dohā* or *caupāī* meter, then it will be culled for verses applicable to *ṭakkar*. More often than not, however, Hindi translations of classical texts are in prose rather than verse form and so cannot be used in chanting. Thus, although the initial impetus for such research might have been a desire to increase the repertoire of verses available for *ṭakkars*, the purpose of study for many *vidvāns* extends beyond collecting verses for *bhajans*. In the eyes of the *vidvāns*, textual study serves to deepen their own understanding of *gyān*, *bhakti*, and *rāmnām*, as well as providing a storehouse of knowledge on which they can draw to continually enrich, renew, and reinvigorate the sect's oral recitations of the *Rāmāyaṇ*.

During the early 1970s three *vidvāns* gathered together verses from a wide variety of texts for use in *bhajans* as well as non-*bhajan* discussions and debates. The compilers also added several couplets of their own creation, publishing the collection under the title *Rām Rasik Gītā*.[32] They had two thousand copies printed and distributed to members of the sect. The fact that the first five pages of this fifty-two page booklet are entirely in Sanskrit, coupled with the inclusion of the compilers' own verses, raised the ire of many sect members, who viewed the booklet as a form of self-aggrandizement, and many *vidvāns* refuse to refer to it at all. Nevertheless, the *Rām Rasik Gītā* has become a useful source of verses for Rāmnāmīs who cannot afford to buy books or who are unable to obtain copies of the original texts from which the booklet's contents are drawn.

The particular form a *ṭakkar* takes depends to a large extent on the subject matter and the *vidvāns* present. *Vidvāns* who know a large repertoire of verses and possess a deep understanding of their subject matter can generate lively interchanges. In *gyān ṭakkars*, *vidvāns* may deliberately take opposing stands on various philosophical issues, such as the impersonal vs. personal understanding of God, the dualism/monism debate, and the disagreement concerning the relationship between God and *māyā*. On the topics of *bhakti* and *nām*, however, a relative consensus exists among *vidvāns*, and the range of viewpoints is accordingly less diversified. The object of such *ṭakkars* seems to consist more in pitting one's talent and the size of one's repertoire of verses against that of the other *vidvāns* than in serious attempts to refute another's point of view.

The following is a portion of a *gyān ṭakkar* that took place during the annual Rāmnāmī festival in 1989.[33] Several thousand Rāmnāmīs had gathered for the three-day festival, in which *bhajan* continues from sunset to sunrise. One evening a young *vidvān* recited the following verse, obviously directed at another *vidvān* seated nearby.

> According to the Vedas, *itihāsas*, and *purāṇas*, God's creation is filled with both good and evil.[34]

Accepting the challenge, the second *vidvān* replied:

> God created all existence as a mixture of good and evil. Swanlike saints drink the nectar of goodness, leaving behind the waters of imperfection.[35]

Stimulated by this response, the first *vidvān* offered two verses consecutively, the second intended to bolster the view presented in the first.

> Planets, medicinal plants, water, wind, and clothing become useful or harmful in accordance with their good or bad associations. Only a clever and thoughtful person can know the difference.

Only when the Creator gives one discriminative wisdom does the mind turn from sin to goodness.[36]

The second *vidvān's* rejoinder was a verse commonly heard in chanting.

Knowing the world to be permeated by Rām's Name, I bow with joined hands.[37]

In the above interchange the challenging Rāmnāmī puts forth the view that the world is dualistic, containing both good and evil. As he goes on to point out, wisdom and discrimination are necessary in order for one to be able to reject the world's dark side. In his initial reply the respondent seems to accept this view, further suggesting that a holy person absorbs the good and is not bothered by the bad. Ultimately, however, he implies that in reality there is no evil, for the world is permeated by none other than Rām's Name. Such a reply is called *samarthak* ("conclusive") since in the eyes of the Rāmnāmīs there can be no rebuttal, only agreement. While the last verse is one commonly repeated in *bhajans*, in the context of this particular *ṭakkar* it was seen as a valid rejoinder and not just an uninspired retreat into platitudes, as it might have been viewed in some other *ṭakkar*.

An intriguing feature of this particular interchange is that the verses are all taken from within the same three pages of the *Mānas*. The ability to conduct a *ṭakkar* with verses drawn entirely, or even predominantly, from one episode in the text is considered by the *vidvāns* to be a sign of both intelligence and cleverness. It suggests that the participants in the *ṭakkar* are sufficiently knowledgeable about the particular event and the various concepts implicit in it to be able to glean verses from a common narrative to support opposing viewpoints.

What I term *līlā ṭakkars* (*ṭakkars* in the form of a *līlā*—"play" or "drama") are a relatively recent variant of the *ṭakkar* form and add a new dimension to the *bhajan* process. During chanting a *vidvān* may adopt the role of one of the major figures in Tulsīdās's Rām story, from Rām himself to Rāvaṇ, the ten-headed demon king who is Rām's staunchest adversary. To indicate his choice, the *vidvān* recites several verses spoken by that character in the *Mānas* while casting challenging glances at one or more of the other *vidvāns*, one of whom is then expected to take on the role of an opposing character.

A *ṭakkar* that took place during the 1989 Rāmnāmī *melā* serves as a good illustration of the dynamic interchange between opposing characters that distinguishes this form of *ṭakkar*. On the second evening of the festival, nearly seventy-five Rāmnāmīs were assembled under one of the many open-sided tents set up for the gathering. As the chanting proceeded one *vidvān* recited several *Mānas* verses attributed to Rāvaṇ, the demon king of Lanka, all the while looking quite intently at a *vidvān* seated nearby. The latter soon acknowledged the challenge and replied with two verses spoken by Aṅgad, a monkey member of Rām's army who engaged in a philosophical argument with Rāvaṇ immediately prior to the war in Lanka. Their roles firmly established, the participants in the *līlā ṭakkar* were now free to recite any verses they chose in order to help further their respective positions in the debate. Among the verses recited by "Rāvaṇ," himself a demon but also a Brahmin, were several spoken by Rām extolling the greatness of Brahmins. (Here the recitation of verses extolling Brahmins was in order because the speaker was playing the role of a demon.) "Aṅgad," on the other hand, quoted from Mārīch, a demon friend of Rāvaṇ, celebrating Rām's power. Soon the discussion left the *Mānas* entirely and concentrated on verses from another text. Ultimately it returned to the *Mānas*, and "Aṅgad" won the debate—an inevitable outcome. Figures such as Rāvaṇ, Bālī, and others whose roles in Tulsīdās's telling are generally negative never win such debates, but then winning is not always the purpose of the *līlā*. It is a sport, a game, in which the *vidvāns* display their mastery of relevant verses and their understanding of various texts and their teachings.

The number of Rāmnāmīs has been declining rapidly during the last decade, essentially because the number of deaths of elder sect members far exceeds the number of new initiates. At the same time, however, the percentage of *vidvāns* is increasing because many of the new, younger members are relatively more literate and are thus encouraged by the older *vidvāns* to study various texts and take part in the *ṭakkars*. As their number increases, many *vidvāns* are gravitating toward smaller *bhajan* gatherings at which they make up the majority of participants—so that their *ṭakkars* are not "interrupted" by the interjection of random verses from sect members unaware of the interchange taking place.

The increase in the number of *vidvāns* and their practice of *ṭakkar* has led to the creation of two levels of oral *Rāmāyaṇ* within the sect: the *Rāmāyaṇ* of the general membership and the individual *Rāmāyaṇs* of the various *vidvāns*. In some ways this is dividing the sect, yet at the same time each level performs an important function. Through group performance, the shared *Rāmāyaṇ* of the sect unifies it and defines its beliefs. It provides the sect with an oral scripture, whose parameters and philosophy are constructed around the beliefs of the sect.

Setting the stage for future development of the shared *Rāmāyaṇ* are the personalized versions of the *vidvāns*. In doing individual study of various texts, both to search for new *ṭakkar* material as well as to expand their own private understanding of *gyān* and *bhakti*, each *vidvān* creates a personalized repertoire of verses that alters his own telling and makes it a unique creation. This process inspires a great deal of experimentation and growth for many of the *vidvāns*. It also provides a diversity of directions and an ever-changing treasury of new verse material for the future growth of the shared *Rāmāyaṇ* of the sect. It assures the continual fluid nature of the Rāmnāmīs' telling of the Rām story.

CONCLUSION

The concepts of *śruti* and *smṛti* have long been used to classify the multiple forms that sacred word has assumed in India. As we have seen, the boundaries of these categories have grown more permeable over the centuries, particularly with the rise of devotional movements and their sectarian texts. Originally used in reference to specific works, both *śruti* and *smṛti* have gradually evolved into more fluid, relational categories capable of subsuming a variety of texts, depending on the status attributed to each text within a particular community. As a result, both categories have become open-ended. While the status of *śruti* was once reserved exclusively for Vedic texts, the category has expanded to include sectarian works that have been vedacized by devotional movements seeking to equate their own scriptures with the Veda.

In the *Mānas* we have an example of a sectarian text that is not only considered equal to the Vedas but has actually challenged their position, superseding them in the eyes of its adherents. The Rāmnāmīs have in turn evolved their own distinctive conception of the *Mānas* and its status in relation to the traditional classifications of sacred word. They celebrate the text as *śruti* insofar as, for the most part, its verses are held to be potent mantras, the meaning of which need not be understood. Just as *Om* is considered the consummate mantra, representing the essence of the Vedas, so *rāmnām* is viewed by the Rāmnāmīs as the consummate mantra of the *Mānas*. It is uncreated, eternal, and intrinsically powerful, and it is the quintessential expression of *śruti* for the present age. Ultimately, it is *rāmnām* that infuses the *Mānas* verses with mantric power and thus gives the *Mānas* its sacred status as *śruti* in the Rāmnāmī community. *Rāmnām* is, moreover, the only irreducible, unalterable element in the *Mānas*. The narrative content of the text is significant in that it conveys the Rām story, but on the level of narrative the text is *smṛti*, not *śruti*. Therefore it can be selectively cited, reinterpreted, elaborated, and even at times altered. The Rāmnāmīs find no contradiction in this dual perspective on the *Mānas* as, on the one hand, sacred and inviolable and, on the other, open to interpretation, criticism, and modification. Defending the community's relationship with the text, an elder Rāmnāmī exclaimed, "The *Rāmāyaṇ* is so great we cannot possibly damage it; we can only make it better!" In the process of recreating the Rām story the Rāmnāmīs have indeed enhanced the vitality of the *Mānas*, broadening the ways in which it is used, and have added but one more dimension to the ever-expanding literary genre that is the *Rāmāyaṇ*.

NOTES

I would like to thank the entire Rāmnāmī Samāj for sharing their beliefs, their practices, and their lives with me. Without such openness, this research would have never been possible. I would also like to thank Professor Barbara Holdrege (University of California, Santa Barbara) for her invaluable advice and editorial assistance in the preparation of this material.

In Hindi, as in many of the regional languages of North India, the final *a* of a word, unless preceded by a double consonant, is dropped. Since this essay deals with the Hindi-speaking Rāmnāmī Samāj, I will generally follow the standard Hindi transliteration of terms, with two exceptions:

(1) The names of Sanskrit texts are given in Sanskrit transliteration.

(2) In transliterating verses I have chosen to retain the final *a* of Hindi words that is dropped in ordinary speech, since it is pronounced in the chanting and in the recitation of verses.

I have chosen to transliterate the Hindi *anusvār* as *ñ*.

1. North Indians refer to Tulsīdās's *Rāmcaritmānas* in a variety of ways, including "Tulsī *Rāmāyaṇ*," "*Mānas*," or simply "*Rāmāyaṇ*." Of these designations "*Mānas*" is by far the most common and will be used throughout the present essay. North Indians generally refer to Vālmīki's Sanskrit *Rāmāyaṇa* as either "Vālmīki *Rāmāyaṇ*" or "Sanskṛt *Rāmāyaṇ*."

2. Since there are no universally accepted demarcations of the categories *śruti* and *smṛti*, I have chosen to begin with the prevailing Western academic definitions, which largely reflect contemporary orthodox Hindu beliefs. Supplementary views expressed by recent Indological scholars will be mentioned in the notes. Brian K. Smith points out that throughout the history of Hinduism, new texts have been composed and given the name "Upaniṣad," thus bringing them into the corpus of *śruti*—a process which clearly contradicts the supposedly bounded nature of the category: *Reflections on Resemblance, Ritual, and Religion* (New York: Oxford University Press, 1989), 21.

3. Both Wendy Doniger O'Flaherty (*Other People's Myths* [New York: Macmillan, 1988], 58) and Sheldon Pollock ("The 'Revelation' of 'Tradition': *Śruti*, *Smṛti*, and the Sanskrit Discourse of Power" in *Lex et Litterae [Festschrift Oscar Botto]*, forthcoming) mention the fact that the chanted Veda was heard by the worshipers as a part of the explanation for the term *śruti*.

4. The innate power of mantras is activated through their recitation by *śrotriyas* ("masters of *śruti*"). This belief in the inherent power of sounds underlies both the later concept of *bīja* ("seed") mantras in the Tantric schools and the devotional sects' belief in the power of the Name of God. O'Flaherty (*Other People's Myths*, 61), Brian K. Smith, and others point out that an understanding of the Vedas was considered by some to be of great importance. However, this was not crucial for the ritual use of the text, which was its primary raison d'être. Barbara A. Holdrege offers an extensive discussion of various conceptions of the Veda and their influence on the modes of preservation and memorization of the Saṃhitās in "Veda and Torah: Ontological Conceptions of Scripture in the Brahmanical and Judaic Traditions" (Ph.D. diss., Harvard University, 1987).

5. Thomas B. Coburn, "'Scripture' in India: Towards a Typology of the Word in Hindu Life," *Journal of the American Academy of Religion* 52, no. 3 (September 1984): 448. Coburn presents an illuminating discussion of various approaches to the understanding of *śruti* and *smṛti* and encourages a rethinking of traditional categorizations. The theoretical approach adopted in this section was to some extent inspired by his article.

6. William Graham, *Beyond the Written Word: Oral Aspects of Scripture in the History of Religion* (Cambridge: Cambridge University Press, 1987), 5.

7. J. L. Brockington, *Righteous Rāma: The Evolution of an Epic* (Delhi: Oxford University Press, 1984), 206–13, 307–27.

8. In contemporary times, the *Mānas* has occasionally been referred to as the "Fifth Veda" or the "Hindi Veda." According to Hindu cosmology, the world is now passing through the Kali Yug, the age of darkness, in which *bhakti* is the highest form of religious practice. Many devotional groups thus maintain that texts such as the *Mānas* that extol *bhakti* have replaced the Vedas in delineating *śruti* for this age.

9. The process of vedacization is discussed in Sheldon Pollock, "From Discourse of Ritual to Discourse of Power in Sanskrit Culture"; and in Philip Lutgendorf, "The Power of Sacred Story: Rāmāyaṇa Recitation in Contemporary North India," in *Ritual and Power*, special issue of the *Journal of Ritual Studies* (4, no. 1 [Summer 1990]), ed. Barbara A. Holdrege.

10. Philip Lutgendorf, "The Power of Sacred Story," p. 138.

11. As previously mentioned, texts of the *smṛti* category are open-ended, i.e., subject to additions, interpolations, etc. As early as the nineteenth century, distinctly marked additions were made to the written text of Tulsīdās's *Mānas* by various publishers. These addenda, usually consisting of commentaries on events in the narrative or supplementary episodes in the life of Rām, most likely had their inception in the repertoires of the *kathāvācaks* (storytellers) and Rāmānandī ascetics who carried the Rām story from village to village. Owing in all probability to their popularity, certain of these additions eventually came to be included in some printed editions as part of the text. Although they are labeled *kṣepak* ("addition, interpolation"), many readers have come to believe them to have been written by Tulsīdās himself.

12. Lutgendorf, "The Power of Sacred Story," pp. 124–26.

13. The account presented here of Parasurām's life and of the formation of the Rāmnāmī sect is based on his oral hagiography, recounted to me by several elder members of the sect.

14. The level of literacy in Madhya Pradesh is one of the lowest in India. At the turn of the century it was less than 10 percent, those classified as literate living primarily in the urban areas. Illiteracy among village *harijans* most likely exceeded 95 percent during this period. Even for those who are literate, understanding the *Mānas* is extremely difficult, for it is written in a medieval dialect of Avadhi, while the Rāmnāmīs speak a contemporary Chhattisgarhi dialect. Although in present times both are considered dialects of Hindi, medieval Avadhi is sufficiently different from modern Hindi dialects to discourage most speakers from gaining more than a cursory understanding of the *Mānas* in its original language. When reading for understanding, rather than for ritual purposes, North Indians often use a text that provides a modern Hindi translation of each verse.

15. It should be noted that individual chanting of *rāmnām* has never been a fundamental part of Rāmnāmī practice. The sect maintains that if one is going to chant *rāmnām*, one should do so in the company of others so that all can partake of its benefits.

16. For a more extensive discussion of the Rāmnāmī Samāj and their various uses of the Name, see Ramdas Lamb, "Rāmnāmīs, *Rāmnām*, and the Role of the Low Caste in the Rām *Bhakti* Tradition" (Ph.D. diss., University of California, Santa Barbara, [1991]).

17. These numbers are approximations based on hundreds of hours spent sitting and listening to Rāmnāmī *bhajan*.

18. In the Rāmnāmīs' view the authoritativeness of a verse or text is determined not by its author but by its content. Sect members cite the example of Rāvaṇ, the demon king of Lanka, who on occasion in the *Mānas* speaks words of great wisdom, thus illustrating that even demons can speak truth. The Rāmnāmīs say that ultimately it is truth they seek, irrespective of its source.

19. Owing to the predominance of the *dohā* (2 lines, 24 beats) and the *caupāī* (4 lines of 4 parts, 64 beats) in the *Mānas*, these two verse forms have set the metrical parameters of the Rāmnāmīs' chanting style and thus have also determined which verses can be incorporated into *bhajans*. For a detailed explanation of the structure of *Mānas* verses, see Philip Lutgendorf, *The Life of a Text: Performing the Rāmcaritmānas of Tulsidas* (Berkeley and Los Angeles: University of California Press, 1991).

20. Most of the supplemental writings used by the Rāmnāmīs are in fact obscure texts with regional popularity at best, discovered by *vidvāns*. Various verses from them have become popular with sect members because their contents and meter happen to make them suitable for chanting.

21. *Nirguṇ bhakti* is the practice of devotion to God, conceived of as not limited by, and therefore transcending, all forms. Most schools of Hindu devotionalism see the divine as *saguṇ*, perceptible to humans through one or several particular forms. Kabīr's *bhakti* is exclusively *nirguṇ* and that of Raghunāthdās primarily *nirguṇ*. For both, the name "Rām" is a primary focus of much devotion.

22. For Hindus Hanumān is obviously more than just a monkey. He is said to be the eleventh incarnation of Śiva and the epitome of devotion. For the Rāmnāmīs, however, the status of any being, human or divine, lies in his or her relationship of subservience to *nirguṇ* Rām.

23. In its original form the verse reads: *Vipra dhenu sura santa hita līnha manuja avatāra* | (*Rāmcaritmānas* 1.192). This is revised by the Rāmnāmīs to: *Rāmnām denā sura santa* . . . |

24. *Citavata pantha raheũñ dina rātī* | *Aba prabhu dekhi jurdānī chātī* ||
Nātha sakala sādhana maiñ hīna | *Kinhi kṛpā jānī jana dīna* || (3.6.2)

25. *Aba mohi bhā barosa Hanumantā* |
Binu Hari kṛpā milahi nahiñ santā || (5.7.2)

26. *Kī tumha Hari dāsanha mahañ koī* | *Moreñ hṛdaya prīti ati hoī* ||
Kī tumha Rāmu dīna anurāgī | *Āyahu mohi karana barḍmāgī* || (5.6.4)

27. *Nātha Dasānana kara maiñ brātā* | *Nisicara bañs janama surtrātā* || (5.45.4)

28. *Dhanya dhanya taiñ dhanya Bibhīṣana* |
Bhayahu tāta nisīcara kula bhūṣana || (6.64.4)

29. It should be noted that *vidvān* is not an official designation. Any sect member who studies the *Mānas* and/or other texts and actively takes part in philosophical dialogues may be called a *vidvān*. Although the term has been in use for over four decades, in recent years many Rāmnāmīs have chosen to refer to active *ṭakkar* participants as *gyānīs* rather than *vidvāns*. This is to emphasize that their primary focus is wisdom, as opposed to intellectual knowledge.

30. Not all verses are selected strictly on the basis of philosophical viewpoint. Many verses are learned simply as a matter of course, as a result of participation in the chanting, and thus are not necessarily in complete harmony with a Rāmnāmī's

own philosophy. A sect member may also memorize certain commonly repeated verses without understanding them, solely out of a desire to join in whenever they are recited.

31. I sat in on one late night *ṭakkar* that involved verses drawn solely from the *Viśrām Sāgar*; it lasted for nearly five hours. The participants were seven erudite *vidvāns*, who continued until after I fell asleep.

32. Śivānandan Rām, Sūr Sādhū Bhāradvāj, and Śrīrām Lahare, *Rām Rasik Gītā* (Raipur: Sriram Lahare, 1979).

33. The Rāmnāmī Samāj holds a *melā*, or festival, every year in a different village in Chhattisgarh. The 1989 *melā* was the eightieth annual gathering.

34. *Kahahiñ beda itihāsa purānā* | *Vidhi prapancu guna avaguna sānā* || (1.6.2)

35. *Jarḍa cetana juna doṣamaya bisva kīnha kartāra* |
Santa hansa guna gahahiñ paya parihari bāri bikāra || (1.6)

In India, enlightened saints, with their ability to distinguish the self from the nonself and good from evil, are often compared to swans (*haṃsas*), who when given a mixture of milk and water are said to have the ability to separate out the milk, leaving behind the water.

36. *Graha bhoṣaja jala pavana paṭa pāi kujoga sujoga* |
Hohiñ kubastu jubastu jaga lakhahiñ sulacchana loga || (1.7A)
Asa bibeka jaba dei Vidhātā | *Taba taji doṣa gunahiñ manu rāta* ||
Kāla subhāu karama bariāī | *Bhaleu prakṛti basa cukai bhalāī* || (1.7.1)

37. The verse as it was chanted was a modification of a *Mānas caupāī*:
Sīyarāmamaya saba jaga jānī | *Karauñ pranāma jori juga pānī* || (1.8.1)

The responding Rāmnāmī replaced "*Sīyarāmamaya*" ("filled with Sītā and Rām") with "*Rāmrām nāmamaya*" ("filled with *rāmnām*").

CONTRIBUTORS

Stuart H. Blackburn, the recipient of a National Endowment for the Humanities grant and a Fulbright fellowship, has done extensive fieldwork on the performance traditions of South India. His book *Singing of Birth and Death: Texts in Performance* (University of Pennsylvania Press, 1989) analyzed a ritual song tradition in southern Tamilnadu. He recently edited *Another Harmony: New Essays on the Folklore of India*, with A. K. Ramanujan (University of California Press, 1986), and *Oral Epics of India*, with Peter Claus, Joyce Flueckiger, and Susan S. Wadley (University of California Press, 1989). Blackburn is currently completing a book on the Kerala shadow puppet performance of the *Rāmāyaṇa*.

Kathleen M. Erndl, Assistant Professor of Religious Studies at Lewis and Clark College, has done research on goddess traditions of Northwest India. Recent publications include "Rapist or Bodyguard, Demon or Devotee? Images of Bhairo in the Mythology and Cult of Vaiṣṇo Devī" in *Criminal Gods and Demon Devotees*, edited by Alf Hiltebeitel (SUNY Press, 1989), "Fire and Wakefulness: The Devī Jagrātā in Contemporary Panjabi Hinduism," *Journal of the American Academy of Religion* (1991), and *Victory to the Mother: The Hindu Goddess of Northwest India in Myth, Ritual, and Symbol* (Oxford University Press, forthcoming). Her current research focuses on the religious life of Hindu women in Kangra, India.

Ramdas Lamb, Associate Professor of Religion at the University of Hawaii, has studied contemporary Hindu devotionalism and religious practice for the past twenty years, having spent nearly half this period doing fieldwork in North and Central India. At present he is preparing his dissertation, "Rāmnāmīs, *Rāmnām*, and the Role of the Low Caste in the Rām *Bhakti* Tradition"

(University of California, Santa Barbara), for publication. It looks at the history of Rām *bhakti* and focuses on the Rāmnāmī Samāj in Madhya Pradesh, India.

Philip Lutgendorf, Associate Professor of Hindi and Modern Indian Studies at the University of Iowa, has researched North Indian oral performance traditions that utilize the Hindi *Rāmāyaṇa*. His publications on the subject include "The View from the Ghats: Traditional Exegesis of a Hindu Epic" in the *Journal of Asian Studies* (1989), "Ram's Story in Shiva's City: Public Arenas and Private Patronage" in *Culture and Power in Banaras: Community, Performance, and Environment, 1800–1980* (University of California Press, 1989), edited by Sandria Freitag, "Ramayan: The Video" in *The Drama Review* (Summer 1990), and *The Life of a Text: Performing the Rāmcaritmānas of Tulsidas* (University of California Press, 1991). He is currently working on a study of the cult of Hanumān.

Patricia Y. Mumme, Assistant Professor of Religion at Denison University, has focused on the Śrīvaiṣṇava theological tradition of medieval Tamilnadu. Her publications include *The Mumukṣuppaṭi of Piḷḷai Lokācārya with Maṇavāḷamāmuni's Commentary* (Ananthacharya Indological Research Institute, 1987), "Grace and Karma in Nammāḻvār's Salvation," in the *Journal of the American Oriental Society* (1987), and *The Śrīvaiṣṇava Theological Dispute: Maṇavāḷamāmuni and Vedānta Deśika* (New Era Publications, 1988). At present she is completing a translation of the *Parantarahasya* of Periyavāccāṉ Piḷḷai.

Velcheru Narayana Rao, an expert in the area of Telugu literature, is Professor of South Asian Studies at the University of Wisconsin–Madison. His scholarly interests in Telugu texts and folklore have led to numerous publications in fields as diverse as medieval devotional Śaivite poetry, modern novels and poetry, folk epics, proverbs and riddles, and classical grammar. His many translations from Telugu to English include, most recently, *For the Lord of the Animals*, with Hank Heifetz (University of California Press, 1987), and *Śiva's Warriors: The Basava Purāṇa of Palkuriki Somanātha*, with Gene Roghair (Princeton University Press, 1990). His latest book, with David Shulman and Sanjay Subrahmanyam, is *Symbols of Substance: Court and State in Nāyaka-Period South India* (Oxford University Press, 1991).

A. K. Ramanujan, scholar and poet as well as recent recipient of a MacArthur Fellowship, is William E. Colvin Professor in the Department of South Asian Languages and Civilizations, the Committee on Social Thought, and the Department of Linguistics at the University of Chicago. In addition to a large number of articles in the fields of South Asian linguistics, Tamil and Kannada literature, and folklore, Ramanujan has published prizewinning volumes of his own poetry. He is also widely known for a series of translations, most recently *Hymns for the Drowning: Poems for Viṣṇu by Nammāḻvār* (Princeton University Press, 1981) and *Poems of Love and War from the Eight Anthologies and the Ten Songs of Classical Tamil* (Columbia University Press, 1985). He and Vinay Dharwadkher have just finished editing *An Anthology of Modern Indian Poetry* (Oxford University Press–Madras, forthcoming). Among Ramanujan's many current projects is a translation of women's oral tales from Kannada.

Frank E. Reynolds, Professor of History of Religions and Buddhist Studies in the Divinity School and the Department of South Asian Languages and Civilizations at the University of Chicago, is a specialist in Thai Buddhism within the context of Theravāda Buddhism in South and Southeast Asia. He has published widely in the fields of Buddhism, South and Southeast Asian studies, and methodology and comparison in the history of religions. Some of his most influential recent books are his monograph *Three Worlds According to King Ruang: A Thai Cosmology*, translated with Mani Reynolds (Asian Humanities Press, 1982), *Cosmogony and the Ethical Order: New Studies in Comparative Ethics*, edited with Robin Lovin (University of Chicago Press, 1985), and *Myth and Philosophy*, edited with David Tracy (SUNY Press, 1990).

Paula Richman, Associate Professor of South Asian Religions at Oberlin College, has focused on rhetorical strategies in Tamil religious texts. Among her publications are *Gender and Religion: On the Complexity of Symbols*, coedited with Caroline Bynum and Stevan Harrell (Beacon Press, 1986), *Women, Branch Stories, and Religious Rhetoric in a Tamil Buddhist Text* (Maxwell School, Syracuse University, 1988), and "Gender and Persuasion: Beauty, Anguish, and Nurturance in the Account of a Tamil Nun," in *Buddhism, Sexuality, and Gender*, edited by José Cabezón (SUNY Press, 1991). Her current projects include a study of Tamil devotional poems called *piḷḷaittamiḻ* and a monograph on the political uses of the *Rāmāyaṇa* in Madras from 1878 to 1973.

Clinton Seely, Associate Professor of Bengali at the University of Chicago, has written several articles on Michael Madhusudan Dutt, as well as pieces on Jibanananda Das and Rabindranath Tagore. Recent books include, in addition to two Bengali language textbooks, *Grace and Mercy in Her Wild Hair: Selected Poems to the Mother Goddess*, translated with Leonard Nathan (Great Eastern Book Co., 1982), *A Poet Apart: A Literary Biography of the Bengali Poet Jibanananda Das (1899–1954)* (University of Delaware Press, 1990), and an edited volume titled *Women, Politics, and Literature in Bengal* (Asian Studies Center, Michigan State University, 1981). At present Seely is working on a translation of *Meghanādavadha Kāvya*.

David Shulman, MacArthur Fellow and Professor in the Department of Indian, Iranian, and Armenian Studies at Hebrew University in Jerusalem, is well known for his writings in the fields of Tamil, Sanskrit, and Telugu literature, religion, and folklore. In addition to numerous articles in these fields, Shulman has published *The King and the Clown in South Indian Myth and Poetry* (Princeton University Press, 1985), *Songs of the Harsh Devotee: The Tēvāram of Cuntaramūrttināyaṉār* (South Asian Studies, University of Pennsylvania, 1990), and *Symbols of Substance: Court and State in Nāyaka-Period South India*, with V. Narayana Rao and Sanjay Subrahmanyam (Oxford University Press, 1991). Among many other projects, Shulman is currently working on a literary and cultural-historical study of the fifteenth-century Telugu poet Śrīnātha and a monograph on medieval Tamil poetic theory.

INDEX